Essays and Cases: Foundations for Media Law

Daniel S. Brown, Jr., Ph.D., Editor

Grove City College
Grove City, Pennsylvania, USA

Published January 2015, first edition.

Shrum + Freeman
Grove City, Pennsylvania, USA.

Official case law for all courts in the United States is found only in the print version of the appropriate court reporter. Decisions by the Supreme Court of the United States are, for example, found in the publication United States Reports. Case law is provided in the present publication for informational and educational purposes, and likely do not reflect current legal developments or verdicts. The editor has made informed choices to exclude some material, such as footnotes and full concurring or dissenting opinions, in the interest of space. Always check official sources in the form of the appropriate court reporter.

A syllabus or summarizing headnote is frequently, but not always, released, at the time the opinion is issued. Care has been taken in the present publication to label the syllabus when it is included by the reporter. The syllabus constitutes no part of the opinion of the Court but has been prepared by the Reporter of Decisions for the convenience of the reader. That is, the syllabus is a tool, not the law. The appropriate court reporter supplies the syllabus, not the court itself. See United States v. Detroit Timber & Lumber Co., 200 U. S. 321, 337.

ISBN: 150750876X
ISBN-13: 978-1507508763

DEDICATION

To my students past and passed.

CONTENTS

III.   Appendices

I. Milestone Essays

1 ENGLISH BILL OF RIGHTS: AN ACT DECLARING THE RIGHTS AND LIBERTIES OF THE SUBJECT (1689)

Whereas the Lords Spiritual and Temporal and Commons assembled at Westminster, lawfully, fully and freely representing all the estates of the people of this realm, did upon the thirteenth day of February in the year of our Lord one thousand six hundred eighty-eight [old style date] present unto their Majesties, then called and known by the names and style of William and Mary, prince and princess of Orange, being present in their proper persons, a certain declaration in writing made by the said Lords and Commons in the words following, viz.:

Whereas the late King James the Second, by the assistance of divers evil counsellors, judges and ministers employed by him, did endeavour to subvert and extirpate the Protestant religion and the laws and liberties of this kingdom;

By assuming and exercising a power of dispensing with and suspending of laws and the execution of laws without consent of Parliament;

By committing and prosecuting divers worthy prelates for humbly petitioning to be excused from concurring to the said assumed power;

By issuing and causing to be executed a commission under the great seal for erecting a court called the Court of Commissioners for Ecclesiastical Causes;

By levying money for and to the use of the Crown by pretence of prerogative for other time and in other manner than the same was granted by Parliament;

By raising and keeping a standing army within this kingdom in time of peace without consent of Parliament, and quartering soldiers contrary to law;

By causing several good subjects being Protestants to be disarmed at the same time when papists were both armed and employed contrary to law;

By violating the freedom of election of members to serve in Parliament;

By prosecutions in the Court of King's Bench for matters and causes cognizable only in

Parliament, and by divers other arbitrary and illegal courses;

And whereas of late years partial corrupt and unqualified persons have been returned and served on juries in trials, and particularly divers jurors in trials for high treason which were not freeholders;

And excessive bail hath been required of persons committed in criminal cases to elude the benefit of the laws made for the liberty of the subjects;

And excessive fines have been imposed;

And illegal and cruel punishments inflicted;

And several grants and promises made of fines and forfeitures before any conviction or judgment against the persons upon whom the same were to be levied;

All which are utterly and directly contrary to the known laws and statutes and freedom of this realm;

And whereas the said late King James the Second having abdicated the government and the throne being thereby vacant, his Highness the prince of Orange (whom it hath pleased Almighty God to make the glorious instrument of delivering this kingdom from popery and arbitrary power) did (by the advice of the Lords Spiritual and Temporal and divers principal persons of the Commons) cause letters to be written to the Lords Spiritual and Temporal being Protestants, and other letters to the several counties, cities, universities, boroughs and cinque ports, for the choosing of such persons to represent them as were of right to be sent to Parliament, to meet and sit at Westminster upon the two and twentieth day of January in this year one thousand six hundred eighty and eight [old style date], in order to such an establishment as that their religion, laws and liberties might not again be in danger of being subverted, upon which letters elections having been accordingly made;

And thereupon the said Lords Spiritual and Temporal and Commons, pursuant to their respective letters and elections, being now assembled in a full and free representative of this nation, taking into their most serious consideration the best means for attaining the ends aforesaid, do in the first place (as their ancestors in like case have usually done) for the vindicating and asserting their ancient rights and liberties declare

That the pretended power of suspending the laws or the execution of laws by regal authority without consent of Parliament is illegal;

That the pretended power of dispensing with laws or the execution of laws by regal authority, as it hath been assumed and exercised of late, is illegal;

That the commission for erecting the late Court of Commissioners for Ecclesiastical Causes, and all other commissions and courts of like nature, are illegal and pernicious;

That levying money for or to the use of the Crown by pretence of prerogative, without grant of Parliament, for longer time, or in other manner than the same is or shall be granted, is illegal;

That it is the right of the subjects to petition the king, and all commitments and prosecutions for such petitioning are illegal;

That the raising or keeping a standing army within the kingdom in time of peace, unless it be with consent of Parliament, is against law;

That the subjects which are Protestants may have arms for their defence suitable to their conditions and as allowed by law;

That election of members of Parliament ought to be free;

That the freedom of speech and debates or proceedings in Parliament ought not to be impeached or questioned in any court or place out of Parliament;

That excessive bail ought not to be required, nor excessive fines imposed, nor cruel and unusual punishments inflicted;

That jurors ought to be duly impanelled and returned, and jurors which pass upon men in trials for high treason ought to be freeholders;

That all grants and promises of fines and forfeitures of particular persons before conviction are illegal and void;

And that for redress of all grievances, and for the amending, strengthening and preserving of the laws, Parliaments ought to be held frequently.

And they do claim, demand and insist upon all and singular the premises as their undoubted rights and liberties, and that no declarations, judgments, doings or proceedings to the prejudice of the people in any of the said premises ought in any wise to be drawn hereafter into consequence or example; to which demand of their rights they are particularly encouraged by the declaration of his Highness the prince of Orange as being the only means for obtaining a full redress and remedy therein. Having therefore an entire confidence that his said Highness the prince of Orange will perfect the deliverance so far advanced by him, and will still preserve them from the violation of their rights which they have here asserted, and from all other attempts upon their religion, rights and liberties, the said Lords Spiritual and Temporal and Commons assembled at Westminster do resolve that William and Mary, prince and princess of Orange, be and be declared king and queen of England, France and Ireland and the dominions thereunto belonging, to hold the crown and royal dignity of the said kingdoms and dominions to them, the said prince and princess, during their lives and the life of the survivor to them, and that the sole and full exercise of the regal power be only in and executed by the said prince of Orange in the names of the said prince and princess during their joint lives, and after their deceases the said crown and royal dignity of the same kingdoms and dominions to be to the heirs of the body of the said princess, and for default of such issue to the Princess Anne of Denmark and the heirs of her body, and for default of such issue to the heirs of the body of the said prince of Orange. And the Lords Spiritual and Temporal and Commons do pray the said prince and princess to accept the same accordingly.

2 *AREOPAGITICA: A SPEECH FOR THE LIBERTY OF UNLICENSED PRINTING TO THE PARLIAMENT OF ENGLAND* BY JOHN MILTON (1644)

> This is true liberty, when free-born men,
> Having to advise the public, may speak free,
> Which he who can, and will, deserves high praise;
> Who neither can, nor will, may hold his peace:
> What can be juster in a state than this?
> --Euripid. Hicetid.

They, who to states and governors of the Commonwealth direct their speech, High Court of Parliament, or, wanting such access in a private condition, write that which they foresee may advance the public good; I suppose them, as at the beginning of no mean endeavor, not a little altered and moved inwardly in their minds: some with doubt of what will be the success, others with fear of what will be the censure; some with hope, others with confidence of what they have to speak. And me perhaps each of these dispositions, as the subject was whereon I entered, may have at other times variously affected; and likely might in these foremost expressions now also disclose which of them swayed most, but that the very attempt of this address thus made, and the thought of whom it hath recourse to, hath got the power within me to a passion, far more welcome than incidental to a preface.

Which though I stay not to confess ere any ask, I shall be blameless, if it be no other than the joy and gratulation which it brings to all who wish and promote their country's liberty; whereof this whole discourse proposed will be a certain testimony, if not a trophy. For this is not the liberty which we can hope, that no grievance ever should arise in the Commonwealth--that let no man in this world expect; but when complaints are freely heard, deeply considered and speedily reformed, then is the utmost bound of civil liberty attained that wise men look for. To which if I now manifest by the very sound of this which I shall utter, that we are already in good part arrived, and yet from such a steep disadvantage of tyranny and superstition grounded into our principles as was beyond the manhood of a Roman recovery, it will be attributed first, as is most due, to the strong assistance of God our deliverer, next to your faithful guidance and undaunted wisdom, Lords and Commons of England. Neither is it in God's esteem the diminution of his glory, when honorable things are spoken of good men and worthy magistrates; which if I now first should begin to do, after so fair a progress of your laudable deeds, and such a long obligement upon the whole realm to your indefatigable virtues, I might be justly reckoned among the tardiest, and the unwillingest of them that praise ye.

Nevertheless there being three principal things, without which all praising is but courtship and flattery: First, when that only is praised which is solidly worth praise: next, when greatest likelihoods are brought that such things are truly and really in those persons to whom they are ascribed: the other, when he who praises, by showing that such his actual persuasion is of whom he writes, can demonstrate that he flatters not; the former two of these I have heretofore endeavored, rescuing the employment from him who went about to impair your merits with a trivial and malignant encomium; the latter as belonging chiefly to mine own acquittal, that whom I so extolled I did not flatter, hath been reserved opportunely to this occasion.

For he who freely magnifies what hath been nobly done, and fears not to declare as freely what might be done better, gives ye the best covenant of his fidelity; and that his loyalest affection and his hope waits on your proceedings. His highest praising is not flattery, and his plainest advice is a kind of praising. For though I should affirm and hold by argument, that it would fare better with truth, with learning and the Commonwealth, if one of your published Orders, which I should name, were called in; yet at the same time it could not but much redound to the lustre of your mild and equal government, when as private persons are hereby animated to think ye better pleased with public advice, than other statists have been delighted heretofore with public flattery. And men will then see what difference there is between the magnanimity of a triennial Parliament, and that jealous haughtiness of prelates and cabin counselors that usurped of late, when as they shall observe ye in the midst of your victories and successes more gently brooking written exceptions against a voted Order than other courts, which had produced nothing worth memory but the weak ostentation of wealth, would have endured the least signified dislike at any sudden proclamation.

If I should thus far presume upon the meek demeanor of your civil and gentle greatness, Lords and Commons, as what your published Order hath directly said, that to gainsay, I might defend myself with ease, if any should accuse me of being new or insolent, did they but know how much better I find ye esteem it to imitate the old and elegant humanity of Greece, than the barbaric pride of a Hunnish and Norwegian stateliness. And out of those ages, to whose polite wisdom and letters we owe that we are not yet Goths and Jutlanders, I could name him who from his private house wrote that discourse to the Parliament of Athens, that persuades them to change the form of democracy which was then established. Such honor was done in those days to men who professed the study of wisdom and eloquence, not only in their own country, but in other lands, that cities and signatories heard them gladly, and with great respect, if they had sought in public to admonish the state. Thus did Dion Prusaeus, a stranger and a private orator, counsel the Rhodians against a former edict; and I abound with other like examples, which to set here would be superfluous.

But if from the industry of a life wholly dedicated to studious labors, and those natural endowments haply not the worst for two and fifty degrees of northern latitude, so much must be derogated, as to count me not equal to any of those who had this privilege, I would obtain to be thought not so inferior, as yourselves are superior to the most of them who received their counsel: and how far you excel them, be assured, Lords and Commons, there can no greater testimony appear, than when your prudent spirit acknowledges and obeys the voice of reason from what quarter soever it be heard speaking; and renders ye as willing to repeal any Act of your own setting forth, as any set forth by your predecessors.

If ye be thus resolved, as it were injury to think ye were not, I know not what should withhold me from presenting ye with a fit instance wherein to show both that love of truth which ye eminently profess, and that uprightness of your judgment which is not wont to be partial to yourselves; by judging over again that Order which ye have ordained to regulate printing:--that no book, pamphlet, or paper shall be henceforth printed, unless the same be first approved and licensed by such, or at least one of such, as shall be thereto appointed. For that part which preserves justly every man's copy to himself, or provides for the poor, I touch not, only wish they be not made pretences to abuse and persecute honest and painful men, who offend not in either of these particulars.

But that other clause of licensing books, which we thought had died with his brother quadragesimal and matrimonial when the prelates expired, I shall now attend with such a homily, as shall lay before ye, first the inventors of it to be those whom ye will be loath to own; next what is to be thought in general of reading, whatever sort the books be; and that this Order avails nothing to the suppressing of scandalous, seditious, and libelous books, which were mainly intended to be suppressed. Last, that it will be primely to the discouragement of all learning, and the stop of truth, not only by disexercising and blunting our abilities in what we know already, but by hindering and cropping the discovery that might be yet further made both in religious and civil wisdom.

I deny not, but that it is of greatest concernment in the Church and Commonwealth, to have a vigilant eye how books demean themselves as well as men; and thereafter to confine, imprison, and do sharpest justice on them as malefactors. For books are not absolutely dead things, but do contain a potency of life in them to be as active as that soul was whose progeny they are; nay, they do preserve as in a vial the purest efficacy and extraction of that living intellect that bred them. I know they are as lively, and as vigorously productive, as those fabulous dragon's teeth; and being sown up and down, may chance to spring up armed men. And yet, on the other hand, unless wariness be used, as good almost kill a man as kill a good book. Who kills a man kills a reasonable creature, God's image; but he who destroys a good book, kills reason itself, kills the image of God, as it were in the eye. Many a man lives a burden to the earth; but a good book is the precious life-blood of a master spirit, embalmed and treasured up on purpose to a life beyond life. 'Tis true, no age can restore a life, whereof perhaps there is no great loss; and revolutions of ages do not oft recover the loss of a rejected truth, for the want of which whole nations fare the worse.

We should be wary therefore what persecution we raise against the living labors of public men, how we spill that seasoned life of man, preserved and stored up in books; since we see a kind of homicide may be thus committed, sometimes a martyrdom, and if it extend to the whole impression, a kind of massacre; whereof the execution ends not in the slaying of an elemental life, but strikes at that ethereal and fifth essence, the breath of reason itself, slays an immortality rather than a life. But lest I should be condemned of introducing license, while I oppose licensing, I refuse not the pains to be so much historical, as will serve to show what hath been done by ancient and famous commonwealths against this disorder, till the very time that this project of licensing crept out of the Inquisition, was catched up by our prelates, and hath caught some of our presbyters.

In Athens, where books and wits were ever busier than in any other part of Greece, I find but only two sorts of writings which the magistrate cared to take notice of; those either blasphemous and atheistical, or libelous. Thus the books of Protagoras were by the judges of Areopagus commanded to be burnt, and himself banished the territory for a discourse begun with his confessing not to know WHETHER THERE WERE GODS, OR WHETHER NOT. And against defaming, it was decreed that none should be traduced by name, as was the manner of Vetus Comoedia, whereby we may guess how they censured libeling. And this course was quick enough, as Cicero writes, to quell both the desperate wits of other atheists, and the open way of defaming, as the event showed. Of other sects and opinions, though tending to voluptuousness, and the denying of divine Providence, they took no heed.

Therefore we do not read that either Epicurus, or that libertine school of Cyrene, or what the Cynic impudence uttered, was ever questioned by the laws. Neither is it recorded that the writings of those old comedians were suppressed, though the acting of them were forbid; and that Plato commended the reading of Aristophanes, the loosest of them all, to his royal scholar Dionysius, is commonly known, and may be excused, if holy Chrysostom, as is reported, nightly studied so much the same author and had the art to cleanse a scurrilous vehemence into the style of a rousing sermon.

That other leading city of Greece, Lacedaemon, considering that Lycurgus their lawgiver was so addicted to elegant learning, as to have been the first that brought out of Ionia the scattered works of Homer, and sent the poet Thales from Crete to prepare and mollify the Spartan surliness with his smooth songs and odes, the better to plant among them law and civility, it is to be wondered how museless and unbookish they were, minding naught but the feats of war. There needed no licensing of books among them, for they disliked all but their own laconic apophthegms, and took a slight occasion to chase Archilochus out of their city, perhaps for composing in a higher strain than their own soldierly ballads and roundels could reach to. Or if it were for his broad verses, they were not therein so cautious but they were as dissolute in their promiscuous conversing; whence Euripides affirms in Andromache, that their women were all unchaste. Thus much may give us light after what sort of books were prohibited among the Greeks.

The Romans also, for many ages trained up only to a military roughness resembling most the Lacedaemonian guise, knew of learning little but what their twelve Tables, and the Pontific College with their augurs and flamens taught them in religion and law; so unacquainted with other learning, that when Carneades and Critolaus, with the Stoic Diogenes, coming ambassadors to Rome, took thereby occasion to give the city a taste of their philosophy, they were suspected for seducers by no less a man than Cato the Censor, who moved it in the Senate to dismiss them speedily, and to banish all such Attic babblers out of Italy. But Scipio and others of the noblest senators withstood him and his old Sabine austerity; honored and admired the men; and the censor himself at last, in his old age, fell to the study of that whereof before he was so scrupulous. And yet at the same time Naevius and Plautus, the first Latin comedians, had filled the city with all the borrowed scenes of Menander and Philemon. Then began to be considered there also what was to be done to libelous books and authors; for Naevius was quickly cast into prison for his unbridled pen, and released by the tribunes upon his recantation; we read also that libels were burnt, and the makers punished by Augustus. The like severity, no doubt, was used, if aught were impiously written against their esteemed gods. Except in these two points, how the world went in books, the magistrate kept no reckoning.

By this time the emperors were become Christians, whose discipline in this point I do not find to have been more severe than what was formerly in practice. The books of those whom they took to be grand heretics were examined, refuted, and condemned in the general Councils; and not till then were prohibited, or burnt, by authority of the emperor. As for the writings of heathen authors, unless they were plain invectives against Christianity, as those of Porphyrius and Proclus, they met with no interdict that can be cited, till about the year 400, in a Carthaginian Council, wherein bishops themselves were forbid to read the books of Gentiles, but heresies they might read: while others long before them, on the contrary, scrupled more the books of heretics than of Gentiles. And that the primitive Councils and bishops were wont only to declare what books were not commendable, passing no further, but leaving it to each one's conscience to read or to lay by, till after the year 800, is observed already by Padre Paolo, the great unmasker of the Trentine Council.

After which time the Popes of Rome, engrossing what they pleased of political rule into their own hands, extended their dominion over men's eyes, as they had before over their judgments, burning and prohibiting to be read what they fancied not; yet sparing in their censures, and the books not many which they so dealt with: till Martin V., by his bull, not only prohibited, but was the first that excommunicated the reading of heretical books; for about that time Wickliffe and Huss, growing terrible, were they who first drove the Papal Court to a stricter policy of prohibiting. Which course Leo X. and his successors followed, until the Council of Trent and the Spanish Inquisition engendering together brought forth, or perfected, those Catalogues and expurging Indexes, that rake through the entrails of many an old good author, with a violation worse than any could be offered to his tomb. Nor did they stay in matters heretical, but any subject that was not to their palate, they either condemned in a Prohibition, or had it straight into the new purgatory of an index.

To fill up the measure of encroachment, their last invention was to ordain that no book, pamphlet, or paper should be printed (as if St. Peter had bequeathed them the keys of the press also out of Paradise) unless it were approved and licensed under the hands of two or three glutton friars.

What advantage is it to be a man, over it is to be a boy at school, if we have only escaped the ferula to come under the fescue of an Imprimatur; if serious and elaborate writings, as if they were no more than the theme of a grammar-lad under his pedagogue, must not be uttered without the cursory eyes of a temporizing and extemporizing licenser? He who is not trusted with his own actions, his drift not being known to be evil, and standing to the hazard of law and penalty, has no great argument to think himself reputed in the Commonwealth wherein he was born for other than a fool or a foreigner. When a man writes to the world, he summons up all his reason and deliberation to assist him; he searches, meditates, is industrious, and likely consults and confers with his judicious friends; after all which done he takes himself to be informed in what he writes, as well as any that writ before him. If, in this the most consummate act of his fidelity and ripeness, no years, no industry, no former proof of his abilities can bring him to that state of maturity, as not to be still mistrusted and suspected, unless he carry all his considerate diligence, all his midnight watchings and expense of Palladian oil, to the hasty view of an unleisured licenser, perhaps much his younger, perhaps his inferior in judgment, perhaps one who never knew the labor of bookwriting, and if he be not repulsed or slighted, must appear in print like a puny with his guardian, and his censor's hand on the back of his title to be his bail and surety that he is no idiot or seducer, it cannot be but a dishonor and derogation to the author, to the book, to the privilege and dignity of learning.

And what if the author shall be one so copious of fancy, as to have many things well worth the adding come into his mind after licensing, while the book is yet under the press, which not seldom happens to the best and most diligent writers; and that perhaps a dozen times in one book? The printer dares not go beyond his licensed copy; so often then must the author trudge to his leave-giver, that those his new insertions may be viewed; and many a jaunt will be made, are that licenser, for it must be the same man, can either be found, or found at leisure; meanwhile either the press must stand still, which is no small damage, or the author lose his most accurate thoughts, and send the book forth worse than he had made it, which to a diligent writer is the greatest melancholy and vexation that can befall.

And how can a man teach with authority, which is the life of teaching; how can he be a doctor in his book as he ought to be, or else had better be silent, when as all he teaches, all he delivers, is but under the tuition, under the correction of his patriarchal licenser to blot or alter what precisely accords not with the hidebound humor which he calls his judgment? When every acute reader, upon the first sight of a pedantic licence, will be ready with these like words to ding the book a quoit's distance from him: I hate a pupil teacher, I endure not an instructor that comes to me under the wardship of an overseeing fist. I know nothing of the licenser, but that I have his own hand here for his arrogance; who shall warrant me his judgment? The State, sir, replies the stationer, but has a quick return: The State shall be my governors, but not my critics; they may be mistaken in the choice of a licenser, as easily as this licenser may be mistaken in an author; this is some common stuff; and he might add from Sir Francis Bacon, THAT SUCH AUTHORIZED BOOKS ARE BUT THE LANGUAGE OF THE TIMES. For though a licenser should happen to be judicious more than ordinary, which will be a great jeopardy of the next succession, yet his very office and his commission enjoins him to let pass nothing but what is vulgarly received already.

Nay, which is more lamentable, if the work of any deceased author, though never so famous in his lifetime and even to this day, come to their hands for licence to be printed, or reprinted, if there be found in his book one sentence of a venturous edge, uttered in the height of zeal (and who knows whether it might not be the dictate of a divine spirit?) yet not suiting with every low decrepit humor of their own, though it were Knox himself, the reformer of a kingdom, that spake it, they will not pardon him their dash: the sense of that great man shall to all posterity be lost, for the fearfulness or the presumptuous rashness of a perfunctory licenser. And to what an author this violence hath been lately done, and in what book of greatest consequence to be faithfully published, I could now instance, but shall forbear till a more convenient season.

Yet if these things be not resented seriously and timely by them who have the remedy in their power, but that such iron-moulds as these shall have authority to gnaw out the choicest periods of most exquisite books, and to commit such a treacherous fraud against the orphan remainders of worthiest men after death, the more sorrow will belong to that hapless race of men, whose misfortune it is to have understanding. Henceforth let no man care to learn, or care to be more than worldly-wise; for certainly in higher matters to be ignorant and slothful, to be a common steadfast dunce, will be the only pleasant life, and only in request. And it is a particular disesteem of every knowing person alive, and most injurious to the written labors and monuments of the dead, so to me it seems an undervaluing and vilifying of the whole nation. I cannot set so light by all the invention, the art, the wit, the grave and solid judgment which is in England, as that it can be comprehended in any twenty capacities how good soever, much less that it should not pass except their superintendence be over it, except it be sifted and strained with their strainers, that it should be uncurrent without their manual stamp. Truth and understanding are not such wares as to be monopolized and traded in by tickets and statutes and standards. We must not think to make a staple commodity of all the knowledge in the land, to mark and licence it like our broadcloth and our woolpacks. What is it but a servitude like that imposed by the Philistines, not to be allowed the sharpening of our own axes and coulters, but we must repair from all quarters to twenty licensing forges? Had anyone written and divulged erroneous things and scandalous to honest life, misusing and forfeiting the esteem had of his reason among men, if after conviction this only censure were adjudged him that he should never henceforth write but what were first examined by an appointed officer, whose hand should be annexed to pass his credit for him that now he might be safely read; it could not be apprehended less than a disgraceful punishment. Whence to include the whole nation, and those that never yet thus offended, under such a diffident and suspectful prohibition, may plainly be understood what a disparagement it is. So much the more, when as debtors and delinquents may walk abroad without a keeper, but unoffensive books must not stir forth without a visible jailer in their title.

Nor is it to the common people less than a reproach; for if we be so jealous over them, as that we dare not trust them with an English pamphlet, what do we but censure them for a giddy, vicious, and ungrounded people; in such a sick and weak state of faith and discretion, as to be able to take nothing down but through the pipe of a licenser? That this is care or love of them, we cannot pretend, when as, in those popish places where the laity are most hated and despised, the same strictness is used over them. Wisdom we cannot call it, because it stops but one breach of licence, nor that neither: when as those corruptions, which it seeks to prevent, break in faster at other doors which cannot be shut.

And in conclusion it reflects to the disrepute of our ministers also, of whose labors we should hope better, and of the proficiency which their flock reaps by them, than that after all this light of the Gospel which is, and is to be, and all this continual preaching, they should still be frequented with such an unprincipled, unedified and laic rabble, as that the whiff of every new pamphlet should stagger them out of their catechism and Christian walking. This may have much reason to discourage the ministers when such a low conceit is had of all their exhortations, and the benefiting of their hearers, as that they are not thought fit to be turned loose to three sheets of paper without a licenser; that all the sermons, all the lectures preached, printed, vented in such numbers, and such volumes, as have now well nigh made all other books unsaleable, should not be armor enough against one single Enchiridion, without the castle of St. Angelo of an Imprimatur.

And lest some should persuade ye, Lords and Commons, that these arguments of learned men's discouragement at this your Order are mere flourishes, and not real, I could recount what I have seen and heard in other countries, where this kind of inquisition tyrannizes; when I have sat among their learned men, for that honor I had, and been counted happy to be born in such a place of philosophic freedom, as they supposed England was, while themselves did nothing but bemoan the servile condition into which learning amongst them was brought; that this was it which had damped the glory of Italian wits; that nothing had been there written now these many years but flattery and fustian. There it was that I found and visited the famous Galileo, grown old, a prisoner to the Inquisition, for thinking in astronomy otherwise than the Franciscan and Dominican licensers thought. And though I knew that England then was groaning loudest under the prelatical yoke, nevertheless I took it as a pledge of future happiness, that other nations were so persuaded of her liberty. Yet was it beyond my hope that those worthies were then breathing in her air, who should be her leaders to such a deliverance, as shall never be forgotten by any revolution of time that this world hath to finish. When that was once begun, it was as little in my fear that what words of complaint I heard among learned men of other parts uttered against the Inquisition, the same I should hear by as learned men at home, uttered in time of Parliament against an order of licensing; and that so generally that, when I had disclosed myself a companion of their discontent, I might say, if without envy, that he whom an honest quaestorship had endeared to the Sicilians was not more by them importuned against Verres, than the favorable opinion which I had among many who honor ye, and are known and respected by ye, loaded me with entreaties and persuasions, that I would not despair to lay together that which just reason should bring into my mind, toward the removal of an undeserved thralldom upon learning. That this is not therefore the disburdening of a particular fancy, but the common grievance of all those who had prepared their minds and studies above the vulgar pitch to advance truth in others, and from others to entertain it, thus much may satisfy.

And in their name I shall for neither friend nor foe conceal what the general murmur is; that if it come to inquisitioning again and licensing, and that we are so timorous of ourselves, and so suspicious of all men, as to fear each book and the shaking of every leaf, before we know what the contents are; if some who but of late were little better than silenced from preaching shall come now to silence us from reading, except what they please, it cannot be guessed what is intended by some but a second tyranny over learning: and will soon put it out of controversy, that bishops and presbyters are the same to us, both name and thing. That those evils of prelaty, which before from five or six and twenty sees were distributively charged upon the whole people, will now light wholly upon learning, is not obscure to us: when as now the pastor of a small unlearned parish on the sudden shall be exalted archbishop over a large diocese of books, and yet not remove, but keep his other cure too, a mystical pluralist. He who but of late cried down the sole ordination of every novice Bachelor of Art, and denied sole jurisdiction over the simplest parishioner, shall now at home in his private chair assume both these over worthiest and most excellent books and ablest authors that write them.

In the meanwhile if anyone would write, and bring his helpful hand to the slow-moving Reformation which we labor under, if Truth have spoken to him before others, or but seemed at least to speak, who hath so bejesuited us that we should trouble that man with asking license to do so worthy a deed? and not consider this, that if it come to prohibiting, there is not aught more likely to be prohibited than truth itself; whose first appearance to our eyes, bleared and dimmed with prejudice and custom, is more unsightly and unplausible than many errors, even as the person is of many a great man slight and contemptuous to see to. And what do they tell us vainly of new opinions, when this very opinion of theirs, that none must be heard but whom they like, is the worst and newest opinion of all others; and is the chief cause why sects and schisms do so much abound, and true knowledge is kept at distance from us; besides yet a greater danger which is in it.

For when God shakes a kingdom with strong and healthful commotions to a general reforming, 'tis not untrue that many sectaries and false teachers are then busiest in seducing; but yet more true it is, that God then raises to his own work men of rare abilities, and more than common industry, not only to look back and revise what hath been taught heretofore, but to gain further and go on some new enlightened steps in the discovery of truth. For such is the order of God's enlightening his Church, to dispense and deal out by degrees his beam, so as our earthly eyes may best sustain it.

Neither is God appointed and confined, where and out of what place these his chosen shall be first heard to speak; for he sees not as man sees, chooses not as man chooses, lest we should devote ourselves again to set places, and assemblies, and outward callings of men; planting our faith one while in the old Convocation house, and another while in the Chapel at Westminster; when all the faith and religion that shall be there canonized is not sufficient without plain convincement, and the charity of patient instruction to supple the least bruise of conscience, to edify the meanest Christian, who desires to walk in the Spirit, and not in the letter of human trust, for all the number of voices that can be there made; no, though Harry VII himself there, with all his liege tombs about him, should lend them voices from the dead, to swell their number.

And if the men be erroneous who appear to be the leading schismatics, what withholds us but our sloth, our self-will, and distrust in the right cause, that we do not give them gentle meetings and gentle dismissions, that we debate not and examine the matter thoroughly with liberal and frequent audience; if not for their sakes, yet for our own? Seeing no man who hath tasted learning, but will confess the many ways of profiting by those who, not contented with stale receipts, are able to manage and set forth new positions to the world. And were they but as the dust and cinders of our feet, so long as in that notion they may yet serve to polish and brighten the armory of Truth, even for that respect they were not utterly to be cast away. But if they be of those whom God hath fitted for the special use of these times with eminent and ample gifts, and those perhaps neither among the priests nor among the Pharisees, and we in the haste of a precipitant zeal shall make no distinction, but resolve to stop their mouths, because we fear they come with new and dangerous opinions, as we commonly forejudge them ere we understand them; no less than woe to us, while, thinking thus to defend the Gospel, we are found the persecutors.

There have been not a few since the beginning of this Parliament, both of the presbytery and others, who by their unlicensed books, to the contempt of an Imprimatur, first broke that triple ice clung about our hearts, and taught the people to see day: I hope that none of those were the persuaders to renew upon us this bondage which they themselves have wrought so much good by contemning. But if neither the check that Moses gave to young Joshua, nor the countermand which our Savior gave to young John, who was so ready to prohibit those whom he thought unlicensed, be not enough to admonish our elders how unacceptable to God their testy mood of prohibiting is; if neither their own remembrance what evil hath abounded in the Church by this set of licensing, and what good they themselves have begun by transgressing it, be not enough, but that they will persuade and execute the most Dominican part of the Inquisition over us, and are already with one foot in the stirrup so active at suppressing, it would be no unequal distribution in the first place to suppress the suppressors themselves: whom the change of their condition hath puffed up, more than their late experience of harder times hath made wise.

And as for regulating the press, let no man think to have the honor of advising ye better than yourselves have done in that Order published next before this, "that no book be printed, unless the printer's and the author's name, or at least the printer's, be registered." Those which otherwise come forth, if they be found mischievous and libelous, the fire and the executioner will be the timeliest and the most effectual remedy that man's prevention can use. For this authentic Spanish policy of licensing books, if I have said aught, will prove the most unlicensed book itself within a short while; and was the immediate image of a Star Chamber decree to that purpose made in those very times when that Court did the rest of those her pious works, for which she is now fallen from the stars with Lucifer. Whereby ye may guess what kind of state prudence, what love of the people, what care of religion or good manners there was at the contriving, although with singular hypocrisy it pretended to bind books to their good behavior. And how it got the upper hand of your precedent Order so well constituted before, if we may believe those men whose profession gives them cause to inquire most, it may be doubted there was in it the fraud of some old patentees and monopolizers in the trade of bookselling; who under pretence of the poor in their Company not to be defrauded, and the just retaining of each man his several copy, which God forbid should be gainsaid, brought divers glossing colors to the House, which were indeed but colors, and serving to no end except it be to exercise a superiority over their neighbors; men who do not therefore labor in an honest profession to which learning is indebted, that they should be made other men's vassals. Another end is thought was aimed at by some of them in procuring by petition this Order, that, having power in their hands, malignant books might the easier scape abroad, as the event shows.

But of these sophisms and elenchs of merchandise I skill not. This I know, that errors in a good government and in a bad are equally almost incident; for what magistrate may not be misinformed, and much the sooner, if liberty of printing be reduced into the power of a few? But to redress willingly and speedily what hath been erred, and in highest authority to esteem a plain advertisement more than others have done a sumptuous bride, is a virtue (honored Lords and Commons) answerable to your highest actions, and whereof none can participate but greatest and wisest men.

3 ON THE FREEDOM OF THE PRESS FROM POOR RICHARD'S ALMANACK BY BENJAMIN FRANKLIN (1757)

While free from Force the Press remains,
Virtue and Freedom chear our Plains,
And Learning Largesses bestows,
And keeps unlicens'd open House.
We to the Nation's publick Mart
Our Works of Wit, and Schemes of Art,
And philosophic Goods, this Way,
Like Water carriage, cheap convey.
This Tree which Knowledge so affords,
Inquisitors with flaming swords
From Lay-Approach with Zeal defend,
Lest their own Paradise should end.

The Press from her fecundous Womb
Brought forth the Arts of Greece and Rome;
Her offspring, skill'd in Logic War,
Truth's Banner wav'd in open Air;
The Monster Superstition fled,
And hid in Shades in Gorgon Head;
And awless Pow'r, the long kept Field,
By Reason quell'd, was forc'd to yield.

This Nurse of Arts, and Freedom's Fence,
To chain, is Treason against Sense:
And Liberty, thy thousand Tongues
None silence who design no Wrongs;
For those who use the Gag's Restraint,
First Rob, before they stop Complaint.

BROWN

4 AMENDMENT ONE (SPEECH AND PRESS): ADAPTED FROM COMMENTARIES 4:150—53 BY WILLIAM BLACKSTONE (1769)

Of a nature very similar to challenges are libels, libelli famosi, which, taken in their largest and most extensive sense, signify any writings, pictures, or the like, of an immoral or illegal tendency; but, in the sense under which we are now to consider them, are malicious defamations of any person, and especially a magistrate, made public by either printing, writing, signs, or pictures, in order to provoke him to wrath, or expose him to public hatred, contempt, and ridicule. The direct tendency of these libels is the breach of the public peace, by stirring up the objects of them to revenge, and perhaps to bloodshed.

The communication of a libel to any one person is a publication in the eye of the law: and therefore the sending an abusive private letter to a man is as much a libel as if it were openly printed, for it equally tends to a breach of the peace. For the same reason it is immaterial with respect to the essence of a libel, whether the matter of it be true or false; since the provocation, and not the falsity, is the thing to be punished criminally: though, doubtless, the falsehood of it may aggravate it's guilt, and enhance it's punishment.

In a civil action, we may remember, a libel must appear to be false, as well as scandalous; for, if the charge be true, the plaintiff has received no private injury, and has no ground to demand a compensation for himself, whatever offence it may be against the public peace: and therefore, upon a civil action, the truth of the accusation may be pleaded in bar of the suit. But, in a criminal prosecution, the tendency which all libels have to create animosities, and to disturb the public peace, is the sole consideration of the law. And therefore, in such prosecutions, the only facts to be considered are, first, the making or publishing of the book or writing; and secondly, whether the matter be criminal: and, if both these points are against the defendant, the offence against the public is complete.

The punishment of such libellers, for either making, repeating, printing, or publishing the libel, is fine, and such corporal punishment as the court in their discretion shall inflict; regarding the quantity of the offence, and the quality of the offender. By the law of the twelve tables at Rome, libels, which affected the reputation of another, were made a capital offence: but, before the reign of Augustus, the punishment became corporal only. Under the emperor Valentinian it was again made capital, not only to write, but to publish, or even to omit destroying them. Our law, in this and many other respects, corresponds rather with the middle age of Roman jurisprudence, when liberty, learning, and humanity, were in their full vigour, than with the cruel edicts that were established in the dark and tyrannical ages of the antient decemviri, or the later emperors.

In this, and the other instances which we have lately considered, where blasphemous, immoral, treasonable, schismatical, seditious, or scandalous libels are punished by the English law, some with a greater, others with a less degree of severity; the liberty of the press, properly understood, is by no means infringed or violated.

The liberty of the press is indeed essential to the nature of a free state: but this consists in laying no previous restraints upon publications, and not in freedom from censure for criminal matter when published. Every freeman has an undoubted right to lay what sentiments he pleases before the public: to forbid this, is to destroy the freedom of the press: but if he publishes what is improper, mischievous, or illegal, he must take the consequence of his own temerity. To subject the press to the restrictive power of a licenser, as was formerly done, both before and since the revolution, is to subject all freedom of sentiment to the prejudices of one man, and make him the arbitrary and infallible judge of all controverted points in learning, religion, and government. But to punish (as the law does at present) any dangerous or offensive writings, which, when published, shall on a fair and impartial trial be adjudged of a pernicious tendency, is necessary for the preservation of peace and good order, of government and religion, the only solid foundations of civil liberty. Thus the will of individuals is still left free; the abuse only of that free will is the object of legal punishment. Neither is any restraint hereby laid upon freedom of thought or enquiry: liberty of private sentiment is still left; the disseminating, or making public, of bad sentiments, destructive of the ends of society, is the crime which society corrects.

A man (says a fine writer on this subject) may be allowed to keep poisons in his closet, but not publicly to vend them as cordials. And to this we may add, that the only plausible argument heretofore used for restraining the just freedom of the press, "that it was necessary to prevent the daily abuse of it," will entirely lose it's force, when it is shewn (by a seasonable exertion of the laws) that the press cannot be abused to any bad purpose, without incurring a suitable punishment: whereas it never can be used to any good one, when under the control of an inspector. So true will it be found, that to censure the licentiousness, is to maintain the liberty, of the press.

5 THE BILL OF RIGHTS AND AMENDMENTS 11-14: THE CONSTITUTION OF THE UNITED STATES OF AMERICA (1789)

Amendment I

Congress shall make no law respecting an establishment of religion, or prohibiting the free exercise thereof; or abridging the freedom of speech, or of the press; or the right of the people peaceably to assemble, and to petition the government for a redress of grievances.

Amendment II

A well regulated militia, being necessary to the security of a free state, the right of the people to keep and bear arms, shall not be infringed.

Amendment III

No soldier shall, in time of peace be quartered in any house, without the consent of the owner, nor in time of war, but in a manner to be prescribed by law.

Amendment IV

The right of the people to be secure in their persons, houses, papers, and effects, against unreasonable searches and seizures, shall not be violated, and no warrants shall issue, but upon probable cause, supported by oath or affirmation, and particularly describing the place to be searched, and the persons or things to be seized.

Amendment V

No person shall be held to answer for a capital, or otherwise infamous crime, unless on a presentment or indictment of a grand jury, except in cases arising in the land or naval forces, or in the militia, when in actual service in time of war or public danger; nor shall any person be subject for the same offense to be twice put in jeopardy of life or limb; nor shall be compelled in any criminal case to be a witness against himself, nor be deprived of life, liberty, or property, without due process of law; nor shall private property be taken for public use, without just compensation.

Amendment VI

In all criminal prosecutions, the accused shall enjoy the right to a speedy and public trial, by an impartial jury of the state and district wherein the crime shall have been committed, which district shall have been previously ascertained by law, and to be informed of the nature and cause of the accusation; to be confronted with the witnesses against him; to have compulsory process for obtaining witnesses in his favor, and to have the assistance of counsel for his defense.

Amendment VII

In suits at common law, where the value in controversy shall exceed twenty dollars, the right of trial by jury shall be preserved, and no fact tried by a jury, shall be otherwise reexamined in any court of the United States, than according to the rules of the common law.

Amendment VIII

Excessive bail shall not be required, nor excessive fines imposed, nor cruel and unusual punishments inflicted.

Amendment IX

The enumeration in the Constitution, of certain rights, shall not be construed to deny or disparage others retained by the people.

Amendment X

The powers not delegated to the United States by the Constitution, nor prohibited by it to the states, are reserved to the states respectively, or to the people.

Amendment XI

Note: Article III, section 2, of the Constitution was modified by amendment 11.

The Judicial power of the United States shall not be construed to extend to any suit in law or equity, commenced or prosecuted against one of the United States by Citizens of another State, or by Citizens or Subjects of any Foreign State.

Amendment XII

Note: A portion of Article II, section 1 of the Constitution was superseded by the 12th amendment.

The Electors shall meet in their respective states and vote by ballot for President and Vice-President, one of whom, at least, shall not be an inhabitant of the same state with themselves; they shall name in their ballots the person voted for as President, and in distinct ballots the person voted for as Vice-President, and they shall make distinct lists of all persons voted for as President, and of all persons voted for as Vice-President, and of the number of votes for each, which lists they shall sign and certify, and transmit sealed to the seat of the government of the United States, directed to the President of the Senate; -- the President of the Senate shall, in the presence of the Senate and House of Representatives, open all the certificates and the votes shall then be counted; -- The person having the greatest number of votes for President, shall be the President, if such number be a majority of the whole number of Electors appointed; and if no person have such majority, then from the persons having the highest numbers not exceeding three on the list of those voted for as President, the House of Representatives shall choose immediately, by ballot, the President. But in choosing the President, the votes shall be taken by states, the representation from each state having one vote; a quorum for this purpose shall consist of a member or members from two-thirds of the states, and a majority of all the states shall be necessary to a choice. [And if the House of Representatives shall not choose a President whenever the right of choice shall devolve upon them, before the fourth day of March next following, then the Vice-President shall act as President, as in case of the death or other constitutional disability of the President. --]* The person having the greatest number of votes as Vice-President, shall be the Vice-President, if such number be a majority of the whole number of Electors appointed, and if no person have a majority, then from the two highest numbers on the list, the Senate shall choose the Vice-President; a quorum for the purpose shall consist of two-thirds of the whole number of Senators, and a majority of the whole number shall be necessary to a choice. But no person constitutionally ineligible to the office of President shall be eligible to that of Vice-President of the United States.

*Superseded by section 3 of the 20th amendment.

Amendment XIII

Note: A portion of Article IV, section 2, of the Constitution was superseded by the 13th amendment.

Section 1. Neither slavery nor involuntary servitude, except as a punishment for crime whereof the party shall have been duly convicted, shall exist within the United States, or any place subject to their jurisdiction.

Section 2. Congress shall have power to enforce this article by appropriate legislation.

Amendment XIV

Note: Article I, section 2, of the Constitution was modified by section 2 of the 14th amendment.

Section 1. All persons born or naturalized in the United States, and subject to the jurisdiction thereof, are citizens of the United States and of the State wherein they reside. No State shall make or enforce any law which shall abridge the privileges or immunities of citizens of the United States; nor shall any State deprive any person of life, liberty, or property, without due process of law; nor deny to any person within its jurisdiction the equal protection of the laws.

Section 2. Representatives shall be apportioned among the several States according to their respective numbers, counting the whole number of persons in each State, excluding Indians not taxed. But when the right to vote at any election for the choice of electors for President and Vice-President of the United States, Representatives in Congress, the Executive and Judicial officers of a State, or the members of the Legislature thereof, is denied to any of the male inhabitants of such State, being twenty-one years of age,* and citizens of the United States, or in any way abridged, except for participation in rebellion, or other crime, the basis of representation therein shall be reduced in the proportion which the number of such male citizens shall bear to the whole number of male citizens twenty-one years of age in such State.

Section 3. No person shall be a Senator or Representative in Congress, or elector of President and Vice-President, or hold any office, civil or military, under the United States, or under any State, who, having previously taken an oath, as a member of Congress, or as an officer of the United States, or as a member of any State legislature, or as an executive or judicial officer of any State, to support the Constitution of the United States, shall have engaged in insurrection or rebellion against the same, or given aid or comfort to the enemies thereof. But Congress may by a vote of two-thirds of each House, remove such disability.

Section 4. The validity of the public debt of the United States, authorized by law, including debts incurred for payment of pensions and bounties for services in suppressing insurrection or rebellion, shall not be questioned. But neither the United States nor any State shall assume or pay any debt or obligation incurred in aid of insurrection or rebellion against the United States, or any claim for the loss or emancipation of any slave; but all such debts, obligations and claims shall be held illegal and void.

Section 5. The Congress shall have the power to enforce, by appropriate legislation, the provisions of this article.

*Changed by section 1 of the 26th amendment.

6 ON LIMITATIONS TO FREEDOM OF SPEECH
BY THOMAS ERSKINE (1797)

A free and unlicensed Press, in the just and legal sense of the expression, has led to all the blessings, both of religion and government, which Great Britain or any part of the world at this moment enjoys, and it is calculated to advance mankind to still higher degrees of civilization and happiness. But this freedom, like every other, must be limited to be enjoyed and like every human advantage, may be defeated by its abuse.

I am well aware that by the communications of a free Press, all the errors of mankind, from age to age, have been dissipated and dispelled; and I recollect that the world, under the banners of reformed Christianity, has struggled through persecution to the noble eminence on which it stands at this moment, shedding the blessings of humanity and science upon the nations of the earth.

It may be asked, then, by what means the reformation would have been effected, if the books of the reformers had been suppressed, and the errors of now exploded superstitions had been supported by the terrors of an unreformed state? Or how, upon such principles, any reformation, civil or religious, can in future be effected? The solution is easy: Let us examine what are the genuine principles of the liberty of the Press, as they regard writings upon general subjects, unconnected with the personal reputations of private men, which are wholly foreign to the present inquiry. They are full of simplicity, and are brought as near perfection, by the law of England, as perhaps is attainable by any of the frail institutions of mankind.

Although every community must establish supreme authorities, founded upon fixed principles, and must give high powers to magistrates to administer laws for the preservation of government, and for the security of those who are to be protected by it; yet as infallibility and perfection belong neither to human individuals nor to human establishments, it ought to be the policy of all free nations, as it is most peculiarly the principle of our own, to permit the most unbounded freedom of discussion, even to the detection of errors in the Constitution of the very government itself; so as that common decorum is observed, which every State must exact from its subjects and which imposes no restraint upon any intellectual composition, fairly, honestly, and decently addressed to the consciences and understandings of men. Upon this principle I have an unquestionable right, a right which the best subjects have exercised, to examine the principles and structure of the Constitution, and by fair, manly reasoning, to question the practice of its administrators. I have a right to consider and to point out errors in the one or in the other; and not merely to reason upon their existence, but to consider the means of their reformation.

By such free, well-intentioned, modest, and dignified communication of sentiments and opinions, all nations have been gradually improved, and milder laws and purer religions have been established. The same principles which vindicate civil controversies, honestly directed, extend their protection to the sharpest contentions on the subject of religious faiths. This rational and legal course of improvement was recognized and ratified by Lord Kenyon as the law of England, in the late trial at Guildhall, where he looked back with gratitude to the labors of the reformers, as the fountains of our religious emancipation, and of the civil blessings that followed in their train. The English Constitution, indeed, does not stop short in the toleration of religious opinions, but liberally extends it to practice. It permits every man, even publicly, to worship God according to his own conscience, though in marked dissent from the national establishment, so as he professes the general faith, which is the sanction of all our moral duties, and the only pledge of our submission to the system which constitutes the State.

Is not this freedom of controversy and freedom of worship sufficient for all the purposes of human happiness and improvement? Can it be necessary for either, that the law should hold out indemnity to those who wholly abjure and revile the government of their country, or the religion on which it rests for its foundation? I expect to hear in answer to what I am now saying, much that will offend me. My learned friend, from the difficulties of his situation, which I know from experience how to feel for very sincerely, may be driven to advance propositions which it may be my duty with much freedom to reply to; and the law will sanction that freedom. But will not the ends of justice be completely answered by my exercise of that right, in terms that are decent, and calculated to expose its defects? Or will my argument suffer, or will public justice be impeded, because neither private honor and justice nor public decorum would endure my telling my very learned friend, because I differ from him in opinion, that he is a fool, a liar, and a scoundrel, in the face of the court? This is just the distinction between a book of free legal controversy, and the book which I am arraigning before you. Every man has a right to investigate, with decency, controversial points of the Christian religion; but no man consistently with a law which only exists under its sanctions has a right to deny its very existence, and to pour forth such shocking and insulting invectives as the lowest establishments in the graduation of civil authority ought not to be subjected to, and which soon would be borne down by insolence and disobedience, if they were.

The same principle pervades the whole system of the law, not merely in its abstract theory, but in its daily and most applauded practice. The intercourse between the sexes, which, properly regulated, not only continues, but humanizes and adorns our natures, is the foundation of all the thousand romances, plays and novels, which are in the hands of everybody. Some of them lead to the confirmation of every virtuous principle; others, though with the same profession, address the imagination in a manner to lead the passions into dangerous excesses; but though the law does not nicely discriminate the various shades which distinguish such works from one another, so as to suffer many to pass, through its liberal spirit, that upon principle ought to be suppressed, would it or does it tolerate, or does any decent man contend that it ought to pass by unpunished, libels of the most shameless obscenity, manifestly pointed to debauch innocent and to blast and poison the morals of the rising generation? This is only another illustration to demonstrate the obvious distinction between the work of an author who fairly exercises the powers of his mind in investigating the religion of government of any country, and him who attacks the rational existence of every religion or government, and brands with absurdity and folly the state which sanctions, and the obedient tools who cherish, the delusion.

But this publication appears to me to be as cruel and mischievous in its effects, as it is manifestly illegal in its principles; because it strikes at the best—sometimes, alas!—the only refuge and consolation amid the distresses and afflictions of the world. The poor and humble, whom it affects to pity, may be stabbed to the heart by it. They have more occasion for firm hopes beyond the grave than the rich and prosperous who have other comforts to render life delightful. I can conceive a distressed but virtuous man, surrounded by his children looking up to him for bread when he has none to give them; sinking under the last day's labor, and unequal to the next, yet still, supported by confidence in the hour when all tears shall be wiped from the eyes of affliction, bearing the burden laid upon him by a mysterious Providence which he adores, and anticipating with exultation the revealed promises of his Creator, when he shall be greater than the greatest, and happier than the happiest of mankind. What a change in such a mind might be wrought by such a merciless publication!

How any man can rationally vindicate the publication of such a book, in a country where the Christian religion is the very foundation of the law of the land, I am totally at a loss to conceive, and have no ideas for the discussion of. How is a tribunal whose whole jurisdiction is founded upon the solemn belief and practice of what is here denied as falsehood, and reprobated as impiety, to deal with such an anomalous defense? Upon what principle is it even offered to the court, whose authority is contemned and mocked at? If the religion proposed to be called in question, is not previously adopted in belief and solemnly acted upon, what authority has the court to pass any judgment at all of acquittal or condemnation? Why am I now or upon any other occasion to submit to his lordship's authority? Why am I now or at any time to address twelve of my equals, as I am now addressing you, with reverence and submission? Under what sanction are the witnesses to give their evidence, without which there can be no trial? Under what obligations can I call upon you, the jury representing your country, to administer justice? Surely upon no other than that you are sworn to administer it, under the oaths you have taken. The whole judicial fabric, from the king's sovereign authority to the lowest office of magistracy, has no other foundation. The whole is built, both in form and substance, upon the same oath of every one of its ministers to do justice, as God shall help them hereafter. What God? And what hereafter? That God, undoubtedly, who has commanded kings to rule, and judges to decree justice; who has said to witnesses, not only by the voice of nature but in revealed commandments, "Thou shalt not bear false testimony against thy neighbor"; and who has enforced obedience to them by the revelation of the unutterable blessings which shall attend their observance, and the awful punishments which shall await upon their transgression.

But it seems this is an age of reason, and the time and the person are at last arrived that are to dissipate the errors which have overspread the past generations of ignorance. The believers in Christianity are many, but it belongs to the few that are wise to correct their credulity. Belief is an act of reason, and superior reason may, therefore, dictate to the weak. In running the mind over the long list of sincere and devout Christians, I cannot help lamenting that Newton had not lived to this day, to have had his shallowness filled up with this new flood of light. But the subject is too awful for irony; I will speak plainly and directly. Newton was a Christian: Newton, whose mind burst forth from the fetters fastened by nature upon our finite conceptions; Newton, whose science was truth, and the foundations of whose knowledge of it was philosophy—not those visionary and arrogant presumptions which too often usurp its name, but philosophy resting upon the basis of mathematics, which, like figures, cannot lie; Newton, who carried the line and rule to the uttermost barriers of creation, and explored the principles by which all created matter exists and is held together. But this extraordinary man, in the might reach of this mind, overlooked, perhaps, the errors which a minuter investigation of the created things on this earth might have taught him.

What shall then be said of Mr. Boyle, who looked into the organic structure of all matter, even to the inanimate substances which the foot treads upon? Such a man may be supposed to have been equally qualified with Mr. Paine to look up through nature to nature's God; yet the result of all his contemplations was the most confirmed and devout belief in all which the other holds in contempt as despicable and driveling superstition. But this error might, perhaps, arise from a want of due attention to the foundations of human judgment, and the structure of that understanding which God has given us for the investigation of truth. Let that question be answered by Mr. Locke, who to the highest pitch of devotion and adoration was a Christian; Mr. Locke, whose office was to detect the errors of thinking, by going up to the very fountains of thought, and to direct into the proper track of reasoning the devious mind of man, by showing him its whole process, from the first perceptions of sense, to the last conclusions of ratiocination, putting a rein upon false opinion, by practical rules for the conduct of human judgment.

But these men, it may be said, were only deep thinkers, and lived in their closets, unaccustomed to the traffic of the world, and to the laws which practically regulate mankind. Gentlemen, in the place where we now sit to administer the justice of this great country, the never-to-be-forgotten Sir Matthew Hale once presided; whose faith in Christianity is an exalted commentary upon its truth and reason, and whose life was a glorious example of its fruits; whose justice, drawn from the pure fountain of the Christian dispensation, will be, in all ages, a subject of the highest reverence and admiration. But it is said by the author, that the Christian fable is but the tale of the more ancient superstitions of the world, and may be easily detected by a proper understanding of the mythologies of the heathens. Did Milton understand those mythologies? Was he less versed than Mr. Paine in the superstitions of the world? No, they were the subject of his immortal song; and, though shut out from all recurrence to them, he poured them forth from the stores of a memory rich with all that man ever knew, and laid them in their order as the illustration of real and exalted faith, the unquestionable source of that fervid genius, which has cast a kind of shade upon most of the other works of man:

He pass'd the flaming bounds of place and time:
The living throne, the sapphire blaze,
Where angels tremble while they gaze,
He saw but blasted with excess of light,
Closed his eyes in endless night.

Thus, you find all that is great, or wise, or splendid, or illustrious, among created things; all the minds gifted beyond ordinary nature, if not inspired by its universal Author for the advancement and dignity of the world, though divided by distant ages, and by clashing opinions, yet joining as it were in one sublime chorus, to celebrate the truths of Christianity; laying upon its holy altars the never-fading offerings of their immortal wisdom.

Against all this concurring testimony, we find suddenly, from the author of this book, that the Bible teaches nothing but "lies, obscenity, cruelty, and injustice." Had he ever read our Savior's sermon on the mount, in which the great principles of our faith and duty are summed up? Let us all but read and practice it, and lies, obscenity, cruelty and injustice, and all human wickedness will be banished from the world!

Gentlemen, there is but one consideration more, which I cannot possibly omit, because I confess it affects me very deeply. The author of this book has written largely on public liberty and government; and this last performance, which I am now prosecuting, has, on that account, been more widely circulated, and principally among those who attached themselves from principle to his former works. This circumstance renders a public attack upon all revealed religion from such a writer infinitely more dangerous. The religious and moral sense of the people of Great Britain is the great anchor which alone can hold the vessel of the state amid the storms which agitate the world; and if the mass of the people were debauched from the principles of religion—the true basis of that humanity, charity, and benevolence, which have been so long the national characteristics—instead of mixing myself, as I sometimes have done, in political reformations, I would retire to the uttermost corners of the earth, to avoid their agitation; and would bear, not only the imperfections and abuses complained of in our own wise establishment, but even the worst government that even existed in the world, rather than go to the work of reformation with a multitude set free from all the charities of Christianity, who had no other sense of God's existence than was to be collected from Mr. Paine's observations of nature, which the mass of mankind have no leisure to contemplate, which promises no future rewards to animate the good in the glorious pursuit of human happiness, nor punishments to deter the wicked from destroying it even in its birth. The people of England are a religious people, and, with the blessing of God, so far as it is in my power, I will lend aid to keep them so.

Gentlemen, I cannot conclude without expressing the deepest regret at all attacks upon the Christian religion by authors who profess to promote the civil liberties of the world. For under what other auspices than Christianity have the lost and subverted liberties of mankind in former ages been reasserted? By what zeal, but the warm zeal of devout Christians, have English liberties been redeemed and consecrated? Under what other sanctions, even in our own days, have liberty and happiness been spreading to the uttermost corners of the earth? What work of civilization, what commonwealth of greatness, has this bald religion of nature ever established? We see, on the contrary, the nations that have no other light than that of nature to direct them, sunk in barbarism, or slaves to arbitrary governments; while under the Christian dispensation, the great career of the world has been slowly but clearly advancing, lighter at every step from the encouraging prophecies of the gospel, and leading, I trust, in the end to universal and eternal happiness. Each generation of mankind can see but a few revolving links of this mighty and mysterious chain; but by doing our several duties in our allotted stations, we are sure that we are fulfilling the purposes of our existence. You, I trust, will fulfill yours this day.

7 ON LIBERTY: OF THE LIBERTY OF THOUGHT AND DISCUSSION BY JOHN STUART MILL (1869)

The time, it is to be hoped, is gone by when any defence would be necessary of the "liberty of the press" as one of the securities against corrupt or tyrannical government. No argument, we may suppose, can now be needed, against permitting a legislature or an executive, not identified in interest with the people, to prescribe opinions to them, and determine what doctrines or what arguments they shall be allowed to hear. This aspect of the question, besides, has been so often and so triumphantly enforced by preceding writers, that it needs not be specially insisted on in this place. [Though the law of England, on the subject of the press, is as servile to this day as it was in the time of the Tudors, there is little danger of its being actually put in force against political discussion, except during some temporary panic, when fear of insurrection drives ministers and judges from their propriety;[1] and, speaking generally, it is not, in constitutional countries, to be apprehended that the government, whether completely responsible to the people or not, will often attempt to control the expression of opinion, except when in doing so it makes itself the organ of the general intolerance of the public. Let us suppose, therefore, that the government is entirely at one with the people, and never thinks of exerting any power of coercion unless in agreement with what it conceives to be their voice. But I deny the right of the people to exercise such coercion, either by themselves or by their government. The power itself is illegitimate. The best government has no more title to it than the worst. It is as noxious, or more noxious, when exerted in accordance with public opinion, than when in opposition to it. If all mankind minus one, were of one opinion, and only one person were of the contrary opinion, mankind would be no more justified in silencing that one person, than he, if he had the power, would be justified in silencing mankind. Were an opinion a personal possession of no value except to the owner; if to be obstructed in the enjoyment of it were simply a private injury, it would make some difference whether the injury was inflicted only on a few persons or on many. But the peculiar evil of silencing the expression of an opinion is, that it is robbing the human race; posterity as well as the existing generation; those who dissent from the opinion, still more than those who hold it. If the opinion is right, they are deprived of the opportunity of exchanging error for truth: if wrong, they lose, what is almost as great a benefit, the clearer perception and livelier impression of truth, produced by its collision with error.]

It is necessary to consider separately these two hypotheses, each of which has a distinct branch of the argument corresponding to it. We can never be sure that the opinion we are endeavouring to stifle is a false opinion; and if we were sure, stifling it would be an evil still.

First: the opinion which it is attempted to suppress by authority may possibly be true. Those who desire to suppress it, of course deny its truth; but they are not infallible. They have no authority to decide the question for all mankind, and exclude every other person from the means of judging. To refuse a hearing to an opinion, because they are sure that it is false, is to assume that their certainty is the same thing as absolute certainty. All silencing of discussion is an assumption of infallibility. Its condemnation may be allowed to rest on this common argument, not the worse for being common.

Unfortunately for the good sense of mankind, the fact of their fallibility is far from carrying the weight in their practical judgment, which is always allowed to it in theory; for while every one well knows himself to be fallible, few think it necessary to take any precautions against their own fallibility, or admit the supposition that any opinion of which they feel very certain, may be one of the examples of the error to which they acknowledge themselves to be liable. Absolute princes, or others who are accustomed to unlimited deference, usually feel this complete confidence in their own opinions on nearly all subjects. People more happily situated, who sometimes hear their opinions disputed, and are not wholly unused to be set right when they are wrong, place the same unbounded reliance only on such of their opinions as are shared by all who surround them, or to whom they habitually defer: for in proportion to a man's want of confidence in his own solitary judgment, does he usually repose, with implicit trust, on the infallibility of "the world" in general. And the world, to each individual, means the part of it with which he comes in contact; his party, his sect, his church, his class of society: the man may be called, by comparison, almost liberal and largeminded to whom it means anything so comprehensive as his own country or his own age. Nor is his faith in this collective authority at all shaken by his being aware that other ages, countries, sects, churches, classes, and parties have thought, and even now think, the exact reverse. He devolves upon his own world the responsibility of being in the right against the dissentient worlds of other people; and it never troubles him that mere accident has decided which of these numerous worlds is the object of his reliance, and that the same causes which make him a Churchman in London, would have made him a Buddhist or a Confucian in Pekin. Yet it is as evident in itself as any amount of argument can make it, that ages are no more infallible than individuals; every age having held many opinions which subsequent ages have deemed not only false but absurd; and it is as certain that many opinions, now general, will be rejected by future ages, as it is that many, once general, are rejected by the present.

The objection likely to be made to this argument, would probably take some such form as the following. There is no greater assumption of infallibility in forbidding the propagation of error, than in any other thing which is done by public authority on its own judgment and responsibility. Judgment is given to men that they may use it. Because it may be used erroneously, are men to be told that they ought not to use it at all? To prohibit what they think pernicious, is not claiming exemption from error, but fulfilling the duty incumbent on them, although fallible, of acting on their conscientious conviction. If we were never to act on our opinions, because those opinions may be wrong, we should leave all our interests uncared for, and all our duties unperformed. An objection which applies to all conduct can be no valid objection to any conduct in particular.

It is the duty of governments, and of individuals, to form the truest opinions they can;

to form them carefully, and never impose them upon others unless they are quite sure of being right. But when they are sure (such reasoners may say), it is not conscientiousness but cowardice to shrink from acting on their opinions, and allow doctrines which they honestly think dangerous to the welfare of mankind, either in this life or in another, to be scattered abroad without restraint, because other people, in less enlightened times, have persecuted opinions now believed to be true. Let us take care, it may be said, not to make the same mistake: but governments and nations have made mistakes in other things, which are not denied to be fit subjects for the exercise of authority: they have laid on bad taxes, made unjust wars. Ought we therefore to lay on no taxes, and, under whatever provocation, make no wars? Men, and governments, must act to the best of their ability. There is no such thing as absolute certainty, but there is assurance sufficient for the purposes of human life. We may, and must, assume our opinion to be true for the guidance of our own conduct: and it is assuming no more when we forbid bad men to pervert society by the propagation of opinions which we regard as false and pernicious.

I answer, that it is assuming very much more. There is the greatest difference between presuming an opinion to be true, because, with every opportunity for contesting it, it has not been refuted, and assuming its truth for the purpose of not permitting its refutation. Complete liberty of contradicting and disproving our opinion, is the very condition which justifies us in assuming its truth for purposes of action; and on no other terms can a being with human faculties have any rational assurance of being right.

When we consider either the history of opinion, or the ordinary conduct of human life, to what is it to be ascribed that the one and the other are no worse than they are? Not certainly to the inherent force of the human understanding; for, on any matter not self-evident, there are ninety-nine persons totally incapable of judging of it, for one who is capable; and the capacity of the hundredth person is only comparative; for the majority of the eminent men of every past generation held many opinions now known to be erroneous, and did or approved numerous things which no one will now justify. Why is it, then, that there is on the whole a preponderance among mankind of rational opinions and rational conduct? If there really is this preponderance — which there must be, unless human affairs are, and have always been, in an almost desperate state — it is owing to a quality of the human mind, the source of everything respectable in man, either as an intellectual or as a moral being, namely, that his errors are corrigible. He is capable of rectifying his mistakes by discussion and experience. Not by experience alone. There must be discussion, to show how experience is to be interpreted. Wrong opinions and practices gradually yield to fact and argument: but facts and arguments, to produce any effect on the mind, must be brought before it. Very few facts are able to tell their own story, without comments to bring out their meaning. The whole strength and value, then, of human judgment, depending on the one property, that it can be set right when it is wrong, reliance can be placed on it only when the means of setting it right are kept constantly at hand. In the case of any person whose judgment is really deserving of confidence, how has it become so? Because he has kept his mind open to criticism of his opinions and conduct. Because it has been his practice to listen to all that could be said against him; to profit by as much of it as was just, and expound to himself, and upon occasion to others, the fallacy of what was fallacious. Because he has felt, that the only way in which a human being can make some approach to knowing the whole of a subject, is by hearing what can be said about it by persons of every variety of opinion, and studying all modes in which it can be looked at by every character of mind. No wise man ever acquired his wisdom in any mode but this; nor is it in the nature of human intellect to become wise in any other manner. The steady habit of correcting and completing his own opinion by collating it with those of others, so far from causing doubt and hesitation in carrying it into practice, is the only stable foundation for a just reliance on it: for, being cognizant of all that can, at least obviously, be said against him, and having taken up his position against all gainsayers knowing that he has sought for objections and difficulties, instead of avoiding them, and has shut out no light which can be thrown upon the subject from any quarter — he has a right to think his judgment better than that of any person, or any multitude, who have not gone through a similar process.

It is not too much to require that what the wisest of mankind, those who are best entitled to trust their own judgment, find necessary to warrant their relying on it, should be submitted to by that miscellaneous collection of a few wise and many foolish individuals, called the public. The most intolerant of churches, the Roman Catholic Church, even at the canonization of a saint, admits, and listens patiently to, a "devil's advocate." The holiest of men, it appears, cannot be admitted to posthumous honors, until all that the devil could say against him is known and weighed. If even the Newtonian philosophy were not permitted to be questioned, mankind could not feel as complete assurance of its truth as they now do. The beliefs which we have most warrant for, have no safeguard to rest on, but a standing invitation to the whole world to prove them unfounded. If the challenge is not accepted, or is accepted and the attempt fails, we are far enough from certainty still; but we have done the best that the existing state of human reason admits of; we have neglected nothing that could give the truth a chance of reaching us: if the lists are kept open, we may hope that if there be a better truth, it will be found when the human mind is capable of receiving it; and in the meantime we may rely on having attained such approach to truth, as is possible in our own day. This is the amount of certainty attainable by a fallible being, and this the sole way of attaining it.

Strange it is, that men should admit the validity of the arguments for free discussion, but object to their being "pushed to an extreme;" not seeing that unless the reasons are good for an extreme case, they are not good for any case. Strange that they should imagine that they are not assuming infallibility when they acknowledge that there should be free discussion on all subjects which can possibly be doubtful, but think that some particular principle or doctrine should be forbidden to be questioned because it is so certain, that is, because they are certain that it is certain. To call any proposition certain, while there is any one who would deny its certainty if permitted, but who is not permitted, is to assume that we ourselves, and those who agree with us, are the judges of certainty, and judges without hearing the other side.

In the present age — which has been described as "destitute of faith, but terrified at scepticism," — in which people feel sure, not so much that their opinions are true, as that they should not know what to do without them — the claims of an opinion to be protected from public attack are rested not so much on its truth, as on its importance to society. There are, it is alleged, certain beliefs, so useful, not to say indispensable to well-being, that it is as much the duty of governments to uphold those beliefs, as to protect any other of the interests of society. In a case of such necessity, and so directly in the line of their duty, something less than infallibility may, it is maintained, warrant, and even bind, governments, to act on their own opinion, confirmed by the general opinion of mankind. It is also often argued, and still oftener thought, that none but bad men would desire to weaken these salutary beliefs; and there can be nothing wrong, it is thought, in restraining bad men, and prohibiting what only such men would wish to practise. This mode of thinking makes the justification of restraints on discussion not a question of the truth of doctrines, but of their usefulness; and flatters itself by that means to escape the responsibility of claiming to be an infallible judge of opinions. But those who thus satisfy themselves, do not perceive that the assumption of infallibility is merely shifted from one point to another. The usefulness of an opinion is itself matter of opinion: as disputable, as open to discussion and requiring discussion as much, as the opinion itself. There is the same need of an infallible judge of opinions to decide an opinion to be noxious, as to decide it to be false, unless the opinion condemned has full opportunity of defending itself. And it will not do to say that the heretic may be allowed to maintain the utility or harmlessness of his opinion, though forbidden to maintain its truth. The truth of an opinion is part of its utility. If we would know whether or not it is desirable that a proposition should be believed, is it possible to exclude the consideration of whether or not it is true? In the opinion, not of bad men, but of the best men, no belief which is contrary to truth can be really useful: and can you prevent such men from urging that plea, when they are charged with culpability for denying some doctrine which they are told is useful, but which they believe to be false? Those who are on the side of received opinions, never fail to take all possible advantage of this plea; you do not find them handling the question of utility as if it could be completely abstracted from that of truth: on the contrary, it is, above all, because their doctrine is "the truth," that the knowledge or the belief of it is held to be so indispensable. There can be no fair discussion of the question of usefulness, when an argument so vital may be employed on one side, but not on the other. And in point of fact, when law or public feeling do not permit the truth of an opinion to be disputed, they are just as little tolerant of a denial of its usefulness. The utmost they allow is an extenuation of its absolute necessity or of the positive guilt of rejecting it.

In order more fully to illustrate the mischief of denying a hearing to opinions because we, in our own judgment, have condemned them, it will be desirable to fix down the discussion to a concrete case; and I choose, by preference, the cases which are least favourable to me — in which the argument against freedom of opinion, both on the score of truth and on that of utility, is considered the strongest. Let the opinions impugned be the belief in a God and in a future state, or any of the commonly received doctrines of morality. To fight the battle on such ground, gives a great advantage to an unfair antagonist; since he will be sure to say (and many who have no desire to be unfair will say it internally), Are these the doctrines which you do not deem sufficiently certain to be taken under the protection of law? Is the belief in a God one of the opinions, to feel sure of which, you hold to be assuming infallibility? But I must be permitted to observe, that it is not the feeling sure of a doctrine (be it what it may) which I call an assumption of infallibility. It is the undertaking to decide that question for others, without allowing them to hear what can be said on the contrary side. And I denounce and reprobate this pretension not the less, if put forth on the side of my most solemn convictions. However positive any one's persuasion may be, not only of the falsity, but of the pernicious consequences — not only of the pernicious consequences, but (to adopt expressions which I altogether condemn) the immorality and impiety of an opinion; yet if, in pursuance of that private judgment, though backed by the public judgment of his country or his cotemporaries, he prevents the opinion from being heard in its defence, he assumes infallibility. And so far from the assumption being less objectionable or less dangerous because the opinion is called immoral or impious, this is the case of all others in which it is most fatal. These are exactly the occasions on which the men of one generation commit those dreadful mistakes which excite the astonishment and horror of posterity. It is among such that we find the instances memorable in history, when the arm of the law has been employed to root out the best men and the noblest doctrines; with deplorable success as to the men, though some of the doctrines have survived to be (as if in mockery) invoked, in defence of similar conduct towards those who dissent from them, or from their received interpretation.

Mankind can hardly be too often reminded, that there was once a man named Socrates, between whom and the legal authorities and public opinion of his time, there took place a memorable collision. Born in an age and country abounding in individual greatness, this man has been handed down to us by those who best knew both him and the age, as the most virtuous man in it; while we know him as the head and prototype of all subsequent teachers of virtue, the source equally of the lofty inspiration of Plato and the judicious utilitarianism of Aristotle, "i maestri di color che sanno," the two headsprings of ethical as of all other philosophy. This acknowledged master of all the eminent thinkers who have since lived — whose fame, still growing after more than two thousand years, all but outweighs the whole remainder of the names which make his native city illustrious — was put to death by his countrymen, after a judicial conviction, for impiety and immorality. Impiety, in denying the gods recognized by the State; indeed his accuser asserted (see the "Apologia") that he believed in no gods at all. Immorality, in being, by his doctrines and instructions, a "corrupter of youth." Of these charges the tribunal, there is every ground for believing, honestly found him guilty, and condemned the man who probably of all then born had deserved best of mankind, to be put to death as a criminal.

To pass from this to the only other instance of judicial iniquity, the mention of which, after the condemnation of Socrates, would not be an anti-climax: the event which took place on Calvary rather more than eighteen hundred years ago. The man who left on the memory of those who witnessed his life and conversation, such an impression of his moral grandeur, that eighteen subsequent centuries have done homage to him as the Almighty in person, was ignominiously put to death, as what? As a blasphemer. Men did not merely mistake their benefactor; they mistook him for the exact contrary of what he was, and treated him as that prodigy of impiety, which they themselves are now held to be, for their treatment of him. The feelings with which mankind now regard these lamentable transactions, especially the latter of the two, render them extremely unjust in their judgment of the unhappy actors. These were, to all appearance, not bad men — not worse than men most commonly are, but rather the contrary; men who possessed in a full, or somewhat more than a full measure, the religious, moral, and patriotic feelings of their time and people: the very kind of men who, in all times, our own included, have every chance of passing through life blameless and respected. The high-priest who rent his garments when the words were pronounced, which, according to all the ideas of his country, constituted the blackest guilt, was in all probability quite as sincere in his horror and indignation, as the generality of respectable and pious men now are in the religious and moral sentiments they profess; and most of those who now shudder at his conduct, if they had lived in his time and been born Jews, would have acted precisely as he did. Orthodox Christians who are tempted to think that those who stoned to death the first martyrs must have been worse men than they themselves are, ought to remember that one of those persecutors was Saint Paul.

Let us add one more example, the most striking of all, if the impressiveness of an error is measured by the wisdom and virtue of him who falls into it. If ever any one, possessed of power, had grounds for thinking himself the best and most enlightened among his cotemporaries, it was the Emperor Marcus Aurelius. Absolute monarch of the whole civilized world, he preserved through life not only the most unblemished justice, but what was less to be expected from his Stoical breeding, the tenderest heart. The few failings which are attributed to him, were all on the side of indulgence: while his writings, the highest ethical product of the ancient mind, differ scarcely perceptibly, if they differ at all, from the most characteristic teachings of Christ. This man, a better Christian in all but the dogmatic sense of the word, than almost any of the ostensibly Christian sovereigns who have since reigned, persecuted Christianity. Placed at the summit of all the previous attainments of humanity, with an open, unfettered intellect, and a character which led him of himself to embody in his moral writings the Christian ideal, he yet failed to see that Christianity was to be a good and not an evil to the world, with his duties to which he was so deeply penetrated. Existing society he knew to be in a deplorable state. But such as it was, he saw or thought he saw, that it was held together and prevented from being worse, by belief and reverence of the received divinities. As a ruler of mankind, he deemed it his duty not to suffer society to fall in pieces; and saw not how, if its existing ties were removed, any others could be formed which could again knit it together. The new religion openly aimed at dissolving these ties: unless, therefore, it was his duty to adopt that religion, it seemed to be his duty to put it down. Inasmuch then as the theology of Christianity did not appear to him true or of divine origin; inasmuch as this strange history of a crucified God was not credible to him, and a system which purported to rest entirely upon a foundation to him so wholly unbelievable, could not be foreseen by him to be that renovating agency which, after all abatements, it has in fact proved to be; the gentlest and most amiable of philosophers and rulers, under a solemn sense of duty, authorized the persecution of Christianity. To my mind this is one of the most tragical facts in all history. It is a bitter thought, how different a thing the Christianity of the world might have been, if the Christian faith had been adopted as the religion of the empire under the auspices of Marcus Aurelius instead of those of Constantine. But it would be equally unjust to him and false to truth, to deny, that no one plea which can be urged for punishing anti-Christian teaching, was wanting to Marcus Aurelius for punishing, as he did, the propagation of Christianity. No Christian more firmly believes that Atheism is false, and tends to the dissolution of society, than Marcus Aurelius believed the same things of Christianity; he who, of all men then living, might have been thought the most capable of appreciating it. Unless any one who approves of punishment for the promulgation of opinions, flatters himself that he is a wiser and better man than Marcus Aurelius — more deeply versed in the wisdom of his time, more elevated in his intellect above it — more earnest in his search for truth, or more single-minded in his devotion to it when found; — let him abstain from that assumption of the joint infallibility of himself and the multitude, which the great Antoninus made with so unfortunate a result.

Aware of the impossibility of defending the use of punishment for restraining irreligious opinions, by any argument which will not justify Marcus Antoninus, the enemies of religious freedom, when hard pressed, occasionally accept this consequence, and say, with Dr. Johnson, that the persecutors of Christianity were in the right; that persecution is an ordeal through which truth ought to pass, and always passes successfully, legal penalties being, in the end, powerless against truth, though sometimes beneficially effective against mischievous errors. This is a form of the argument for religious intolerance, sufficiently remarkable not to be passed without notice.

A theory which maintains that truth may justifiably be persecuted because persecution cannot possibly do it any harm, cannot be charged with being intentionally hostile to the reception of new truths; but we cannot commend the generosity of its dealing with the persons to whom mankind are indebted for them. To discover to the world something which deeply concerns it, and of which it was previously ignorant; to prove to it that it had been mistaken on some vital point of temporal or spiritual interest, is as important a service as a human being can render to his fellow-creatures, and in certain cases, as in those of the early Christians and of the Reformers, those who think with Dr. Johnson believe it to have been the most precious gift which could be bestowed on mankind. That the authors of such splendid benefits should be requited by martyrdom; that their reward should be to be dealt with as the vilest of criminals, is not, upon this theory, a deplorable error and misfortune, for which humanity should mourn in sackcloth and ashes, but the normal and justifiable state of things. The propounder of a new truth, according to this doctrine, should stand, as stood, in the legislation of the Locrians, the proposer of a new law, with a halter round his neck, to be instantly tightened if the public assembly did not, on hearing his reasons, then and there adopt his proposition. People who defend this mode of treating benefactors, can not be supposed to set much value on the benefit; and I believe this view of the subject is mostly confined to the sort of persons who think that new truths may have been desirable once, but that we have had enough of them now.

But, indeed, the dictum that truth always triumphs over persecution, is one of those pleasant falsehoods which men repeat after one another till they pass into commonplaces, but which all experience refutes. History teems with instances of truth put down by persecution. If not suppressed forever, it may be thrown back for centuries. To speak only of religious opinions: the Reformation broke out at least twenty times before Luther, and was put down. Arnold of Brescia was put down. Fra Dolcino was put down. Savonarola was put down. The Albigeois were put down. The Vaudois were put down. The Lollards were put down. The Hussites were put down. Even after the era of Luther, wherever persecution was persisted in, it was successful. In Spain, Italy, Flanders, the Austrian empire, Protestantism was rooted out; and, most likely, would have been so in England, had Queen Mary lived, or Queen Elizabeth died. Persecution has always succeeded, save where the heretics were too strong a party to be effectually persecuted. No reasonable person can doubt that Christianity might have been extirpated in the Roman empire. It spread, and became predominant, because the persecutions were only occasional, lasting but a short time, and separated by long intervals of almost undisturbed propagandism. It is a piece of idle sentimentality that truth, merely as truth, has any inherent power denied to error, of prevailing against the dungeon and the stake. Men are not more zealous for truth than they often are for error, and a sufficient application of legal or even of social penalties will generally succeed in stopping the propagation of either. The real advantage which truth has, consists in this, that when an opinion is true, it may be extinguished once, twice, or many times, but in the course of ages there will generally be found persons to rediscover it, until some one of its reappearances falls on a time when from favourable circumstances it escapes persecution until it has made such head as to withstand all subsequent attempts to suppress it.

It will be said, that we do not now put to death the introducers of new opinions: we are not like our fathers who slew the prophets, we even build sepulchres to them. It is true we no longer put heretics to death; and the amount of penal infliction which modern feeling would probably tolerate, even against the most obnoxious opinions, is not sufficient to extirpate them. But let us not flatter ourselves that we are yet free from the stain even of legal persecution. Penalties for opinion, or at least for its expression, still exist by law; and their enforcement is not, even in these times, so unexampled as to make it at all incredible that they may some day be revived in full force. In the year 1857, at the summer assizes of the county of Cornwall, an unfortunate man,[2] said to be of unexceptionable conduct in all relations of life, was sentenced to twenty-one months imprisonment, for uttering, and writing on a gate, some offensive words concerning Christianity. Within a month of the same time, at the Old Bailey, two persons, on two separate occasions,[3] were rejected as jurymen, and one of them grossly insulted by the judge and one of the counsel, because they honestly declared that they had no theological belief; and a third, a foreigner,[4] for the same reason, was denied justice against a thief. This refusal of redress took place in virtue of the legal doctrine, that no person can be allowed to give evidence in a court of justice, who does not profess belief in a God (any god is sufficient) and in a future state; which is equivalent to declaring such persons to be outlaws, excluded from the protection of the tribunals; who may not only be robbed or assaulted with impunity, if no one but themselves, or persons of similar opinions, be present, but any one else may be robbed or assaulted with impunity, if the proof of the fact depends on their evidence. The assumption on which this is grounded, is that the oath is worthless, of a person who does not believe in a future state; a proposition which betokens much ignorance of history in those who assent to it (since it is historically true that a large proportion of infidels in all ages have been persons of distinguished integrity and honor); and would be maintained by no one who had the smallest conception how many of the persons in greatest repute with the world, both for virtues and for attainments, are well known, at least to their intimates, to be unbelievers. The rule, besides, is suicidal, and cuts away its own foundation. Under pretence that atheists must be liars, it admits the testimony of all atheists who are willing to lie, and rejects only those who brave the obloquy of publicly confessing a detested creed rather than affirm a falsehood. A rule thus self-convicted of absurdity so far as regards its professed purpose, can be kept in force only as a badge of hatred, a relic of persecution; a persecution, too, having the peculiarity that the qualification for undergoing it is the being clearly proved not to deserve it. The rule, and the theory it implies, are hardly less insulting to believers than to infidels. For if he who does not believe in a future state necessarily lies, it follows that they who do believe are only prevented from lying, if prevented they are, by the fear of hell. We will not do the authors and abettors of the rule the injury of supposing, that the conception which they have formed of Christian virtue is drawn from their own consciousness.

These, indeed, are but rags and remnants of persecution, and may be thought to be not so much an indication of the wish to persecute, as an example of that very frequent infirmity of English minds, which makes them take a preposterous pleasure in the assertion of a bad principle, when they are no longer bad enough to desire to carry it really into practice. But unhappily there is no security in the state of the public mind, that the suspension of worse forms of legal persecution, which has lasted for about the space of a generation, will continue. In this age the quiet surface of routine is as often ruffled by attempts to resuscitate past evils, as to introduce new benefits. What is boasted of at the present time as the revival of religion, is always, in narrow and uncultivated minds, at least as much the revival of bigotry; and where there is the strongest permanent leaven of intolerance in the feelings of a people, which at all times abides in the middle classes of this country, it needs but little to provoke them into actively persecuting those whom they have never ceased to think proper objects of persecution.[5] For it is this — it is the opinions men entertain, and the feelings they cherish, respecting those who disown the beliefs they deem important, which makes this country not a place of mental freedom. For a long time past, the chief mischief of the legal penalties is that they strengthen the social stigma. It is that stigma which is really effective, and so effective is it, that the profession of opinions which are under the ban of society is much less common in England, than is, in many other countries, the avowal of those which incur risk of judicial punishment. In respect to all persons but those whose pecuniary circumstances make them independent of the good will of other people, opinion, on this subject, is as efficacious as law; men might as well be imprisoned, as excluded from the means of earning their bread. Those whose bread is already secured, and who desire no favors from men in power, or from bodies of men, or from the public, have nothing to fear from the open avowal of any opinions, but to be ill-thought of and illspoken of, and this it ought not to require a very heroic mould to enable them to bear. There is no room for any appeal ad misericordiam in behalf of such persons. But though we do not now inflict so much evil on those who think differently from us, as it was formerly our custom to do, it may be that we do ourselves as much evil as ever by our treatment of them. Socrates was put to death, but the Socratic philosophy rose like the sun in heaven, and spread its illumination over the whole intellectual firmament. Christians were cast to the lions, but the Christian Church grew up a stately and spreading tree, overtopping the older and less vigorous growths, and stifling them by its shade. Our merely social intolerance, kills no one, roots out no opinions, but induces men to disguise them, or to abstain from any active effort for their diffusion. With us, heretical opinions do not perceptibly gain or even lose, ground in each decade or generation; they never blaze out far and wide, but continue to smoulder in the narrow circles of thinking and studious persons among whom they originate, without ever lighting up the general affairs of mankind with either a true or a deceptive light. And thus is kept up a state of things very satisfactory to some minds, because, without the unpleasant process of fining or imprisoning anybody, it maintains all prevailing opinions outwardly undisturbed, while it does not absolutely interdict the exercise of reason by dissentients afflicted with the malady of thought. A convenient plan for having peace in the intellectual world, and keeping all things going on therein very much as they do already. But the price paid for this sort of intellectual pacification, is the sacrifice of the entire moral courage of the human mind. A state of things in which a large portion of the most active and inquiring intellects find it advisable to keep the genuine principles and grounds of their convictions within their own breasts, and attempt, in what they address to the public, to fit as much as they can of their own conclusions to premises which they have internally renounced, cannot send forth the open, fearless characters, and logical, consistent intellects who once adorned the thinking world. The sort of men who can be looked for under it, are either mere conformers to commonplace, or time-servers for truth whose arguments on all great subjects are meant for their hearers, and are not those which have convinced themselves. Those who avoid this alternative, do so by narrowing their thoughts and interests to things which can be spoken of without venturing within the region of principles, that is, to small practical matters, which would come right of themselves, if but the minds of mankind were strengthened and enlarged, and which will never be made effectually right until then; while that which would strengthen and enlarge men's minds, free and daring speculation on the highest subjects, is abandoned.

Those in whose eyes this reticence on the part of heretics is no evil, should consider in the first place, that in consequence of it there is never any fair and thorough discussion of heretical opinions; and that such of them as could not stand such a discussion, though they may be prevented from spreading, do not disappear. But it is not the minds of heretics that are deteriorated most, by the ban placed on all inquiry which does not end in the orthodox conclusions. The greatest harm done is to those who are not heretics, and whose whole mental development is cramped, and their reason cowed, by the fear of heresy. Who can compute what the world loses in the multitude of promising intellects combined with timid characters, who dare not follow out any bold, vigorous, independent train of thought, lest it should land them in something which would admit of being considered irreligious or immoral? Among them we may occasionally see some man of deep conscientiousness, and subtile and refined understanding, who spends a life in sophisticating with an intellect which he cannot silence, and exhausts the resources of ingenuity in attempting to reconcile the promptings of his conscience and reason with orthodoxy, which yet he does not, perhaps, to the end succeed in doing. No one can be a great thinker who does not recognize, that as a thinker it is his first duty to follow his intellect to whatever conclusions it may lead. Truth gains more even by the errors of one who, with due study and preparation, thinks for himself, than by the true opinions of those who only hold them because they do not suffer themselves to think. Not that it is solely, or chiefly, to form great thinkers, that freedom of thinking is required. On the contrary, it is as much, and even more indispensable, to enable average human beings to attain the mental stature which they are capable of. There have been, and may again be, great individual thinkers, in a general atmosphere of mental slavery. But there never has been, nor ever will be, in that atmosphere, an intellectually active people. Where any people has made a temporary approach to such a character, it has been because the dread of heterodox speculation was for a time suspended. Where there is a tacit convention that principles are not to be disputed; where the discussion of the greatest questions which can occupy humanity is considered to be closed, we cannot hope to find that generally high scale of mental activity which has made some periods of history so remarkable. Never when controversy avoided the subjects which are large and important enough to kindle enthusiasm, was the mind of a people stirred up from its foundations, and the impulse given which raised even persons of the most ordinary intellect to something of the dignity of thinking beings. Of such we have had an example in the condition of Europe during the times immediately following the Reformation; another, though limited to the Continent and to a more cultivated class, in the speculative movement of the latter half of the eighteenth century; and a third, of still briefer duration, in the intellectual fermentation of Germany during the Goethian and Fichtean period. These periods differed widely in the particular opinions which they developed; but were alike in this, that during all three the yoke of authority was broken. In each, an old mental despotism had been thrown off, and no new one had yet taken its place. The impulse given at these three periods has made Europe what it now is. Every single improvement which has taken place either in the human mind or in institutions, may be traced distinctly to one or other of them. Appearances have for some time indicated that all three impulses are well-nigh spent; and we can expect no fresh start, until we again assert our mental freedom.

Let us now pass to the second division of the argument, and dismissing the Supposition that any of the received opinions may be false, let us assume them to be true, and examine into the worth of the manner in which they are likely to be held, when their truth is not freely and openly canvassed. However unwillingly a person who has a strong opinion may admit the possibility that his opinion may be false, he ought to be moved by the consideration that however true it may be, if it is not fully, frequently, and fearlessly discussed, it will be held as a dead dogma, not a living truth.

There is a class of persons (happily not quite so numerous as formerly) who think it enough if a person assents undoubtingly to what they think true, though he has no knowledge whatever of the grounds of the opinion, and could not make a tenable defence of it against the most superficial objections. Such persons, if they can once get their creed taught from authority, naturally think that no good, and some harm, comes of its being allowed to be questioned. Where their influence prevails, they make it nearly impossible for the received opinion to be rejected wisely and considerately, though it may still be rejected rashly and ignorantly; for to shut out discussion entirely is seldom possible, and when it once gets in, beliefs not grounded on conviction are apt to give way before the slightest semblance of an argument. Waiving, however, this possibility — assuming that the true opinion abides in the mind, but abides as a prejudice, a belief independent of, and proof against, argument — this is not the way in which truth ought to be held by a rational being. This is not knowing the truth. Truth, thus held, is but one superstition the more, accidentally clinging to the words which enunciate a truth.

If the intellect and judgment of mankind ought to be cultivated, a thing which Protestants at least do not deny, on what can these faculties be more appropriately exercised by any one, than on the things which concern him so much that it is considered necessary for him to hold opinions on them? If the cultivation of the understanding consists in one thing more than in another, it is surely in learning the grounds of one's own opinions. Whatever people believe, on subjects on which it is of the first importance to believe rightly, they ought to be able to defend against at least the common objections. But, some one may say, "Let them be taught the grounds of their opinions. It does not follow that opinions must be merely parroted because they are never heard controverted. Persons who learn geometry do not simply commit the theorems to memory, but understand and learn likewise the demonstrations; and it would be absurd to say that they remain ignorant of the grounds of geometrical truths, because they never hear any one deny, and attempt to disprove them." Undoubtedly: and such teaching suffices on a subject like mathematics, where there is nothing at all to be said on the wrong side of the question. The peculiarity of the evidence of mathematical truths is, that all the argument is on one side. There are no objections, and no answers to objections. But on every subject on which difference of opinion is possible, the truth depends on a balance to be struck between two sets of conflicting reasons. Even in natural philosophy, there is always some other explanation possible of the same facts; some geocentric theory instead of heliocentric, some phlogiston instead of oxygen; and it has to be shown why that other theory cannot be the true one: and until this is shown and until we know how it is shown, we do not understand the grounds of our opinion. But when we turn to subjects infinitely more complicated, to morals, religion, politics, social relations, and the business of life, three-fourths of the arguments for every disputed opinion consist in dispelling the appearances which favor some opinion different from it. The greatest orator, save one, of antiquity, has left it on record that he always studied his adversary's case with as great, if not with still greater, intensity than even his own. What Cicero practised as the means of forensic success, requires to be imitated by all who study any subject in order to arrive at the truth. He who knows only his own side of the case, knows little of that. His reasons may be good, and no one may have been able to refute them. But if he is equally unable to refute the reasons on the opposite side; if he does not so much as know what they are, he has no ground for preferring either opinion. The rational position for him would be suspension of judgment, and unless he contents himself with that, he is either led by authority, or adopts, like the generality of the world, the side to which he feels most inclination. Nor is it enough that he should hear the arguments of adversaries from his own teachers, presented as they state them, and accompanied by what they offer as refutations. This is not the way to do justice to the arguments, or bring them into real contact with his own mind. He must be able to hear them from persons who actually believe them; who defend them in earnest, and do their very utmost for them. He must know them in their most plausible and persuasive form; he must feel the whole force of the difficulty which the true view of the subject has to encounter and dispose of, else he will never really possess himself of the portion of truth which meets and removes that difficulty. Ninety-nine in a hundred of what are called educated men are in this condition, even of those who can argue fluently for their opinions. Their conclusion may be true, but it might be false for anything they know: they have never thrown themselves into the mental position of those who think differently from them, and considered what such persons may have to say; and consequently they do not, in any proper sense of the word, know the doctrine which they themselves profess. They do not know those parts of it which explain and justify the remainder; the considerations which show that a fact which seemingly conflicts with another is reconcilable with it, or that, of two apparently strong reasons, one and not the other ought to be preferred. All that part of the truth which turns the scale, and decides the judgment of a completely informed mind, they are strangers to; nor is it ever really known, but to those who have attended equally and impartially to both sides, and endeavored to see the reasons of both in the strongest light. So essential is this discipline to a real understanding of moral and human subjects, that if opponents of all important truths do not exist, it is indispensable to imagine them and supply them with the strongest arguments which the most skilful devil's advocate can conjure up.

To abate the force of these considerations, an enemy of free discussion may be supposed to say, that there is no necessity for mankind in general to know and understand all that can be said against or for their opinions by philosophers and theologians. That it is not needful for common men to be able to expose all the misstatements or fallacies of an ingenious opponent. That it is enough if there is always somebody capable of answering them, so that nothing likely to mislead uninstructed persons remains unrefuted. That simple minds, having been taught the obvious grounds of the truths inculcated on them, may trust to authority for the rest, and being aware that they have neither knowledge nor talent to resolve every difficulty which can be raised, may repose in the assurance that all those which have been raised have been or can be answered, by those who are specially trained to the task.

Conceding to this view of the subject the utmost that can be claimed for it by those most easily satisfied with the amount of understanding of truth which ought to accompany the belief of it; even so, the argument for free discussion is no way weakened. For even this doctrine acknowledges that mankind ought to have a rational assurance that all objections have been satisfactorily answered; and how are they to be answered if that which requires to be answered is not spoken? or how can the answer be known to be satisfactory, if the objectors have no opportunity of showing that it is unsatisfactory? If not the public, at least the philosophers and theologians who are to resolve the difficulties, must make themselves familiar with those difficulties in their most puzzling form; and this cannot be accomplished unless they are freely stated, and placed in the most advantageous light which they admit of. The Catholic Church has its own way of dealing with this embarrassing problem. It makes a broad separation between those who can be permitted to receive its doctrines on conviction, and those who must accept them on trust. Neither, indeed, are allowed any choice as to what they will accept; but the clergy, such at least as can be fully confided in, may admissibly and meritoriously make themselves acquainted with the arguments of opponents, in order to answer them, and may, therefore, read heretical books; the laity, not unless by special permission, hard to be obtained. This discipline recognizes a knowledge of the enemy's case as beneficial to the teachers, but finds means, consistent with this, of denying it to the rest of the world: thus giving to the elite more mental culture, though not more mental freedom, than it allows to the mass. By this device it succeeds in obtaining the kind of mental superiority which its purposes require; for though culture without freedom never made a large and liberal mind, it can make a clever nisi prius advocate of a cause. But in countries professing Protestantism, this resource is denied; since Protestants hold, at least in theory, that the responsibility for the choice of a religion must be borne by each for himself, and cannot be thrown off upon teachers. Besides, in the present state of the world, it is practically impossible that writings which are read by the instructed can be kept from the uninstructed. If the teachers of mankind are to be cognizant of all that they ought to know, everything must be free to be written and published without restraint.

If, however, the mischievous operation of the absence of free discussion, when the received opinions are true, were confined to leaving men ignorant of the grounds of those opinions, it might be thought that this, if an intellectual, is no moral evil, and does not affect the worth of the opinions, regarded in their influence on the character. The fact, however, is, that not only the grounds of the opinion are forgotten in the absence of discussion, but too often the meaning of the opinion itself. The words which convey it, cease to suggest ideas, or suggest only a small portion of those they were originally employed to communicate. Instead of a vivid conception and a living belief, there remain only a few phrases retained by rote; or, if any part, the shell and husk only of the meaning is retained, the finer essence being lost. The great chapter in human history which this fact occupies and fills, cannot be too earnestly studied and meditated on.

It is illustrated in the experience of almost all ethical doctrines and religious creeds. They are all full of meaning and vitality to those who originate them, and to the direct disciples of the originators. Their meaning continues to be felt in undiminished strength, and is perhaps brought out into even fuller consciousness, so long as the struggle lasts to give the doctrine or creed an ascendency over other creeds. At last it either prevails, and becomes the general opinion, or its progress stops; it keeps possession of the ground it has gained, but ceases to spread further. When either of these results has become apparent, controversy on the subject flags, and gradually dies away. The doctrine has taken its place, if not as a received opinion, as one of the admitted sects or divisions of opinion: those who hold it have generally inherited, not adopted it; and conversion from one of these doctrines to another, being now an exceptional fact, occupies little place in the thoughts of their professors. Instead of being, as at first, constantly on the alert either to defend themselves against the world, or to bring the world over to them, they have subsided into acquiescence, and neither listen, when they can help it, to arguments against their creed, nor trouble dissentients (if there be such) with arguments in its favor. From this time may usually be dated the decline in the living power of the doctrine. We often hear the teachers of all creeds lamenting the difficulty of keeping up in the minds of believers a lively apprehension of the truth which they nominally recognize, so that it may penetrate the feelings, and acquire a real mastery over the conduct. No such difficulty is complained of while the creed is still fighting for its existence: even the weaker combatants then know and feel what they are fighting for, and the difference between it and other doctrines; and in that period of every creed's existence, not a few persons may be found, who have realized its fundamental principles in all the forms of thought, have weighed and considered them in all their important bearings, and have experienced the full effect on the character, which belief in that creed ought to produce in a mind thoroughly imbued with it. But when it has come to be an hereditary creed, and to be received passively, not actively — when the mind is no longer compelled, in the same degree as at first, to exercise its vital powers on the questions which its belief presents to it, there is a progressive tendency to forget all of the belief except the formularies, or to give it a dull and torpid assent, as if accepting it on trust dispensed with the necessity of realizing it in consciousness, or testing it by personal experience; until it almost ceases to connect itself at all with the inner life of the human being. Then are seen the cases, so frequent in this age of the world as almost to form the majority, in which the creed remains as it were outside the mind, encrusting and petrifying it against all other influences addressed to the higher parts of our nature; manifesting its power by not suffering any fresh and living conviction to get in, but itself doing nothing for the mind or heart, except standing sentinel over them to keep them vacant.

To what an extent doctrines intrinsically fitted to make the deepest impression upon the mind may remain in it as dead beliefs, without being ever realized in the imagination, the feelings, or the understanding, is exemplified by the manner in which the majority of believers hold the doctrines of Christianity. By Christianity I here mean what is accounted such by all churches and sects — the maxims and precepts contained in the New Testament. These are considered sacred, and accepted as laws, by all professing Christians. Yet it is scarcely too much to say that not one Christian in a thousand guides or tests his individual conduct by reference to those laws. The standard to which he does refer it, is the custom of his nation, his class, or his religious profession. He has thus, on the one hand, a collection of ethical maxims, which he believes to have been vouchsafed to him by infallible wisdom as rules for his government; and on the other, a set of every-day judgments and practices, which go a certain length with some of those maxims, not so great a length with others, stand in direct opposition to some, and are, on the whole, a compromise between the Christian creed and the interests and suggestions of worldly life. To the first of these standards he gives his homage; to the other his real allegiance. All Christians believe that the blessed are the poor and humble, and those who are illused by the world; that it is easier for a camel to pass through the eye of a needle than for a rich man to enter the kingdom of heaven; that they should judge not, lest they be judged; that they should swear not at all; that they should love their neighbor as themselves; that if one take their cloak, they should give him their coat also; that they should take no thought for the morrow; that if they would be perfect, they should sell all that they have and give it to the poor. They are not insincere when they say that they believe these things. They do believe them, as people believe what they have always heard lauded and never discussed. But in the sense of that living belief which regulates conduct, they believe these doctrines just up to the point to which it is usual to act upon them. The doctrines in their integrity are serviceable to pelt adversaries with; and it is understood that they are to be put forward (when possible) as the reasons for whatever people do that they think laudable. But any one who reminded them that the maxims require an infinity of things which they never even think of doing would gain nothing but to be classed among those very unpopular characters who affect to be better than other people. The doctrines have no hold on ordinary believers — are not a power in their minds. They have an habitual respect for the sound of them, but no feeling which spreads from the words to the things signified, and forces the mind to take them in, and make them conform to the formula. Whenever conduct is concerned, they look round for Mr. A and B to direct them how far to go in obeying Christ.

Now we may be well assured that the case was not thus, but far otherwise, with the early Christians. Had it been thus, Christianity never would have expanded from an obscure sect of the despised Hebrews into the religion of the Roman empire. When their enemies said, "See how these Christians love one another" (a remark not likely to be made by anybody now), they assuredly had a much livelier feeling of the meaning of their creed than they have ever had since. And to this cause, probably, it is chiefly owing that Christianity now makes so little progress in extending its domain, and after eighteen centuries, is still nearly confined to Europeans and the descendants of Europeans. Even with the strictly religious, who are much in earnest about their doctrines, and attach a greater amount of meaning to many of them than people in general, it commonly happens that the part which is thus comparatively active in their minds is that which was made by Calvin, or Knox, or some such person much nearer in character to themselves. The sayings of Christ coexist passively in their minds, producing hardly any effect beyond what is caused by mere listening to words so amiable and bland. There are many reasons, doubtless, why doctrines which are the badge of a sect retain more of their vitality than those common to all recognized sects, and why more pains are taken by teachers to keep their meaning alive; but one reason certainly is, that the peculiar doctrines are more questioned, and have to be oftener defended against open gainsayers. Both teachers and learners go to sleep at their post, as soon as there is no enemy in the field.

The same thing holds true, generally speaking, of all traditional doctrines — those of prudence and knowledge of life, as well as of morals or religion. All languages and literatures are full of general observations on life, both as to what it is, and how to conduct oneself in it; observations which everybody knows, which everybody repeats, or hears with acquiescence, which are received as truisms, yet of which most people first truly learn the meaning, when experience, generally of a painful kind, has made it a reality to them. How often, when smarting under some unforeseen misfortune or disappointment, does a person call to mind some proverb or common saying familiar to him all his life, the meaning of which, if he had ever before felt it as he does now, would have saved him from the calamity. There are indeed reasons for this, other than the absence of discussion: there are many truths of which the full meaning cannot be realized, until personal experience has brought it home. But much more of the meaning even of these would have been understood, and what was understood would have been far more deeply impressed on the mind, if the man had been accustomed to hear it argued pro and con by people who did understand it. The fatal tendency of mankind to leave off thinking about a thing when it is no longer doubtful, is the cause of half their errors. A contemporary author has well spoken of "the deep slumber of a decided opinion."

But what! (it may be asked) Is the absence of unanimity an indispensable condition of true knowledge? Is it necessary that some part of mankind should persist in error, to enable any to realize the truth? Does a belief cease to be real and vital as soon as it is generally received — and is a proposition never thoroughly understood and felt unless some doubt of it remains? As soon as mankind have unanimously accepted a truth, does the truth perish within them? The highest aim and best result of improved intelligence, it has hitherto been thought, is to unite mankind more and more in the acknowledgment of all important truths: and does the intelligence only last as long as it has not achieved its object? Do the fruits of conquest perish by the very completeness of the victory?

I affirm no such thing. As mankind improve, the number of doctrines which are no longer disputed or doubted will be constantly on the increase: and the well-being of mankind may almost be measured by the number and gravity of the truths which have reached the point of being uncontested. The cessation, on one question after another, of serious controversy, is one of the necessary incidents of the consolidation of opinion; a consolidation as salutary in the case of true opinions, as it is dangerous and noxious when the opinions are erroneous. But though this gradual narrowing of the bounds of diversity of opinion is necessary in both senses of the term, being at once inevitable and indispensable, we are not therefore obliged to conclude that all its consequences must be beneficial. The loss of so important an aid to the intelligent and living apprehension of a truth, as is afforded by the necessity of explaining it to, or defending it against, opponents, though not sufficient to outweigh, is no trifling drawback from, the benefit of its universal recognition. Where this advantage can no longer be had, I confess I should like to see the teachers of mankind endeavoring to provide a substitute for it; some contrivance for making the difficulties of the question as present to the learner's consciousness, as if they were pressed upon him by a dissentient champion, eager for his conversion.

But instead of seeking contrivances for this purpose, they have lost those they formerly had. The Socratic dialectics, so magnificently exemplified in the dialogues of Plato, were a contrivance of this description. They were essentially a negative discussion of the great questions of philosophy and life, directed with consummate skill to the purpose of convincing any one who had merely adopted the commonplaces of received opinion, that he did not understand the subject — that he as yet attached no definite meaning to the doctrines he professed; in order that, becoming aware of his ignorance, he might be put in the way to attain a stable belief, resting on a clear apprehension both of the meaning of doctrines and of their evidence. The school disputations of the Middle Ages had a somewhat similar object. They were intended to make sure that the pupil understood his own opinion, and (by necessary correlation) the opinion opposed to it, and could enforce the grounds of the one and confute those of the other. These last-mentioned contests had indeed the incurable defect, that the premises appealed to were taken from authority, not from reason; and, as a discipline to the mind, they were in every respect inferior to the powerful dialectics which formed the intellects of the "Socratici viri:" but the modern mind owes far more to both than it is generally willing to admit, and the present modes of education contain nothing which in the smallest degree supplies the place either of the one or of the other. A person who derives all his instruction from teachers or books, even if he escape the besetting temptation of contenting himself with cram, is under no compulsion to hear both sides; accordingly it is far from a frequent accomplishment, even among thinkers, to know both sides; and the weakest part of what everybody says in defence of his opinion, is what he intends as a reply to antagonists. It is the fashion of the present time to disparage negative logic -- that which points out weaknesses in theory or errors in practice, without establishing positive truths. Such negative criticism would indeed be poor enough as an ultimate result; but as a means to attaining any positive knowledge or conviction worthy the name, it cannot be valued too highly; and until people are again systematically trained to it, there will be few great thinkers, and a low general average of intellect, in any but the mathematical and physical departments of speculation. On any other subject no one's opinions deserve the name of knowledge, except so far as he has either had forced upon him by others, or gone through of himself, the same mental process which would have been required of him in carrying on an active controversy with opponents. That, therefore, which when absent, it is so indispensable, but so difficult, to create, how worse than absurd is it to forego, when spontaneously offering itself! If there are any persons who contest a received opinion, or who will do so if law or opinion will let them, let us thank them for it, open our minds to listen to them, and rejoice that there is some one to do for us what we otherwise ought, if we have any regard for either the certainty or the vitality of our convictions, to do with much greater labor for ourselves.

It still remains to speak of one of the principal causes which make diversity of opinion advantageous, and will continue to do so until mankind shall have entered a stage of intellectual advancement which at present seems at an incalculable distance. We have hitherto considered only two possibilities: that the received opinion may be false, and some other opinion, consequently, true; or that, the received opinion being true, a conflict with the opposite error is essential to a clear apprehension and deep feeling of its truth. But there is a commoner case than either of these; when the conflicting doctrines, instead of being one true and the other false, share the truth between them; and the nonconforming opinion is needed to supply the remainder of the truth, of which the received doctrine embodies only a part. Popular opinions, on subjects not palpable to sense, are often true, but seldom or never the whole truth. They are a part of the truth; sometimes a greater, sometimes a smaller part, but exaggerated, distorted, and disjoined from the truths by which they ought to be accompanied and limited. Heretical opinions, on the other hand, are generally some of these suppressed and neglected truths, bursting the bonds which kept them down, and either seeking reconciliation with the truth contained in the common opinion, or fronting it as enemies, and setting themselves up, with similar exclusiveness, as the whole truth. The latter case is hitherto the most frequent, as, in the human mind, one-sidedness has always been the rule, and many-sidedness the exception. Hence, even in revolutions of opinion, one part of the truth usually sets while another rises. Even progress, which ought to superadd, for the most part only substitutes one partial and incomplete truth for another; improvement consisting chiefly in this, that the new fragment of truth is more wanted, more adapted to the needs of the time, than that which it displaces. Such being the partial character of prevailing opinions, even when resting on a true foundation; every opinion which embodies somewhat of the portion of truth which the common opinion omits, ought to be considered precious, with whatever amount of error and confusion that truth may be blended. No sober judge of human affairs will feel bound to be indignant because those who force on our notice truths which we should otherwise have overlooked, overlook some of those which we see. Rather, he will think that so long as popular truth is one-sided, it is more desirable than otherwise that unpopular truth should have one-sided asserters too; such being usually the most energetic, and the most likely to compel reluctant attention to the fragment of wisdom which they proclaim as if it were the whole.

Thus, in the eighteenth century, when nearly all the instructed, and all those of the uninstructed who were led by them, were lost in admiration of what is called civilization, and of the marvels of modern science, literature, and philosophy, and while greatly overrating the amount of unlikeness between the men of modern and those of ancient times, indulged the belief that the whole of the difference was in their own favor; with what a salutary shock did the paradoxes of Rousseau explode like bombshells in the midst, dislocating the compact mass of one-sided opinion, and forcing its elements to recombine in a better form and with additional ingredients. Not that the current opinions were on the whole farther from the truth than Rousseau's were; on the contrary, they were nearer to it; they contained more of positive truth, and very much less of error. Nevertheless there lay in Rousseau's doctrine, and has floated down the stream of opinion along with it, a considerable amount of exactly those truths which the popular opinion wanted; and these are the deposit which was left behind when the flood subsided. The superior worth of simplicity of life, the enervating and demoralizing effect of the trammels and hypocrisies of artificial society, are ideas which have never been entirely absent from cultivated minds since Rousseau wrote; and they will in time produce their due effect, though at present needing to be asserted as much as ever, and to be asserted by deeds, for words, on this subject, have nearly exhausted their power.

In politics, again, it is almost a commonplace, that a party of order or stability, and a party of progress or reform, are both necessary elements of a healthy state of political life; until the one or the other shall have so enlarged its mental grasp as to be a party equally of order and of progress, knowing and distinguishing what is fit to be preserved from what ought to be swept away. Each of these modes of thinking derives its utility from the deficiencies of the other; but it is in a great measure the opposition of the other that keeps each within the limits of reason and sanity. Unless opinions favorable to democracy and to aristocracy, to property and to equality, to co-operation and to competition, to luxury and to abstinence, to sociality and individuality, to liberty and discipline, and all the other standing antagonisms of practical life, are expressed with equal freedom, and enforced and defended with equal talent and energy, there is no chance of both elements obtaining their due; one scale is sure to go up, and the other down. Truth, in the great practical concerns of life, is so much a question of the reconciling and combining of opposites, that very few have minds sufficiently capacious and impartial to make the adjustment with an approach to correctness, and it has to be made by the rough process of a struggle between combatants fighting under hostile banners. On any of the great open questions just enumerated, if either of the two opinions has a better claim than the other, not merely to be tolerated, but to be encouraged and countenanced, it is the one which happens at the particular time and place to be in a minority. That is the opinion which, for the time being, represents the neglected interests, the side of human well-being which is in danger of obtaining less than its share. I am aware that there is not, in this country, any intolerance of differences of opinion on most of these topics. They are adduced to show, by admitted and multiplied examples, the universality of the fact, that only through diversity of opinion is there, in the existing state of human intellect, a chance of fair play to all sides of the truth. When there are persons to be found, who form an exception to the apparent unanimity of the world on any subject, even if the world is in the right, it is always probable that dissentients have something worth hearing to say for themselves, and that truth would lose something by their silence.

It may be objected, "But some received principles, especially on the highest and most vital subjects, are more than half-truths. The Christian morality, for instance, is the whole truth on that subject and if any one teaches a morality which varies from it, he is wholly in error." As this is of all cases the most important in practice, none can be fitter to test the general maxim. But before pronouncing what Christian morality is or is not, it would be desirable to decide what is meant by Christian morality. If it means the morality of the New Testament, I wonder that any one who derives his knowledge of this from the book itself, can suppose that it was announced, or intended, as a complete doctrine of morals. The Gospel always refers to a preexisting morality, and confines its precepts to the particulars in which that morality was to be corrected, or superseded by a wider and higher; expressing itself, moreover, in terms most general, often impossible to be interpreted literally, and possessing rather the impressiveness of poetry or eloquence than the precision of legislation. To extract from it a body of ethical doctrine, has never been possible without eking it out from the Old Testament, that is, from a system elaborate indeed, but in many respects barbarous, and intended only for a barbarous people. St. Paul, a declared enemy to this Judaical mode of interpreting the doctrine and filling up the scheme of his Master, equally assumes a preexisting morality, namely, that of the Greeks and Romans; and his advice to Christians is in a great measure a system of accommodation to that; even to the extent of giving an apparent sanction to slavery. What is called Christian, but should rather be termed theological, morality, was not the work of Christ or the Apostles, but is of much later origin, having been gradually built up by the Catholic Church of the first five centuries, and though not implicitly adopted by moderns and Protestants, has been much less modified by them than might have been expected. For the most part, indeed, they have contented themselves with cutting off the additions which had been made to it in the Middle Ages, each sect supplying the place by fresh additions, adapted to its own character and tendencies. That mankind owe a great debt to this morality, and to its early teachers, I should be the last person to deny; but I do not scruple to say of it, that it is, in many important points, incomplete and one-sided, and that unless ideas and feelings, not sanctioned by it, had contributed to the formation of European life and character, human affairs would have been in a worse condition than they now are. Christian morality (so called) has all the characters of a reaction; it is, in great part, a protest against Paganism. Its ideal is negative rather than positive; passive rather than active; Innocence rather than Nobleness; Abstinence from Evil, rather than energetic Pursuit of Good: in its precepts (as has been well said) "thou shalt not" predominates unduly over "thou shalt." In its horror of sensuality, it made an idol of asceticism, which has been gradually compromised away into one of legality. It holds out the hope of heaven and the threat of hell, as the appointed and appropriate motives to a virtuous life: in this falling far below the best of the ancients, and doing what lies in it to give to human morality an essentially selfish character, by disconnecting each man's feelings of duty from the interests of his fellow-creatures, except so far as a self-interested inducement is offered to him for consulting them. It is essentially a doctrine of passive obedience; it inculcates submission to all authorities found established; who indeed are not to be actively obeyed when they command what religion forbids, but who are not to be resisted, far less rebelled against, for any amount of wrong to ourselves. And while, in the morality of the best Pagan nations, duty to the State holds even a disproportionate place, infringing on the just liberty of the individual; in purely Christian ethics that grand department of duty is scarcely noticed or acknowledged. It is in the Koran, not the New Testament, that we read the maxim — "A ruler who appoints any man to an office, when there is in his dominions another man better qualified for it, sins against God and against the State." What little recognition the idea of obligation to the public obtains in modern morality, is derived from Greek and Roman sources, not from Christian; as, even in the morality of private life, whatever exists of magnanimity, high-mindedness, personal dignity, even the sense of honor, is derived from the purely human, not the religious part of our education, and never could have grown out of a standard of ethics in which the only worth, professedly recognized, is that of obedience.

I am as far as any one from pretending that these defects are necessarily inherent in the Christian ethics, in every manner in which it can be conceived, or that the many requisites of a complete moral doctrine which it does not contain, do not admit of being reconciled with it. Far less would I insinuate this of the doctrines and precepts of Christ himself. I believe that the sayings of Christ are all, that I can see any evidence of their having been intended to be; that they are irreconcilable with nothing which a comprehensive morality requires; that everything which is excellent in ethics may be brought within them, with no greater violence to their language than has been done to it by all who have attempted to deduce from them any practical system of conduct whatever. But it is quite consistent with this, to believe that they contain and were meant to contain, only a part of the truth; that many essential elements of the highest morality are among the things which are not provided for, nor intended to be provided for, in the recorded deliverances of the Founder of Christianity, and which have been entirely thrown aside in the system of ethics erected on the basis of those deliverances by the Christian Church. And this being so, I think it a great error to persist in attempting to find in the Christian doctrine that complete rule for our guidance, which its author intended it to sanction and enforce, but only partially to provide. I believe, too, that this narrow theory is becoming a grave practical evil, detracting greatly from the value of the moral training and instruction, which so many wellmeaning persons are now at length exerting themselves to promote. I much fear that by attempting to form the mind and feelings on an exclusively religious type, and discarding those secular standards (as for want of a better name they may be called) which heretofore coexisted with and supplemented the Christian ethics, receiving some of its spirit, and infusing into it some of theirs, there will result, and is even now resulting, a low, abject, servile type of character, which, submit itself as it may to what it deems the Supreme Will, is incapable of rising to or sympathizing in the conception of Supreme Goodness. I believe that other ethics than any one which can be evolved from exclusively Christian sources, must exist side by side with Christian ethics to produce the moral regeneration of mankind; and that the Christian system is no exception to the rule that in an imperfect state of the human mind, the interests of truth require a diversity of opinions. It is not necessary that in ceasing to ignore the moral truths not contained in Christianity, men should ignore any of those which it does contain. Such prejudice, or oversight, when it occurs, is altogether an evil; but it is one from which we cannot hope to be always exempt, and must be regarded as the price paid for an inestimable good. The exclusive pretension made by a part of the truth to be the whole, must and ought to be protested against, and if a reactionary impulse should make the protestors unjust in their turn, this one-sidedness, like the other, may be lamented, but must be tolerated. If Christians would teach infidels to be just to Christianity, they should themselves be just to infidelity. It can do truth no service to blink the fact, known to all who have the most ordinary acquaintance with literary history, that a large portion of the noblest and most valuable moral teaching has been the work, not only of men who did not know, but of men who knew and rejected, the Christian faith.

I do not pretend that the most unlimited use of the freedom of enunciating all possible opinions would put an end to the evils of religious or philosophical sectarianism. Every truth which men of narrow capacity are in earnest about, is sure to be asserted, inculcated, and in many ways even acted on, as if no other truth existed in the world, or at all events none that could limit or qualify the first. I acknowledge that the tendency of all opinions to become sectarian is not cured by the freest discussion, but is often heightened and exacerbated thereby; the truth which ought to have been, but was not, seen, being rejected all the more violently because proclaimed by persons regarded as opponents. But it is not on the impassioned partisan, it is on the calmer and more disinterested bystander, that this collision of opinions works its salutary effect. Not the violent conflict between parts of the truth, but the quiet suppression of half of it, is the formidable evil: there is always hope when people are forced to listen to both sides; it is when they attend only to one that errors harden into prejudices, and truth itself ceases to have the effect of truth, by being exaggerated into falsehood. And since there are few mental attributes more rare than that judicial faculty which can sit in intelligent judgment between two sides of a question, of which only one is represented by an advocate before it, truth has no chance but in proportion as every side of it, every opinion which embodies any fraction of the truth, not only finds advocates, but is so advocated as to be listened to.

We have now recognized the necessity to the mental wellbeing of mankind (on which all their other well-being depends) of freedom of opinion, and freedom of the expression of opinion, on four distinct grounds; which we will now briefly recapitulate.

First, if any opinion is compelled to silence, that opinion may, for aught we can certainly know, be true. To deny this is to assume our own infallibility.

Secondly, though the silenced opinion be an error, it may, and very commonly does, contain a portion of truth; and since the general or prevailing opinion on any object is rarely or never the whole truth, it is only by the collision of adverse opinions that the remainder of the truth has any chance of being supplied.

Thirdly, even if the received opinion be not only true, but the whole truth; unless it is suffered to be, and actually is, vigorously and earnestly contested, it will, by most of those who receive it, be held in the manner of a prejudice, with little comprehension or feeling of its rational grounds. And not only this, but, fourthly, the meaning of the doctrine itself will be in danger of being lost, or enfeebled, and deprived of its vital effect on the character and conduct: the dogma becoming a mere formal profession, inefficacious for good, but cumbering the ground, and preventing the growth of any real and heartfelt conviction, from reason or personal experience.

Before quitting the subject of freedom of opinion, it is fit to take notice of those who say, that the free expression of all opinions should be permitted, on condition that the manner be temperate, and do not pass the bounds of fair discussion. Much might be said on the impossibility of fixing where these supposed bounds are to be placed; for if the test be offence to those whose opinion is attacked, I think experience testifies that this offence is given whenever the attack is telling and powerful, and that every opponent who pushes them hard, and whom they find it difficult to answer, appears to them, if he shows any strong feeling on the subject, an intemperate opponent. But this, though an important consideration in a practical point of view, merges in a more fundamental objection. Undoubtedly the manner of asserting an opinion, even though it be a true one, may be very objectionable, and may justly incur severe censure. But the principal offences of the kind are such as it is mostly impossible, unless by accidental self-betrayal, to bring home to conviction. The gravest of them is, to argue sophistically, to suppress facts or arguments, to misstate the elements of the case, or misrepresent the opposite opinion. But all this, even to the most aggravated degree, is so continually done in perfect good faith, by persons who are not considered, and in many other respects may not deserve to be considered, ignorant or incompetent, that it is rarely possible on adequate grounds conscientiously to stamp the misrepresentation as morally culpable; and still less could law presume to interfere with this kind of controversial misconduct. With regard to what is commonly meant by intemperate discussion, namely, invective, sarcasm, personality, and the like, the denunciation of these weapons would deserve more sympathy if it were ever proposed to interdict them equally to both sides; but it is only desired to restrain the employment of them against the prevailing opinion: against the unprevailing they may not only be used without general disapproval, but will be likely to obtain for him who uses them the praise of honest zeal and righteous indignation. Yet whatever mischief arises from their use, is greatest when they are employed against the comparatively defenceless; and whatever unfair advantage can be derived by any opinion from this mode of asserting it, accrues almost exclusively to received opinions. The worst offence of this kind which can be committed by a polemic, is to stigmatize those who hold the contrary opinion as bad and immoral men. To calumny of this sort, those who hold any unpopular opinion are peculiarly exposed, because they are in general few and uninfluential, and nobody but themselves feels much interest in seeing justice done them; but this weapon is, from the nature of the case, denied to those who attack a prevailing opinion: they can neither use it with safety to themselves, nor if they could, would it do anything but recoil on their own cause. In general, opinions contrary to those commonly received can only obtain a hearing by studied moderation of language, and the most cautious avoidance of unnecessary offence, from which they hardly ever deviate even in a slight degree without losing ground: while unmeasured vituperation employed on the side of the prevailing opinion, really does deter people from professing contrary opinions, and from listening to those who profess them. For the interest, therefore, of truth and justice, it is far more important to restrain this employment of vituperative language than the other; and, for example, if it were necessary to choose, there would be much more need to discourage offensive attacks on infidelity, than on religion. It is, however, obvious that law and authority have no business with restraining either, while opinion ought, in every instance, to determine its verdict by the circumstances of the individual case; condemning every one, on whichever side of the argument he places himself, in whose mode of advocacy either want of candor, or malignity, bigotry or intolerance of feeling manifest themselves, but not inferring these vices from the side which a person takes, though it be the contrary side of the question to our own; and giving merited honor to every one, whatever opinion he may hold, who has calmness to see and honesty to state what his opponents and their opinions really are, exaggerating nothing to their discredit, keeping nothing back which tells, or can be supposed to tell, in their favor. This is the real morality of public discussion; and if often violated, I am happy to think that there are many controversialists who to a great extent observe it, and a still greater number who conscientiously strive towards it.

8 THE EUROPEAN CONVENTION ON HUMAN RIGHTS, COUNCIL OF EUROPE, MEETING IN ROME (1950)

The Governments signatory hereto, being Members of the Council of Europe, Considering the Universal Declaration of Human Rights proclaimed by the General Assembly of the United Nations on 10 December 1948; Considering that this Declaration aims at securing the universal and effective recognition and observance of the Rights therein declared; Considering that the aim of the Council of Europe is the achievement of greater unity between its Members and that one of the methods by which the aim is to be pursued is the maintenance and further realization of Human Rights and Fundamental Freedoms; Reaffirming their profound belief in those Fundamental Freedoms which are the foundation of justice and peace in the world and are best maintained on the one hand by an effective political democracy and on the other by a common understanding and observance of the Human Rights upon which they depend; Being resolved, as the Governments of European countries which are like-minded and have a common heritage of political traditions, ideals, freedom and the rule of law to take the first steps for the collective enforcement of certain of the Rights stated in the Universal Declaration; Have agreed as follows:

. . . .

ARTICLE 8
1.   Everyone has the right to respect for his private and family life, his home and his correspondence.
2.   There shall be no interference by a public authority with the exercise of this right except such as is in accordance with the law and is necessary in a democratic society in the interests of national security, public safety or the economic well-being of the country, for the prevention of disorder or crime, for the protection of health or morals, or for the protection of the rights and freedoms of others.

ARTICLE 9
1.   Everyone has the right to freedom of thought, conscience and religion; this right includes freedom to change his religion or belief, and freedom, either alone or in community with others and in public or private, to manifest his religion or belief, in worship, teaching, practice and observance.
2.   Freedom to manifest one's religion or beliefs shall be subject only to such limitations as are prescribed by law and are necessary in a democratic society in the interests of public safety, for the protection of public order, health or morals, or the protection of the rights and freedoms of others.

ARTICLE 10

1.   Everyone has the right to freedom of expression. This right shall include freedom to hold opinions and to receive and impart information and ideas without interference by public authority and regardless of frontiers. This article shall not prevent States from requiring the licensing of broadcasting, television or cinema enterprises.

2.   The exercise of these freedoms, since it carries with it duties and responsibilities, may be subject to such formalities, conditions, restrictions or penalties as are prescribed by law and are necessary in a democratic society, in the interests of national security, territorial integrity or public safety, for the prevention of disorder or crime, for the protection of health or morals, for the protection of the reputation or the rights of others, for preventing the disclosure of information received in confidence, or for maintaining the authority and impartiality of the judiciary.

ARTICLE 11

1.   Everyone has the right to freedom of peaceful assembly and to freedom of association with others, including the right to form and to join trade unions for the protection of his interests.

2.   No restrictions shall be placed on the exercise of these rights other than such as are prescribed by law and are necessary in a democratic society in the interests of national security or public safety, for the prevention of disorder or crime, for the protection of health or morals or for the protection of the rights and freedoms of others. this article shall not prevent the imposition of lawful restrictions on the exercise of these rights by members of the armed forces, of the police or of the administration of the State.

II. Landmark Cases

9 SCHENCK V. UNITED STATES
SUPREME COURT OF THE UNITED STATES
249 U.S. 47
Argued January 9, 10, 1919
Decided March 3, 1919

Syllabus

Evidence held sufficient to connect the defendants with the mailing of printed circulars in pursuance of a conspiracy to obstruct the recruiting and enlistment service, contrary to the Espionage Act of June 15, 1917. P. 49. [48]

Incriminating document seized under a search warrant directed against a Socialist headquarters, held admissible in evidence, consistently with the Fourth and Fifth Amendment, in a criminal prosecution against the general secretary of a Socialist party, who had charge of the office. P. 50 .

Words which, ordinarily and in many places, would be within the freedom of speech protected by the First Amendment may become subject to prohibition when of such a nature and used in such circumstances a to create a clear and present danger that they will bring about the substantive evils which Congress has a right to prevent. The character of every act depends upon the circumstances in which it is done. P. 51 .

A conspiracy to circulate among men called and accepted for military service under the Selective Service Act of May 18, 1917, a circular tending to influence them to obstruct the draft, with the intent to effect that result, and followed by the sending of such circulars, is within the power of Congress to punish, and is punishable under the Espionage Act, § 4, although unsuccessful. P. 52 .

The word "recruiting," as used in the Espionage Act, § 3, means the gaining of fresh supplies of men for the military forces, as well by draft a otherwise. P. 52

The amendment of the Espionage Act by the Act of May 16, 1918, c. 75, 40 Stat. 553, did not affect the prosecution of offenses under the former. P. 53 .

Affirmed.

MR. JUSTICE HOLMES delivered the opinion of the court.

This is an indictment in three counts. The first charges a conspiracy to violate the Espionage Act of June 15, 1917, c. 30, § 3, 40 Stat. 217, 219, by causing and attempting [49] to cause insubordination, &c., in the military and naval forces of the United States, and to obstruct the recruiting and enlistment service of the United States, when the United States was at war with the German Empire, to-wit, that the defendants willfully conspired to have printed and circulated to men who had been called and accepted for military service under the Act of May 18, 1917, a document set forth and alleged to be calculated to cause such insubordination and obstruction. The count alleges overt acts in pursuance of the conspiracy, ending in the distribution of the document set forth. The second count alleges a conspiracy to commit an offence against the United States, to-wit, to use the mails for the transmission of matter declared to be nonmailable by Title XII, § 2 of the Act of June 15, 1917, to-wit, the above mentioned document, with an averment of the same overt acts. The third count charges an unlawful use of the mails for the transmission of the same matter and otherwise as above. The defendants were found guilty on all the counts. They set up the First Amendment to the Constitution forbidding Congress to make any law abridging the freedom of speech, or of the press, and bringing the case here on that ground have argued some other points also of which we must dispose.

It is argued that the evidence, if admissible, was not sufficient to prove that the defendant Schenck was concerned in sending the documents. According to the testimony, Schenck said he was general secretary of the Socialist party, and had charge of the Socialist headquarters from which the documents were sent. He identified a book found there as the minutes of the Executive Committee of the party. The book showed a resolution of August 13, 1917, that 15,000 leaflets should be printed on the other side of one of them in use, to be mailed to men who had passed exemption boards, and for distribution. Schenck personally attended to the printing. On [50] August 20, the general secretary's report said "Obtained new leaflets from printer and started work addressing envelopes" &c., and there was a resolve that Comrade Schenck be allowed $125 for sending leaflets through the mail. He said that he had about fifteen or sixteen thousand printed. There were files of the circular in question in the inner office which he said were printed on the other side of the one sided circular, and were there for distribution. Other copies were proved to have been sent through the mails to drafted men. Without going into confirmatory details that were proved, no reasonable man could doubt that the defendant Schenck was largely instrumental in sending the circulars about. As to the defendant Baer, there was evidence that she was a member of the Executive Board, and that the minutes of its transactions were hers. The argument as to the sufficiency of the evidence that the defendants conspired to send the documents only impairs the seriousness of the real defence.

It is objected that the documentary evidence was not admissible because obtained upon a search warrant, valid so far as appears. The contrary is established. *Adams v. New York*, 192 U.S. 585; *Weeks v. United States*, 232 U.S. 383, 395, 396. The search warrant did not issue against the defendant, but against the Socialist headquarters at 1326 Arch Street, and it would seem that the documents technically were not even in the defendants' possession. See *Johnson v. United States*, 228 U.S. 457. Notwithstanding some protest in argument, the notion that evidence even directly proceeding from the defendant in a criminal proceeding is excluded in all cases by the Fifth Amendment is plainly unsound. *Holt v. United States*, 218 U.S. 245, 252, 253.

The document in question, upon its first printed side, recited the first section of the Thirteenth Amendment, said that the idea embodied in it was violated by the Conscription Act, and that a conscript is little better than a [51] convict. In impassioned language, it intimated that conscription was despotism in its worst form, and a monstrous wrong against humanity in the interest of Wall Street's chosen few. It said "Do not submit to intimidation," but in form, at least, confined itself to peaceful measures such as a petition for the repeal of the act. The other and later printed side of the sheet was headed "Assert Your Rights." It stated reasons for alleging that anyone violated the Constitution when he refused to recognize "your right to assert your opposition to the draft," and went on "If you do not assert and support your rights, you are helping to deny or disparage rights which it is the solemn duty of all citizens and residents of the United States to retain." It described the arguments on the other side as coming from cunning politicians and a mercenary capitalist press, and even silent consent to the conscription law as helping to support an infamous conspiracy. It denied the power to send our citizens away to foreign shores to shoot up the people of other lands, and added that words could not express the condemnation such cold-blooded ruthlessness deserves, &c., &c., winding up, "You must do your share to maintain, support and uphold the rights of the people of this country." Of course, the document would not have been sent unless it had been intended to have some effect, and we do not see what effect it could be expected to have upon persons subject to the draft except to influence them to obstruct the carrying of it out. The defendants do not deny that the jury might find against them on this point.

But it is said, suppose that that was the tendency of this circular, it is protected by the First Amendment to the Constitution. Two of the strongest expressions are said to be quoted respectively from well known public men. It well may be that the prohibition of laws abridging the freedom of speech is not confined to previous restraints, although to prevent them may have been the [52] main purpose, as intimated in *Patterson v. Colorado*, 205 U.S. 454, 462. We admit that, in many places and in ordinary times, the defendants, in saying all that was said in the circular, would have been within their constitutional rights. But the character of every act depends upon the circumstances in which it is done. *Aikens v. Wisconsin*, 195 U.S. 194, 205, 206. The most stringent protection of free speech would not protect a man in falsely shouting fire in a theatre and causing a panic. It does not even protect a man from an injunction against uttering words that may have all the effect of force. *Gompers v. Bucks Stove & Range Co.*, 221 U.S. 418, 439. The question in every case is whether the words used are used in such circumstances and are of such a nature as to create a clear and present danger that they will bring about the substantive evils that Congress has a right to prevent. It is a question of proximity and degree. When a nation is at war, many things that might be said in time of peace are such a hindrance to its effort that their utterance will not be endured so long as men fight, and that no Court could regard them as protected by any constitutional right. It seems to be admitted that, if an actual obstruction of the recruiting service were proved, liability for words that produced that effect might be enforced. The statute of 1917, in § 4, punishes conspiracies to obstruct, as well as actual obstruction. If the act (speaking, or circulating a paper), its tendency, and the intent with which it is done are the same, we perceive no ground for saying that success alone warrants making the act a crime. *Goldman v. United States*, 245 U.S. 474, 477. Indeed, that case might be said to dispose of the present contention if the precedent covers all *media concludendi*. But, as the right to free speech was not referred to specially, we have thought fit to add a few words.

It was not argued that a conspiracy to obstruct the draft was not within the words of the Act of 1917. The [53] words are "obstruct the recruiting or enlistment service," and it might be suggested that they refer only to making it hard to get volunteers. Recruiting heretofore usually having been accomplished by getting volunteers, the word is apt to call up that method only in our minds. But recruiting is gaining fresh supplies for the forces, as well by draft as otherwise. It is put as an alternative to enlistment or voluntary enrollment in this act. The fact that the Act of 1917 was enlarged by the amending Act of May 16, 1918, c. 75, 40 Stat. 553, of course, does not affect the present indictment, and would not even if the former act had been repealed. Rev.Stats., § 13.

Judgments affirmed.

10 GITLOW V. NEW YORK
SUPREME COURT OF THE UNITED STATES
268 U.S. 652
Argued April 12, 1923
Reargued November 23, 1923
Decided June 8, 1925

Syllabus

1. Assumed, for the purposes of the case, that freedom of speech and of the press are among the personal rights and liberties protected by the due process clause of the Fourteenth Amendment from impairment by the States. P. 666.

2. Freedom of speech and of the press, as secured by the Constitution, is not an absolute right to speak or publish without responsibility whatever one may choose or an immunity for every possible use of language. P. 666.

3. That a State, in the exercise of its police power, may punish those who abuse this freedom by utterances inimical to the public welfare, tending to corrupt public morals, incite to crime or disturb the public peace, is not open to question. P. 667.

4. For yet more imperative reasons, a State may punish utterances endangering the foundations of organized government and threatening its overthrow by unlawful means. P. 667.

5. A statute punishing utterances advocating the overthrow of organized government by force, violence and unlawful means, imports a legislative determination that such utterances are so inimical to the general welfare and involve such danger of substantive evil that they may be penalized under the police power; and this determination must be given great weight, and every presumption be indulged in favor of the validity of the statute. P. 668.

6. Such utterances present sufficient danger to the public peace and security of the State to bring their punishment clearly within the range of legislative discretion, even if the effect of a given utterance can not accurately be foreseen. P. 669.

7. A State can not reasonably be required to defer taking measures against these

revolutionary utterances until they lead to actual disturbances of the peace or imminent danger of the State's destruction. P. 669.

8. The New York statute punishing those who advocate, advise or teach the duty, necessity or propriety of overthrowing or overturning organized government by force, violence, or any unlawful means, or who print, publish, or knowingly circulate any book [653], paper, etc., advocating, advising or teaching the doctrine that organized government should be so overthrown, does not penalize the utterance or publication of abstract doctrine or academic discussion having no quality of incitement to any concrete action, but denounces the advocacy of action for accomplishing the overthrow of organized government by unlawful means, and is constitutional as applied to a printed "Manifesto" advocating and urging mass action which shall progressively foment industrial disturbances and, through political mass strikes and revolutionary mass action overthrow and destroy organized parliamentary government; even though the advocacy was in general terms and not addressed to particular immediate acts or to particular persons. Pp. 654, 672.

9. The statute being constitutional, it may constitutionally be applied to every utterance -- not too trivial to be beneath the notice of the law -- which is of such a character and used with such intent and purpose as to bring it within the prohibition of the statute; and the question whether the specific utterance in question was likely to bring about the substantive evil aimed at by the statute, is not open to consideration. *Schenck v. United States*, 249 U.S. 47, explained. P. 670.

195 App. Div. 773; 234 N.Y., 132, 539, affirmed. [654]

MR. JUSTICE SANFORD delivered the opinion of the Court.

Benjamin Gitlow was indicted in the Supreme Court of New York, with three others, for the statutory crime of criminal anarchy. New York Penal Laws, §§ 160, 161. [note 1] He was separately tried, convicted, and sentenced to imprisonment. The judgment was affirmed by the Appellate Division and by the Court of Appeals. 195 App. Div. 773; 234 N. Y. 132 and 539. The case is here on writ of error to the Supreme Court, to which the record was remitted. 260 U.S. 703.

The contention here is that the statute, by its terms and as applied in this case, is repugnant to the due process clause of the Fourteenth Amendment. Its material provisions are:

"§ 160. Criminal anarchy defined. Criminal anarchy is the doctrine that organized government should be overthrown by force or violence, or by assassination of the executive head or of any of the executive officials of government, or by any unlawful means. The advocacy of such doctrine either by word of mouth or writing is a felony.

"§ 161. Advocacy of criminal anarchy. Any person who:

"1. By word of mouth or writing advocates, advises or teaches the duty, necessity or propriety of overthrowing or overturning organized government by force or violence, or by assassination of the executive head or of any of the executive officials of government, or by any unlawful means; or,

"2. Prints, publishes, edits, issues or knowingly circulates, sells, distributes or publicly displays any book, paper, document, or written or printed matter in any [655] form, containing or advocating, advising or teaching the doctrine that organized government should be overthrown by force, violence or any unlawful means . . . ,

"Is guilty of a felony and punishable" by imprisonment or fine, or both.

The indictment was in two counts. The first charged that the defendant had advocated, advised and taught the duty, necessity and propriety of overthrowing and overturning organized government by force, violence and unlawful means, by certain writings therein set forth entitled "The Left Wing Manifesto"; the second that he had printed, published and knowingly circulated and distributed a certain paper called "The Revolutionary Age," containing the writings set forth in the first count advocating, advising and teaching the doctrine that organized government should be overthrown by force, violence and unlawful means.

The following facts were established on the trial by undisputed evidence and admissions: The defendant is a member of the Left Wing Section of the Socialist Party, a dissenting branch or faction of that party formed in opposition to its dominant policy of "moderate Socialism." Membership in both is open to aliens as well as citizens. The Left Wing Section was organized nationally at a conference in New York City in June, 1919, attended by ninety delegates from twenty different States. The conference elected a National Council, of which the defendant was a member, and left to it the adoption of a "Manifesto." This was published in The Revolutionary Age, the official organ of the Left Wing. The defendant was on the board of managers of the paper and was its business manager. He arranged for the printing of the paper and took to the printer the manuscript of the first issue which contained the Left Wing Manifesto, and also a Communist Program and a Program of the Left Wing that had been adopted by the conference. Sixteen thousand [656] copies were printed, which were delivered at the premises in New York City used as the office of the Revolutionary Age and the headquarters of the Left Wing, and occupied by the defendant and other officials. These copies were paid for by the defendant, as business manager of the paper. Employees at this office wrapped and mailed out copies of the paper under the defendant's direction; and copies were sold from this office. It was admitted that the defendant signed a card subscribing to the Manifesto and Program of the Left Wing, which all applicants were required to sign before being admitted to membership; that he went to different parts of the State to speak to branches of the Socialist Party about the principles of the Left Wing and advocated their adoption; and that he was responsible for the Manifesto as it appeared, that "he knew of the publication, in a general way and he knew of its publication afterwards, and is responsible for its circulation."

There was no evidence of any effect resulting from the publication and circulation of the Manifesto.

No witnesses were offered in behalf of the defendant.

Extracts from the Manifesto are set forth in the margin. [note 2] Coupled with a review of the rise of Socialism, it [657] condemned the dominant "moderate Socialism" for its recognition of the necessity of the democratic parliamentary state; repudiated its policy of introducing Socialism by legislative measures; and advocated, in plain and unequivocal language, the necessity of accomplishing the "Communist Revolution" by a militant and "revolutionary Socialism", based on "the class struggle" and mobilizing [658] the "power of the proletariat in action," through mass industrial revolts developing into mass political strikes and "revolutionary mass action", for the purpose of conquering and destroying the parliamentary state and establishing in its place, through a "revolutionary dictatorship of the proletariat", the system of Communist Socialism. The then recent strikes in Seattle and Winnipeg [note 3] were cited as instances of a development already verging on revolutionary action and suggestive of proletarian [659] dictatorship, in which the strike-workers were "trying to usurp the functions of municipal government"; and revolutionary Socialism, it was urged, must use these mass industrial revolts to broaden the strike, make it general and militant, and develop it into mass political strikes and revolutionary mass action for the annihilation of the parliamentary state.

At the outset of the trial the defendant's counsel objected to the introduction of any evidence under the [660] indictment on the grounds that, as a matter of law, the Manifesto "is not in contravention of the statute," and that "the statute is in contravention of" the due process clause of the Fourteenth Amendment. This objection was denied. They also moved, at the close of the evidence, to dismiss the indictment and direct an acquittal "on the grounds stated in the first objection to evidence", [661] and again on the grounds that "the indictment does not charge an offense" and the evidence "does not show an offense." These motions were also denied.

The court, among other things, charged the jury, in substance, that they must determine what was the intent, purpose and fair meaning of the Manifesto; that its words must be taken in their ordinary meaning, as they would be understood by people whom it might reach; that a mere statement or analysis of social and economic facts and historical incidents, in the nature of an essay, accompanied by prophecy as to the future course of events, but with no teaching, advice or advocacy of action, would not constitute the advocacy, advice or teaching of a doctrine for the overthrow of government within the meaning of the statute; that a mere statement that unlawful acts might accomplish such a purpose would be insufficient, unless there was a teaching, advising and advocacy of employing such unlawful acts for the purpose of overthrowing government; and that if the jury had a reasonable doubt that the Manifesto did teach, advocate or advise the duty, necessity or propriety of using unlawful means for the overthrowing of organized government, the defendant was entitled to an acquittal.

The defendant's counsel submitted two requests to charge which embodied in substance the statement that to constitute criminal anarchy within the meaning of the statute it was necessary that the language used or published should advocate, teach or advise the duty, necessity or propriety of doing "some definite or immediate act or acts" of force, violence or unlawfulness directed toward the overthrowing of organized government. These were denied further than had been charged. Two other requests to charge embodied in substance the statement that to constitute guilt the language used or published must be "reasonably and ordinarily calculated to incite certain persons" to acts of force, violence or unlawfulness, [662] with the object of overthrowing organized government. These were also denied.

The Appellate Division, after setting forth extracts from the Manifesto and referring to the Left Wing and Communist Programs published in the same issue of the Revolutionary Age, said: [note 4] "It is perfectly plain that the plan and purpose advocated . . . contemplate the overthrow and destruction of the governments of the United States and of all the States, not by the free action of the majority of the people through the ballot box in electing representatives to authorize a change of government by amending or changing the Constitution, . . . but by immediately organizing the industrial proletariat into militant Socialist unions and at the earliest opportunity through mass strike and force and violence, if necessary, compelling the government to cease to function, and then through a proletarian dictatorship, taking charge of and appropriating all property and administering it and governing through such dictatorship until such time as the proletariat is permitted to administer and govern it. . . . The articles in question are not a discussion of ideas and theories. They advocate a doctrine deliberately determined upon and planned for militantly disseminating a propaganda advocating that it is the duty and necessity of the proletariat engaged in industrial pursuits to organize to such an extent that, by massed strike, the wheels of government may ultimately be stopped and the government overthrown . . ."

The Court of Appeals held that the Manifesto "advocated the overthrow of this government by violence, or by unlawful means." [note 5] In one of the opinions representing [663] the views of a majority of the court, [note 6] it was said: "It will be seen . . . that this defendant through the manifesto . . . advocated the destruction of the state and the establishment of the dictatorship of the proletariat. . . . To advocate . . . the commission of this conspiracy or action by mass strike whereby government is crippled, the administration of justice paralyzed, and the health, morals and welfare of a community endangered, and this for the purpose of bringing about a revolution in the state, is to advocate the overthrow of organized government by unlawful means." In the other [note 7] it was said: "As we read this manifesto . . . we feel entirely clear that the jury were justified in rejecting the view that it was a mere academic and harmless discussion of the advantages of communism and advanced socialism" and "in regarding it as a justification and advocacy of action by one class which would destroy the rights of all other classes and overthrow the state itself by use of revolutionary mass strikes. It is true that there is no advocacy in specific terms of the use of . . . force or violence. There was no need to be. Some things are so commonly incident to others that they do not need to be mentioned when the underlying purpose is described."

And both the Appellate Division and the Court of Appeals held the statute constitutional.

The specification of the errors relied on relates solely to the specific rulings of the trial court in the matters hereinbefore set out. [note 8] The correctness of the verdict is not [664] questioned, as the case was submitted to the jury. The sole contention here is, essentially, that as there was no evidence of any concrete result flowing from the publication of the Manifesto or of circumstances showing the likelihood of such result, the statute as construed and applied by the trial court penalizes the mere utterance, as such, of "doctrine" having no quality of incitement, without regard either to the circumstances of its utterance or to the likelihood of unlawful sequences; and that, as the exercise of the right of free expression with relation to government is only punishable "in circumstances involving likelihood of substantive evil," the statute contravenes the due process clause of the Fourteenth Amendment. The argument in support of this contention rests primarily upon the following propositions: 1st, That the "liberty" protected by the Fourteenth Amendment includes the liberty of speech and of the press; and 2nd, That while liberty of expression "is not absolute," it may be restrained "only in circumstances where its exercise bears a causal relation with some substantive evil, consummated, attempted or likely," and as the statute "takes no account of circumstances," it unduly restrains this liberty and is therefore unconstitutional.

The precise question presented, and the only question which we can consider under this writ of error, then is, whether the statute, as construed and applied in this case by the state courts, deprived the defendant of his liberty of expression in violation of the due process clause of the Fourteenth Amendment.

The statute does not penalize the utterance or publication of abstract "doctrine" or academic discussion having no quality of incitement to any concrete action. It is not aimed against mere historical or philosophical essays. It does not restrain the advocacy of changes in the form of government by constitutional and lawful means. What it prohibits is language advocating, advising or teaching [665] the overthrow of organized government by unlawful means. These words imply urging to action. Advocacy is defined in the Century Dictionary as: "1. The act of pleading for, supporting, or recommending; active espousal." It is not the abstract "doctrine" of overthrowing organized government by unlawful means which is denounced by the statute, but the advocacy of action for the accomplishment of that purpose. It was so construed and applied by the trial judge, who specifically charged the jury that: "A mere grouping of historical events and a prophetic deduction from them would neither constitute advocacy, advice or teaching of a doctrine for the overthrow of government by force, violence or unlawful means. [And] if it were a mere essay on the subject, as suggested by counsel, based upon deductions from alleged historical events, with no teaching, advice or advocacy of action, it would not constitute a violation of the statute. . . ."

The Manifesto, plainly, is neither the statement of abstract doctrine nor, as suggested by counsel, mere prediction that industrial disturbances and revolutionary mass strikes will result spontaneously in an inevitable process of evolution in the economic system. It advocates and urges in fervent language mass action which shall progressively foment industrial disturbances and through political mass strikes and revolutionary mass action overthrow and destroy organized parliamentary government. It concludes with a call to action in these words: "The proletariat revolution and the Communist reconstruction of society -- *the struggle for these* -- is now indispensable. . . . The Communist International calls the proletariat of the world to the final struggle!" This is not the expression of philosophical abstraction, the mere prediction of future events; it is the language of direct incitement.

The means advocated for bringing about the destruction of organized parliamentary government, namely, mass industrial [666] revolts usurping the functions of municipal government, political mass strikes directed against the parliamentary state, and revolutionary mass action for its final destruction, necessarily imply the use of force and violence, and in their essential nature are inherently unlawful in a constitutional government of law and order. That the jury were warranted in finding that the Manifesto advocated not merely the abstract doctrine of overthrowing organized government by force, violence and unlawful means, but action to that end, is clear.

For present purposes we may and do assume that freedom of speech and of the press -- which are protected by the First Amendment from abridgment by Congress -- are among the fundamental personal rights and "liberties" protected by the due process clause of the Fourteenth Amendment from impairment by the States. We do not regard the incidental statement in *Prudential Ins. Co. Cheek*, 259 U.S. 530, 543, that the Fourteenth Amendment imposes no restrictions on the States concerning freedom of speech, as determinative of this question. [note 9]

It is a fundamental principle, long established, that the freedom of speech and of the press which is secured by the Constitution, does not confer an absolute right to speak or publish, without responsibility, whatever one may choose, or an unrestricted and unbridled license that gives immunity for every possible use of language and prevents the punishment of those who abuse this freedom. 2 Story on the Constitution, 5th ed., § 1580, p. 634; *Robertson v. Baldwin*, 165 U.S. 275, 281; *Patterson v. Colorado*, 205 U.S. 454, 462; *Fox v. Washington*, 236 U.S. 273, 276; [667] *Schenck v. United States*, 249 U.S. 47, 52; *Frohwerk v. United States*, 249 U.S. 204, 206; Debs v. United States, 249 U.S. 211, 213; *Schaefer v. United States*, 251 U.S. 466, 474; *Gilbert v. Minnesota*, 254 U.S. 325, 332; *Warren v. United States*, (C. C. A.) 183 Fed. 718, 721. Reasonably limited, it was said by Story in the passage cited, this freedom is an inestimable privilege in a free government; without such limitation, it might become the scourge of the republic.

That a State in the exercise of its police power may punish those who abuse this freedom by utterances inimical to the public welfare, tending to corrupt public morals, incite to crime, or disturb the public peace, is not open to question. *Robertson v. Baldwin, supra*, p. 281; *Patterson v. Colorado, supra*, p. 462; *Fox v. Washington, supra*, p. 277; *Gilbert v. Minnesota, supra*, p. 339; *People v. Most*, 171 N. Y. 423, 431; *State v. Holm*, 139 Minn. 267, 275; *State v. Hennessy*, 114 Wash. 351, 359; *State v. Boyd*, 86 N. J. L. 75, 79; *State v. McKee*, 73 Conn. 18, 27. Thus it was held by this Court in the Fox Case, that a State may punish publications advocating and encouraging a breach of its criminal laws; and, in the Gilbert Case, that a State may punish utterances teaching or advocating that its citizens should not assist the United States in prosecuting or carrying on war with its public enemies.

And, for yet more imperative reasons, a State may punish utterances endangering the foundations of organized government and threatening its overthrow by unlawful means. These imperil its own existence as a constitutional State. Freedom of speech and press, said Story (*supra*) does not protect disturbances to the public peace or the attempt to subvert the government. It does not protect publications or teachings which tend to subvert or imperil the government or to impede or hinder it in the performance of its governmental duties. *State v.* [668] *Holm, supra*, p. 275. It does not protect publications prompting the overthrow of government by force; the punishment of those who publish articles which tend to destroy organized society being essential to the security of freedom and the stability of the State. *People v. Most, supra*, pp. 431, 432. And a State may penalize utterances which openly advocate the overthrow of the representative and constitutional form of government of the United States and the several States, by violence or other unlawful means. *People v. Lloyd*, 304 Ill. 23, 34. See also, *State v. Tachin*, 92 N. J. L. 269, 274; and *People v. Steelik*, 187 Cal. 361, 375. In short this freedom does not deprive a State of the primary and essential right of self preservation; which, so long as human governments endure, they cannot be denied. *Turner v. Williams*, 194 U.S. 279, 294. In *Toledo Newspaper Co. v. United States*, 247 U.S. 402, 419, it was said: "The safeguarding and fructification of free and constitutional institutions is the very basis and mainstay upon which the freedom of the press rests, and that freedom, therefore, does not and cannot be held to include the right virtually to destroy such institutions."

By enacting the present statute the State has determined, through its legislative body, that utterances advocating the overthrow of organized government by force, violence and unlawful means, are so inimical to the general welfare and involve such danger of substantive evil that they may be penalized in the exercise of its police power. That determination must be given great weight. Every presumption is to be indulged in favor of the validity of the statute. *Mugler v. Kansas,* 123 U.S. 623, 661. And the case is to be considered "in the light of the principle that the State is primarily the judge of regulations required in the interest of public safety and welfare;" and that its police "statutes may only be declared unconstitutional where they are arbitrary or unreasonable [669] attempts to exercise authority vested in the State in the public interest." *Great Northern Ry. v. Clara City,* 246 U.S. 434, 439. That utterances inciting to the overthrow of organized government by unlawful means, present a sufficient danger of substantive evil to bring their punishment within the range of legislative discretion, is clear. Such utterances, by their very nature, involve danger to the public peace and to the security of the State. They threaten breaches of the peace and ultimate revolution. And the immediate danger is none the less real and substantial, because the effect of a given utterance cannot be accurately foreseen. The State cannot reasonably be required to measure the danger from every such utterance in the nice balance of a jeweler's scale. A single revolutionary spark may kindle a fire that, smouldering for a time, may burst into a sweeping and destructive conflagration. It cannot be said that the State is acting arbitrarily or unreasonably when in the exercise of its judgment as to the measures necessary to protect the public peace and safety, it seeks to extinguish the spark without waiting until it has enkindled the flame or blazed into the conflagration. It cannot reasonably be required to defer the adoption of measures for its own peace and safety until the revolutionary utterances lead to actual disturbances of the public peace or imminent and immediate danger of its own destruction; but it may, in the exercise of its judgment, suppress the threatened danger in its incipiency. In *People v. Lloyd, supra,* p. 35, it was aptly said: "Manifestly, the legislature has authority to forbid the advocacy of a doctrine designed and intended to overthrow the government without waiting until there is a present and imminent danger of the success of the plan advocated. If the State were compelled to wait until the apprehended danger became certain, then its right to protect itself would come into being simultaneously with the overthrow of the government, when there [670] would be neither prosecuting officers nor courts for the enforcement of the law."

We cannot hold that the present statute is an arbitrary or unreasonable exercise of the police power of the State unwarrantably infringing the freedom of speech or press; and we must and do sustain its constitutionality.

This being so it may be applied to every utterance -- not too trivial to be beneath the notice of the law -- which is of such a character and used with such intent and purpose as to bring it within the prohibition of the statute. This principle is illustrated in *Fox v. Washington, supra,* p. 277; *Abrams v. United States,* 250 U.S. 616, 624; *Schaefer v. United States, supra,* pp. 479, 480; *Pierce v. United States,* 252 U.S. 239, 250, 251; [note 10] and *Gilbert v. Minnesota, supra,* p. 333. In other words, when the legislative body has determined generally, in the constitutional exercise of its discretion, that utterances of a certain kind involve such danger of substantive evil that they may be punished, the question whether any specific utterance coming within the prohibited class is likely, in and of itself, to bring about the substantive evil, is not open to consideration. It is sufficient that the statute itself be constitutional and that the use of the language comes within its prohibition.

It is clear that the question in such cases is entirely different from that involved in those cases where the statute merely prohibits certain acts involving the danger of substantive evil, without any reference to language itself, and it is sought to apply its provisions to language [671] used by the defendant for the purpose of bringing about the prohibited results. There, if it be contended that the statute cannot be applied to the language used by the defendant because of its protection by the freedom of speech or press, it must necessarily be found, as an original question, without any previous determination by the legislative body, whether the specific language used involved such likelihood of bringing about the substantive evil as to deprive it of the constitutional protection. In such cases it has been held that the general provisions of the statute may be constitutionally applied to the specific utterance of the defendant if its natural tendency and probable effect was to bring about the substantive evil which the legislative body might prevent. *Schenck v. United States, supra*, p. 51; *Debs v. United States*, supra, pp. 215, 216. And the general statement in the *Schenck Case* (p. 52) that the "question in every case is whether the words are used in such circumstances and are of such a nature as to create a clear and present danger that they will bring about the substantive evils," -- upon which great reliance is placed in the defendant's argument -- was manifestly intended, as shown by the context, to apply only in cases of this class, and has no application to those like the present, where the legislative body itself has previously determined the danger of substantive evil arising from utterances of a specified character.

The defendant's brief does not separately discuss any of the rulings of the trial court. It is only necessary to say that, applying the general rules already stated, we find that none of them involved any invasion of the constitutional rights of the defendant. It was not necessary, within the meaning of the statute, that the defendant should have advocated "some definite or immediate act or acts" of force, violence or unlawfulness. It was sufficient if such acts were advocated in general terms; and it was not essential that their immediate execution should [672] have been advocated. Nor was it necessary that the language should have been "reasonably and ordinarily calculated to incite certain persons" to acts of force, violence or unlawfulness. The advocacy need not be addressed to specific persons. Thus, the publication and circulation of a newspaper article may be an encouragement or endeavor to persuade to murder, although not addressed to any person in particular. *Queen v. Most*, L. R., 7 Q. B. D. 244.

We need not enter upon a consideration of the English common law rule of seditious libel or the Federal Sedition Act of 1798, to which reference is made in the defendant's brief. These are so unlike the present statute, that we think the decisions under them cast no helpful light upon the questions here.

And finding, for the reasons stated, that the statute is not in itself unconstitutional, and that it has not been applied in the present case in derogation of any constitutional right, the judgment of the Court of Appeals is Affirmed.

11 NEAR V. MINNESOTA
SUPREME COURT OF THE UNITED STATES
283 U.S. 697
Argued January 30, 1931
Decided June 1, 1931

Syllabus

1. A Minnesota statute declares that one who engages "in the business of regularly and customarily producing, publishing," etc., "a malicious, scandalous and defamatory newspaper, magazine or other periodical," is guilty of a nuisance, and authorizes suits, in the name of the State, in which such periodicals may be abated and their publishers enjoined from future violations. In such a suit, malice may be inferred from the fact of publication. The defendant is permitted to prove, as a defense, that his publications were true and published "with good motives and for justifiable ends." Disobedience of an injunction is punishable as a contempt. Held unconstitutional, as applied to publications charging neglect of duty and corruption upon the part of law-enforcing officers of the State. Pp. 704, 709, 712, 722.

2. Liberty of the press is within the liberty safeguarded by the due process clause of the Fourteenth Amendment from invasion by state action. P. 707.

3. Liberty of the press is not an absolute right, and the State may punish its abuse. P. 708.

4. In passing upon the constitutionality of the statute, the court has regard for substance, and not for form; the statute must be tested by its operation and effect. P. 708. [698]

5. Cutting through mere details of procedure, the operation and effect of the statute is that public authorities may bring a publisher before a judge upon a charge of conducting a business of publishing scandalous and defamatory matter -- in particular, that the matter consists of charges against public officials of official dereliction -- and, unless the publisher is able and disposed to satisfy the judge that the charges are true and are published with good motives and for justifiable ends, his newspaper or periodical is suppressed and further publication is made punishable as a contempt. This is the essence of censorship. P. 713.

6. A statute authorizing such proceedings in restraint of publication is inconsistent with

the conception of the liberty of the press as historically conceived and guaranteed. P. 713.

7. The chief purpose of the guaranty is to prevent previous restraints upon publication. The libeler, however, remains criminally and civilly responsible for his libels. P. 713.

8. There are undoubtedly limitations upon the immunity from previous restraint of the press, but they are not applicable in this case. P. 715.

9. The liberty of the press has been especially cherished in this country as respects publications censuring public officials and charging official misconduct. P. 716.

10. Public officers find their remedies for false accusations in actions for redress and punishment under the libel laws, and not in proceedings to restrain the publication of newspapers and periodicals. P. 718.

11. The fact that the liberty of the press may be abused by miscreant purveyors of scandal does not make any the less necessary the immunity from previous restraint in dealing with official misconduct. P. 720.

12. Characterizing the publication of charges of official misconduct as a "business," and the business as a nuisance, does not avoid the constitutional guaranty; nor does it matter that the periodical is largely or chiefly devoted to such charges. P. 720.

13. The guaranty against previous restraint extends to publications charging official derelictions that amount to crimes. P. 720.

14. Permitting the publisher to show in defense that the matter published is true and is published with good motives and for justifiable ends does not justify the statute. P. 721.

15. Nor can it be sustained as a measure for preserving the public peace and preventing assaults and crime. Pp. 721, 722.

179 Minn. 40; 228 N.W. 326, reversed. [699]

MR. CHIEF JUSTICE HUGHES delivered the opinion of the Court.

Chapter 285 of the Session Laws of Minnesota for the year 1925 [note 1] provides for the abatement, as a public nuisance, of a "malicious, scandalous and defamatory newspaper, [702] magazine or other periodical." Section one of the Act is as follows:

Section 1. Any person who, as an individual, or as a member or employee of a firm, or association or organization, or as an officer, director, member or employee of a corporation, shall be engaged in the business of regularly or customarily producing, publishing or circulating, having in possession, selling or giving away

(a) an obscene, lewd and lascivious newspaper, magazine, or other periodical, or

(b) a malicious, scandalous and defamatory newspaper, magazine or other periodical, is guilty of a nuisance, and all persons guilty of such nuisance may be enjoined, as hereinafter provided.

Participation in such business shall constitute a commission of such nuisance and render the participant liable and subject to the proceedings, orders and judgments provided for in this Act. Ownership, in whole or in part, directly or indirectly, of any such periodical, or of any stock or interest in any corporation or organization which owns the same in whole or in part, or which publishes the same, shall constitute such participation.

In actions brought under (b) above, there shall be available the defense that the truth was published with good motives and for justifiable ends and in such actions the plaintiff shall not have the right to report (sic) to issues or editions of periodicals taking place more than three months before the commencement of the action.

Section two provides that, whenever any such nuisance is committed or exists, the County Attorney of any county where any such periodical is published or circulated, or, in case of his failure or refusal to proceed upon written request in good faith of a reputable citizen, the Attorney General, or, upon like failure or refusal of the latter, any citizen of the county may maintain an action in the district court of the county in the name of the State to enjoin [703] perpetually the persons committing or maintaining any such nuisance from further committing or maintaining it. Upon such evidence as the court shall deem sufficient, a temporary injunction may be granted. The defendants have the right to plead by demurrer or answer, and the plaintiff may demur or reply as in other cases.

The action, by section three, is to be " governed by the practice and procedure applicable to civil actions for injunctions," and, after trial, the court may enter judgment permanently enjoining the defendants found guilty of violating the Act from continuing the violation, and, "in and by such judgment, such nuisance may be wholly abated." The court is empowered, as in other cases of contempt, to punish disobedience to a temporary or permanent injunction by fine of not more than $1,000 or by imprisonment in the county jail for not more than twelve months.

Under this statute, clause (b), the County Attorney of Hennepin County brought this action to enjoin the publication of what was described as a " malicious, scandalous and defamatory newspaper, magazine and periodical" known as " The Saturday Press," published by the defendants in the city of Minneapolis. The complaint alleged that the defendants, on September 24, 1927, and on eight subsequent dates in October and November, 1927, published and circulated editions of that periodical which were "largely devoted to malicious, scandalous and defamatory articles" concerning Charles G. Davis, Frank W. Brunskill, the Minneapolis Tribune, the Minneapolis Journal, Melvin C. Passolt, George E. Leach, the Jewish Race, the members of the Grand Jury of Hennepin County impaneled in November, 1927, and then holding office, and other persons, as more fully appeared in exhibits annexed to the complaint, consisting of copies of the articles described and constituting 327 pages of the record. While the complaint did not so allege, it [704] appears from the briefs of both parties that Charles G. Davis was a special law enforcement officer employed by a civic organization, that George E. Leach was Mayor of Minneapolis, that Frank W. Brunskill was its Chief of Police, and that Floyd B. Olson (the relator in this action) was County Attorney.

Without attempting to summarize the contents of the voluminous exhibits attached to the complaint, we deem it sufficient to say that the articles charged in substance that a Jewish gangster was in control of gambling, bootlegging and racketeering in Minneapolis, and that law enforcing officers and agencies were not energetically performing their duties. Most of the charges were directed against the Chief of Police; he was charged with gross neglect of duty, illicit relations with gangsters, and with participation in graft. The County Attorney was charged with knowing the existing conditions and with failure to take adequate measures to remedy them. The Mayor was accused of inefficiency and dereliction. One member of the grand jury was stated to be in sympathy with the gangsters. A special grand jury and a special prosecutor were demanded to deal with the situation in general, and, in particular, to investigate an attempt to assassinate one Guilford, one of the original defendants, who, it appears from the articles, was shot by gangsters after the first issue of the periodical had been published. There is no question but that the articles made serious accusations against the public officers named and others in connection with the prevalence of crimes and the failure to expose and punish them.

At the beginning of the action, on November 22, 1927, and upon the verified complaint, an order was made directing the defendants to show cause why a temporary injunction should not issue and meanwhile forbidding the defendants to publish, circulate or have in their possession any editions of the periodical from September [705] 24, 1927, to November 19, 1927, inclusive, and from publishing, circulating, or having in their possession, "any future editions of said The Saturday Press" and "any publication, known by any other name whatsoever containing malicious, scandalous and defamatory matter of the kind alleged in plaintiff's complaint herein or otherwise."

The defendants demurred to the complaint upon the ground that it did not state facts sufficient to constitute a cause of action, and on this demurrer challenged the constitutionality of the statute. The District Court overruled the demurrer and certified the question of constitutionality to the Supreme Court of the State. The Supreme Court sustained the statute (174 Minn. 457, 219 N.W. 770), and it is conceded by the appellee that the Act was thus held to be valid over the objection that it violated not only the state constitution, but also the Fourteenth Amendment of the Constitution of the United States.

Thereupon, the defendant Near, the present appellant, answered the complaint. He averred that he was the sole owner and proprietor of the publication in question. He admitted the publication of the articles in the issues described in the complaint, but denied that they were malicious, scandalous or defamatory as alleged. He expressly invoked the protection of the due process clause of the Fourteenth Amendment. The case then came on for trial. The plaintiff offered in evidence the verified complaint, together with the issues of the publication in question, which were attached to the complaint as exhibits. The defendant objected to the introduction of the evidence, invoking the constitutional provisions to which his answer referred. The objection was overruled, no further evidence was presented, and the plaintiff rested. The defendant then rested without offering evidence. The plaintiff moved that the court direct the issue of a permanent injunction, and this was done. [706]

The District Court made findings of fact which followed the allegations of the complaint and found in general terms that the editions in question were "chiefly devoted to malicious, scandalous and defamatory articles" concerning the individuals named. The court further found that the defendants, through these publications, "did engage in the business of regularly and customarily producing, publishing and circulating a malicious, scandalous and defamatory newspaper," and that "the said publication" "under said name of The Saturday

Press, or any other name, constitutes a public nuisance under the laws of the State." Judgment was thereupon entered adjudging that "the newspaper, magazine and periodical known as The Saturday Press," as a public nuisance, "be and is hereby abated." The Judgment perpetually enjoined the defendants "from producing, editing, publishing, circulating, having in their possession, selling or giving away any publication whatsoever which is a malicious, scandalous or defamatory newspaper, as defined by law," and also "from further conducting said nuisance under the name and title of said The Saturday Press or any other name or title."

The defendant Near appealed from this judgment to the Supreme Court of the State, again asserting his right under the Federal Constitution, and the judgment was affirmed upon the authority of the former decision. 179 Minn. 40, 228 N.W. 326. With respect to the contention that the judgment went too far, and prevented the defendants from publishing any kind of a newspaper, the court observed that the assignments of error did not go to the form of the judgment, and that the lower court had not been asked to modify it. The court added that it saw no reason "for defendants to construe the judgment as restraining them from operating a newspaper in harmony with the public welfare, to which all must yield," that the allegations of the complaint had been [707] found to be true, and, though this was an equitable action, defendants had not indicated a desire "to conduct their business in the usual and legitimate manner."

From the judgment as thus affirmed, the defendant Near appeals to this Court.

This statute, for the suppression as a public nuisance of a newspaper or periodical, is unusual, if not unique, and raises questions of grave importance transcending the local interests involved in the particular action. It is no longer open to doubt that the liberty of the press, and of speech, is within the liberty safeguarded by the due process clause of the Fourteenth Amendment from invasion by state action. It was found impossible to conclude that this essential personal liberty of the citizen was left unprotected by the general guaranty of fundamental rights of person and property. *Gitlow v. New York*, 268 U.S. 652, 666; *Whitney v. California*, 274 U.S. 357, 362, 373; *Fiske v. Kansas*, 274 U.S. 380, 382; *Stromberg v. California*, ante, p. 359. In maintaining this guaranty, the authority of the State to enact laws to promote the health, safety, morals and general welfare of its people is necessarily admitted. The limits of this sovereign power must always be determined with appropriate regard to the particular subject of its exercise. Thus, while recognizing the broad discretion of the legislature in fixing rates to be charged by those undertaking a public service, this Court has decided that the owner cannot constitutionally be deprived of his right to a fair return, because that is deemed to be of the essence of ownership. *Railroad Commission Cases*, 116 U.S. 307, 331; *Northern Pacific Ry. Co. v. North Dakota*, 236 U.S. 585, 596. So, while liberty of contract is not an absolute right, and the wide field of activity in the making of contracts is subject to legislative supervision (*Frisbie v. United States*, 157 U.S. 161, 165), this Court has held that the power of the State stops short of interference with what are deemed [708] to be certain indispensable requirements of the liberty assured, notably with respect to the fixing of prices and wages. *Tyson Bros. v. Banton*, 273 U.S. 418; *Ribnik v. McBride*, 277 U.S. 350; *Adkins v. Children's Hospital*, 261 U.S. 525, 560, 561. Liberty of speech, and of the press, is also not an absolute right, and the State may punish its abuse. *Whitney v. California, supra; Stromberg v. California, supra*. Liberty, in each of its phases, has its history and connotation, and, in the present instance, the inquiry is as to the historic conception of the liberty of the press and whether the statute under review violates the essential attributes of that liberty.

The appellee insists that the questions of the application of the statute to appellant's periodical, and of the construction of the judgment of the trial court, are not presented for review; that appellant's sole attack was upon the constitutionality of the statute, however it might be applied. The appellee contends that no question either of motive in the publication, or whether the decree goes beyond the direction of the statute, is before us. The appellant replies that, in his view, the plain terms of the statute were not departed from in this case, and that, even if they were, the statute is nevertheless unconstitutional under any reasonable construction of its terms. The appellant states that he has not argued that the temporary and permanent injunctions were broader than were warranted by the statute; he insists that what was done was properly done if the statute is valid, and that the action taken under the statute is a fair indication of its scope.

With respect to these contentions, it is enough to say that, in passing upon constitutional questions, the court has regard to substance, and not to mere matters of form, and that, in accordance with familiar principles, the statute must be tested by its operation and effect. *Henderson v. Mayor*, 92 U.S. 259, 268; *Bailey v. Alabama*, 219 [709] U.S. 219, 244; *United States v. Reynolds*, 235 U.S. 133, 148, 149; *St. Louis Southwestern R. Co. v. Arkansas*, 235 U.S. 350, 362; *Mountain Timber Co. v. Washington*, 243 U.S. 219, 237. That operation and effect we think is clearly shown by the record in this case. We are not concerned with mere errors of the trial court, if there be such, in going beyond the direction of the statute as construed by the Supreme Court of the State. It is thus important to note precisely the purpose and effect of the statute as the state court has construed it.

First. The statute is not aimed at the redress of individual or private wrongs. Remedies for libel remain available and unaffected. The statute, said the state court, "is not directed at threatened libel, but at an existing business which, generally speaking, involves more than libel." It is aimed at the distribution of scandalous matter as "detrimental to public morals and to the general welfare," tending "to disturb the peace of the community" and "to provoke assaults and the commission of crime." In order to obtain an injunction to suppress the future publication of the newspaper or periodical, it is not necessary to prove the falsity of the charges that have been made in the publication condemned. In the present action, there was no allegation that the matter published was not true. It is alleged, and the statute requires the allegation, that the publication was "malicious." But, as in prosecutions for libel, there is no requirement of proof by the State of malice in fact, as distinguished from malice inferred from the mere publication of the defamatory matter.[note 2] The judgment in this case proceeded upon the mere proof of publication. The statute permits the defense not of the truth alone, but only that the truth was published with good motives and [710] for justifiable ends. It is apparent that, under the statute, the publication is to be regarded as defamatory if it injures reputation, and that it is scandalous if it circulates charges of reprehensible conduct, whether criminal or otherwise, and the publication is thus deemed to invite public reprobation and to constitute a public scandal. The court sharply defined the purpose of the statute, bringing out the precise point, in these words: "There is no constitutional right to publish a fact merely because it is true. It is a matter of common knowledge that prosecutions under the criminal libel statutes do not result in efficient repression or suppression of the evils of scandal. Men who are the victims of such assaults seldom resort to the courts. This is especially true if their sins are exposed and the only question relates to whether it was done with good motives and for justifiable ends. This law is not for the protection of the person attacked, nor to punish the wrongdoer. It is for the protection of the public welfare."

Second. The statute is directed not simply at the circulation of scandalous and defamatory statements with regard to private citizens, but at the continued publication by newspapers and periodicals of charges against public officers of corruption, malfeasance in office, or serious neglect of duty. Such charges, by their very nature, create a public scandal. They are scandalous and defamatory within the meaning of the statute, which has its normal operation in relation to publications dealing prominently and chiefly with the alleged derelictions of public officers. [note 3] [711]

Third. The object of the statute is not punishment, in the ordinary sense, but suppression of the offending newspaper or periodical. The reason for the enactment, as the state court has said, is that prosecutions to enforce penal statutes for libel do not result in "efficient repression or suppression of the evils of scandal." Describing the business of publication as a public nuisance does not obscure the substance of the proceeding which the statute authorizes. It is the continued publication of scandalous and defamatory matter that constitutes the business and the declared nuisance. In the case of public officers, it is the reiteration of charges of official misconduct, and the fact that the newspaper or periodical is principally devoted to that purpose, that exposes it to suppression. In the present instance, the proof was that nine editions of the newspaper or periodical in question were published on successive dates, and that they were chiefly devoted to charges against public officers and in relation to the prevalence and protection of crime. In such a case, these officers are not left to their ordinary remedy in a suit for libel, or the authorities to a prosecution for criminal libel. Under this statute, a publisher of a newspaper or periodical, undertaking to conduct a campaign to expose and to censure official derelictions, and devoting his publication principally to that purpose, must face not simply the possibility of a verdict against him in a suit or prosecution for libel, but a determination that his newspaper or periodical is a public nuisance to be abated, and that this abatement and suppression will follow unless he is prepared with legal evidence to prove the truth of the charges and also to satisfy the court that, in [712] addition to being true, the matter was published with good motives and for justifiable ends.

This suppression is accomplished by enjoining publication, and that restraint is the object and effect of the statute.

Fourth. The statute not only operates to suppress the offending newspaper or periodical, but to put the publisher under an effective censorship. When a newspaper or periodical is found to be "malicious, scandalous, and defamatory," and is suppressed as such, resumption of publication is punishable as a contempt of court by fine or imprisonment. Thus, where a newspaper or periodical has been suppressed because of the circulation of charges against public officers of official misconduct, it would seem to be clear that the renewal of the publication of such charges would constitute a contempt, and that the judgment would lay a permanent restraint upon the publisher, to escape which he must satisfy the court as to the character of a new publication. Whether he would be permitted again to publish matter deemed to be derogatory to the same or other public officers would depend upon the court's ruling. In the present instance, the judgment restrained the defendants from "publishing, circulating, having in their possession, selling or giving away any publication whatsoever which is a malicious, scandalous or defamatory newspaper, as defined by the law." The law gives no definition except that covered by the words "scandalous and defamatory," and publications charging official misconduct are of that class. While the court, answering the objection that the judgment was too broad, saw no reason for construing it as restraining the defendants "from operating a newspaper in harmony with the public welfare to which all must yield," and said that the defendants had not indicated "any desire to conduct their business in the usual and legitimate manner," the manifest inference is that, at least with respect to a [713] new publication directed against official misconduct, the defendant would be held, under penalty of punishment for contempt as provided in the statute, to a manner of publication which the court considered to be "usual and legitimate" and consistent with the public welfare.

If we cut through mere details of procedure, the operation and effect of the statute, in substance, is that public authorities may bring the owner or publisher of a newspaper or periodical before a judge upon a charge of conducting a business of publishing scandalous and defamatory matter -- in particular, that the matter consists of charges against public officers of official dereliction -- and, unless the owner or publisher is able and disposed to bring competent evidence to satisfy the judge that the charges are true and are published with good motives and for justifiable ends, his newspaper or periodical is suppressed and further publication is made punishable as a contempt. This is of the essence of censorship.

The question is whether a statute authorizing such proceedings in restraint of publication is consistent with the conception of the liberty of the press as historically conceived and guaranteed. In determining the extent of the constitutional protection, it has been generally, if not universally, considered that it is the chief purpose of the guaranty to prevent previous restraints upon publication. The struggle in England, directed against the legislative power of the licenser, resulted in renunciation of the censorship of the press. [note 4] The liberty deemed to be established was thus described by Blackstone: "The liberty of the press is indeed essential to the nature of a free state; but this consists in laying no previous restraints upon publications, and not in freedom from censure for criminal matter when published. Every freeman has an [714] undoubted right to lay what sentiments he pleases before the public; to forbid this is to destroy the freedom of the press; but if he publishes what is improper, mischievous or illegal, he must take the consequence of his own temerity." 4 Bl.Com. 151, 152; see Story on the Constitution, §§ 1884, 1889. The distinction was early pointed out "between the extent of the freedom with respect to censorship under our constitutional system and that enjoyed in "England. Here, as Madison said, "the great and essential rights of the people are secured against legislative as well as against executive ambition. "They are secured not by laws paramount to prerogative, but by constitutions paramount to laws. This security of "the freedom of the press requires that it should be exempt not only from previous restraint by the Executive, a in "Great Britain, but from legislative restraint also." Report on the Virginia Resolutions, Madison's Works, vol. IV, p. 543. This Court said, in *Patterson v. "Colorado*, 205 U.S. 454, 462: "In the first place, the main purpose of such constitutional provisions is "to prevent all such previous restraints "upon publications as had been practiced by other governments," and they do not prevent the subsequent "punishment of such as may be deemed ·contrary to the public welfare. *Commonwealth v. Blanding*, 3 Pick. 304, "313, 314; *Respublica v. Oswald*, 1 Dallas 319, 325. The preliminary freedom extends as well to the false as to "the true; the subsequent punishment may extend as well to the true as to the false. This was the law of criminal "libel apart from statute in most cases, if not in all. *Commonwealth v. Blanding*, ubi sup.; 4 Bl.Com. 150."

The criticism upon Blackstone's statement has not been because immunity from previous restraint upon "publication has not been regarded as deserving of special emphasis, but chiefly because that immunity cannot be "deemed to exhaust the conception of the liberty guaranteed by [715] state and federal constitutions. The point of "criticism has been "that the mere exemption from previous restraints cannot be all that is secured by the "constitutional provisions", and that "the liberty of the press might be rendered a mockery and a delusion, and the phrase itself a byword, if, while "every man was at liberty to publish what he pleased, the public authorities might nevertheless punish him for "harmless publications." 2 Cooley, Const.Lim., 8th ed., p. 885. But it is recognized that punishment for the abuse of the liberty accorded "to the press is essential to the protection of the public, and that the common law rules that subject the libeler to "responsibility for the public offense, as well as for the private injury, are not abolished by the protection extended "in our constitutions. Id., pp. 883, 884. The law of criminal libel rests upon that secure foundation. There is also "the conceded authority of courts to punish for contempt when publications directly tend to prevent the proper "discharge of judicial functions. *Patterson v. Colorado, supra; Toledo Newspaper Co. v. United States*, 247 U.S. "402, 419. [note 5] In the present case, we have no occasion to inquire as to the permissible scope of subsequent "punishment. For whatever wrong the appellant has committed or may commit by his publications the State "appropriately affords both public and private redress by its libel laws. As has been noted, the statute in question "does not deal with punishments; it provides for no punishment, except in case of contempt for violation of the "court's order, but for suppression and injunction, that is, for restraint upon publication.

The objection has also been made that the principle as to immunity from previous restraint is stated too [716] "broadly, if every such restraint is deemed to be prohibited. That is undoubtedly true; the protection even as to "previous restraint is not absolutely unlimited. But the limitation has been recognized only in exceptional cases: "When a nation is at war, many things that might be said in time of peace are such a hindrance to its effort that their "utterance will not be endured so long as men fight, and that no Court could regard them as protected by any "constitutional right." *Schenck v. United States*, 249 U.S. 47, 52. No one would question but that a government might prevent actual "obstruction to its recruiting service or the publication of the sailing dates of transports or the number and location "of troops. [note 6] On similar grounds, the primary requirements of decency may be enforced against obscene "publications. The security of the community life may be protected against incitements to acts of violence and the "overthrow by force of orderly government. The constitutional guaranty of free speech does not "protect a man from an injunction against uttering words that may have all the effect of force. *Gompers v. Buck "Stove & Range Co.*, 221 U.S. 418, 439." *Schenck v. United States, supra.* These limitations are not applicable here. Nor are we now concerned with "questions as to the extent of authority to prevent publications in order to protect private rights according to the "principles governing the exercise of the jurisdiction of courts of equity. [note 7]

The exceptional nature of its limitations places in a strong light the general conception that liberty of the press, "historically considered and taken up by the Federal Constitution, has meant, principally, although not exclusively, "immunity from previous restraints or censorship. The conception of the liberty of the press in this country had "broadened with the exigencies of the colonial [717] period and with the efforts to secure freedom from "oppressive administration. [note 8] That liberty was especially cherished for the immunity it afforded from previous "restraint of the publication of censure of public officers and charges of official misconduct. As was said by Chief "Justice Parker, in *Commonwealth v.*

Blanding, 3 Pick. 304, 313, with respect to the constitution of "Massachusetts: "Besides, it is well understood, and received as a commentary on this provision for the liberty of the press, that it "was intended to prevent all such previous restraints upon publications as had been practiced by other "governments, and in early times here, to stifle the efforts of patriots towards enlightening their fellow subjects "upon their rights and the duties of rulers. The liberty of the press was to be unrestrained, but he who used it was "to be responsible in case of its abuse." In the letter sent by the Continental Congress (October 26, 1774) to the Inhabitants of Quebec, referring to the ""five great rights," it was said: [note 9] "The last right we shall mention regards the freedom of the press. The importance of this consists, besides the "advancement of truth, science, morality, and arts in general, in its diffusion of liberal sentiments on the "administration of Government, its ready communication of thoughts between subjects, and its consequential "promotion of union among them whereby oppressive officers are shamed or intimidated into more honourable and "just modes of conducting affairs." Madison, who was the leading spirit in preparation of the First amendment of the Federal Constitution, thus described the practice and sentiment which led to the guaranties of liberty of the press in state constitutions:

In every State, probably, in the Union, the press has exerted a freedom in canvassing the merits and measures of public men of every description which has not been confined to the strict limits of the common law. On this footing the freedom of the press has stood; on this footing it yet stands. . . . Some degree of abuse is inseparable from the proper use of everything, and in no instance is this more true than in that of the press. It has accordingly been decided by the practice of the States that it is better to leave a few of its noxious branches to their luxuriant growth than, by pruning them away, to injure the vigour of those yielding the proper fruits. And can the wisdom of this policy be doubted by any who reflect that to the press alone, chequered as it is with abuses, the world is indebted for all the triumphs which have been gained by reason and humanity over error and oppression; who reflect that to the same beneficent source the United States owe much of the lights which conducted them to the ranks of a free and independent nation, and which have improved their political system into a shape so auspicious to their happiness? Had "Sedition Acts," forbidding every publication that might bring the constituted agents into contempt or disrepute, or that might excite the hatred of the people against the authors of unjust or pernicious measures, been uniformly enforced against the press, might not the United States have been languishing at this day under the infirmities of a sickly Confederation? Might they not, possibly, be miserable colonies, groaning under a foreign yoke?

The fact that, for approximately one hundred and fifty years, there has been almost an entire absence of attempts to impose previous restraints upon publications relating to the malfeasance of public officers is significant of the deep-seated conviction that such restraints would violate constitutional right. Public officers, whose character and [719] conduct remain open to debate and free discussion in the press, find their remedies for false accusations in actions under libel laws providing for redress and punishment, and not in proceedings to restrain the publication of newspapers and periodicals. The general principle that the constitutional guaranty of the liberty of the press gives immunity from previous restraints has been approved in many decisions under the provisions of state constitutions. [note 11]

The importance of this immunity has not lessened. While reckless assaults upon public men, and efforts to bring obloquy upon those who are endeavoring faithfully to discharge official duties, exert a baleful influence and deserve the severest condemnation in public opinion, it cannot be said that this abuse is greater, and it is believed to be less, than that which characterized the period in which our institutions took shape. Meanwhile, the administration of government has become more complex, the opportunities for malfeasance and corruption have multiplied, crime has grown to most serious proportions, and the danger of its protection by unfaithful officials and of the impairment of the fundamental security of life and [720] property by criminal alliances and official neglect, emphasizes the primary need of a vigilant and courageous press, especially in great cities. The fact that the liberty of the press may be abused by miscreant purveyors of scandal does not make any the less necessary the immunity of the press from previous restraint in dealing with official misconduct. Subsequent punishment for such abuses as may exist is the appropriate remedy consistent with constitutional privilege.

In attempted justification of the statute, it is said that it deals not with publication per se, but with the "business" of publishing defamation. If, however, the publisher has a constitutional right to publish, without previous restraint, an edition of his newspaper charging official derelictions, it cannot be denied that he may publish subsequent editions for the same purpose. He does not lose his right by exercising it. If his right exists, it may be exercised in publishing nine editions, as in this case, as well as in one edition. If previous restraint is permissible, it may be imposed at once; indeed, the wrong may be as serious in one publication as in several. Characterizing the publication as a business, and the business as a nuisance, does not permit an invasion of the constitutional immunity against restraint. Similarly, it does not matter that the newspaper or periodical is found to be "largely" or "chiefly" devoted to the publication of such derelictions. If the publisher has a right, without previous restraint, to publish them, his right cannot be deemed to be dependent upon his publishing something else, more or less, with the matter to which objection is made.

Nor can it be said that the constitutional freedom from previous restraint is lost because charges are made of derelictions which constitute crimes. With the multiplying provisions of penal codes, and of municipal charters and ordinances carrying penal sanctions, the conduct of [721] public officers is very largely within the purview of criminal statutes. The freedom of the press from previous restraint has never been regarded as limited to such animadversions as lay outside the range of penal enactments. Historically, there is no such limitation; it is inconsistent with the reason which underlies the privilege, as the privilege so limited would be of slight value for the purposes for which it came to be established.

The statute in question cannot be justified by reason of the fact that the publisher is permitted to show, before injunction issues, that the matter published is true and is published with good motives and for justifiable ends. If such a statute, authorizing suppression and injunction on such a basis, is constitutionally valid, it would be equally permissible for the legislature to provide that at any time the publisher of any newspaper could be brought before a court, or even an administrative officer (as the constitutional protection may not be regarded as resting on mere procedural details) and required to produce proof of the truth of his publication, or of what he intended to publish, and of his motives, or stand enjoined. If this can be done, the legislature may provide machinery for determining in the complete exercise of its discretion what are justifiable ends, and restrain publication accordingly. And it would be but a step to a complete system of censorship. The recognition of authority to impose previous restraint upon publication in order to protect the community against the circulation of charges of misconduct, and especially of official misconduct, necessarily would carry with it the admission of the authority of the censor against which the constitutional barrier was erected. The preliminary freedom, by virtue of the very reason for its existence, does not depend, as this Court has said, on proof of truth. *Patterson v. Colorado, supra.*

Equally unavailing is the insistence that the statute is designed to prevent the circulation of scandal which tends [722] to disturb the public peace and to provoke assaults and the commission of crime. Charges of reprehensible conduct, and in particular of official malfeasance, unquestionably create a public scandal, but the theory of the constitutional guaranty is that even a more serious public evil would be caused by authority to prevent publication. "To prohibit the intent to excite those unfavorable sentiments against those who administer the Government is equivalent to a prohibition of the actual excitement of them, and to prohibit the actual excitement of them is equivalent to a prohibition of discussions having that tendency and effect, which, again, is equivalent to a protection of those who administer the Government, if they should at any time deserve the contempt or hatred of the people, against being exposed to it by free animadversions on their characters and conduct."[note 12] There is nothing new in the fact that charges of reprehensible conduct may create resentment and the disposition to resort to violent means of redress, but this well understood tendency did not alter the determination to protect the press against censorship and restraint upon publication. As was said in *New Yorker Staats-Zeitung v. Nolan,* 89 N.J. Eq. 387, 388, 105 Atl. 72: "If the township may prevent the circulation of a newspaper for no reason other than that some of its inhabitants may violently disagree with it, and resent its circulation by resorting to physical violence, there is no limit to what may be prohibited." The danger of violent reactions becomes greater with effective organization of defiant groups resenting exposure, and if this consideration warranted legislative interference with the initial freedom of publication, the constitutional protection would be reduced to a mere form of words.

For these reasons we hold the statute, so far as it authorized the proceedings in this action under clause (b) [723] of section one, to be an infringement of the liberty of the press guaranteed by the Fourteenth Amendment. We should add that this decision rests upon the operation and effect of the statute, without regard to the question of the truth of the charges contained in the particular periodical. The fact that the public officers named in this case, and those associated with the charges of official dereliction, may be deemed to be impeccable cannot affect the conclusion that the statute imposes an unconstitutional restraint upon publication.

Judgment reversed.

12 CHAPLINSKY V. NEW HAMPSHIRE
SUPREME COURT OF THE UNITED STATES
315 U.S. 568
Argued February 5, 1942
Decided March 9, 1942

Syllabus

1. That part of c. 378, § 2, of the Public Laws of New Hampshire which forbids under penalty that any person shall address "any offensive, derisive or annoying word to any other person who is lawfully in any street or other public place," or "call him by any offensive or derisive name," was construed by the Supreme Court of the State, in this case and before this case arose, as limited to the use in a public place of words directly tending to cause a breach of the peace by provoking the person addressed to acts of violence.

Held:

(1) That, so construed, it is sufficiently definite and specific to comply with requirements of due process of law. P. 573.

(2) That as applied to a person who, on a public street, addressed another as a "damned Fascist" and a "damned racketeer," it does not substantially or unreasonably impinge upon freedom of speech. P. 574.

(3) The refusal of the state court to admit evidence offered by the defendant tending to prove provocation and evidence bearing on the truth or falsity of the utterances charged is open to no constitutional objection. P. 574.

2. The Court notices judicially that the appellations "damned racketeer" and "damned Fascist" are epithets likely to provoke the average person to retaliation, and thereby cause a breach of the peace. P. 574.

91 N. H. 310, 18 A. 2d 754, affirmed.

[569] MR. JUSTICE MURPHY delivered the opinion of the Court.

Appellant, a member of the sect known as Jehovah's Witnesses, was convicted in the municipal court of Rochester, New Hampshire, for violation of Chapter 378, § 2, of the Public Laws of New Hampshire:

"No person shall address any offensive, derisive or annoying word to any other person who is lawfully in any street or other public place, nor call him by any offensive or derisive name, nor make any noise or exclamation in his presence and hearing with intent to deride, offend or annoy him, or to prevent him from pursuing his lawful business or occupation."

The complaint charged that appellant, "with force and arms, in a certain public place in said city of Rochester, to wit, on the public sidewalk on the easterly side of Wakefield Street, near unto the entrance of the City Hall, did unlawfully repeat, the words following, addressed to the complainant, that is to say, 'You are a God damned racketeer' and 'a damned Fascist and the whole government of Rochester are Fascists or agents of Fascists,' the same being offensive, derisive and annoying words and names."

Upon appeal there was a trial de novo of appellant before a jury in the Superior Court. He was found guilty and the judgment of conviction was affirmed by the Supreme Court of the State. 91 N.H. 310, 18 A. 2d 754.

By motions and exceptions, appellant raised the questions that the statute was invalid under the Fourteenth Amendment of the Constitution of the United States, in that it placed an unreasonable restraint on freedom of speech, freedom of the press, and freedom of worship, and because it was vague and indefinite. These contentions were overruled and the case comes here on appeal.

There is no substantial dispute over the facts. Chaplinsky was distributing the literature of his sect on the streets [570] of Rochester on a busy Saturday afternoon. Members of the local citizenry complained to the City Marshal, Bowering, that Chaplinsky was denouncing all religion as a "racket." Bowering told them that Chaplinsky was lawfully engaged, and then warned Chaplinsky that the crowd was getting restless. Some time later, a disturbance occurred and the traffic officer on duty at the busy intersection started with Chaplinsky for the police station, but did not inform him that he was under arrest or that he was going to be arrested. On the way, they encountered Marshal Bowering, who had been advised that a riot was under way and was therefore hurrying to the scene. Bowering repeated his earlier warning to Chaplinsky, who then addressed to Bowering the words set forth in the complaint.

Chaplinsky's version of the affair was slightly different. He testified that, when he met Bowering, he asked him to arrest the ones responsible for the disturbance. In reply, Bowering cursed him and told him to come along. Appellant admitted that he said the words charged in the complaint, with the exception of the name of the Deity.

Over appellant's objection the trial court excluded, as immaterial, testimony relating to appellant's mission "to preach the true facts of the Bible," his treatment at the hands of the crowd, and the alleged neglect of duty on the part of the police. This action was approved by the court below, which held that neither provocation nor the truth of the utterance would constitute a defense to the charge.

It is now clear that "Freedom of speech and freedom of the press, which are protected by the First Amendment from infringement by Congress, are among the fundamental personal rights and liberties which are protected by the Fourteenth Amendment from invasion by state [571] action." *Lovell v. Griffin*, 303 U.S. 444, 450.[note 1] Freedom of worship is similarly sheltered. *Cantwell v. Connecticut*, 310 U.S. 296, 303.

Appellant assails the statute as a violation of all three freedoms, speech, press and worship, but only an attack on the basis of free speech is warranted. The spoken, not the written, word is involved. And we cannot conceive that cursing a public officer is the exercise of religion in any sense of the term. But even if the activities of the appellant which preceded the incident could be viewed as religious in character, and therefore entitled to the protection of the Fourteenth Amendment, they would not cloak him with immunity from the legal consequences for concomitant acts committed in violation of a valid criminal statute. We turn, therefore, to an examination of the statute itself.

Allowing the broadest scope to the language and purpose of the Fourteenth Amendment, it is well understood that the right of free speech is not absolute at all times and under all circumstances.[note 2] There are certain well-defined and narrowly limited classes of speech, the prevention [572] and punishment of which have never been thought to raise any Constitutional problem.[note 3] These include the lewd and obscene, the profane, the libelous, and the insulting or "fighting" words--those which by their very utterance inflict injury or tend to incite an immediate breach of the peace.[note 4] It has been well observed that such utterances are no essential part of any exposition of ideas, and are of such slight social value as a step to truth that any benefit that may be derived from them is clearly outweighed by the social interest in order and morality.[note 5] "Resort to epithets or personal abuse is not in any proper sense communication of information or opinion safeguarded by the Constitution, and its punishment as a criminal act would raise no question under that instrument." *Cantwell v. Connecticut*, 310 U.S. 296, 309-310.

The state statute here challenged comes to us authoritatively construed by the highest court of New Hampshire. It has two provisions--the first relates to words or names addressed to another in a public place; the second refers to noises and exclamations. The court said: "The two provisions are distinct. One may stand separately from the other. Assuming, without holding, that the second were unconstitutional, the first could stand if constitutional." We accept that construction of severability and limit our consideration to the first provision of the statute.[note 6]

[573] On the authority of its earlier decisions, the state court declared that the statute's purpose was to preserve the public peace, no words being "forbidden except such as have a direct tendency to cause acts of violence by the persons to whom, individually, the remark is addressed." [note 7] It was further said: "The word 'offensive' is not to be defined in terms of what a particular addressee thinks. . . . The test is what men of common intelligence would understand would be words likely to cause an average addressee to fight. . . . The English language has a number of words and expressions which by general consent are 'fighting words' when said without a disarming smile. . . . Such words, as ordinary men know, are likely to cause a fight. So are threatening, profane or obscene revilings. Derisive and annoying words can be taken as coming within the purview of the statute as heretofore interpreted only when they have this characteristic of plainly tending to excite the addressee to a breach of the peace. . . . The statute, as construed, does no more than prohibit the face-

to-face words plainly likely to cause a breach of the peace by the addressee, words whose speaking constitutes a breach of the peace by the speaker--including 'classical fighting words', words in current use less 'classical' but equally likely to cause violence, and other disorderly words, including profanity, obscenity and threats."

We are unable to say that the limited scope of the statute as thus construed contravenes the Constitutional right of free expression. It is a statute narrowly drawn and limited to define and punish specific conduct lying within the domain of state power, the use in a public place of words likely to cause a breach of the peace. Cf. *Cantwell v. Connecticut*, 310 U.S. 296, 311; *Thornhill v. Alabama*, [574] 310 U.S. 88, 105. This conclusion necessarily disposes of appellant's contention that the statute is so vague and indefinite as to render a conviction thereunder a violation of due process. A statute punishing verbal acts, carefully drawn so as not unduly to impair liberty of expression, is not too vague for a criminal law. Cf. *Fox v. Washington*, 236 U.S. 273, 277.[note 8]

Nor can we say that the application of the statute to the facts disclosed by the record substantially or unreasonably impinges upon the privilege of free speech. Argument is unnecessary to demonstrate that the appellations "damned racketeer" and "damned Fascist" are epithets likely to provoke the average person to retaliation, and thereby cause a breach of the peace.

The refusal of the state court to admit evidence of provocation and evidence bearing on the truth or falsity of the utterances, is open to no Constitutional objection. Whether the facts sought to be proved by such evidence constitute a defense to the charge, or may be shown in mitigation, are questions for the state court to determine. Our function is fulfilled by a determination that the challenged statute, on its face and as applied, does not contravene the Fourteenth Amendment.

Affirmed.

Footnotes to the Majority Opinion

1. See also *Bridges v. California*, 314 U.S. 252; *Cantwell v. Connecticut*, 310 U.S. 296, 303; *Thornhill v. Alabama*, 310 U.S. 88, 95; *Schneider v. State*, 308 U.S. 147, 160; *De Jonge v. Oregon*, 299 U.S. 353, 364; *Grosjean v. American Press Co.*, 297 U.S. 233, 243; *Near v. Minnesota*, 283 U.S. 697, 707; *Stromberg v. California*, 283 U.S. 359, 368; *Whitney v. California*, 274 U.S. 357, 362, 371, 373; *Gitlow v. New York*, 268 U.S. 652, 666.

Appellant here pitches his argument on the due process clause of the Fourteenth Amendment.

2. *Schenck v. United States*, 249 U.S. 47; *Whitney v. California*, 274 U.S. 357, 373 (Brandeis, J., concurring); *Stromberg v. California*, 283 U.S. 359; *Near v. Minnesota*, 283 U.S. 697; *De Jonge v. Oregon*, 299 U.S. 353; *Herndon v. Lowry*, 301 U.S. 242; *Cantwell v. Connecticut*, 310 U.S. 296.

3. The protection of the First Amendment, mirrored in the Fourteenth, is not limited to the Blackstonian idea that freedom of the press means only freedom from restraint prior to publication. *Near v. Minnesota*, 283 U.S. 697, 714-715.

4. Chafee, Free Speech in the United States (1941), 149.

5. Chafee, op. cit., 150.

6. Since the complaint charged appellant only with violating the first provision of the statute, the problem of *Stromberg v. California*, 283 U.S. 359, is not present.

7. *State v. Brown*, 68 N. H. 200, 38 A. 731; *State v. McConnell*, 70 N. H. 294, 47 A. 267.

8. We do not have here the problem of *Lanzetta v. New Jersey*, 306 U.S. 451. Even if the interpretative gloss placed on the statute by the court below be disregarded, the statute had been previously construed as intended to preserve the public peace by punishing conduct, the direct tendency of which was to provoke the person against whom it was directed to acts of violence. *State v. Brown*, 68 N. H. 200, 38 A. 731 (1894).

Appellant need not therefore have been a prophet to understand what the statute condemned. Cf. *Herndon v. Lowry*, 301 U.S. 242. See *Nash v. United States*, 229 U.S. 373, 377.

13 ROTH V. UNITED STATES
SUPREME COURT OF THE UNITED STATES
354 U.S. 476
Argued April 22, 1957
Decided June 24, 1957

Together with No. 61, *Alberts v. California*, appeal from the Superior Court of California, Los Angeles County, Appellate Department, argued and decided on the same dates.

Syllabus

1. In the *Roth* case, the constitutionality of 18 U. S. C. § 1461, which makes punishable the mailing of material that is "obscene, lewd, lascivious, or filthy . . . or other publication of an indecent character," and Roth's conviction thereunder for mailing an obscene book and obscene circulars and advertising, are sustained. Pp. 479-494.

2. In the *Alberts* case, the constitutionality of § 311 of West's California Penal Code Ann., 1955, which, inter alia, makes it a misdemeanor to keep for sale, or to advertise, material that is "obscene or indecent," and Alberts' conviction thereunder for lewdly keeping for sale obscene and indecent books and for writing, composing, and publishing an obscene advertisement of them, are sustained. Pp. 479-494.

3. Obscenity is not within the area of constitutionally protected freedom of speech or press--either (1) under the First Amendment, as to the Federal Government, or (2) under the Due Process Clause of the Fourteenth Amendment, as to the States. Pp. 481-485.

(a) In the light of history, it is apparent that the unconditional phrasing of the First Amendment was not intended to protect every utterance. Pp. 482-483.

(b) The protection given speech and press was fashioned to assure unfettered interchange of ideas for the bringing about of political and social changes desired by the people. P. 484.

(c) All ideas having even the slightest redeeming social importance--unorthodox ideas, controversial ideas, even ideas hateful to the prevailing climate of opinion--have the full protection of the guaranties, unless excludable because they encroach upon the limited area of more important interests; but implicit in the history of the First Amendment is the rejection of obscenity as utterly without redeeming social importance. Pp. 484-485. [477]

4. Since obscenity is not protected, constitutional guaranties were not violated in these cases merely because, under the trial judges' instructions to the juries, convictions could be had without proof either that the obscene material would perceptibly create a clear and present danger of antisocial conduct, or probably would induce its recipients to such conduct. *Beauharnais v. Illinois,* 343 U.S. 250. Pp. 485-490.

(a) Sex and obscenity are not synonymous. Obscene material is material which deals with sex in a manner appealing to prurient interest--i. e., material having a tendency to excite lustful thoughts. P. 487.

(b) It is vital that the standards for judging obscenity safeguard the protection of freedom of speech and press for material which does not treat sex in a manner appealing to prurient interest. Pp. 487-488.

(c) The standard for judging obscenity, adequate to withstand the charge of constitutional infirmity, is whether, to the average person, applying contemporary community standards, the dominant theme of the material, taken as a whole, appeals to prurient interest. Pp. 488-489.

(d) In these cases, both trial courts sufficiently followed the proper standard and used the proper definition of obscenity. Pp. 489-490.

5. When applied according to the proper standard for judging obscenity, 18 U. S. C. § 1461, which makes punishable the mailing of material that is "obscene, lewd, lascivious, or filthy . . . or other publication of an indecent character," does not (1) violate the freedom of speech or press guaranteed by the First Amendment, or (2) violate the constitutional requirements of due process by failing to provide reasonably ascertainable standards of guilt. Pp. 491-492.

6. When applied according to the proper standard for judging obscenity, § 311 of West's California Penal Code Ann., 1955, which, inter alia, makes it a misdemeanor to keep for sale or to advertise material that is "obscene or indecent," does not (1) violate the freedom of speech or press guaranteed by the Fourteenth Amendment against encroachment by the States, or (2) violate the constitutional requirements of due process by failing to provide reasonably ascertainable standards of guilt. 491-492.

7. The federal obscenity statute, 18 U. S. C. § 1461, punishing the use of the mails for obscene material, is a proper exercise of the postal power delegated to Congress by Art. I, § 8, cl. 7; and it [478] does not unconstitutionally encroach upon the powers reserved to the States by the Ninth and Tenth Amendments. Pp. 492-493.

8. The California obscenity statute here involved is not repugnant to Art. I, § 8, cl. 7, since it does not impose a burden upon, or interfere with, the federal postal functions--even when applied to a mail-order business. Pp. 493-494.

237 F.2d 796, affirmed. 138 Cal. App. 2d Supp. 909, 292 P. 2d 90, affirmed. [479]

MR. JUSTICE BRENNAN delivered the opinion of the Court.

The constitutionality of a criminal obscenity statute is the question in each of these cases. In *Roth*, the primary constitutional question is whether the federal obscenity statute [note 1] violates the provision of the First Amendment that "Congress shall make no law . . . abridging the freedom of speech, or of the press . . . ." In *Alberts*, the primary constitutional question is whether the obscenity provisions of the California Penal Code [note 2] invade the freedoms of speech and press as they may be incorporated in [480] the liberty protected from state action by the Due Process Clause of the Fourteenth Amendment.

Other constitutional questions are: whether these statutes violate due process, [note 3] because too vague to support conviction for crime; whether power to punish speech and press offensive to decency and morality is in the States alone, so that the federal obscenity statute violates the Ninth and Tenth Amendments (raised in *Roth*); and whether Congress, by enacting the federal obscenity statute, under the power delegated by Art. I, § 8, cl. 7, to establish post offices and post roads, pre-empted the regulation of the subject matter (raised in *Alberts*).

Roth conducted a business in New York in the publication and sale of books, photographs and magazines. He used circulars and advertising matter to solicit sales. He was convicted by a jury in the District Court for the Southern District of New York upon 4 counts of a 26-count indictment charging him with mailing obscene circulars and advertising, and an obscene book, in violation of the federal obscenity statute. His conviction was affirmed by the Court of Appeals for the Second Circuit. [note 4] We granted certiorari. [note 5] [481]

Alberts conducted a mail-order business from Los Angeles. He was convicted by the Judge of the Municipal Court of the Beverly Hills Judicial District (having waived a jury trial) under a misdemeanor complaint which charged him with lewdly keeping for sale obscene and indecent books, and with writing, composing and publishing an obscene advertisement of them, in violation of the California Penal Code. The conviction was affirmed by the Appellate Department of the Superior Court of the State of California in and for the County of Los Angeles. [note 6] We noted probable jurisdiction. [note 7]

The dispositive question is whether obscenity is utterance within the area of protected speech and press. [note 8] Although this is the first time the question has been squarely presented to this Court, either under the First Amendment or under the Fourteenth Amendment, expressions found in numerous opinions indicate that this Court has always assumed that obscenity is not protected by the freedoms of speech and press. *Ex parte Jackson*, 96 U.S. 727, 736-737; *United States v. Chase*, 135 U.S. 255, 261; *Robertson v. Baldwin*, 165 U.S. 275, 281; *Public Clearing House v. Coyne*, 194 U.S. 497, 508; *Hoke v. United States*, 227 U.S. 308, 322; *Near v. Minnesota*, 283 U.S. 697, 716; *Chaplinsky v. New Hampshire*, 315 U.S. 568, 571-572; *Hannegan v. Esquire, Inc.*, 327 U.S. 146, 158; *Winters v. New York*, 333 U.S. 507, 510; *Beauharnais v. Illinois*, 343 U.S. 250, 266.[note 9] [482]

The guaranties of freedom of expression [note 10] in effect in 10 of the 14 States which by 1792 had ratified the Constitution, gave no absolute protection for every utterance. Thirteen of the 14 States provided for the prosecution of libel, [note 11] and all of those States made either blasphemy or profanity, or both, statutory crimes. [note 12] As early as

[483] 1712, Massachusetts made it criminal to publish "any filthy, obscene, or profane song, pamphlet, libel or mock sermon" in imitation or mimicking of religious services. Acts and Laws of the Province of Mass. Bay, c. CV, § 8 (1712), Mass. Bay Colony Charters & Laws 399 (1814). Thus, profanity and obscenity were related offenses.

In light of this history, it is apparent that the unconditional phrasing of the First Amendment was not intended to protect every utterance. This phrasing did not prevent this Court from concluding that libelous utterances are not within the area of constitutionally protected speech. *Beauharnais v. Illinois*, 343 U.S. 250, 266. At the time of the adoption of the First Amendment, obscenity law was not as fully developed as libel law, but there is sufficiently contemporaneous evidence to show that obscenity, too, was outside the protection intended for speech and press. [note 13] [484]

The protection given speech and press was fashioned to assure unfettered interchange of ideas for the bringing about of political and social changes desired by the people. This objective was made explicit as early as 1774 in a letter of the Continental Congress to the inhabitants of Quebec:

"The last right we shall mention, regards the freedom of the press. The importance of this consists, besides the advancement of truth, science, morality, and arts in general, in its diffusion of liberal sentiments on the administration of Government, its ready communication of thoughts between subjects, and its consequential promotion of union among them, whereby oppressive officers are shamed or intimidated, into more honourable and just modes of conducting affairs." 1 Journals of the Continental Congress 108 (1774).

All ideas having even the slightest redeeming social importance--unorthodox ideas, controversial ideas, even ideas hateful to the prevailing climate of opinion--have the full protection of the guaranties, unless excludable because they encroach upon the limited area of more important interests. [note 14] But implicit in the history of the First Amendment is the rejection of obscenity as utterly without redeeming social importance. This rejection for [485] that reason is mirrored in the universal judgment that obscenity should be restrained, reflected in the international agreement of over 50 nations, [note 15] in the obscenity laws of all of the 48 States, [note 16] and in the 20 obscenity laws enacted by the Congress from 1842 to 1956. [note 17] This is the same judgment expressed by this Court in *Chaplinsky v. New Hampshire*, 315 U.S. 568, 571-572:

". . . There are certain well-defined and narrowly limited classes of speech, the prevention and punishment of which have never been thought to raise any Constitutional problem. *These include the lewd and obscene . . . . It has been well observed that such utterances are no essential part of any exposition of ideas, and are of such slight social value as a step to truth that any benefit that may be derived from them is clearly outweighed by the social interest in order and morality. . . .*" (Emphasis added.)

We hold that obscenity is not within the area of constitutionally protected speech or press.

It is strenuously urged that these obscenity statutes offend the constitutional guaranties because they punish [486] incitation to impure sexual thoughts, not shown to be related to any overt antisocial conduct which is or may be incited in the persons stimulated to such thoughts. In *Roth*, the trial judge instructed the jury: "The words 'obscene, lewd and lascivious' as used in the law, signify that form of immorality which has relation to sexual impurity and has a tendency to excite lustful thoughts." (Emphasis added.) In *Alberts*, the trial judge applied the test laid down in *People v. Wepplo*, 78 Cal. App. 2d Supp. 959, 178 P. 2d 853, namely, whether the material has "a substantial tendency to deprave or corrupt its readers by inciting lascivious thoughts or arousing lustful desires." (Emphasis added.) It is insisted that the constitutional guaranties are violated because convictions may be had without proof either that obscene material will perceptibly create a clear and present danger of antisocial conduct, [note 18] or will probably induce its recipients to such conduct. [note 19] But, in light of our holding that obscenity is not protected speech, the complete answer to this argument is in the holding of this Court in *Beauharnais v. Illinois, supra,* at 266:

"Libelous utterances not being within the area of constitutionally protected speech, it is unnecessary, either for us or for the State courts, to consider the issues behind the phrase 'clear and present danger.' Certainly no one would contend that obscene speech, [487] for example, may be punished only upon a showing of such circumstances. Libel, as we have seen, is in the same class."

However, sex and obscenity are not synonymous. Obscene material is material which deals with sex in a manner appealing to prurient interest. [note 20] The portrayal of sex, e. g., in art, literature and scientific works, [note 21] is not itself sufficient reason to deny material the constitutional protection of freedom of speech and press. Sex, a great and mysterious motive force in human life, has indisputably been a subject of absorbing interest to mankind through the ages; it is one of the vital problems of human interest and public concern. As to all such problems, [488] this Court said in *Thornhill v. Alabama*, 310 U.S. 88, 101-102:

"The freedom of speech and of the press guaranteed by the Constitution embraces at the least the liberty to discuss publicly and truthfully *all matters of public concern* without previous restraint or fear of subsequent punishment. The exigencies of the colonial period and the efforts to secure freedom from oppressive administration developed a broadened conception of these liberties as adequate to supply the public need for *information and education with respect to the significant issues of the times.* . . . Freedom of discussion, if it would fulfill its historic function in this nation, must embrace *all issues about which information is needed or appropriate to enable the members of society to cope with the exigencies of their period."* (Emphasis added.)

The fundamental freedoms of speech and press have contributed greatly to the development and well-being of our free society and are indispensable to its continued growth. [note 22] Ceaseless vigilance is the watchword to prevent their erosion by Congress or by the States. The door barring federal and state intrusion into this area cannot be left ajar; it must be kept tightly closed and opened only the slightest crack necessary to prevent encroachment upon more important interests. [note 23] It is therefore vital that the standards for judging obscenity safeguard the protection of freedom of speech and press for material which does not treat sex in a manner appealing to prurient interest.

The early leading standard of obscenity allowed material to be judged merely by the effect of an isolated [489] excerpt upon particularly susceptible persons. *Regina v. Hicklin*, [1868] L. R. 3 Q. B. 360. [note 24] Some American courts adopted this standard [note 25] but later decisions have rejected it and substituted this test: whether to the average person, applying contemporary community standards, the dominant theme of the material taken as a whole appeals to prurient interest. [note 26] The Hicklin test, judging obscenity by the effect of isolated passages upon the most susceptible persons, might well encompass material legitimately treating with sex, and so it must be rejected as unconstitutionally restrictive of the freedoms of speech and press. On the other hand, the substituted standard provides safeguards adequate to withstand the charge of constitutional infirmity.

Both trial courts below sufficiently followed the proper standard. Both courts used the proper definition of obscenity. In addition, in the *Alberts* case, in ruling on a motion to dismiss, the trial judge indicated that, as the [490] trier of facts, he was judging each item as a whole as it would affect the normal person, [note 27] and in *Roth*, the trial judge instructed the jury as follows:

". . . The test is not whether it would arouse sexual desires or sexual impure thoughts in those comprising a particular segment of the community, the young, the immature or the highly prudish or would leave another segment, the scientific or highly educated or the so-called worldly-wise and sophisticated indifferent and unmoved. . . .

"The test in each case is the effect of the book, picture or publication considered as a whole, not upon any particular class, but upon all those whom it is likely to reach. In other words, you determine its impact upon the average person in the community. The books, pictures and circulars must be judged as a whole, in their entire context, and you are not to consider detached or separate portions in reaching a conclusion. You judge the circulars, pictures and publications which have been put in evidence by present-day standards of the community. You may ask yourselves does it offend the common conscience of the community by present-day standards.

. . . .

"In this case, ladies and gentlemen of the jury, you and you alone are the exclusive judges of what the common conscience of the community is, and in determining that conscience you are to consider the community as a whole, young and old, educated and uneducated, the religious and the irreligious--men, women and children." [491]

It is argued that the statutes do not provide reasonably ascertainable standards of guilt and therefore violate the constitutional requirements of due process. *Winters v. New York*, 333 U.S. 507. The federal obscenity statute makes punishable the mailing of material that is "obscene, lewd, lascivious, or filthy . . . or other publication of an indecent character." [note 28] The California statute makes punishable, inter alia, the keeping for sale or advertising material that is "obscene or indecent." The thrust of the argument is that these words are not sufficiently precise because they do not mean the same thing to all people, all the time, everywhere.

Many decisions have recognized that these terms of obscenity statutes are not precise. [note 29] This Court, however, has consistently held that lack of precision is not itself offensive to the requirements of due process. ". . . The Constitution does not require impossible standards"; all that is required is that the language "conveys sufficiently definite warning as to the proscribed conduct when measured by common understanding and practices. . . ." *United States v. Petrillo*, 332 U.S. 1, 7-8. These words, applied according to the proper standard for judging obscenity, already discussed, give adequate warning of the conduct proscribed and mark ". . . boundaries sufficiently distinct for judges and juries fairly to administer the law . . . . That there may be marginal cases in which it is difficult to determine the side of the line on [492] which a particular fact situation falls is not sufficient reason to hold the language too ambiguous to define a criminal offense. . . ." *Id.*, at 7. See also *United States v. Harriss*, 347 U.S. 612, 624, n. 15; *Boyce Motor Lines, Inc. v. United States*, 342 U.S. 337, 340; *United States v. Ragen*, 314 U.S. 513, 523-524; *United States v. Wurzbach*, 280 U.S. 396; *Hygrade Provision Co. v. Sherman*, 266 U.S. 497; *Fox v. Washington*, 236 U.S. 273; *Nash v. United States*, 229 U.S. 373. [note 30]

In summary, then, we hold that these statutes, applied according to the proper standard for judging obscenity, do not offend constitutional safeguards against convictions based upon protected material, or fail to give men in acting adequate notice of what is prohibited.

Roth's argument that the federal obscenity statute unconstitutionally encroaches upon the powers reserved by the Ninth and Tenth Amendments to the States and to the people to punish speech and press where offensive to decency and morality is hinged upon his contention that obscenity is expression not excepted from the sweep of the provision of the First Amendment that "Congress shall make no law . . . abridging the freedom of speech, or of the press . . . ." (Emphasis added.) That argument falls in light of our holding that obscenity is not expression protected by the First Amendment. [note 31] We [493] therefore hold that the federal obscenity statute punishing the use of the mails for obscene material is a proper exercise of the postal power delegated to Congress by Art. I, § 8, cl. 7. [note 32] In *United Public Workers v. Mitchell*, 330 U.S. 75, 95-96, this Court said:

". . . The powers granted by the Constitution to the Federal Government are subtracted from the totality of sovereignty originally in the states and the people. Therefore, when objection is made that the exercise of a federal power infringes upon rights reserved by the Ninth and Tenth Amendments, the inquiry must be directed toward the granted power under which the action of the Union was taken. If granted power is found, necessarily the objection of invasion of those rights, reserved by the Ninth and Tenth Amendments, must fail. . . ."

Alberts argues that because his was a mail-order business, the California statute is repugnant to Art. I, § 8, cl. 7, under which the Congress allegedly pre-empted the regulatory field by enacting the federal obscenity statute punishing the mailing or advertising by mail of obscene material. The federal statute deals only with actual [494] mailing; it does not eliminate the power of the state to punish "keeping for sale" or "advertising" obscene material. The state statute in no way imposes a burden or interferes with the federal postal functions. ". . . The decided cases which indicate the limits of state regulatory power in relation to the federal mail service involve situations where state regulation involved a direct, physical interference with federal activities under the postal power or some direct, immediate burden on the performance of the postal functions. . . ." *Railway Mail Assn. v. Corsi*, 326 U.S. 88, 96.

The judgments are Affirmed.

14 NEW YORK TIMES CO. V. SULLIVAN
SUPREME COURT OF THE UNITED STATES
376 U.S. 254
Argued January 6, 1964
Decided March 9, 1964

Syllabus

Respondent, an elected official in Montgomery, Alabama, brought suit in a state court alleging that he had been libeled by an advertisement in corporate petitioner's newspaper, the text of which appeared over the names of the four individual petitioners and many others. The advertisement included statements, some of which were false, about police action allegedly directed against students who participated in a civil rights demonstration and against a leader of the civil rights movement; respondent claimed the statements referred to him because his duties included supervision of the police department. The trial judge instructed the jury that such statements were "libelous per se," legal injury being implied without proof of actual damages, and that, for the purpose of compensatory damages, malice was presumed, so that such damages could be awarded against petitioners if the statements were found to have been published by them and to have related to respondent. As to punitive damages, the judge instructed that mere negligence was not evidence of actual malice, and would not justify an award of punitive damages; he refused to instruct that actual intent to harm or recklessness had to be found before punitive damages could be awarded, or that a verdict for respondent should differentiate between compensatory and punitive damages. The jury found for respondent, and the State Supreme Court affirmed.

Held: A State cannot, under the First and Fourteenth Amendments, award damages to a public official for defamatory falsehood relating to his official conduct unless he proves "actual malice"--that the statement was made with knowledge of its falsity or with reckless disregard of whether it was true or false. Pp. 265-292.

(a) Application by state courts of a rule of law, whether statutory or not, to award a judgment in a civil action, is "state action" under the Fourteenth Amendment. P. 265.

(b) Expression does not lose constitutional protection to which it would otherwise be entitled because it appears in the form of a paid advertisement. Pp. 265-266. [255]

(c) Factual error, content defamatory of official reputation, or both, are insufficient to warrant an award of damages for false statements unless "actual malice"--knowledge that statements are false or in reckless disregard of the truth--is alleged and proved. Pp. 279-283.

(d) State court judgment entered upon a general verdict which does not differentiate between punitive damages, as to which, under state law, actual malice must be proved, and general damages, as to which it is "presumed," precludes any determination as to the basis of the verdict, and requires reversal, where presumption of malice is inconsistent with federal constitutional requirements. P. 284.

(e) The evidence was constitutionally insufficient to support the judgment for respondent, since it failed to support a finding that the statements were made with actual malice or that they related to respondent. Pp. 285-292.

273 Ala. 656, 144 So.2d 25, reversed and remanded. [256]

MR. JUSTICE BRENNAN delivered the opinion of the Court.

We are required in this case to determine for the first time the extent to which the constitutional protection for speech and press limit a State's power to award damages in a libel action brought by a public official against critics of his official conduct.

Respondent L.B. Sullivan is one of the three elected Commissioners of the City of Montgomery, Alabama. He testified that he was "Commissioner of Public Affairs and the duties are supervision of the Police Department, Fire Department, Department of Cemetery and Department of Scales." He brought this civil libel action against the four individual petitioners, who are Negroes and Alabama clergymen, and against petitioner the New York Times Company, a New York corporation which publishes the New York Times, a daily newspaper. A jury in the Circuit Court of Montgomery County awarded him damages of $500,000, the full amount claimed, against all the petitioners, and the Supreme Court of Alabama affirmed. 273 Ala. 656, 144 So.2d 25.

Respondent's complaint alleged that he had been libeled by statements in a full-page advertisement that was carried in the New York Times on March 29, 1960. [note 1] Entitled "Heed Their Rising Voices," the advertisement began by stating that, "As the whole world knows by now, thousands of Southern Negro students are engaged in widespread nonviolent demonstrations in positive affirmation of the right to live in human dignity as guaranteed by the U.S. Constitution and the Bill of Rights." It went on to charge that, "in their efforts to uphold these guarantees, they are being met by an unprecedented wave of terror by those who would deny and negate that document which the whole world looks upon as setting the pattern for modern freedom. . . .' Succeeding [257] paragraphs purported to illustrate the "wave of terror" by describing certain alleged events. The text concluded with an appeal for funds for three purposes: support of the student movement, "the struggle for the right to vote," and the legal defense of Dr. Martin Luther King, Jr., leader of the movement, against a perjury indictment then pending in Montgomery.

The text appeared over the names of 64 persons, many widely known for their activities in public affairs, religion, trade unions, and the performing arts. Below these names, and under a line reading "We in the south who are struggling daily for dignity and freedom warmly endorse this appeal," appeared the names of the four individual petitioners and of 16 other persons, all but two of whom were identified as clergymen in various Southern cities. The advertisement was signed at the bottom of the page by the "Committee to Defend Martin Luther King and the Struggle for Freedom in the South," and the officers of the Committee were listed.

Of the 10 paragraphs of text in the advertisement, the third and a portion of the sixth were the basis of respondent's claim of libel. They read as follows:

Third paragraph:

In Montgomery, Alabama, after students sang "My Country, 'Tis of Thee" on the State Capitol steps, their leaders were expelled from school, and truckloads of police armed with shotguns and tear-gas ringed the Alabama State College Campus. When the entire student body protested to state authorities by refusing to reregister, their dining hall was padlocked in an attempt to starve them into submission.

Sixth paragraph:

Again and again, the Southern violators have answered Dr. King's peaceful protests with intimidation and violence. They have bombed his home, almost killing his wife and child. They have [258] assaulted his person. They have arrested him seven times--for "speeding," "loitering" and similar "offenses." And now they have charged him with "perjury"--a felony under which they could imprison him for ten years. . . .

Although neither of these statements mentions respondent by name, he contended that the word "police" in the third paragraph referred to him as the Montgomery Commissioner who supervised the Police Department, so that he was being accused of "ringing" the campus with police. He further claimed that the paragraph would be read as imputing to the police, and hence to him, the padlocking of the dining hall in order to starve the students into submission. [note 2] As to the sixth paragraph, he contended that, since arrests are ordinarily made by the police, the statement "They have arrested [Dr. King] seven times" would be read as referring to him; he further contended that the "They" who did the arresting would be equated with the "They" who committed the other described acts and with the "Southern violators." Thus, he argued, the paragraph would be read as accusing the Montgomery police, and hence him, of answering Dr. King's protests with "intimidation and violence," bombing his home, assaulting his person, and charging him with perjury. Respondent and six other Montgomery residents testified that they read some or all of the statements as referring to him in his capacity as Commissioner.

It is uncontroverted that some of the statements contained in the two paragraphs were not accurate descriptions of events which occurred in Montgomery. Although Negro students staged a demonstration on the State Capitol steps, they sang the National Anthem and not "My [259] Country, 'Tis of Thee." Although nine students were expelled by the State Board of Education, this was not for leading the demonstration at the Capitol, but for demanding service at a lunch counter in the Montgomery County Courthouse on another day. Not the entire student body, but most of it, had protested the expulsion, not by refusing to register, but by boycotting classes on a single day; virtually all the students did register for the ensuing semester. The campus dining hall was not padlocked on any occasion, and the only students who may have been barred from eating there were the few who had neither signed a preregistration application nor requested temporary meal tickets. Although the police were deployed near the campus in large numbers on three occasions, they did not at any time "ring" the campus, and they were not called to the campus in connection with the demonstration on the State Capitol steps, as the third paragraph implied. Dr. King had not been arrested seven times, but only four, and although he claimed to have been assaulted some years earlier in connection with his arrest for loitering outside a courtroom, one of the officers who made the arrest denied that there was such an assault.

On the premise that the charges in the sixth paragraph could be read as referring to him, respondent was allowed to prove that he had not participated in the events described. Although Dr. King's home had, in fact, been bombed twice when his wife and child were there, both of these occasions antedated respondent's tenure as Commissioner, and the police were not only not implicated in the bombings, but had made every effort to apprehend those who were. Three of Dr. King's four arrests took place before respondent became Commissioner. Although Dr. King had, in fact, been indicted (he was subsequently acquitted) on two counts of perjury, each of which carried a possible five-year sentence, respondent had nothing to do with procuring the indictment. [260]

Respondent made no effort to prove that he suffered actual pecuniary loss as a result of the alleged libel. [note 3] One of his witnesses, a former employer, testified that, if he had believed the statements, he doubted whether he "would want to be associated with anybody who would be a party to such things that are stated in that ad," and that he would not reemploy respondent if he believed "that he allowed the Police Department to do the things that the paper say he did." But neither this witness nor any of the others testified that he had actually believed the statements in their supposed reference to respondent. The cost of the advertisement was approximately $4800, and it was published by the Times upon an order from a New York advertising agency acting for the signatory Committee. The agency submitted the advertisement with a letter from A. Philip Randolph, Chairman of the Committee, certifying that the persons whose names appeared on the advertisement had given their permission. Mr. Randolph was known to the Times' Advertising Acceptability Department as a responsible person, and, in accepting the letter as sufficient proof of authorization, it followed its established practice. There was testimony that the copy of the advertisement which accompanied the letter listed only the 64 names appearing under the text, and that the statement, "We in the south . . . warmly endorse this appeal," and the list of names thereunder, which included those of the individual petitioners, were subsequently added when the first proof of the advertisement was received. Each of the individual petitioners testified that he had not authorized the use of his name, and that he had been unaware of its use until receipt of respondent's demand for a retraction. The manager of the Advertising Acceptability [261] Department testified that he had approved the advertisement for publication because he knew nothing to cause him to believe that anything in it was false, and because it bore the endorsement of "a number of people who are well known and whose reputation" he "had no reason to question." Neither he nor anyone else at the Times made an effort to confirm the accuracy of the advertisement, either by checking it against recent Times news stories relating to some of the described events or by any other means.

Alabama law denies a public officer recovery of punitive damages in a libel action brought on account of a publication concerning his official conduct unless he first makes a written demand for a public retraction and the defendant fails or refuses to comply. Alabama

Code, Tit. 7, § 914. Respondent served such a demand upon each of the petitioners. None of the individual petitioners responded to the demand, primarily because each took the position that he had not authorized the use of his name on the advertisement, and therefore had not published the statements that respondent alleged had libeled him. The Times did not publish a retraction in response to the demand, but wrote respondent a letter stating, among other things, that "we . . . are somewhat puzzled as to how you think the statements in any way reflect on you," and "you might, if you desire, let us know in what respect you claim that the statements in the advertisement reflect on you." Respondent filed this suit a few days later without answering the letter. The Times did, however, subsequently publish a retraction of the advertisement upon the demand of Governor John Patterson of Alabama, who asserted that the publication charged him with "grave misconduct and . . . improper actions and omissions as Governor of Alabama and Ex-Officio Chairman of the State Board of Education of Alabama." When asked to explain why there has been a retraction for the Governor but not for respondent, the Secretary of the Times testified: "We did that because we didn't want anything that was published by The Times to be a reflection on the State of Alabama, and the Governor was, as far as we could see, the embodiment of the State of Alabama and the proper representative of the State, and, furthermore, we had by that time learned more of the actual facts which the and purported to recite and, finally, the ad did refer to the action of the State authorities and the Board of Education, presumably of which the Governor is the ex-officio chairman. . . . ." On the other hand, he testified that he did not think that "any of the language in there referred to Mr. Sullivan."

The trial judge submitted the case to the jury under instructions that the statements in the advertisement were "libelous per se," and were not privileged, so that petitioners might be held liable if the jury found that they had published the advertisement and that the statements were made "of and concerning" respondent. The jury was instructed that, because the statements were libelous per se, "the law . . . implies legal injury from the bare fact of publication itself," "falsity and malice are presumed," "general damages need not be alleged or proved, but are presumed," and "punitive damages may be awarded by the jury even though the amount of actual damages is neither found nor shown." An award of punitive damages--as distinguished from "general" damages, which are compensatory in nature--apparently requires proof of actual malice under Alabama law, and the judge charged that "mere negligence or carelessness is not evidence of actual malice or malice in fact, and does not justify an award of exemplary or punitive damages." He refused to charge, however, that the jury must be "convinced" of malice, in the sense of "actual intent" to harm or "gross negligence and recklessness," to make such an award, and he also refused to require that a verdict for respondent differentiate between compensatory and punitive damages. The judge rejected petitioners' contention [263] that his rulings abridged the freedoms of speech and of the press that are guaranteed by the First and Fourteenth Amendments.

In affirming the judgment, the Supreme Court of Alabama sustained the trial judge's rulings and instructions in all respects. 273 Ala. 656, 144 So.2d 25. It held that, "where the words published tend to injure a person libeled by them in his reputation, profession, trade or business, or charge him with an indictable offense, or tend to bring the individual into public contempt," they are "libelous per se"; that "the matter complained of is, under the above doctrine, libelous per se, if it was published of and concerning the plaintiff", and that it was actionable without "proof of pecuniary injury . . . . such injury being implied." *Id.* at 673, 676, 144 So.2d at 37, 41. It approved the trial court's ruling that the jury could find the statements to have been made "of and concerning" respondent, stating: "We think it common knowledge that the average person knows that municipal agents, such as police and firemen, and others, are under the control and direction of the city governing body, and, more particularly, under the direction and control of a single commissioner. In measuring the performance or deficiencies of such groups, praise or criticism is usually attached to the official in complete control of the body." *Id.* at 674-675, 144 So.2d at 39. In sustaining the trial court's determination that the verdict was not excessive, the court said that malice could be inferred from the Times' "irresponsibility" in printing the advertisement while "the Times, in its own files, had articles already published which would have demonstrated the falsity of the allegations in the advertisement"; from the Times' failure to retract for respondent while retracting for the Governor, whereas the falsity of some of the allegations was then known to the Times and "the matter contained in the advertisement was equally false as to both parties", and from the testimony of the Times' Secretary that, [264] apart from the statement that the dining hall was padlocked, he thought the two paragraphs were "substantially correct." *Id.* at 686-687, 144 So.2d at 50-51. The court reaffirmed a statement in an earlier opinion that "There is no legal measure of damages in cases of this character." *Id.* at 686, 144 So.2d at 50. It rejected petitioners' constitutional contentions with the brief statements that "The First Amendment of the U.S. Constitution does not protect libelous publications," and "The Fourteenth Amendment is directed against State action, and not private action." *Id.* at 676, 144 So.2d at 40.

Because of the importance of the constitutional issues involved, we granted the separate petitions for certiorari of the individual petitioners and of the Times. 371 U.S. 946. We reverse the judgment. We hold that the rule of law applied by the Alabama courts is constitutionally deficient for failure to provide the safeguards for freedom of speech and of the press that are required by the First and Fourteenth Amendments in a libel action brought by a public official against critics of his official conduct.[note 4] We [265] further hold that, under the proper safeguards, the evidence presented in this case is constitutionally insufficient to support the judgment for respondent.

I

We may dispose at the outset of two grounds asserted to insulate the judgment of the Alabama courts from constitutional scrutiny. The first is the proposition relied on by the State Supreme Court--that "The Fourteenth Amendment is directed against State action, and not private action." That proposition has no application to this case. Although this is a civil lawsuit between private parties, the Alabama courts have applied a state rule of law which petitioners claim to impose invalid restrictions on their constitutional freedoms of speech and press. It matters not that that law has been applied in a civil action and that it is common law only, though supplemented by statute. See, e.g., Alabama Code, Tit. 7, §§ 908-917. The test is not the form in which state power has been applied but, whatever the form, whether such power has, in fact, been exercised. See *Ex parte Virginia*, 100 U.S. 339, 346-347; *American Federation of Labor v. Swing*, 312 U.S. 321.

The second contention is that the constitutional guarantees of freedom of speech and of the press are inapplicable here, at least so far as the Times is concerned, because the allegedly libelous statements were published as part of a paid, "commercial" advertisement. The argument relies on *Valentine v. Chrestensen*, 316 U.S. 52, where the Court held that a city ordinance forbidding street distribution of commercial and business advertising matter did not abridge the First Amendment freedoms, even as applied to a handbill having a commercial message on one side but a protest against certain official action, on the other. The reliance is wholly misplaced. The Court in Chrestensen reaffirmed the constitutional protection for "the freedom of communicating [266] information and disseminating opinion"; its holding was based upon the factual conclusions that the handbill was "purely commercial advertising" and that the protest against official action had been added only to evade the ordinance.

The publication here was not a "commercial" advertisement in the sense in which the word was used in Chrestensen. It communicated information, expressed opinion, recited grievances, protested claimed abuses, and sought financial support on behalf of a movement whose existence and objectives are matters of the highest public interest and concern. See *NAACP v. Button*, 371 U.S. 415, 435. That the Times was paid for publishing the advertisement is as immaterial in this connection as is the fact that newspapers and books are sold. *Smith v. California*, 361 U.S. 147, 150; cf. *Bantam Books, Inc., v. Sullivan*, 372 U.S. 58, 64, n. 6. Any other conclusion would discourage newspapers from carrying "editorial advertisements" of this type, and so might shut off an important outlet for the promulgation of information and ideas by persons who do not themselves have access to publishing facilities--who wish to exercise their freedom of speech even though they are not members of the press. Cf. *Lovell v. Griffin*, 303 U.S. 444, 452; *Schneider v. State*, 308 U.S. 147, 164. The effect would be to shackle the First Amendment in its attempt to secure "the widest possible dissemination of information from diverse and antagonistic sources." *Associated Press v. United States*, 326 U.S. 1, 20. To avoid placing such a handicap upon the freedoms of expression, we hold that, if the allegedly libelous statements would otherwise be constitutionally protected from the present judgment, they do not forfeit that protection because they were published in the form of a paid advertisement. [note 5] [267]

II

Under Alabama law, as applied in this case, a publication is "libelous per se" if the words "tend to injure a person . . . in his reputation" or to "bring [him] into public contempt"; the trial court stated that the standard was met if the words are such as to "injure him in his public office, or impute misconduct to him in his office, or want of official integrity, or want of fidelity to a public trust. . . ." The jury must find that the words were published "of and concerning" the plaintiff, but, where the plaintiff is a public official, his place in the governmental hierarchy is sufficient evidence to support a finding that his reputation has been affected by statements that reflect upon the agency of which he is in charge. Once "libel per se" has been established, the defendant has no defense as to stated facts unless he can persuade the jury that they were true in all their particulars. *Alabama Ride Co. v. Vance*, 235 Ala. 263, 178 So. 438 (1938); *Johnson Publishing Co. v. Davis*, 271 Ala. 474, 494 495, 124 So.2d 441, 457-458 (1960). His privilege of "fair comment" for expressions of opinion depends on the truth of the facts upon which the comment is based. *Parsons v. Age-Herald Publishing Co.*, 181 Ala. 439, 450, 61 So. 345, 350 (1913). Unless he can discharge the burden of proving truth, general damages are presumed, and may be awarded without proof of pecuniary injury. A showing of actual malice is apparently a prerequisite to recovery of punitive damages, and the defendant may, in any event, forestall a punitive award by a retraction meeting the statutory requirements. Good motives and belief in truth do not negate an inference of malice, but are relevant only in mitigation of punitive damages if the jury chooses to accord them weight. *Johnson Publishing Co. v. Davis, supra*, 271 Ala., at 495, 124 So.2d at 458. [268]

The question before us is whether this rule of liability, as applied to an action brought by a public official against critics of his official conduct, abridges the freedom of speech and of the press that is guaranteed by the First and Fourteenth Amendments.

Respondent relies heavily, as did the Alabama courts, on statements of this Court to the effect that the Constitution does not protect libelous publications.[note 6] Those statements do not foreclose our inquiry here. None of the cases sustained the use of libel laws to impose sanctions upon expression critical of the official conduct of public officials. The dictum in *Pennekamp v. Florida*, 328 U.S. 331, 348-349, that "when the statements amount to defamation, a judge has such remedy in damages for libel as do other public servants," implied no view as to what remedy might constitutionally be afforded to public officials. In *Beauharnais v. Illinois*, 343 U.S. 250, the Court sustained an Illinois criminal libel statute as applied to a publication held to be both defamatory of a racial group and "liable to cause violence and disorder." But the Court was careful to note that it "retains and exercises authority to nullify action which encroaches on freedom of utterance under the guise of punishing libel"; for "public men, are, as it were, public property," and "discussion cannot be denied and the right, as well as the duty, of criticism must not be stifled." *Id.,* at 263-264, and n. 18. In the only previous case that did present the question of constitutional limitations upon the power to award damages for libel of a public official, the Court was equally divided and the question was not decided. *Schenectady Union Pub. Co. v. Sweeney*, 316 U.S. 642. In deciding the question now, we are compelled by neither precedent nor policy to give any more weight to the epithet "libel" than we have to other "mere labels" of state law. *N. A. A. C. P. v. Button*, 371 U.S. 415, 429. Like insurrection,[note 7] contempt,[note 8] advocacy of unlawful acts,[note 9] breach of the peace,[note 10] obscenity,[note 11] solicitation of legal business,[note 12] and the various other formulae for the repression of expression that have been challenged in this court, libel can claim no talismanic immunity from constitutional limitations. It must be measured by standards that satisfy the First Amendment.

The general proposition that freedom of expression upon public questions is secured by the First Amendment has long been settled by our decisions. The constitutional safeguard, we have said, "was fashioned to assure unfettered interchange of ideas for the bringing about of political and social changes desired by the people." *Roth v. United States*, 354 U.S. 476, 484. "The maintenance of the opportunity for free political discussion to the end that government may be responsive to the will of the people and that changes may be obtained by lawful means, an opportunity essential to the security of the Republic, is a fundamental principle of our constitutional system." *Stromberg v. California*, 283 U.S. 359, 369. "[I]t is a prized American privilege to speak one's mind, although not always with perfect good taste, on all public institutions," *Bridges v. California*, 314 U.S. 252, 270, and this opportunity is to be afforded for "vigorous advocacy" no less than "abstract discussion." *NAACP v. Button*, 371 U.S. 415, 429. [270] The First Amendment, said Judge Learned Hand, "presupposes that right conclusions are more likely to be gathered out of a multitude of tongues than through any kind of authoritative selection. To many, this is, and always will be, folly, but we have staked upon it our all." *United States v. Associated Press*, 52 F.Supp. 362, 372 (D.C.S.D.N.Y.1943). Mr. Justice Brandeis, in his concurring opinion in *Whitney v. California*, 274 U.S. 357, 375-376, gave the principle its classic formulation:

Those who won our independence believed . . . that public discussion is a political duty, and that this should be a fundamental principle of the American government. They recognized the risks to which all human institutions are subject. But they knew that order cannot be secured merely through fear of punishment for its infraction; that it is hazardous to discourage thought, hope and imagination; that fear breeds repression; that repression breeds hate; that hate menaces stable government; that the path of safety lies in the opportunity to discuss freely supposed grievances and proposed remedies, and that the fitting remedy for evil counsels is good ones. Believing in the power of reason as applied through public discussion, they eschewed silence coerced by law--the argument of force in its worst form. Recognizing the occasional tyrannies of governing majorities, they amended the Constitution so that free speech and assembly should be guaranteed.

Thus, we consider this case against the background of a profound national commitment to the principle that debate on public issues should be uninhibited, robust, and wide-open, and that it may well include vehement, caustic, and sometimes unpleasantly sharp attacks on government and public officials. See *Terminiello v. Chicago*, 337 U.S. 1, 4; *De Jonge v. Oregon*, 299 U.S. 353, [271] 365. The present advertisement, as an expression of grievance and protest on one of the major public issues of our time, would seem clearly to qualify for the constitutional protection. The question is whether it forfeits that protection by the falsity of some of its factual statements and by its alleged defamation of respondent.

Authoritative interpretations of the First Amendment guarantees have consistently refused to recognize an exception for any test of truth--whether administered by judges, juries, or administrative officials--and especially one that puts the burden of proving truth on the speaker. Cf. *Speiser v. Randall*, 357 U.S. 513, 525-526. The constitutional protection does not turn upon "the truth, popularity, or social utility of the ideas and beliefs which are offered." *NAACP v. Button*, 371 U.S. 415, 445. As Madison said, "Some degree of abuse is inseparable from the proper use of every thing, and in no instance is this more true than in that of the press." 4 Elliot's Debates on the Federal Constitution (1876), p. 571. In *Cantwell v. Connecticut*, 310 U.S. 296, 310, the Court declared:

In the realm of religious faith, and in that of political belief, sharp differences arise. In both fields, the tenets of one man may seem the rankest error to his neighbor. To persuade others to his own point of view, the pleader, as we know, at times resorts to exaggeration, to vilification of men who have been, or are, prominent in church or state, and even to false statement. But the people of this nation have ordained, in the light of history, that, in spite of the probability of excesses and abuses, these liberties are, in the long view, essential to enlightened opinion and right conduct on the part of the citizens of a democracy.

That erroneous statement is inevitable in free debate, and that it must be protected if the freedoms of expression [272] are to have the "breathing space" that they "need . . . to survive," *NAACP v. Button*, 371 U.S. 415, 433, was also recognized by the Court of Appeals for the District of Columbia Circuit in *Sweeney v. Patterson*, 76 U.S.App.D.C. 23, 24, 128 F.2d 457, 458 (1942), cert. denied, 317 U.S. 678. Judge Edgerton spoke for a unanimous court which affirmed the dismissal of a Congressman's libel suit based upon a newspaper article charging him with anti-Semitism in opposing a judicial appointment. He said:

Cases which impose liability for erroneous reports of the political conduct of officials reflect the obsolete doctrine that the governed must not criticize their governors. . . . The interest of the public here outweighs the interest of appellant or any other individual. The protection of the public requires not merely discussion, but information. Political conduct and views which some respectable people approve, and others condemn, are constantly imputed to Congressmen. Errors of fact, particularly in regard to a man's mental states and processes, are inevitable. . . . Whatever is added to the field of libel is taken from the field of free debate. [note 13]

Injury to official reputation affords no more warrant for repressing speech that would otherwise be free than does factual error. Where judicial officers are involved, this Court has held that concern for the dignity and [273] reputation of the courts does not justify the punishment as criminal contempt of criticism of the judge or his decision. *Bridges v. California,* 314 U.S. 252. This is true even though the utterance contains "half-truths" and "misinformation." *Pennekamp v. Florida,* 328 U.S. 331, 342, 343, n. 5, 345. Such repression can be justified, if at all, only by a clear and present danger of the obstruction of justice. See also *Craig v. Harney,* 331 U.S. 367; *Wood v. Georgia,* 370 U.S. 375. If judges are to be treated as "men of fortitude, able to thrive in a hardy climate," *Craig v. Harney, supra,* 331 U.S. at 376, surely the same must be true of other government officials, such as elected city commissioners. [note 14] Criticism of their official conduct does not lose its constitutional protection merely because it is effective criticism, and hence diminishes their official reputations.

If neither factual error nor defamatory content suffices to remove the constitutional shield from criticism of official conduct, the combination of the two elements is no less inadequate. This is the lesson to be drawn from the great controversy over the Sedition Act of 1798, 1 Stat. 596, which first crystallized a national awareness of the central meaning of the First Amendment. See Levy, Legacy of Suppression (1960), at 258 et seq.; Smith, Freedom's Fetters (1956), at 426, 431, and passim. That statute made it a crime, punishable by a $5,000 fine and five years in prison, "if any person shall write, print, utter or publish . . . any false, scandalous and malicious [274] writing or writings against the government of the United States, or either house of the Congress . . . or the President . . . with intent to defame . . . or to bring them, or either of them, into contempt or disrepute; or to excite against them, or either or any of them, the hatred of the good people of the United States." The Act allowed the defendant the defense of truth, and provided that the jury were to be judges both of the law and the facts. Despite these qualifications, the Act was vigorously condemned as unconstitutional in an attack joined in by Jefferson and Madison. In the famous Virginia Resolutions of 1798, the General Assembly of Virginia resolved that it doth particularly protest against the palpable and alarming infractions of the Constitution in the two late cases of the "Alien and Sedition Acts," passed at the last session of Congress. . . . [The Sedition Act] exercises . . . a power not delegated by the Constitution, but, on the contrary, expressly and positively forbidden by one of the amendments thereto--a power which, more than any other, ought to produce universal alarm because it is leveled against the right of freely examining public characters and measures, and of free communication among the people thereon, which has ever been justly deemed the only effectual guardian of every other right. 4 Elliot's Debates, *supra,* pp. 553-554.

Madison prepared the Report in support of the protest. His premise was that the Constitution created a form of government under which "The people, not the government, possess the absolute sovereignty." The structure of the government dispersed power in reflection of the people's distrust of concentrated power, and of power itself at all levels. This form of government was "altogether different" from the British form, under which the Crown was sovereign and the people were subjects. "Is [275] it not natural and necessary, under such different circumstances," he asked, "that a different degree of freedom in the use of the press should be contemplated?" *Id.*, pp. 569-570. Earlier, in a debate in the House of Representatives, Madison had said: "If we advert to the nature of Republican Government, we shall find that the censorial power is in the people over the Government, and not in the Government over the people." 4 Annals of Congress, p. 934 (1794). Of the exercise of that power by the press, his Report said: "In every state, probably, in the Union, the press has exerted a freedom in canvassing the merits and measures of public men, of every description, which has not been confined to the strict limits of the common law. On this footing, the freedom of the press has stood; on this foundation it yet stands. . . ." 4 Elliot's Debates, *supra*, p. 570. The right of free public discussion of the stewardship of public officials was thus, in Madison's view, a fundamental principle of the American form of government.

Although the Sedition Act was never tested in this Court, [note 16] the attack upon its validity has carried the day in the court of history. Fines levied in its prosecution were repaid by Act of Congress on the ground that it was unconstitutional. See, e.g., Act of July 4, 1840, c. 45, 6 Stat. 802, accompanied by H.R.Rep. No. 86, 26th Cong., 1st Sess. (1840). Calhoun, reporting to the Senate on February 4, 1836, assumed that its invalidity was a matter "which no one now doubts." Report with Senate bill No. 122, 24th Cong., 1st Sess., p. 3. Jefferson, as President, pardoned those who had been convicted and sentenced under the Act and remitted their fines, stating: "I discharged every person under punishment or prosecution under the sedition law because I considered, and now consider, that law to be a nullity, as absolute and as palpable as if Congress had ordered us to fall down and worship a golden image." Letter to Mrs. Adams, July 22, 1804, 4 Jefferson's Works (Washington ed.), pp. 555, 556. The invalidity of the Act has also been assumed by Justices of this Court. See Holmes, J., dissenting and joined by Brandeis, J., in *Abrams v. United States*, 250 U.S. 616, 630; Jackson, J., dissenting in *Beauharnais v. Illinois*, 343 U.S. 250, 288-289; Douglas, The Right of the People (1958), p. 47. See also Cooley, Constitutional Limitations (8th ed., Carrington, 1927), pp. 899-900; Chafee, Free Speech in the United States (1942), pp. 27-28. These views reflect a broad consensus that the Act, because of the restraint it imposed upon criticism of government and public officials, was inconsistent with the First Amendment.

There is no force in respondent's argument that the constitutional limitations implicit in the history of the Sedition Act apply only to Congress, and not to the States. It is true that the First Amendment was originally addressed only to action by the Federal Government, and [277] that Jefferson, for one, while denying the power of Congress "to controul the freedom of the press," recognized such a power in the States. See the 1804 Letter to Abigail Adams quoted in *Dennis v. United States*, 341 U.S. 494, 522, n. 4 (concurring opinion). But this distinction was eliminated with the adoption of the Fourteenth Amendment and the application to the States of the First Amendment's restrictions. See, e.g., *Gitlow v. New York*, 268 U.S. 652, 666; *Schneider v. State*, 308 U.S. 147, 160; *Bridges v. California*, 314 U.S. 252, 268; *Edwards v. South Carolina*, 372 U.S. 229, 235.

What a State may not constitutionally bring about by means of a criminal statute is likewise beyond the reach of its civil law of libel. [note 17] The fear of damage awards under a rule such as that invoked by the Alabama courts here may be markedly more inhibiting than the fear of prosecution under a criminal statute. See *City of Chicago v. Tribune Co.*, 307 Ill. 595, 607, 139 N.E. 86, 90 (1923). Alabama, for example, has a criminal libel law which subjects to prosecution "any person who speaks, writes, or prints of and concerning another any accusation falsely and maliciously importing the commission by such person of a felony, or any other indictable offense involving moral turpitude," and which allows as punishment upon conviction a fine not exceeding $500 and a prison sentence of six months. Alabama Code, Tit. 14, § 350. Presumably, a person charged with violation of this statute enjoys ordinary criminal law safeguards such as the requirements of an indictment and of proof beyond a reasonable doubt. These safeguards are not available to the defendant in a civil action. The judgment awarded in this case--without the need for any proof of actual pecuniary loss--was one thousand times greater than the maximum fine provided by the Alabama criminal statute, and one hundred times greater than that provided by the Sedition Act. [278] And since there is no double jeopardy limitation applicable to civil lawsuits, this is not the only judgment that may be awarded against petitioners for the same publication. [note 18] Whether or not a newspaper can survive a succession of such judgments, the pall of fear and timidity imposed upon those who would give voice to public criticism is an atmosphere in which the First Amendment freedoms cannot survive. Plainly the Alabama law of civil libel is "a form of regulation that creates hazards to protected freedoms markedly greater than those that attend reliance upon the criminal law." *Bantam Books, Inc. v. Sullivan,* 372 U.S. 58, 70.

The state rule of law is not saved by its allowance of the defense of truth. A defense for erroneous statements honestly made is no less essential here than was the requirement of proof of guilty knowledge which, in *Smith v. California,* 361 U.S. 147, we held indispensable to a valid conviction of a bookseller for possessing obscene writings for sale. We said:

For, if the bookseller is criminally liable without knowledge of the contents, . . . He will tend to restrict the books he sells to those he has inspected, and thus the State will have imposed a restriction upon the distribution of constitutionally protected, as well as obscene, literature. . . . And the bookseller's burden would become the public's burden, for, by restricting him, the public's access to reading matter would be restricted. . . . [H]is timidity in the face of his absolute criminal liability thus would tend to restrict the public's access to forms of the printed word which the State could not constitutionally [279] suppress directly. The bookseller's self-censorship, compelled by the State, would be a censorship affecting the whole public, hardly less virulent for being privately administered. Through it, the distribution of all books, both obscene and not obscene, would be impeded. (361 U.S. 147, 153-154.)

A rule compelling the critic of official conduct to guarantee the truth of all his factual assertions--and to do so on pain of libel judgments virtually unlimited in amount--leads to a comparable "self-censorship." Allowance of the defense of truth, with the burden of proving it on the defendant, does not mean that only false speech will be deterred. [note 19] Even courts accepting this defense as an adequate safeguard have recognized the difficulties of adducing legal proofs that the alleged libel was true in all its factual particulars. See, e.g., *Post Publishing Co. v. Hallam,* 59 F. 530, 540 (C.A. 6th Cir. 1893); see also Noel, Defamation of Public Officers and Candidates, 49 Col.L.Rev. 875, 892 (1949). Under such a rule, would-be critics of official conduct may be deterred from voicing their criticism, even though it is believed to be true and even though it is, in fact, true, because of doubt whether it can be proved in court or fear of the expense of having to do so. They tend to make only statements which "steer far wider of the unlawful zone." *Speiser v. Randall, supra,* 357 U.S. at 526. The rule thus dampens the vigor and limits the variety of public debate. It is inconsistent with the First and Fourteenth Amendments.

The constitutional guarantees require, we think, a federal rule that prohibits a public official from recovering damages for a defamatory falsehood relating to his official conduct unless he proves that the statement was made [280] with "actual malice"--that is, with knowledge that it was false or with reckless disregard of whether it was false or not. An oft-cited statement of a like rule, which has been adopted by a number of state courts, [note 20] is found in the Kansas case of *Coleman v. MacLennan*, 78 Kan. 711, 98 P. 281 (1908). The State Attorney General, a candidate for reelection and a member of the commission charged with the management and control of the state school fund, sued a newspaper publisher for alleged libel in an article purporting to state facts relating to his official conduct in connection with a school-fund transaction. The defendant pleaded privilege and the trial judge, over the plaintiff's objection, instructed the jury that where an article is published and circulated among voters for the sole purpose of giving what the defendant [281] believes to be truthful information concerning a candidate for public office and for the purpose of enabling such voters to cast their ballot more intelligently, and the whole thing is done in good faith and without malice, the article is privileged, although the principal matters contained in the article may be untrue, in fact, and derogatory to the character of the plaintiff, and in such a case the burden is on the plaintiff to show actual malice in the publication of the article.

In answer to a special question, the jury found that the plaintiff had not proved actual malice, and a general verdict was returned for the defendant. On appeal, the Supreme Court of Kansas, in an opinion by Justice Burch, reasoned as follows (78 Kan., at 724, 98 P. at 286):

It is of the utmost consequence that the people should discuss the character and qualifications of candidates for their suffrages. The importance to the state and to society of such discussions is so vast, and the advantages derived are so great, that they more than counterbalance the inconvenience of private persons whose conduct may be involved, and occasional injury to the reputations of individuals must yield to the public welfare, although at times such injury may be great. The public benefit from publicity is so great, and the chance of injury to private character so small, that such discussion must be privileged.

The court thus sustained the trial court's instruction as a correct statement of the law, saying:

In such a case the occasion gives rise to a privilege, qualified to this extent: any one claiming to be defamed by the communication must show actual malice or go remediless. This privilege extends to a great variety of subjects, and includes matters of [282] public concern, public men, and candidates for office. 78 Kan. at 723, 98 P. at 285.

Such a privilege for criticism of official conduct [note 21] is appropriately analogous to the protection accorded a public official when he is sued for libel by a private citizen. In *Barr v. Matteo*, 360 U.S. 564, 575, this Court held the utterance of a federal official to be absolutely privileged if made "within the outer perimeter" of his duties. The States accord the same immunity to statements of their highest officers, although some differentiate their lesser officials and qualify the privilege they enjoy. [note 22] But all hold that all officials are protected unless actual malice can be proved. The reason for the official privilege is said to be that the threat of damage suits would otherwise "inhibit the fearless, vigorous, and effective administration of policies of government" and "dampen the ardor of all but the most resolute, or the most irresponsible, in the unflinching discharge of their duties." *Barr v. Matteo, supra,* 360 U.S. at 571. Analogous considerations support the privilege for the citizen-critic of government. It is as much his duty to criticize as it is the official's duty to administer. See *Whitney v. California,* 274 U.S. 357, 375 (concurring opinion of Mr. Justice Brandeis), quoted *supra,* p. 270. As Madison said, see *supra* p. 275, "the censorial power is in the people over the Government, and not in the Government over the people." It would give public servants an unjustified preference over the public they serve, if critics of official conduct [283] did not have a fair equivalent of the immunity granted to the officials themselves.

We conclude that such a privilege is required by the First and Fourteenth Amendments.

III

We hold today that the Constitution delimits a State's power to award damages for libel in actions brought by public officials against critics of their official conduct. Since this is such an action, [note 23] the rule requiring proof of actual malice is applicable. While Alabama law apparently requires proof of actual malice for an award of punitive damages, [note 24] where general damages are concerned malice is "presumed." Such a presumption is inconsistent [284] with the federal rule. "The power to create presumptions is not a means of escape from constitutional restrictions," *Bailey v. Alabama,* 219 U.S. 219, 239, "the showing of malice required for the forfeiture of the privilege is not presumed but is a matter for proof by the plaintiff. . . ." *Lawrence v. Fox,* 357 Mich. 134, 146, 97 N.W.2d 719, 725 (1959). [note 25] Since the trial judge did not instruct the jury to differentiate between general and punitive damages, it may be that the verdict was wholly an award of one or the other. But it is impossible to know, in view of the general verdict returned. Because of this uncertainty, the judgment must be reversed and the case remanded. *Stromberg v. California,* 283 U.S. 359, 367-368; *Williams v. North Carolina,* 317 U.S. 287, 291-292; see *Yates v. United States,* 354 U.S. 298, 311-312; *Cramer v. United States,* 325 U.S. 1, 36, n. 45.

Since respondent may seek a new trial, we deem that considerations of effective judicial administration require us to review the evidence in the present record to determine whether it could constitutionally support a judgment for respondent. This Court's duty is not limited to the elaboration of constitutional principles; we must also in proper cases review the evidence to make certain that those principles have been constitutionally applied. This is such a case, particularly since the question is one of alleged trespass across "the line between speech unconditionally guaranteed and speech which may legitimately be regulated." *Speiser v. Randall,* 357 U.S. 513, 525. In cases where that line must be drawn, the rule is that we "examine for ourselves the statements in issue and the circumstances under which they were made to see . . . whether they are of a character which the principles of the First Amendment, as adopted by the Due Process Clause of the Fourteenth Amendment, protect." *Pennekamp v. Florida,* 328 U.S. 331, 335; see also *One, Inc., v. Olesen,* 355 U.S. 371; *Sunshine Book Co. v. Summerfield,* 355 U.S. 372. We must "make an independent examination of the whole record," *Edwards v. South Carolina,* 372 U.S. 229, 235, so as to assure ourselves that the judgment does not constitute a forbidden intrusion on the field of free expression.[note 26]

Applying these standards, we consider that the proof presented to show actual malice lacks the convincing [286] clarity which the constitutional standard demands, and hence that it would not constitutionally sustain the judgment for respondent under the proper rule of law. The case of the individual petitioners requires little discussion. Even assuming that they could constitutionally be found to have authorized the use of their names on the advertisement, there was no evidence whatever that they were aware of any erroneous statements or were in any way reckless in that regard. The judgment against them is thus without constitutional support.

As to the Times, we similarly conclude that the facts do not support a finding of actual malice. The statement by the Times' Secretary that, apart from the padlocking allegation, he thought the advertisement was "substantially correct," affords no constitutional warrant for the Alabama Supreme Court's conclusion that it was a "cavalier ignoring of the falsity of the advertisement [from which] the jury could not have but been impressed with the bad faith of The Times, and its maliciousness inferable therefrom." The statement does not indicate malice at the time of the publication; even if the advertisement was not "substantially correct"--although respondent's own proofs tend to show that it was--that opinion was at least a reasonable one, and there was no evidence to impeach the witness' good faith in holding it. The Times' failure to retract upon respondent's demand, although it later retracted upon the demand of Governor Patterson, is likewise not adequate evidence of malice for constitutional purposes. Whether or not a failure to retract may ever constitute such evidence, there are two reasons why it does not here. First, the letter written by the Times reflected a reasonable doubt on its part as to whether the advertisement could reasonably be taken to refer to respondent at all. Second, it was not a final refusal, since it asked for an explanation on this point--a request that respondent chose to ignore. Nor does the retraction upon the demand of the Governor supply the [287] necessary proof. It may be doubted that a failure to retract, which is not itself evidence of malice, can retroactively become such by virtue of a retraction subsequently made to another party. But, in any event, that did not happen here, since the explanation given by the Times' Secretary for the distinction drawn between respondent and the Governor was a reasonable one, the good faith of which was not impeached.

Finally, there is evidence that the Times published the advertisement without checking its accuracy against the news stories in the Times' own files. The mere presence of the stories in the files does not, of course, establish that the Times "knew" the advertisement was false, since the state of mind required for actual malice would have to be brought home to the persons in the Times' organization having responsibility for the publication of the advertisement. With respect to the failure of those persons to make the check, the record shows that they relied upon their knowledge of the good reputation of many of those whose names were listed as sponsors of the advertisement, and upon the letter from A. Philip Randolph, known to them as a responsible individual, certifying that the use of the names was authorized. There was testimony that the persons handling the advertisement saw nothing in it that would render it unacceptable under the Times' policy of rejecting advertisements containing "attacks of a personal character"; [note 27] their failure to reject it on this ground was not unreasonable. We think [288] the evidence against the Times supports, at most, a finding of negligence in failing to discover the misstatements, and is constitutionally insufficient to show the recklessness that is required for a finding of actual malice. Cf. *Charles Parker Co. v. Silver City Crystal Co.*, 142 Conn. 605, 618, 116 A.2d 440, 446 (1955); *Phoenix Newspapers, Inc., v. Choisser*, 82 Ariz. 271, 277-278, 312 P.2d 150, 154-155 (1957).

We also think the evidence was constitutionally defective in another respect: it was incapable of supporting the jury's finding that the allegedly libelous statements were made "of and concerning" respondent. Respondent relies on the words of the advertisement and the testimony of six witnesses to establish a connection between it and himself. Thus, in his brief to this Court, he states:

The reference to respondent as police commissioner is clear from the ad. In addition, the jury heard the testimony of a newspaper editor . . . ; a real estate and insurance man . . . ; the sales manager of a men's clothing store . . . ; a food equipment man . . . ; a service station operator . . . , and the operator of a truck line for whom respondent had formerly worked. . . . Each of these witnesses stated that he associated the statements with respondent. . . . (Citations to record omitted.)

There was no reference to respondent in the advertisement, either by name or official position. A number of the allegedly libelous statements--the charges that the dining hall was padlocked and that Dr. King's home was bombed, his person assaulted, and a perjury prosecution instituted against him--did not even concern the police; despite the ingenuity of the arguments which would attach this significance to the word "They," it is plain that these statements could not reasonably be read as accusing respondent of personal involvement in the acts [289] in question. The statements upon which respondent principally relies as referring to him are the two allegations that did concern the police or police functions: that "truckloads of police . . . ringed the Alabama State College Campus" after the demonstration on the State Capitol steps, and that Dr. King had been "arrested . . . seven times." These statements were false only in that the police had been "deployed near" the campus, but had not actually "ringed" it, and had not gone there in connection with the State Capitol demonstration, and in that Dr. King had been arrested only four times. The ruling that these discrepancies between what was true and what was asserted were sufficient to injure respondent's reputation may itself raise constitutional problems, but we need not consider them here. Although the statements may be taken as referring to the police, they did not, on their face, make even an oblique reference to respondent as an individual. Support for the asserted reference must, therefore, be sought in the testimony of respondent's witnesses. But none of them suggested any basis for the belief that respondent himself was attacked in the advertisement beyond the bare fact that he was in overall charge of the Police Department and thus bore official responsibility for police conduct; to the extent that some of the witnesses thought respondent to have been charged with ordering or approving the conduct or otherwise being personally involved in it, they based this notion not on any statements in the advertisement, and not on any evidence that he had, in fact, been so involved, but solely on the unsupported assumption that, because of his official position, he must have been. [note 28] This reliance on the bare [290] fact of respondent's official position [note 29] was made explicit by the Supreme Court of Alabama. That court, in holding that the trial court "did not err in overruling the demurrer [of the Times] in the aspect that the libelous [291] matter was not of and concerning the [plaintiff,]" based its ruling on the proposition that:

We think it common knowledge that the average person knows that municipal agents, such as police and firemen, and others, are under the control and direction of the city governing body, and more particularly under the direction and control of a single commissioner. In measuring the performance or deficiencies of such groups, praise or criticism is usually attached to the official in complete control of the body. 273 Ala., at 674-675, 144 So.2d at 39.

This proposition has disquieting implications for criticism of governmental conduct. For good reason, "no court of last resort in this country has ever held, or even suggested, that prosecutions for libel on government have any place in the American system of jurisprudence." *City of Chicago v. Tribune Co.*, 307 Ill. 595, 601, 139 N.E. [292] 86, 88 (1923). The present proposition would sidestep this obstacle by transmuting criticism of government, however impersonal it may seem on its face, into personal criticism, and hence potential libel, of the officials of whom the government is composed. There is no legal alchemy by which a State may thus create the cause of action that would otherwise be denied for a publication which, as respondent himself said of the advertisement, "reflects not only on me but on the other Commissioners and the community." Raising as it does the possibility that a good faith critic of government will be penalized for his criticism, the proposition relied on by the Alabama courts strikes at the very center of the constitutionally protected area of free expression. [note 30] We hold that such a proposition may not constitutionally be utilized to establish that an otherwise impersonal attack on governmental operations was a libel of an official responsible for those operations. Since it was relied on exclusively here, and there was no other evidence to connect the statements with respondent, the evidence was constitutionally insufficient to support a finding that the statements referred to respondent.

The judgment of the Supreme Court of Alabama is reversed, and the case is remanded to that court for further proceedings not inconsistent with this opinion.

Reversed and remanded. [293]

15 CURTIS PUBLISHING CO. V. BUTTS
SUPREME COURT OF THE UNITED STATES
388 U.S. 130
87 S. Ct. 1975
Argued February 23, 1967
Decided June 12, 1967

* Together with No. 150, *Associated Press v. Walker*, on certiorari to the Court of Civil Appeals of Texas, 2d Supreme Judicial District.

Syllabus

In No. 37, respondent brought a diversity libel action in federal court seeking compensatory and punitive damages for an article which was published in petitioner's magazine accusing respondent of conspiring to "fix" a football game between the University of Alabama and the University of Georgia, where he was privately employed as the athletic director. The article was based upon an affidavit concerning a telephone conversation between respondent and the Alabama coach which the affiant, Burnett, had accidentally overheard. Respondent challenged the truth of the article and claimed a serious departure by the magazine from good investigative standards of the accuracy of its charges amounting to reckless and wanton conduct. He submitted evidence at the trial showing, inter alia, that petitioner's magazine, which had instituted a policy of "sophisticated muckraking," knew that Burnett was on criminal probation but had published the story without any independent support for his affidavit; that it did not before publication view his notes (the information in which, if not valueless, would be readily available to any coach); that the magazine did not interview a person with Burnett when the phone call was overheard, view the game films, or check for any adjustments in Alabama's plans after the information was divulged; and that the magazine assigned the story to a writer not a football expert and made no effort to have such an expert check the story. The jury was instructed on the issue of truth as a defense and was also instructed that it could award punitive damages and could assess the reliability and the nature of the sources of the magazine's information and its care in checking the assertions, considerations relevant to determining whether the magazine had proceeded with "wanton and reckless indifference." The jury returned a verdict of general and punitive damages which was reduced by remittitur. The trial court rejected the defense's new trial motion based on *New York Times Co. v. Sullivan*, 376 U.S. 254 (which was decided after the filing of the complaint in and trial of this case), holding that decision inapplicable to one like petitioner not a public official. It also held the evidence amply supported the conclusion that the magazine had acted in reckless disregard of whether the article was false or not. The Court of Appeals affirmed on the merits. It did not reach the constitutional claim based on *New York Times,* holding that petitioner had waived the right to make that challenge since some of its lawyers had been involved in the latter case, yet the defense was based solely on the issue of truth. In No. 150, petitioner, a news association, published a dispatch about a massive riot on the University of Mississippi campus attending federal efforts to enforce a court decree ordering a Negro's enrollment. The dispatch stated that respondent, a politically prominent figure whose statements on federal intervention had been widely publicized, had taken command of the violent crowd and led a charge against federal marshals trying to enforce the court's decree, had encouraged violence and given technical advice to the rioters. Respondent brought a libel action in the Texas state courts for compensatory and punitive damages. Petitioner's defense was based on truth and constitutional rights. The evidence showed that the dispatch had been made on the scene and almost immediately reported to the petitioner by a competent correspondent. There was no significant showing of improper preparation of the dispatch, or any prejudice by petitioner or its correspondent. The jury was instructed that compensatory damages could be awarded if the dispatch was not substantially true and that punitive damages could be added if the article was actuated by ill will or entire want of care. The jury returned a verdict for both compensatory and punitive damages. The trial court refused to enter an award for the latter. The court held *New York Times* inapplicable but that if applicable it would require a verdict for the petitioner since there was no evidence of malice. Both sides appealed. The Texas Court of Civil Appeals affirmed and the Texas Supreme Court denied review. *Held:* The judgment in No. 37 is affirmed. The judgment in No. 150 is reversed and the case remanded. Pp. 133-174.

No. 37, 351 F. 2d 702, affirmed; No. 150, 393 S. W. 2d 671, reversed and remanded.

MR. JUSTICE HARLAN, joined by MR. JUSTICE CLARK, MR. JUSTICE STEWART, and MR. JUSTICE FORTAS, concluded that:

1. Petitioner's failure in No. 37 to raise the constitutional defense before trial constituted no waiver of its right to do so after *New York Times* was decided. Pp. 142-145.

2. The *New York Times* rule prohibiting a public official from recovering damages for defamatory falsehood relating to his official conduct absent actual malice as therein defined, though necessary there to protect against prosecutions close to seditious libel for criticizing official conduct, should not be inexorably applied to defamation actions by "public figures" like those here, where different considerations are present. Pp. 148, 152-154.

3. A "public figure" who is not a public official may recover damages for defamatory falsehood substantially endangering his reputation on a showing of highly unreasonable conduct constituting an extreme departure from the standards of investigation and reporting ordinarily adhered to by responsible publishers. P. 155.

4. In view of the court's instructions in No. 37, the jury must have decided that the magazine's investigation was grossly inadequate, and the evidence amply supported a finding of the highly unreasonable conduct referred to above. Pp. 156-158.

5. In No. 150, where the courts found the evidence insufficient to support more than a finding of even ordinary negligence, respondent is not entitled to damages. Pp. 158-159.

6. Misconduct sufficient to justify compensatory damages also justifies punitive damages; the same constitutional standards apply to both. Pp. 159-161.

THE CHIEF JUSTICE concluded that:

1. The *New York Times* standard applies to defamation actions by "public figures" as well as those by "public officials." Pp. 162-165.

2. The judgment in No. 150, being in clear conflict with *New York Times*, must be reversed. P. 165.

3. Retrial of No. 37 is not necessary since the jury's verdict therein in view of instructions which invoked the elements later held necessary in *New York Times* most probably was based on the requirement of reckless disregard for the truth enunciated in that case. Pp. 165-167.

4. The overlapping of counsel in No. 37 with counsel in *New York Times* and in a libel action against petitioner by the Alabama coach, in which a First Amendment defense was also made, compels the conclusion that the failure to defend on those grounds here was deliberate. Pp. 167-168.

5. The evidence shows that petitioner in No. 37 acted in reckless disregard for the truth. Pp. 168-170.

MR. JUSTICE BLACK, joined by MR. JUSTICE DOUGLAS, concluded that in order to dispose of No. 150 he concurs in the grounds stated by THE CHIEF JUSTICE which are summarized in paragraphs 1 and 2, *supra*, of THE CHIEF JUSTICE's conclusions but does not recede from his previously expressed views about the much wider press and speech freedoms of the First and Fourteenth Amendments. P. 170.

MR. JUSTICE BRENNAN, joined by MR. JUSTICE WHITE, concluded that the grounds stated by THE CHIEF JUSTICE which are summarized in paragraphs 1 and 2, *supra*, of THE CHIEF JUSTICE's conclusions in No. 150 govern that case. P. 172. [133]

MR. JUSTICE HARLAN announced the judgments of the Court and delivered an opinion in which MR. JUSTICE CLARK, MR. JUSTICE STEWART, and MR. JUSTICE FORTAS join. +

In *New York Times Co. v. Sullivan*, 376 U.S. 254, 279-280, this Court held that "the constitutional guarantees [134] [of freedom of speech and press] require . . . a federal rule that prohibits a public official from recovering damages for a defamatory falsehood relating to his official conduct unless he proves that the statement was made with 'actual malice'-- that is, with knowledge that it was false or with reckless disregard of whether it was false or not." We brought these two cases here, 385 U.S. 811, 385 U.S. 812, to consider the impact of that decision on libel actions instituted by persons who are not public officials, but who are "public figures" and involved in issues in which the public has a justified and important interest. The sweep of the *New York Times* rule in libel actions brought under state law was a question expressly reserved in that case, 376 U.S., at 283, n. 23, and while that question has been involved in later cases, *Garrison v. Louisiana*, 379 U.S. 64; *Rosenblatt v. Baer*, 383 U.S. 75; *Time, Inc. v. Hill*, 385 U.S. 374, it has not been fully settled.

The matter has, however, been passed on by a considerable number of state and lower federal courts and has produced a sharp division of opinion as to whether the *New York Times* rule should apply only in actions brought by public officials or whether it has a longer reach. Compare, e.g., *Pearson v. Fairbanks Publishing Co.*, 413 P. 2d 711 (Alaska), with *Clark v. Pearson*, 248 F.Supp. 188.[note 1] [135] The resolution of the uncertainty in this area of libel actions requires, at bottom, some further exploration and clarification of the relationship between libel law and the freedom of speech and press, lest the *New York Times* rule become a talisman which gives the press constitutionally adequate protection only in a limited field, or, what would be equally unfortunate, one which goes far to immunize the press from having to make just reparation for the infliction of needless injury upon honor and reputation through false publication. These two libel actions, although they arise out of quite different sets of circumstances, provide that opportunity. We think they are best treated together in one opinion.

I

No. 37, *Curtis Publishing Co. v. Butts,* stems from an article published in petitioner's Saturday Evening Post which accused respondent of conspiring to "fix" a football game between the University of Georgia and the University of Alabama, played in 1962. At the time of the article, Butts was the athletic director of the University of Georgia and had overall responsibility for the administration of its athletic program. Georgia is a state university, but Butts was employed by the Georgia Athletic Association, a private corporation, rather than by the State itself.[note 2] Butts had previously served as head [136] football coach of the University and was a well-known and respected figure in coaching ranks. He had maintained an interest in coaching and was negotiating for a position with a professional team at the time of publication.

The article was entitled "The Story of a College Football Fix" and prefaced by a note from the editors stating: "Not since the Chicago White Sox threw the 1919 World Series has there been a sports story as shocking as this one. . . . Before the University of Georgia played the University of Alabama . . . Wally Butts . . . gave [to its coach] . . . Georgia's plays, defensive patterns, all the significant secrets Georgia's football team possessed." The text revealed that one George Burnett, an Atlanta insurance salesman, had accidentally overheard, because of electronic error, a telephone conversation between Butts and the head coach of the University of Alabama, Paul Bryant, which took place approximately one week prior to the game. Burnett was said to have listened while "Butts outlined Georgia's offensive plays . . . and told . . . how Georgia planned to defend . . . . Butts mentioned both players and plays by name." The readers were told that Burnett had made notes of the conversation, and specific examples of the divulged secrets were set out.

The article went on to discuss the game and the players' reaction to the game, concluding that "the Georgia players, their moves analyzed and forecast like those of rats in a maze, took a frightful physical beating," and said that the players, and other sideline observers, were aware that Alabama was privy to Georgia's secrets. It set out the series of events commencing with Burnett's later presentation of his notes to the Georgia head coach, [137] Johnny Griffith, and culminating in Butts' resignation from the University's athletic affairs, for health and business reasons. The article's conclusion made clear its expected impact:

"The chances are that Wally Butts will never help any football team again. . . . The investigation by university and Southeastern Conference officials is continuing; motion pictures of other games are being scrutinized; where it will end no one so far can say. But careers will be ruined, that is sure."

Butts brought this diversity libel action in the federal courts in Georgia seeking $5,000,000 compensatory and $5,000,000 punitive damages. The complaint was filed, and the trial completed, before this Court handed down its decision in *New York Times*, and the only defense raised by petitioner Curtis was one of substantial truth. No constitutional defenses were interposed although Curtis' counsel were aware of the progress of the *New York Times* case, and although general constitutional defenses had been raised by Curtis in a libel action instituted by the Alabama coach who was a state employee.

Evidence at trial was directed both to the truth of the article and to its preparation. The latter point was put in issue by the claim for punitive damages which required a finding of "malice" under Georgia law. The evidence showed that Burnett had indeed overheard a conversation between Butts and the Alabama coach, but the content of that conversation was hotly disputed. It was Butts' contention that the conversation had been general football talk and that nothing Burnett had overheard would have been of any particular value to an opposing coach. Expert witnesses supported Butts by analyzing Burnett's notes and the films of the game itself. The Saturday Evening Post's version of the game and of the players' remarks about the game was severely contradicted. [138]

The evidence on the preparation of the article, on which we shall focus in more detail later, cast serious doubt on the adequacy of the investigation underlying the article. It was Butts' contention that the magazine had departed greatly from the standards of good investigation and reporting and that this was especially reprehensible, amounting to reckless and wanton conduct, in light of the devastating nature of the article's assertions.

The jury was instructed that in order for the defense of truth to be sustained it was "necessary that the truth be substantially portrayed in those parts of the article which libel the plaintiff." The "sting of the libel" was said to be "the charge that the plaintiff rigged and fixed the 1962 Georgia-Alabama game by giving Coach Bryant [of Alabama] information which was calculated to or could have affected the outcome of the game." The jury was also instructed that it could award punitive damages "to deter the wrong-doer from repeating the trespass" in an amount within its sole discretion if it found that actual malice had been proved.[note 3]

The jury returned a verdict for $60,000 in general damages and for $3,000,000 in punitive damages. The trial court reduced the total to $460,000 by remittitur. Soon thereafter we handed down our decision in *New York Times* and Curtis immediately brought it to the attention of the trial court by a motion for new trial. The trial judge rejected Curtis' motion on two grounds. He [139] first held that *New York Times* was inapplicable because Butts was not a public official. He also held that "there was ample evidence from which a jury could have concluded that there was reckless disregard by defendant of whether the article was false or not."

Curtis appealed to the Court of Appeals for the Fifth Circuit which affirmed the judgment of the District Court by a two-to-one vote. The majority there did not reach the merits of petitioner's constitutional claim, holding that Curtis had "clearly waived any right it may have had to challenge the verdict and judgment on any of the constitutional grounds asserted in Times," 351 F.2d 702, 713, on the basis of *Michel v. Louisiana*, 350 U.S. 91. It found Curtis chargeable with knowledge of the constitutional limitations on libel law at the time it filed its pleadings below because of its "interlocking battery of able and distinguished attorneys" some of whom were involved in the *New York Times* litigation. This holding rendered the compensatory damage decision purely one of state law and no error was found in its application. Turning to the punitive damage award, the majority upheld it as stemming from the "enlightened conscience" of the jury as adjusted by the lawful action of the trial judge. It was in "complete accord" with the trial court's determination that the evidence justified the finding "that what the Post did was done with reckless disregard of whether the article was false or not." 351 F.2d, at 719.

Judge Rives dissented, arguing that the record did not support a finding of knowing waiver of constitutional defenses. He concluded that the *New York Times* rule was applicable because Butts was involved in activities of great interest to the public. He would have reversed because "the jury might well have understood the district court's charge to allow recovery on a showing of [140] intent to inflict harm or even the culpably negligent infliction of harm, rather than the intent to inflict harm through falsehood . . . ." 351 F.2d, at 723.

Rehearing was denied, 351 F.2d, at 733, and we granted certiorari, as indicated above. For reasons given below, we would affirm.

II

No. 150, *Associated Press v. Walker*, arose out of the distribution of a news dispatch giving an eyewitness account of events on the campus of the University of Mississippi on the night of September 30, 1962, when a massive riot erupted because of federal efforts to enforce a court decree ordering the enrollment of a Negro, James Meredith, as a student in the University. The dispatch stated that respondent Walker, who was present on the campus, had taken command of the violent crowd and had personally led a charge against federal marshals sent there to effectuate the court's decree and to assist in preserving order. It also described Walker as encouraging rioters to use violence and giving them technical advice on combating the effects of tear gas.

Walker was a private citizen at the time of the riot and publication. He had pursued a long and honorable career in the United States Army before resigning to engage in political activity, and had, in fact, been in command of the federal troops during the school segregation confrontation at Little Rock, Arkansas, in 1957. He was acutely interested in the issue of physical federal intervention, and had made a number of strong statements against such action which had received wide publicity. Walker had his own following, the "Friends of Walker," and could fairly be deemed a man of some political prominence.

Walker initiated this libel action in the state courts of Texas, seeking a total of $2,000,000 in compensatory and punitive damages. Associated Press raised both the [141] defense of truth and constitutional defenses. At trial both sides attempted to reconstruct the stormy events on the campus of the University of Mississippi. Walker admitted his presence on the campus and conceded that he had spoken to a group of students. He claimed, however, that he had counseled restraint and peaceful protest, and exercised no control whatever over the crowd which had rejected his plea. He denied categorically taking part in any charge against the federal marshals.

There was little evidence relating to the preparation of the news dispatch. It was clear, however, that the author of this dispatch, Van Savell, was actually present during the events described and had reported them almost immediately to the Associated Press office in Atlanta. A discrepancy was shown between an oral account given the office and a later written dispatch, but it related solely to whether Walker had spoken to the group before or after approaching the marshals. No other showing of improper preparation was attempted, nor was there any evidence of personal prejudice or incompetency on the part of Savell or the Associated Press.

The jury was instructed that an award of compensatory damages could be made if the dispatch was not substantially true,[note 4]and that punitive damages could be added if the article was actuated by "ill will, bad or evil motive, or that entire want of care which would raise the belief that the act or omission complained of was the result of a conscious indifference to the right or welfare of the person to be affected by it."

A verdict of $500,000 compensatory damages and $300,000 punitive damages was returned. The trial judge, however, found that there was "no evidence to support the jury's answers that there was actual malice" [142] and refused to enter the punitive award. He concluded that the failure further to investigate the minor discrepancy between the oral and written versions of the incident could not "be construed as that entire want of care which would amount to a conscious indifference to the rights of plaintiff. Negligence, it may have been; malice, it was not. Moreover, the mere fact that AP permitted a young reporter to cover the story of the riot is not evidence of malice." (Emphasis in original.) The trial judge also noted that this lack of "malice" would require a verdict for the Associated Press if *New York Times* were applicable. But he rejected its applicability since there were "no compelling reasons of public policy requiring additional defenses to suits for libel. Truth alone should be an adequate defense."

Both sides appealed and the Texas Court of Civil Appeals affirmed both the award of compensatory damages and the striking of punitive damages. It stated without elaboration that *New York Times* was inapplicable. As to the punitive damage award, the plea for reinstatement was refused because "in view of all the surrounding circumstances, the rapid and confused occurrence of events on the occasion in question, and in the light of all the evidence, we hold that appellee failed to prove malice . . . ." 393 S. W. 2d 671, 683.

The Supreme Court of Texas denied a writ of error, and we granted certiorari, as already indicated. For reasons given below, we would reverse.

III

Before we reach the constitutional arguments put forward by the respective petitioners, we must first determine whether Curtis has waived its right to assert such arguments by failing to assert them before trial. As our dispositions of *Rosenblatt v. Baer*, 383 U.S. 75, [143] and other cases involving constitutional questions indicate,[note 5] the mere failure to interpose such a defense prior to the announcement of a decision which might support it cannot prevent a litigant from later invoking such a ground. Of course it is equally clear that even constitutional objections may be waived by a failure to raise them at a proper time, *Michel v. Louisiana, supra,* at 99,[note 6] but an effective waiver must, as was said in *Johnson v. Zerbst,* 304 U.S. 458, 464, be one of a "known right or privilege."

Butts makes two arguments in support of his contention that Curtis' failure to raise constitutional defenses amounted to a knowing waiver. The first is that the general state of the law at the time of this trial was such that Curtis should, in the words of the Fifth Circuit majority, have seen "the handwriting on the wall." 351 F.2d, at 734. We cannot accept this contention. Although our decision in *New York Times* did draw upon earlier precedents in state law, e.g., *Coleman v. MacLennan,* 78 Kan. 711, 98 P. 281, and there were intimations in a prior opinion and the extra-judicial comments of one Justice,[note 7] that some applications of libel law might be in conflict with the guarantees of free speech and press, there was strong precedent indicating that civil libel actions [144] were immune from general constitutional scrutiny.[note 8] Given the state of the law prior to our decision in *New York Times,* we do not think it unreasonable for a lawyer trying a case of this kind, where the plaintiff was not even a public official under state law, to have looked solely to the defenses provided by state libel law. Nor do we think that the previous grant of certiorari in *New York Times* alone indicates a different conclusion. The questions presented for review there were premised on Sullivan's status as an elected public official, and elected officials traditionally have been subject to special rules of libel law.[note 9]

Butts' second contention is that whatever defenses might reasonably have been apparent to the average lawyer, some of Curtis' trial attorneys were involved in the *New York Times* litigation and thus should have been especially alert to constitutional contentions. This was the argument which swayed the Court of Appeals, but we do not find it convincing.

First, as a general matter, we think it inadvisable to determine whether a "right or privilege" is "known" by relying on information outside the record concerning the special legal knowledge of particular attorneys. Second, even a lawyer fully cognizant of the record and briefs in the *New York Times* litigation might reasonably have expected the resolution of that case to have no impact [145] on this litigation, since the arguments advanced there depended so heavily on the analogy to seditious libel. We think that it was our eventual resolution of *New York Times,* rather than its facts and the arguments presented by counsel, which brought out the constitutional question here. We would not hold that Curtis waived a "known right" before it was aware of the *New York Times* decision. It is agreed that Curtis' presentation of the constitutional issue after our decision in *New York Times* was prompt.

Our rejection of Butts' arguments is supported by factors which point to the justice of that conclusion. See *Hormel v. Helvering,* 312 U.S. 552, 556-557. Curtis' constitutional points were raised early enough so that this Court has had the benefit of some ventilation of them by the courts below. The resolution of the merits of Curtis' contentions by the District Court makes it evident that Butts was not prejudiced by the time at which Curtis raised its argument, for it cannot be asserted that an earlier interposition would have resulted in any different proceedings below.[note 10] Finally the constitutional protection which Butts contends that Curtis has waived safeguards a freedom which is the "matrix, the indispensable condition, of nearly every other form of freedom." *Palko v. Connecticut,* 302 U.S. 319, 327. Where the ultimate effect of sustaining a claim of waiver might be an imposition on that valued freedom, we are unwilling to find waiver in circumstances which fall short of being clear and compelling. Cf. *New York Times Co. v. Connor,* 365 F.2d 567, 572.

[146]

IV

We thus turn to a consideration, on the merits, of the constitutional claims raised by *Curtis* in *Butts* and by the Associated Press in *Walker*. Powerful arguments are brought to bear for the extension of the *New York Times* rule in both cases. In Butts it is contended that the facts are on all fours with those of *Rosenblatt v. Baer, supra*, since Butts was charged with the important responsibility of managing the athletic affairs of a state university. It is argued that while the Athletic Association is financially independent from the State and Butts was not technically a state employee, as was Baer, his role in state administration was so significant that this technical distinction from Rosenblatt should be ignored. Even if this factor is to be given some weight, we are told that the public interest in education in general, and in the conduct of the athletic affairs of educational institutions in particular, justifies constitutional protection of discussion of persons involved in it equivalent to the protection afforded discussion of public officials.

A similar argument is raised in the Walker case where the important public interest in being informed about the events and personalities involved in the Mississippi riot is pressed. In that case we are also urged to recognize that Walker's claims to the protection of libel laws are limited since he thrust himself into the "vortex" of the controversy.

We are urged by the respondents, Butts and Walker, to recognize society's "pervasive and strong interest in preventing and redressing attacks upon reputation," and the "important social values which underlie the law of defamation." *Rosenblatt v. Baer, supra*, at 86. It is pointed out that the publicity in these instances was not directed at employees of government and that these cases cannot be analogized to seditious libel prosecutions. *Id.*, at 92 (STEWART, J., concurring). We are [147] told that "the rule that permits satisfaction of the deep-seated need for vindication of honor is not a mere historic relic, but promotes the law's civilizing function of providing an acceptable substitute for violence in the settlement of disputes," *Afro-American Publishing Co. v. Jaffe*, 125 U. S. App. D. C. 70, 81, 366 F.2d 649, 660, and that:

"Newspapers, magazines, and broadcasting companies are businesses conducted for profit and often make very large ones. Like other enterprises that inflict damage in the course of performing a service highly useful to the public . . . they must pay the freight; and injured persons should not be relegated [to remedies which] make collection of their claims difficult or impossible unless strong policy considerations demand." *Buckley v. New York Post Corp.*, 373 F.2d 175, 182.

We fully recognize the force of these competing considerations and the fact that an accommodation between them is necessary not only in these cases, but in all libel actions arising from a publication concerning public issues. In *Time, Inc. v. Hill*, 385 U.S. 374, 388, we held that "the guarantees for speech and press are not the preserve of political expression or comment upon public affairs . . ." and affirmed that freedom of discussion "must embrace all issues about which information is needed or appropriate to enable the members of society to cope with the exigencies of their period." *Thornhill v. Alabama*, 310 U.S. 88, 102. This carries out the intent of the Founders who felt that a free press would advance "truth, science, morality, and arts in general" as well as responsible government. Letter to the Inhabitants of Quebec, 1 Journals of the Continental Cong. 108. From the point of view of deciding whether a constitutional interest of free speech and press is properly involved in the resolution of a libel question a rational [148] distinction "cannot be founded on the assumption that criticism of private citizens who seek to lead in the determination of . . . policy will be less important to the public interest than will criticism of government officials." *Pauling v. Globe-Democrat Publishing Co.*, 362 F.2d 188, 196.

On the other hand, to take the rule found appropriate in *New York Times* to resolve the "tension" between the particular constitutional interest there involved and the interests of personal reputation and press responsibility, *Rosenblatt v. Baer, supra,* at 86, as being applicable throughout the realm of the broader constitutional interest, would be to attribute to this aspect of *New York Times* an unintended inexorability at the threshold of this new constitutional development. In *Time, Inc. v. Hill, supra,* at 390, we counseled against "blind application of *New York Times Co. v. Sullivan*" and considered "the factors which arise in the particular context." Here we must undertake a parallel evaluation.[note 11]

The modern history of the guarantee of freedom of speech and press mainly has been one of a search for the outer limits of that right. From the fountainhead opinions of Justices Holmes and Brandeis in Schenck, Abrams, and Whitney,[note 12] which considered the problem when the disruptive effects of speech might strip the protection from the speaker, to our recent decision in *Adderley v. Florida,* 385 U.S. 39, where we found freedom of speech not to include a freedom to trespass, the Court's primary concern has been to determine the extent of the right and the surrounding safeguards necessary to give it "breathing space." *NAACP v.* [149] *Button,* 371 U.S. 415, 433. That concern has perhaps omitted from searching consideration the "real problem" of defining or delimiting the right itself. See Freund, Mr. Justice Black and the Judicial Function, 14 U. C. L. A. L. Rev. 467, 471.

It is significant that the guarantee of freedom of speech and press falls between the religious guarantees and the guarantee of the right to petition for redress of grievances in the text of the First Amendment, the principles of which are carried to the States by the Fourteenth Amendment. It partakes of the nature of both, for it is as much a guarantee to individuals of their personal right to make their thoughts public and put them before the community, see Holt, Of the Liberty of the Press, in Nelson, Freedom of the Press from Hamilton to the Warren Court 18-19, as it is a social necessity required for the "maintenance of our political system and an open society." *Time, Inc. v. Hill, supra,* at 389. It is because of the personal nature of this right that we have rejected all manner of prior restraint on publication, *Near v. Minnesota,* 283 U.S. 697, despite strong arguments that if the material was unprotected the time of suppression was immaterial. Pound, Equitable Relief Against Defamation and Injuries to Personality, 29 Harv. L. Rev. 640. The dissemination of the individual's opinions on matters of public interest is for us, in the historic words of the Declaration of Independence, an "unalienable right" that "governments are instituted among men to secure." History shows us that the Founders were not always convinced that unlimited discussion of public issues would be "for the benefit of all of us" [note 13] but that they firmly adhered to the proposition that the "true liberty of the press" permitted "every man to publish [150] his opinion." *Respublica v. Oswald,* 1 Dall. 319, 325 (Pa.).

The fact that dissemination of information and opinion on questions of public concern is ordinarily a legitimate, protected and indeed cherished activity does not mean, however, that one may in all respects carry on that activity exempt from sanctions designed to safeguard the legitimate interests of others. A business "is not immune from regulation because it is an agency of the press. The publisher of a newspaper has no special immunity from the application of general laws. He has no special privilege to invade the rights and liberties of others." *Associated Press v. Labor Board*, 301 U.S. 103, 132-133. Federal securities regulation, [note 14] mail fraud statutes,[note 15] and common-law actions for deceit and misrepresentation [note 16] are only some examples of our understanding that the right to communicate information of public interest is not "unconditional." See Note, Freedom of Expression in a Commercial Context, 78 Harv. L. Rev. 1191. However, as our decision in *New York Times* makes explicit, while protected activity may in some respects be subjected to sanctions, it is not open to all forms of regulation. The guarantees of freedom of speech and press were not designed to prevent "the censorship of the press merely, but any action of the government by means of which it might prevent such free and general discussion of public matters as seems absolutely essential . . . ." 2 Cooley, Constitutional Limitations 886 (8th ed.). Our touchstones are that acceptable [151] limitations must neither affect "the impartial distribution of news" and ideas, *Associated Press v. Labor Board, supra,* at 133, nor because of their history or impact constitute a special burden on the press, *Grosjean v. American Press Co., Inc.,* 297 U.S. 233, nor deprive our free society of the stimulating benefit of varied ideas because their purveyors fear physical or economic retribution solely because of what they choose to think and publish.

The history of libel law leaves little doubt that it originated in soil entirely different from that which nurtured these constitutional values. Early libel was primarily a criminal remedy, the function of which was to make punishable any writing which tended to bring into disrepute the state, established religion, or any individual likely to be provoked to a breach of the peace because of the words. Truth was no defense in such actions and while a proof of truth might prevent recovery in a civil action, this limitation is more readily explained as a manifestation of judicial reluctance to enrich an undeserving plaintiff than by the supposition that the defendant was protected by the truth of the publication. The same truthful statement might be the basis of a criminal libel action. See *Commonwealth v. Clap,* 4 Mass. 163; see generally Veeder, The History and Theory of the Law of Defamation, 3 Col. L. Rev. 546, 4 Col. L. Rev. 33.

The law of libel has, of course, changed substantially since the early days of the Republic, and this change is "the direct consequence of the friction between it . . . and the highly cherished right of free speech." *State v. Browne,* 86 N. J. Super. 217, 228, 206 A. 2d 591, 597. The emphasis has shifted from criminal to civil remedies, from the protection of absolute social values to the safeguarding of valid personal interests. Truth has become an absolute defense in almost all cases,[note 17] and privileges designed to foster free communication are almost universally [152] recognized.[note 18] But the basic theory of libel has not changed, and words defamatory of another are still placed "in the same class with the use of explosives or the keeping of dangerous animals." Prosser, The Law of Torts § 108, at 792. Thus some antithesis between freedom of speech and press and libel actions persists, for libel remains premised on the content of speech and limits the freedom of the publisher to express certain sentiments, at least without guaranteeing legal proof of their substantial accuracy.

While the truth of the underlying facts might be said to mark the line between publications which are of significant social value and those which might be suppressed without serious social harm and thus resolve the antithesis on a neutral ground, we have rejected, in prior cases involving materials and persons commanding justified and important public interest, the argument that a finding of falsity alone should strip protections from the publisher. *New York Times Co. v. Sullivan, supra,* at 272. We have recognized "the inevitability of some error in the situation presented in free debate," *Time, Inc. v. Hill, supra,* at 406 (opinion of this writer), and that "putting to the pre-existing prejudices of a jury the determination of what is 'true' may effectively institute a system of censorship."

Our resolution of *New York Times Co. v. Sullivan,* in the context of the numerous statutes and cases which allow ideologically neutral, and generally applicable regulatory measures to be applied to publication, makes clear, however, that neither the interests of the publisher nor those of society necessarily preclude a damage award [153] based on improper conduct which creates a false publication. It is the conduct element, therefore, on which we must principally focus if we are successfully to resolve the antithesis between civil libel actions and the freedom of speech and press. Impositions based on misconduct can be neutral with respect to content of the speech involved, free of historical taint, and adjusted to strike a fair balance between the interests of the community in free circulation of information and those of individuals in seeking recompense for harm done by the circulation of defamatory falsehood.

In *New York Times* we were adjudicating in an area which lay close to seditious libel, and history dictated extreme caution in imposing liability. The plaintiff in that case was an official whose position in government was such "that the public [had] an independent interest in the qualifications and performance of the person who [held] it." *Rosenblatt v. Baer, supra,* at 86. Such officials usually enjoy a privilege against libel actions for their utterances, see, e.g., *Barr v. Matteo,* 360 U.S. 564, and there were analogous considerations involved in *New York Times, supra,* at 282. Thus we invoked "the hypothesis that speech can rebut speech, propaganda will answer propaganda, free debate of ideas will result in the wisest governmental policies," *Dennis v. United States,* 341 U.S. 494, 503, and limited recovery to those cases where "calculated falsehood" placed the publisher "at odds with the premises of democratic government and with the orderly manner in which economic, social, or political change is to be effected." *Garrison v. Louisiana,* 379 U.S. 64, 75. That is to say, such officials were permitted to recover in libel only when they could prove that the publication involved was deliberately falsified, or published recklessly despite the publisher's awareness of probable falsity. Investigatory failures alone were held insufficient to satisfy this standard. See New York [154] Times, at 286-288, 292; *Garrison v. Louisiana, supra,* at 73-75, 79.

In the cases we decide today none of the particular considerations involved in *New York Times* is present. These actions cannot be analogized to prosecutions for seditious libel. Neither plaintiff has any position in government which would permit a recovery by him to be viewed as a vindication of governmental policy. Neither was entitled to a special privilege protecting his utterances against accountability in libel. We are prompted, therefore, to seek guidance from the rules of liability which prevail in our society with respect to compensation of persons injured by the improper performance of a legitimate activity by another. Under these rules, a departure from the kind of care society may expect from a reasonable man performing such activity leaves the actor open to a judicial shifting of loss. In defining these rules, and especially in formulating the standards for determining the degree of care to be expected in the circumstances, courts have consistently given much attention to the importance of defendants' activities. Prosser, The Law of Torts § 31, at 151. The courts have also, especially in libel cases, investigated the plaintiff's position to determine whether he has a legitimate call upon the court for protection in light of his prior activities and means of self-defense. See *Brewer v. Hearst Publishing Co.*, 185 F.2d 846; *Flanagan v. Nicholson Publishing Co.*, 137 La. 588, 68 So. 964. We note that the public interest in the circulation of the materials here involved, and the publisher's interest in circulating them, is not less than that involved in *New York Times*. And both Butts and Walker commanded a substantial amount of independent public interest at the time of the publications; both, in our opinion, would have been labeled "public figures" under ordinary tort rules. See *Spahn v. Julian Messner, Inc.*, 18 N. Y. 2d 324, 221 N. E. 2d 543, remanded [155] on other grounds, 387 U.S. 239. Butts may have attained that status by position alone and Walker by his purposeful activity amounting to a thrusting of his personality into the "vortex" of an important public controversy, but both commanded sufficient continuing public interest and had sufficient access to the means of counterargument to be able "to expose through discussion the falsehood and fallacies" of the defamatory statements. *Whitney v. California*, 274 U.S. 357, 377 (Brandeis, J., dissenting).

These similarities and differences between libel actions involving persons who are public officials and libel actions involving those circumstanced as were Butts and Walker, viewed in light of the principles of liability which are of general applicability in our society, lead us to the conclusion that libel actions of the present kind cannot be left entirely to state libel laws, unlimited by any overriding constitutional safeguard, but that the rigorous federal requirements of *New York Times* are not the only appropriate accommodation of the conflicting interests at stake. We consider and would hold that a "public figure" who is not a public official may also recover damages for a defamatory falsehood whose substance makes substantial danger to reputation apparent, on a showing of highly unreasonable conduct constituting an extreme departure from the standards of investigation and reporting ordinarily adhered to by responsible publishers. Cf. Sulzberger, Responsibility and Freedom, in Nelson, Freedom of the Press from Hamilton to the Warren Court 409, 412.

Nothing in this opinion is meant to affect the holdings in *New York Times* and its progeny, including our recent decision in *Time, Inc. v. Hill*.[note 19] [156]

V

Having set forth the standard by which we believe the constitutionality of the damage awards in these cases must be judged, we turn now, as the Court did in *New York Times*, to the question whether the evidence and findings below meet that standard. We find the standard satisfied in No. 37, *Butts*, and not satisfied by either the evidence or the findings in No. 150, *Walker*.

The Butts jury was instructed, in considering punitive damages, to assess "the reliability, the nature of the sources of the defendant's information, its acceptance or rejection of the sources, and its care in checking upon assertions." These considerations were said to be relevant to a determination whether defendant had proceeded with "wanton and reckless indifference." In this light we consider that the jury must have decided that the investigation undertaken by the Saturday Evening Post, upon which much evidence and argument was centered,[note 20] was grossly inadequate in the circumstances. The impact of a jury instruction "is not to be ascertained by merely considering isolated statements but by taking into view all the instructions given and the tendencies of the proof in the case to which they could possibly be applied." *Seaboard Air Line R. Co. v. Padgett*, 236 U.S. 668, 672.

This jury finding was found to be supported by the evidence by the trial judge and the majority in the Fifth Circuit. Given the extended history of the case, the amount of the evidence pointing to serious deficiencies in Investigatory procedures, and the severe harm inflicted on Butts, we would not feel justified in ordering a retrial of the compensatory damage issue, either on the theory that this aspect of the case was submitted to the jury under the issue of "truth,"[note 21] or on the very slim possibility that the jury finding regarding punitive damages might have been based on Curtis' attitude toward Butts rather than on Curtis' conduct.

The evidence showed that the Butts story was in no sense "hot news" and the editors of the magazine recognized the need for a thorough investigation of the serious charges. Elementary precautions were, nevertheless, ignored. The Saturday Evening Post knew that Burnett had been placed on probation in connection with bad check charges, but proceeded to publish the story on the basis of his affidavit without substantial independent support. Burnett's notes were not even viewed by any of the magazine's personnel prior to publication. John Carmichael who was supposed to have been with Burnett when the phone call was overheard was not interviewed. No attempt was made to screen the films of the game to see if Burnett's information was accurate, and no attempt was made to find out whether Alabama had adjusted its plans after the alleged divulgence of information. [158]

The Post writer assigned to the story was not a football expert and no attempt was made to check the story with someone knowledgeable in the sport. At trial such experts indicated that the information in the Burnett notes was either such that it would be evident to any opposing coach from game films regularly exchanged or valueless. Those assisting the Post writer in his investigation were already deeply involved in another libel action, based on a different article, brought against Curtis Publishing Co. by the Alabama coach and unlikely to be the source of a complete and objective investigation. The Saturday Evening Post was anxious to change its image by instituting a policy of "sophisticated muckraking," and the pressure to produce a successful expose might have induced a stretching of standards. In short, the evidence is ample to support a finding of highly unreasonable conduct constituting an extreme departure from the standards of investigation and reporting ordinarily adhered to by responsible publishers.

The situation in Walker is considerably different. There the trial court found the evidence insufficient to support more than a finding of even ordinary negligence and the Court of Civil Appeals supported the trial court's view of the evidence. Ordinarily we would, under the governing constitutional standard, reverse the decision below on the concurrent findings rule. *Graver Tank & Mfg. Co. v. Linde Air Products Co.*, 336 U.S. 271, 275. But, as in *New York Times,* we think it better to face for ourselves the question whether there is sufficient evidence to support the finding we would require.

In contrast to the Butts article, the dispatch which concerns us in Walker was news which required immediate dissemination. The Associated Press received the information from a correspondent who was present at the scene of the events and gave every indication of being trustworthy and competent. His dispatches in this instance, [159] with one minor exception, were internally consistent and would not have seemed unreasonable to one familiar with General Walker's prior publicized statements on the underlying controversy. Considering the necessity for rapid dissemination, nothing in this series of events gives the slightest hint of a severe departure from accepted publishing standards. We therefore conclude that General Walker should not be entitled to damages from the Associated Press.

VI

We come finally to Curtis' contention that whether or not it can be required to compensate Butts for any injury it may have caused him, it cannot be subjected to an assessment for punitive damages limited only by the "enlightened conscience" of the community. Curtis recognizes that the Constitution presents no general bar to the assessment of punitive damages in a civil case, *Day v. Woodworth*, 13 How. 363, 370-371, but contends that an unlimited punitive award against a magazine publisher constitutes an effective prior restraint by giving the jury the power to destroy the publisher's business. We cannot accept this reasoning. Publishers like Curtis engage in a wide variety of activities which may [160] lead to tort suits where punitive damages are a possibility. To exempt a publisher, because of the nature of his calling, from an imposition generally exacted from other members of the community, would be to extend a protection not required by the constitutional guarantee. *Associated Press v. Labor Board*, 301 U.S. 103. We think the constitutional guarantee of freedom of speech and press is adequately served by judicial control over excessive jury verdicts, manifested in this instance by the trial court's remittitur, and by the general rule that a verdict based on jury prejudice cannot be sustained even when punitive damages are warranted. See, e.g., *Minneapolis, St. P. & S. S. M. R. Co. v. Moquin*, 283 U.S. 520, 521.

Despite this conclusion, it might be argued that an award of punitive damages cannot be justified constitutionally by the same degree of misconduct required to support a compensatory award. The usual rule in libel actions, and other state-created tort actions, is that a higher degree of fault is necessary to sustain a punitive imposition than a compensatory award. And it might be asserted that the need to compensate the injured plaintiff is not relevant to the issue of punitive damages in libel since an award of general damages compensates for any possible pecuniary and intangible harm. Thus the argument would be that the strong speech and press interest in publishing material on public issues, which we have recognized as parallel to the interest in publishing political criticism present in *New York Times*, must be served by a limitation on punitive damages restricting them to cases of "actual malice" as defined in *New York Times* and *Garrison v. Louisiana, supra*. We find the force of any such argument quite insufficient to overcome the compelling contrary considerations, and there is, moreover, nothing in any of our past cases which suggests that compensatory and punitive damages are subject to different constitutional standards of misconduct. [161]

Where a publisher's departure from standards of press responsibility is severe enough to strip from him the constitutional protection our decision acknowledges, we think it entirely proper for the State to act not only for the protection of the individual injured but to safeguard all those similarly situated against like abuse. Moreover, punitive damages require a finding of "ill will" under general libel law and it is not unjust that a publisher be forced to pay for the "venting of his spleen" in a manner which does not meet even the minimum standards required for constitutional protection. Especially in those cases where circumstances outside the publication itself reduce its impact sufficiently to make a compensatory imposition an inordinately light burden, punitive damages serve a wholly legitimate purpose in the protection of individual reputation. We would hold, therefore, that misconduct sufficient to justify the award of compensatory damages also justifies the imposition of a punitive award, subject of course to the limitation that such award is not demonstrated to be founded on the mere prejudice of the jury. As we have already noted (*supra*, pp. 156-158) the case on punitive damages was put to the jury under instructions which satisfied the constitutional test we would apply in cases of this kind, and the evidence amply supported the jury's findings.[note 23]

The judgment of the Court of Appeals for the Fifth Circuit in No. 37 is affirmed.

The judgment of the [162] Texas Court of Civil Appeals in No. 150 is reversed and the case is remanded to that court for further proceedings not inconsistent with the opinions that have been filed herein by THE CHIEF JUSTICE, MR. JUSTICE BLACK, and MR. JUSTICE BRENNAN.

16 BRANDENBURG V. OHIO, 395 U.S. 444 (1969)
395 U.S. 444
BRANDENBURG v. OHIO.
APPEAL FROM THE SUPREME COURT OF OHIO.
No. 492.
Argued February 27, 1969
Decided June 9, 1969

Appellant, a Ku Klux Klan leader, was convicted under the Ohio Criminal Syndicalism statute for "advocat[ing] . . . the duty, necessity, or propriety of crime, sabotage, violence, or unlawful methods of terrorism as a means of accomplishing industrial or political reform" and for "voluntarily assembl[ing] with any society, group or assemblage of persons formed to teach or advocate the doctrines of criminal syndicalism." Neither the indictment nor the trial judge's instructions refined the statute's definition of the crime in terms of mere advocacy not distinguished from incitement to imminent lawless action. Held: Since the statute, by its words and as applied, purports to punish mere advocacy and to forbid, on pain of criminal punishment, assembly with others merely to advocate the described type of action, it falls within the condemnation of the First and Fourteenth Amendments. Freedoms of speech and press do not permit a State to forbid advocacy of the use of force or of law violation except where such advocacy is directed to inciting or producing imminent lawless action and is likely to incite or produce such action. Whitney v. California, 274 U.S. 357 , overruled.

Reversed.

Allen Brown argued the cause for appellant. With him on the briefs were Norman Dorsen, Melvin L. Wulf, Eleanor Holmes Norton, and Bernard A. Berkman.

Leonard Kirschner argued the cause for appellee. With him on the brief was Melvin G. Rueger.

Paul W. Brown, Attorney General of Ohio, pro se, and Leo J. Conway, Assistant Attorney General, filed a brief for the Attorney General as amicus curiae.

PER CURIAM.

The appellant, a leader of a Ku Klux Klan group, was convicted under the Ohio Criminal Syndicalism statute for "advocat[ing] . . . the duty, necessity, or propriety [395 U.S. 444, 445] of crime, sabotage, violence, or unlawful methods of terrorism as a means of accomplishing industrial or political reform" and for "voluntarily assembl[ing] with any society, group, or assemblage of persons formed to teach or advocate the doctrines of criminal syndicalism." Ohio Rev. Code Ann. 2923.13. He was fined $1,000 and sentenced to one to 10 years' imprisonment. The appellant challenged the constitutionality of the criminal syndicalism statute under the First and Fourteenth Amendments to the United States Constitution, but the intermediate appellate court of Ohio affirmed his conviction without opinion. The Supreme Court of Ohio dismissed his appeal, sua sponte, "for the reason that no substantial constitutional question exists herein." It did not file an opinion or explain its conclusions. Appeal was taken to this Court, and we noted probable jurisdiction. 393 U.S. 948 (1968). We reverse.

The record shows that a man, identified at trial as the appellant, telephoned an announcer-reporter on the staff of a Cincinnati television station and invited him to come to a Ku Klux Klan "rally" to be held at a farm in Hamilton County. With the cooperation of the organizers, the reporter and a cameraman attended the meeting and filmed the events. Portions of the films were later broadcast on the local station and on a national network.

The prosecution's case rested on the films and on testimony identifying the appellant as the person who communicated with the reporter and who spoke at the rally. The State also introduced into evidence several articles appearing in the film, including a pistol, a rifle, a shotgun, ammunition, a Bible, and a red hood worn by the speaker in the films.

One film showed 12 hooded figures, some of whom carried firearms. They were gathered around a large wooden cross, which they burned. No one was present [395 U.S. 444, 446] other than the participants and the newsmen who made the film. Most of the words uttered during the scene were incomprehensible when the film was projected, but scattered phrases could be understood that were derogatory of Negroes and, in one instance, of Jews. 1 Another scene on the same film showed the appellant, in Klan regalia, making a speech. The speech, in full, was as follows:

"This is an organizers' meeting. We have had quite a few members here today which are - we have hundreds, hundreds of members throughout the State of Ohio. I can quote from a newspaper clipping from the Columbus, Ohio Dispatch, five weeks ago Sunday morning. The Klan has more members in the State of Ohio than does any other organization. We're not a revengent organization, but if our President, our Congress, our Supreme Court, continues to suppress the white, Caucasian race, it's possible that there might have to be some revengeance taken.

"We are marching on Congress July the Fourth, four hundred thousand strong. From there we are dividing into two groups, one group to march on St. Augustine, Florida, the other group to march into Mississippi. Thank you." [395 U.S. 444, 447]

The second film showed six hooded figures one of whom, later identified as the appellant, repeated a speech very similar to that recorded on the first film. The reference to the possibility of "revengeance" was omittted[�], and one sentence was added: "Personally, I believe the nigger should be returned to Africa, the Jew returned to Israel." Though some of the figures in the films carried weapons, the speaker did not.

The Ohio Criminal Syndicalism Statute was enacted in 1919. From 1917 to 1920, identical or quite similar laws were adopted by 20 States and two territories. E. Dowell, A

History of Criminal Syndicalism Legislation in the United States 21 (1939). In 1927, this Court sustained the constitutionality of California's Criminal Syndicalism Act, Cal. Penal Code 11400-11402, the text of which is quite similar to that of the laws of Ohio. Whitney v. California, 274 U.S. 357 (1927). The Court upheld the statute on the ground that, without more, "advocating" violent means to effect political and economic change involves such danger to the security of the State that the State may outlaw it. Cf. Fiske v. Kansas, 274 U.S. 380 (1927). But Whitney has been thoroughly discredited by later decisions. See Dennis v. United States, 341 U.S. 494 , at 507 (1951). These later decisions have fashioned the principle that the constitutional guarantees of free speech and free press do not permit a State to forbid or proscribe advocacy of the use of force or of law violation except where such advocacy is directed to inciting or producing imminent lawless action and is likely to incite or produce such action. 2 As we[395 U.S. 444, 448] said in Noto v. United States, 367 U.S. 290, 297 -298 (1961), "the mere abstract teaching . . . of the moral propriety or even moral necessity for a resort to force and violence, is not the same as preparing a group for violent action and steeling it to such action." See also Herndon v. Lowry,301 U.S. 242, 259 - 261 (1937); Bond v. Floyd, 385 U.S. 116, 134 (1966). A statute which fails to draw this distinction impermissibly intrudes upon the freedoms guaranteed by the First and Fourteenth Amendments. It sweeps within its condemnation speech which our Constitution has immunized from governmental control. Cf. Yates v. United States, 354 U.S. 298 (1957); De Jonge v. Oregon, 299 U.S. 353 (1937); Stromberg v. California, 283 U.S. 359 (1931). See also United States v. Robel, 389 U.S. 258(1967); Keyishian v. Board of Regents, 385 U.S. 589 (1967); Elfbrandt v. Russell, 384 U.S. 11 (1966); Aptheker v. Secretary of State, 378 U.S. 500 (1964); Baggett v. Bullitt, 377 U.S. 360 (1964).

Measured by this test, Ohio's Criminal Syndicalism Act cannot be sustained. The Act punishes persons who "advocate or teach the duty, necessity, or propriety" of violence "as a means of accomplishing industrial or political reform"; or who publish or circulate or display any book or paper containing such advocacy; or who "justify" the commission of violent acts "with intent to exemplify, spread or advocate the propriety of the doctrines of criminal syndicalism"; or who "voluntarily assemble" with a group formed "to teach or advocate the doctrines of criminal syndicalism." Neither the indictment nor the trial judge's instructions to the jury in any way refined the statute's bald definition of the crime [395 U.S. 444, 449] in terms of mere advocacy not distinguished from incitement to imminent lawless action. 3

Accordingly, we are here confronted with a statute which, by its own words and as applied, purports to punish mere advocacy and to forbid, on pain of criminal punishment, assembly with others merely to advocate the described type of action. 4 Such a statute falls within the condemnation of the First and Fourteenth Amendments. The contrary teaching of Whitney v. California, supra, cannot be supported, and that decision is therefore overruled.

Reversed.

Footnotes

[Footnote �] ERRATA: "omittted" should be "omitted."

[Footnote 1] The significant portions that could be understood were:

"How far is the nigger going to - yeah."

"This is what we are going to do to the niggers."

"A dirty nigger."

"Send the Jews back to Israel."

"Let's give them back to the dark garden."

"Save America."

"Let's go back to constitutional betterment."

"Bury the niggers."

"We intend to do our part."

"Give us our state rights."

"Freedom for the whites."

"Nigger will have to fight for every inch he gets from now on."

[Footnote 2] It was on the theory that the Smith Act, 54 Stat. 670, 18 U.S.C. 2385, embodied such a principle and that it had been applied only in conformity with it that this Court sustained the Act's constitutionality. Dennis v. United States, 341 U.S. 494 (1951). That this was the basis for Dennis was emphasized in Yates v. United States, 354 U.S. 298, 320 -324 (1957), in which the Court overturned convictions [395 U.S. 444, 448] for advocacy of the forcible overthrow of the Government under the Smith Act, because the trial judge's instructions had allowed conviction for mere advocacy, unrelated to its tendency to produce forcible action.

[Footnote 3] The first count of the indictment charged that appellant "did unlawfully by word of mouth advocate the necessity, or propriety of crime, violence, or unlawful methods of terrorism as a means of accomplishing political reform . . . ." The second count charged that appellant "did unlawfully voluntarily assemble with a group or assemblage of persons formed to advocate the doctrines of criminal syndicalism . . . ." The trial judge's charge merely followed the language of the indictment. No construction of the statute by the Ohio courts has brought it within constitutionally permissible limits. The Ohio Supreme Court has considered the statute in only one previous case, State v. Kassay, 126 Ohio St. 177, 184 N. E. 521 (1932), where the constitutionality of the statute was sustained.

[Footnote 4] Statutes affecting the right of assembly, like those touching on freedom of speech, must observe the established distinctions between mere advocacy and incitement to imminent lawless action, for as Chief Justice Hughes wrote in De Jonge v. Oregon, supra, at 364:

"The right of peaceable assembly is a right cognate to those of free speech and free press and is equally fundamental." See also United States v. Cruikshank, 92 U.S. 542, 552 (1876); Hague v. CIO, 307 U.S. 496, 513 , 519 (1939); NAACP v. Alabama ex rel. Patterson, 357 U.S. 449, 460 -461 (1958).

17 NEW YORK TIMES CO. V. UNITED STATES
403 U.S. 713
ARGUED JUNE 26, 1971
DECIDED JUNE 30, 1971

[Together with No. 1885, United States v. Washington Post Co. et al., on certiorari to the United States Court of Appeals for the District of Columbia Circuit.]

The United States, which brought these actions to enjoin publication in the New York Times and in the Washington Post of certain classified material, has not met the "heavy burden of showing justification for the enforcement of such a [prior] restraint."

PER CURIAM.

We granted certiorari in these cases in which the United States seeks to enjoin the New York Times and the Washington Post from publishing the contents of a classified study entitled "History of U.S. Decision-Making Process on Viet Nam Policy." Post, pp. 942, 943.

"Any system of prior restraints of expression comes to this Court bearing a heavy presumption against its constitutional validity." Bantam Books, Inc. v. Sullivan, 372 U.S. 58, 70 (1963); see also Near v. Minnesota, 283 U.S. 697 (1931). The Government "thus carries a heavy burden of showing justification for the imposition of such a restraint." Organization for a Better Austin v. Keefe, 402 U.S. 415, 419(1971). The District Court for the Southern District of New York in the New York Times case and the District Court for the District of Columbia and the Court of Appeals for the District of Columbia Circuit in the Washington Post case held that the Government had not met that burden. We agree.

The judgment of the Court of Appeals for the District of Columbia Circuit is therefore affirmed. The order of the Court of Appeals for the Second Circuit is reversed and the case is remanded with directions to enter a judgment affirming the judgment of the District Court for the Southern District of New York. The stays entered June 25, 1971, by the Court are vacated. The judgments shall issue forthwith.

So ordered.

MR. JUSTICE BLACK, with whom MR. JUSTICE DOUGLAS joins, concurring.

I adhere to the view that the Government's case against the Washington Post should have been dismissed and that the injunction against the New York Times should have been vacated without oral argument when the cases were first presented to this Court. I believe [403 U.S. 713, 715] that every moment's continuance of the injunctions against these newspapers amounts to a flagrant, indefensible, and continuing violation of the First Amendment. Furthermore, after oral argument, I agree completely that we must affirm the judgment of the Court of Appeals for the District of Columbia Circuit and reverse the judgment of the Court of Appeals for the Second Circuit for the reasons stated by my Brothers DOUGLAS and BRENNAN. In my view it is unfortunate that some of my Brethren are apparently willing to hold that the publication of news may sometimes be enjoined. Such a holding would make a shambles of the First Amendment.

Our Government was launched in 1789 with the adoption of the Constitution. The Bill of Rights, including the First Amendment, followed in 1791. Now, for the first time in the 182 years since the founding of the Republic, the federal courts are asked to hold that the First Amendment does not mean what it says, but rather means that the Government can halt the publication of current news of vital importance to the people of this country.

In seeking injunctions against these newspapers and in its presentation to the Court, the Executive Branch seems to have forgotten the essential purpose and history of the First Amendment. When the Constitution was adopted, many people strongly opposed it because the document contained no Bill of Rights to safeguard certain basic freedoms. 1 They especially feared that the [403 U.S. 713, 716] new powers granted to a central government might be interpreted to permit the government to curtail freedom of religion, press, assembly, and speech. In response to an overwhelming public clamor, James Madison offered a series of amendments to satisfy citizens that these great liberties would remain safe and beyond the power of government to abridge. Madison proposed what later became the First Amendment in three parts, two of which are set out below, and one of which proclaimed: "The people shall not be deprived or abridged of their right to speak, to write, or to publish their sentiments; and the freedom of the press, as one of the great bulwarks of liberty, shall be inviolable." 2 (Emphasis added.) The amendments were offered to curtail and restrict the general powers granted to the Executive, Legislative, and Judicial Branches two years before in the original Constitution. The Bill of Rights changed the original Constitution into a new charter under which no branch of government could abridge the people's freedoms of press, speech, religion, and assembly. Yet the Solicitor General argues and some members of the Court appear to agree that the general powers of the Government adopted in the original Constitution should be interpreted to limit and restrict the specific and emphatic guarantees of the Bill of Rights adopted later. I can imagine no greater perversion of history. Madison and the other Framers of the First Amendment, able men [403 U.S. 713, 717] that they were, wrote in language they earnestly believed could never be misunderstood: "Congress shall make no law . . . abridging the freedom . . . of the press . . . ." Both the history and language of the First Amendment support the view that the press must be left free to publish news, whatever the source, without censorship, injunctions, or prior restraints.

In the First Amendment the Founding Fathers gave the free press the protection it must have to fulfill its essential role in our democracy. The press was to serve the governed, not the governors. The Government's power to censor the press was abolished so that the press would remain forever free to censure the Government. The press was protected so that it could bare the secrets of government and inform the people. Only a free and unrestrained press can effectively expose deception in government. And paramount among the responsibilities of a free press is the duty to prevent any part of the government from deceiving the people and sending them off to distant lands to die of foreign fevers and foreign shot and shell. In my view, far from deserving condemnation for their courageous reporting, the New York Times, the Washington Post, and other newspapers should be commended for serving the purpose that the Founding Fathers saw so clearly. In revealing the workings of government that led to the Vietnam war, the newspapers nobly did precisely that which the Founders hoped and trusted they would do.

The Government's case here is based on premises entirely different from those that guided the Framers of the First Amendment. The Solicitor General has carefully and emphatically stated:

"Now, Mr. Justice [BLACK], your construction of . . . [the First Amendment] is well known, and I certainly respect it. You say that no law means no law, and that should be obvious. I can only [403 U.S. 713, 718] say, Mr. Justice, that to me it is equally obvious that `no law' does not mean `no law', and I would seek to persuade the Court that is true. . . . [T]here are other parts of the Constitution that grant powers and responsibilities to the Executive, and . . . the First Amendment was not intended to make it impossible for the Executive to function or to protect the security of the United States." 3

And the Government argues in its brief that in spite of the First Amendment, "[t]he authority of the Executive Department to protect the nation against publication of information whose disclosure would endanger the national security stems from two interrelated sources: the constitutional power of the President over the conduct of foreign affairs and his authority as Commander-in-Chief." 4

In other words, we are asked to hold that despite the First Amendment's emphatic command, the Executive Branch, the Congress, and the Judiciary can make laws enjoining publication of current news and abridging freedom of the press in the name of "national security." The Government does not even attempt to rely on any act of Congress. Instead it makes the bold and dangerously far-reaching contention that the courts should take it upon themselves to "make" a law abridging freedom of the press in the name of equity, presidential power and national security, even when the representatives of the people in Congress have adhered to the command of the First Amendment and refused to make such a law. 5 See concurring opinion of MR. JUSTICE DOUGLAS, [403 U.S. 713, 719] post, at 721-722. To find that the President has "inherent power" to halt the publication of news by resort to the courts would wipe out the First Amendment and destroy the fundamental liberty and security of the very people the Government hopes to make "secure." No one can read the history of the adoption of the First Amendment without being convinced beyond any doubt that it was injunctions like those sought here that Madison and his collaborators intended to outlaw in this Nation for all time.

The word "security" is a broad, vague generality whose contours should not be invoked to abrogate the fundamental law embodied in the First Amendment. The guarding of military and diplomatic secrets at the expense of informed representative government provides no real security for our Republic. The Framers of the First Amendment, fully aware of both the need to defend a new nation and the abuses of the English and Colonial governments, sought to give this new society strength and security by providing that freedom of speech, press, religion, and assembly should not be abridged. This thought was eloquently expressed in 1937 by Mr. Chief Justice Hughes - great man and great Chief Justice that he was - when the Court held a man could not be punished for attending a meeting run by Communists.

"The greater the importance of safeguarding the community from incitements to the overthrow of our institutions by force and violence, the more imperative is the need to preserve inviolate the constitutional rights of free speech, free press and free [403 U.S. 713, 720] assembly in order to maintain the opportunity for free political discussion, to the end that government may be responsive to the will of the people and that changes, if desired, may be obtained by peaceful means. Therein lies the security of the Republic, the very foundation of constitutional government." 6

Footnotes

[Footnote 1] In introducing the Bill of Rights in the House of Representatives, Madison said: "[B]ut I believe that the great mass of the people who opposed [the Constitution], disliked it because it did not contain effectual provisions against the encroachments on particular rights . . . ." 1 Annals of Cong. 433. Congressman Goodhue added: "[I]t is the wish of many of our constituents, that something should be added to the Constitution, to secure in a stronger manner their liberties from the inroads of power." Id., at 426.

[Footnote 2] The other parts were:

"The civil rights of none shall be abridged on account of religious belief or worship, nor shall any national religion be established, nor shall the full and equal rights of conscience be in any manner, or on any pretext, infringed."

"The people shall not be restrained from peaceably assembling and consulting for their common good; nor from applying to the Legislature by petitions, or remonstrances, for redress of their grievances." 1 Annals of Cong. 434.

[Footnote 3] Tr. of Oral Arg. 76.

[Footnote 4] Brief for the United States 13-14.

[Footnote 5] Compare the views of the Solicitor General with those of James Madison, the author of the First Amendment. When speaking of the Bill of Rights in the House of Representatives, Madison said: "If they [the first ten amendments] are incorporated into the Constitution, [403 U.S. 713, 719] independent tribunals of justice will consider themselves in a peculiar manner the guardians of those rights; they will be an impenetrable bulwark against every assumption of power in the Legislative or Executive; they will be naturally led to resist every encroachment upon rights expressly stipulated for in the Constitution by the declaration of rights." 1 Annals of Cong. 439.

[Footnote 6] De Jonge v. Oregon, 299 U.S. 353, 365 .

. . .

[Additional concurring decisions were published in which the Justices revealed their own reasoning in more detail.]

18 MILLER V. CALIFORNIA, 413 U.S. 15 (1973)

No. 70-73

Argued January 18-19, 1972

Reargued November 7, 1972

Decided June 21, 1973

413 U.S. 15

APPEAL FROM THE APPELLATE DEPARTMENT, SUPERIOR COURT OF CALIFORNIA, COUNTY OF ORANGE

Syllabus

Appellant was convicted of mailing unsolicited sexually explicit material in violation of a California statute that approximately incorporated the obscenity test formulated in *Memoirs v. Massachusetts,*383 U. S. 413, 383 U. S. 418 (plurality opinion). The trial court instructed the jury to evaluate the materials by the contemporary community standards of California. Appellant's conviction was affirmed on appeal. In lieu of the obscenity criteria enunciated by the *Memoirs* plurality, it is *held:*

1. Obscene material is not protected by the First Amendment. *Roth v. United States,*354 U. S. 476, reaffirmed. A work may be subject to state regulation where that work, taken as a whole, appeals to the prurient interest in sex; portrays, in a patently offensive way, sexual conduct specifically defined by the applicable state law; and, taken as a whole, does not have serious literary, artistic, political, or scientific value. Pp. 413 U. S. 23-24.

2. The basic guidelines for the trier of fact must be: (a) whether "the average person, applying contemporary community standards" would find that the work, taken as a whole, appeals to the prurient interest, *Roth, supra,* at 354 U. S. 489, (b) whether the work depicts or describes, in a patently offensive way, sexual conduct specifically defined by the applicable state law, and (c) whether the work, taken as a whole, lacks serious literary, artistic, political, or scientific value. If a state obscenity law is thus limited, First Amendment values are adequately protected by ultimate independent appellate review of constitutional claims when necessary. Pp. 413 U. S. 24-25.

3. The test of "utterly without redeeming social value" articulated in *Memoirs, supra,* is rejected as a constitutional standard. Pp. 413 U. S. 24-25.

4. The jury may measure the essentially factual issues of prurient appeal and patent offensiveness by the standard that prevails in the forum community, and need not employ a "national standard." Pp. 413 U. S. 30-34.

Vacated and remanded.

BURGER, C.J., delivered the opinion of the Court, in which WHITE, BLACKMUN, POWELL, and REHNQUIST, JJ., joined. DOUGLAS, J., filed a dissenting opinion, *post*, p. 413 U. S. 37. BRENNAN, J., filed a dissenting opinion, in which STEWART and MARSHALL, JJ., joined, *post*, p. 413 U. S. 47.

MR. CHIEF JUSTICE BURGER delivered the opinion of the Court.

This is one of a group of "obscenity-pornography" cases being reviewed by the Court in a reexamination of standards enunciated in earlier cases involving what Mr. Justice Harlan called "the intractable obscenity problem." *Interstate Circuit, Inc. v. Dallas,*390 U. S. 676,390 U. S. 704 (1968) (concurring and dissenting).

Appellant conducted a mass mailing campaign to advertise the sale of illustrated books, euphemistically called "adult" material. After a jury trial, he was convicted of violating California Penal Code § 311.2(a), a misdemeanor, by knowingly distributing obscene matter, [Footnote 1] and the Appellate Department, Superior Court of California, County of Orange, summarily affirmed the judgment without opinion. Appellant's conviction was specifically based on his conduct in causing five unsolicited advertising brochures to be sent through the mail in an envelope addressed to a restaurant in Newport Beach, California. The envelope was opened by the manager of the restaurant and his mother. They had not requested the brochures; they complained to the police.

The brochures advertise four books entitled "Intercourse," "Man-Woman," "Sex Orgies Illustrated," and "An Illustrated History of Pornography," and a film entitled "Marital Intercourse." While the brochures contain some descriptive printed material, primarily they consist of pictures and drawings very explicitly depicting men and women in groups of two or more engaging in a variety of sexual activities, with genitals often prominently displayed.

I

This case involves the application of a State's criminal obscenity statute to a situation in which sexually explicit materials have been thrust by aggressive sales action upon unwilling recipients who had in no way indicated any desire to receive such materials. This Court has recognized that the States have a legitimate interest in prohibiting dissemination or exhibition of obscene material [Footnote 2] when the mode of dissemination carries with it a significant danger of offending the sensibilities of unwilling recipients or of exposure to juveniles. *Stanley v. Georgia,*394 U. S. 557, 394 U. S. 567 (1969); *Ginsberg v. New York,*390 U. S. 629, 390 U. S. 637-643 (1968);*Interstate Circuit, Inc. v. Dallas, supra,* at 390 U. S. 690; *Redrup v. New York,*386 U. S. 767, 386 U. S. 769 (1967); *Jacobellis v. Ohio,*378 U. S. 184, 378 U. S. 195 (1964). *See Rabe v. Washington,*405 U. S. 313, 405 U. S. 317 (1972) (BURGER, C.J., concurring);*United States v. Reidel,*402 U. S. 351, 402 U. S. 360-362 (1971) (opinion of MARSHALL, J.);*Joseph Burstyn, Inc. v. Wilson,*343 U. S. 495, 343 U. S. 502 (1952); *Breard v. Alexandria,*341 U. S. 622, 341 U. S. 644 645 (1951); *Kovacs v. Cooper,*336 U. S. 77, 336 U. S. 88-

89 (1949); *Prince v. Massachusetts,*321 U. S. 158, 321 U. S. 169-170 (1944). *Cf. Butler v. Michigan,*352 U. S. 380, 352 U. S. 382-383 (1957); *Public Utilities Comm'n v. Pollak,*343 U. S. 451, 343 U. S. 464-465 (1952) It is in this context that we are called on to define the standards which must be used to identify obscene material that a State may regulate without infringing on the First Amendment as applicable to the States through the Fourteenth Amendment.

The dissent of MR. JUSTICE BRENNAN reviews the background of the obscenity problem, but since the Court now undertakes to formulate standards more concrete than those in the past, it is useful for us to focus on two of the landmark cases in the somewhat tortured history of the Court's obscenity decisions. In *Roth v. United States,*354 U. S. 476 (1957), the Court sustained a conviction under a federal statute punishing the mailing of "obscene, lewd, lascivious or filthy . . ." materials. The key to that holding was the Court's rejection of the claim that obscene materials were protected by the First Amendment. Five Justices joined in the opinion stating:

"All ideas having even the slightest redeeming social importance -- unorthodox ideas, controversial ideas, even ideas hateful to the prevailing climate of opinion -- have the full protection of the [First Amendment] guaranties, unless excludable because they encroach upon the limited area of more important interests. But implicit in the history of the First Amendment is the rejection of obscenity as utterly without redeeming social importance. . . . This is the same judgment expressed by this Court in *Chaplinsky v. New Hampshire,*315 U. S. 568, 315 U. S. 571-572: "

". . . There are certain well defined and narrowly limited classes of speech, the prevention and punishment of which have never been thought to raise any Constitutional problem. *These include the lewd and obscene. . . . It has been well observed that such utterances are no essential part of any exposition of ideas, and are of such slight social value as a step to truth that any benefit that may be derived from them is clearly outweighed by the social interest in order and morality. . . ."*
[Emphasis by Court in *Roth* opinion.]

"We hold that obscenity is not within the area of constitutionally protected speech or press." 354 U.S. at 354 U. S. 48 85.

Nine years later, in *Memoirs v. Massachusetts,*383 U. S. 413 (1966), the Court veered sharply away from the *Roth* concept and, with only three Justices in the plurality opinion, articulated a new test of obscenity. The plurality held that, under the *Roth* definition,

"as elaborated in subsequent cases, three elements must coalesce: it must be established that (a) the dominant theme of the material, taken as a whole, appeals to a prurient interest in sex; (b) the material is patently offensive because it affronts contemporary community standards relating to the description or representation of sexual matters; and (c) the material is utterly without redeeming social value."

Id. at 383 U. S. 418. The sharpness of the break with *Roth,* represented by the third element of the *Memoirs* test and emphasized by MR. JUSTICE WHITE's dissent, *id.* at 383 U. S. 460-462, was further underscored when the *Memoirs* plurality went on to state:

"The Supreme Judicial Court erred in holding that a book need not be 'unqualifiedly worthless before it can be deemed obscene.' A book cannot be proscribed unless it is found to be *utterly* without redeeming social value."

Id. at 383 U. S. 419 (emphasis in original).

While *Roth* presumed "obscenity" to be "utterly without redeeming social importance," *Memoirs* required that to prove obscenity it must be affirmatively established that the material is "*utterly* without redeeming social value." Thus, even as they repeated the words of *Roth*, the *Memoirs* plurality produced a drastically altered test that called on the prosecution to prove a negative,*i.e.*, that the material was "*utterly* without redeeming social value" -- a burden virtually impossible to discharge under our criminal standards of proof. Such considerations caused Mr. Justice Harlan to wonder if the "*utterly* without redeeming social value" test had any meaning at all. *See Memoirs v. Massachusetts, id.* at 383 U. S. 459 (Harlan, J., dissenting). *See also id.* at 383 U. S. 461 (WHITE, J., dissenting); *United States v. Groner,* 479 F.2d 577, 579581 (CA5 1973).

Apart from the initial formulation in the *Roth* case, no majority of the Court has at any given time been able to agree on a standard to determine what constitutes obscene, pornographic material subject to regulation under the States' police power. *See, e.g., Redrup v. New York,* 386 U.S. at 386 U. S. 770-771. We have seen "a variety of views among the members of the Court unmatched in any other course of constitutional adjudication." *Interstate Circuit, Inc. v. Dallas,* 390 U.S. at 390 U. S. 704-705 (Harlan, J., concurring and dissenting) (footnote omitted). [Footnote 3] This is not remarkable, for in the area of freedom of speech and press the courts must always remain sensitive to any infringement on genuinely serious literary, artistic, political, or scientific expression. This is an area in which there are few eternal verities.

The case we now review was tried on the theory that the California Penal Code § 311 approximately incorporates the three-stage*Memoirs* test, *supra.* But now the *Memoirs* test has been abandoned as unworkable by its author, [Footnote 4] and no Member of the Court today supports the *Memoirs* formulation.

II

This much has been categorically settled by the Court, that obscene material is unprotected by the First Amendment. *Kois v. Wisconsin,*408 U. S. 229 (1972); *United States v. Reidel,* 402 U.S. at 402 U. S. 354; *Roth v. United States, supra,* at 354 U. S. 485. [Footnote 5] "The First and Fourteenth Amendments have never been treated as absolutes [footnote omitted]." *Breard v. Alexandria,* 341 U.S. at 341 U. S. 642, and cases cited. *See Times Film Corp. v. Chicago,*365 U. S. 43, 365 U. S. 47-50 (1961); *Joseph Burstyn, Inc. v. Wilson,* 343 U.S. at 343 U. S. 502. We acknowledge, however, the inherent dangers of undertaking to regulate any form of expression. State statutes designed to regulate obscene materials must be carefully limited. *See Interstate Circuit, Inc. v. Dallas, supra,* at 390 U. S. 682-685. As a result, we now confine the permissible scope of such regulation to works which depict or describe sexual conduct. That conduct must be specifically defined by the applicable state law, as written or authoritatively construed. [Footnote 6] A state offense must also be limited to works which, taken as a whole, appeal to the prurient interest in sex, which portray sexual conduct in a patently offensive way, and which, taken as a whole, do not have serious literary, artistic, political, or scientific value.

The basic guidelines for the trier of fact must be: (a) whether "the average person, applying contemporary community standards" would find that the work, taken as a whole, appeals to the prurient interest, *Kois v. Wisconsin, supra,* at 408 U. S. 230, quoting *Roth v. United States, supra,* at 354 U. S. 489; (b) whether the work depicts or describes, in a patently offensive way, sexual conduct specifically defined by the applicable state law; and (c) whether the work, taken as a whole, lacks serious literary, artistic, political, or scientific value. We do not adopt as a constitutional standard the "utterly without redeeming social value" test of *Memoirs v. Massachusetts,* 383 U.S. at 383 U. S. 419; that concept has never commanded the adherence of more than three Justices at one time. [Footnote 7] *See supra* at 413 U. S. 21. If a state law that regulates obscene material is thus limited, as written or construed, the First Amendment values applicable to the States through the Fourteenth Amendment are adequately protected by the ultimate power of appellate courts to conduct an independent review of constitutional claims when necessary. *See Kois v. Wisconsin, supra,* at 408 U. S. 232; *Memoirs v. Massachusetts, supra,* at 383 U. S. 459-460 (Harlan, J., dissenting); *Jacobellis v. Ohio,* 378 U.S. at 204 (Harlan, J., dissenting); *New York Times Co. v. Sullivan,* 376 U. S. 254, 376 U. S. 284-285 (1964); *Roth v. United States, supra,* at 354 U. S. 497-498 (Harlan, J., concurring and dissenting).

We emphasize that it is not our function to propose regulatory schemes for the States. That must await their concrete legislative efforts. It is possible, however, to give a few plain examples of what a state statute could define for regulation under part (b) of the standard announced in this opinion, *supra:*

(a) Patently offensive representations or descriptions of ultimate sexual acts, normal or perverted, actual or simulated.

(b) Patently offensive representations or descriptions of masturbation, excretory functions, and lewd exhibition of the genitals.

Sex and nudity may not be exploited without limit by films or pictures exhibited or sold in places of public accommodation any more than live sex and nudity can be exhibited or sold without limit in such public places. [Footnote 8] At a minimum, prurient, patently offensive depiction or description of sexual conduct must have serious literary, artistic, political, or scientific value to merit First Amendment protection. *See Kois v. Wisconsin, supra,* at 408 U. S. 230-232; *Roth v. United States, supra,* at 354 U. S. 487; *Thornhill v. Alabama,* 310 U. S. 88, 310 U. S. 101-102 (1940). For example, medical books for the education of physicians and related personnel necessarily use graphic illustrations and descriptions of human anatomy. In resolving the inevitably sensitive questions of fact and law, we must continue to rely on the jury system, accompanied by the safeguards that judges, rules of evidence, presumption of innocence, and other protective features provide, as we do with rape, murder, and a host of other offenses against society and its individual members. [Footnote 9]

MR. JUSTICE BRENNAN, author of the opinions of the Court, or the plurality opinions, in *Roth v. United States, supra; Jacobellis v. Ohio, supra; Ginzburg v. United States,* 383 U. S. 463 (1966), *Mishkin v. New York,* 383 U. S. 502 (1966); and *Memoirs v. Massachusetts, supra,* has abandoned his former position and now maintains that no formulation of this Court, the Congress, or the States can adequately distinguish obscene material unprotected by the First Amendment from protected expression, *Paris Adult Theatre I v. Slaton, post,* p. 413

U. S. 73(BRENNAN, J., dissenting). Paradoxically, MR. JUSTICE BRENNAN indicates that suppression of unprotected obscene material is permissible to avoid exposure to unconsenting adults, as in this case, and to juveniles, although he gives no indication of how the division between protected and nonprotected materials may be drawn with greater precision for these purposes than for regulation of commercial exposure to consenting adults only. Nor does he indicate where in the Constitution he finds the authority to distinguish between a willing "adult" one month past the state law age of majority and a willing "juvenile" one month younger.

Under the holdings announced today, no one will be subject to prosecution for the sale or exposure of obscene materials unless these materials depict or describe patently offensive "hard core" sexual conduct specifically defined by the regulating state law, as written or construed. We are satisfied that these specific prerequisites will provide fair notice to a dealer in such materials that his public and commercial activities may bring prosecution. *See Roth v. United States, supra*, at 354 U. S. 491-492. *Cf. Ginsberg v. New York*, 390 U.S. at 390 U. S. 643. [Footnote 10] If the inability to define regulated materials with ultimate, god-like precision altogether removes the power of the States or the Congress to regulate, then "hard core" pornography may be exposed without limit to the juvenile, the passerby, and the consenting adult alike, as, indeed, MR. JUSTICE DOUGLAS contends. As to MR. JUSTICE DOUGLAS' position, *see United States v. Thirty-seven Photographs*, 402 U. S. 363, 402 U. S. 379-380 (1971) (Black, J., joined by DOUGLAS, J., dissenting); *Ginzburg v. United States, supra*, at 383 U. S. 476, 383 U. S. 491-492 (Black, J., and DOUGLAS, J., dissenting); *Jacobellis v. Ohio, supra*, at 378 U. S. 196 (Black, J., joined by DOUGLAS, J., concurring); *Roth, supra*, at 354 U. S. 508-514 (DOUGLAS, J., dissenting). In this belief, however, MR. JUSTICE DOUGLAS now stands alone.

MR. JUSTICE BRENNAN also emphasizes "institutional stress" in justification of his change of view. Noting that "[t]he number of obscenity cases on our docket gives ample testimony to the burden that has been placed upon this Court," he quite rightly remarks that the examination of contested materials "is hardly a source of edification to the members of this Court." *Paris Adult Theatre I v. Slaton, post*, at 413 U. S. 92, 413 U. S. 93. He also notes, and we agree, that "uncertainty of the standards creates a continuing source of tension between state and federal courts. . . ."

"The problem is . . . that one cannot say with certainty that material is obscene until at least five members of this Court, applying inevitably obscure standards, have pronounced it so."

It is certainly true that the absence, since *Roth*, of a single majority view of this Court as to proper standards for testing obscenity has placed a strain on both state and federal courts. But today, for the first time since *Roth* was decided in 1957, a majority of this Court has agreed on concrete guidelines to isolate "hard core" pornography from expression protected by the First Amendment. Now we may abandon the casual practice of *Redrup v. New York*, 386 U. S. 767 (1967), and attempt to provide positive guidance to federal and state courts alike.

This may not be an easy road, free from difficulty. But no amount of "fatigue" should lead us to adopt a convenient "institutional" rationale -- an absolutist, "anything goes" view of the First Amendment -- because it will lighten our burdens. [Footnote 11] "Such an abnegation of judicial supervision in this field would be inconsistent with our duty to uphold the constitutional guarantees." *Jacobellis v. Ohio, supra,* at378 U. S. 187-188 (opinion of BRENNAN, J.). Nor should we remedy "tension between state and federal courts" by arbitrarily depriving the States of a power reserved to them under the Constitution, a power which they have enjoyed and exercised continuously from before the adoption of the First Amendment to this day. *See Roth v. United States, supra,* at 354 U. S. 482-485.

"Our duty admits of no 'substitute for facing up to the tough individual problems of constitutional judgment involved in every obscenity case.' [*Roth v. United States, supra,* at 354 U. S. 498]; *see Manual Enterprises, Inc. v. Day,*370 U. S. 478, 370 U. S. 488 (opinion of Harlan, J.) [footnote omitted]."

Jacobellis v. Ohio, supra, at 378 U. S. 188 (opinion of BRENNAN, J.).

III

Under a National Constitution, fundamental First Amendment limitations on the powers of the States do not vary from community to community, but this does not mean that there are, or should or can be, fixed, uniform national standards of precisely what appeals to the "prurient interest" or is "patently offensive." These are essentially questions of fact, and our Nation is simply too big and too diverse for this Court to reasonably expect that such standards could be articulated for all 50 States in a single formulation, even assuming the prerequisite consensus exists. When triers of fact are asked to decide whether "the average person, applying contemporary community standards" would consider certain materials "prurient," it would be unrealistic to require that the answer be based on some abstract formulation. The adversary system, with lay jurors as the usual ultimate factfinders in criminal prosecutions, has historically permitted triers of fact to draw on the standards of their community, guided always by limiting instructions on the law. To require a State to structure obscenity proceedings around evidence of a *national* "community standard" would be an exercise in futility.

As noted before, this case was tried on the theory that the California obscenity statute sought to incorporate the tripartite test of *Memoirs.*This, a "national" standard of First Amendment protection enumerated by a plurality of this Court, was correctly regarded at the time of trial as limiting state prosecution under the controlling case law. The jury, however, was explicitly instructed that, in determining whether the "dominant theme of the material as a whole . . . appeals to the prurient interest," and, in determining whether the material "goes substantially beyond customary limits of candor and affronts contemporary community standards of decency," it was to apply "contemporary community standards of the State of California."

During the trial, both the prosecution and the defense assumed that the relevant "community standards" in making the factual determination of obscenity were those of the State of California, not some hypothetical standard of the entire United States of America. Defense counsel at trial never objected to the testimony of the State's expert on community standards [Footnote 12] or to the instructions of the trial judge on "state-wide" standards. On appeal to the Appellate Department, Superior Court of California, County of Orange, appellant for the first time contended that application of state, rather than national, standards violated the First and Fourteenth Amendments.

We conclude that neither the State's alleged failure to offer evidence of "national standards," nor the trial court's charge that the jury consider state community standards, were constitutional errors. Nothing in the First Amendment requires that a jury must consider hypothetical and unascertainable "national standards" when attempting to determine whether certain materials are obscene as a matter of fact. Mr. Chief Justice Warren pointedly commented in his dissent in *Jacobellis v. Ohio, supra,* at 378 U. S. 200:

"It is my belief that, when the Court said in *Roth* that obscenity is to be defined by reference to 'community standards,' it meant community standards -- not a national standard, as is sometimes argued. I believe that there is no provable 'national standard.' . . . At all events, this Court has not been able to enunciate one, and it would be unreasonable to expect local courts to divine one."

It is neither realistic nor constitutionally sound to read the First Amendment as requiring that the people of Maine or Mississippi accept public depiction of conduct found tolerable in Las Vegas, or New York City. [Footnote 13] *See Hoyt v. Minnesota,* 399 U.S. at 524-525 (1970) (BLACKMUN, J., dissenting); *Walker v. Ohio,* 398 U.S. at 434 (1970) (BURGER, C.J., dissenting); *id.* at 434-435 (Harlan, J., dissenting); *Cain v. Kentucky,* 397 U. S. 319 (1970) (BURGER, C.J., dissenting); *id.* at 397 U. S. 319-320 (Harlan, J., dissenting); *United States v. Groner,* 479 F.2d at 581-583; O'Meara & Shaffer, Obscenity in The Supreme Court: A Note on *Jacobellis v. Ohio,* 40 Notre Dame Law. 1, 6-7 (1964). *See also Memoirs v. Massachusetts,* 383 U.S. at 383 U. S. 458(Harlan, J., dissenting); *Jacobellis v. Ohio, supra,* at 378 U. S. 203-204 (Harlan, J., dissenting); *Roth v. United States, supra,* at 354 U. S. 505-506 (Harlan, J., concurring and dissenting). People in different States vary in their tastes and attitudes, and this diversity is not to be strangled by the absolutism of imposed uniformity. As the Court made clear in *Mishkin v. New York,* 383 U.S. at 383 U. S. 508-509, the primary concern with requiring a jury to apply the standard of "the average person, applying contemporary community standards" is to be certain that, so far as material is not aimed at a deviant group, it will be judged by its impact on an average person, rather than a particularly susceptible or sensitive person -- or indeed a totally insensitive one. *See Roth v. United States, supra,* at 354 U. S. 489. *Cf.* the now discredited test in *Regina v. Hicklin,* [1868] L.R. 3 Q.B. 360. We hold that the requirement that the jury evaluate the materials with reference to "contemporary standards of the State of California" serves this protective purpose and is constitutionally adequate. [Footnote 14]

IV

The dissenting Justices sound the alarm of repression. But, in our view, to equate the free and robust exchange of ideas and political debate with commercial exploitation of obscene material demeans the grand conception of the First Amendment and its high purposes in the historic struggle for freedom. It is a "misuse of the great guarantees of free speech and free press. . . ." *Breard v. Alexandria,* 341 U.S. at 341 U. S. 645. The First Amendment protects works which, taken as a whole, have serious literary, artistic, political, or scientific value, regardless of whether the government or a majority of the people approve of the ideas these works represent.

"The protection given speech and press was fashioned to assure unfettered interchange of *ideas* for the bringing about of political and social changes desired by the people,"

Roth v. United States, supra, at 354 U. S. 484 (emphasis added). *See Kois v. Wisconsin,* 408 U.S.

at 408 U. S. 230-232; *Thornhill v. Alabama,* 310 U.S. at 310 U. S. 101-102. But the public portrayal of hard-core sexual conduct for its own sake, and for the ensuing commercial gain, is a different matter. [Footnote 15]

There is no evidence, empirical or historical, that the stern 19th century American censorship of public distribution and display of material relating to sex, *see Roth v. United States, supra,* at 354 U. S. 482-485, in any way limited or affected expression of serious literary, artistic, political, or scientific ideas. On the contrary, it is beyond any question that the era following Thomas Jefferson to Theodore Roosevelt was an "extraordinarily vigorous period" not just in economics and politics, but in *belles lettres* and in "the outlying fields of social and political philosophies." [Footnote 16] We do not see the harsh hand of censorship of ideas -- good or bad, sound or unsound -- and "repression" of political liberty lurking in every state regulation of commercial exploitation of human interest in sex.

MR. JUSTICE BRENNAN finds "it is hard to see how state-ordered regimentation of our minds can ever be forestalled." *Paris Adult Theatre I v. Slaton, post,* at 413 U. S. 110 (BRENNAN, J., dissenting). These doleful anticipations assume that courts cannot distinguish commerce in ideas, protected by the First Amendment, from commercial exploitation of obscene material. Moreover, state regulation of hard-core pornography so as to make it unavailable to nonadults, a regulation which MR. JUSTICE BRENNAN finds constitutionally permissible, has all the elements of "censorship" for adults; indeed even more rigid enforcement techniques may be called for with such dichotomy of regulation. *See Interstate Circuit, Inc. v. Dallas,* 390 U.S. at 390 U. S. 690. [Footnote 17] One can concede that the "sexual revolution" of recent years may have had useful byproducts in striking layers of prudery from a subject long irrationally kept from needed ventilation. But it does not follow that no regulation of patently offensive "hard core" materials is needed or permissible; civilized people do not allow unregulated access to heroin because it is a derivative of medicinal morphlne.

In sum, we (a) reaffirm the *Roth* holding that obscene material is not protected by the First Amendment; (b) hold that such material can be regulated by the States, subject to the specific safeguards enunciated above, without a showing that the material is "utterly without redeeming social value"; and (c) hold that obscenity is to be determined by applying "contemporary community standards," *see Kois v. Wisconsin, supra,* at 408 U. S. 230, and *Roth v. United States, supra,* at 354 U. S. 489, not "national standards." The judgment of the Appellate Department of the Superior Court, Orange County, California, is vacated and the case remanded to that court for further proceedings not inconsistent with the First Amendment standards established by this opinion. *See United States v. 12 200-ft. Reels of Film, post* at 413 U. S. 130 n. 7.

Vacated and remanded.

[Footnote 1]
At the time of the commission of the alleged offense, which was prior to June 25, 1969, §§ 311.2(a) and 311 of the California Penal Code read in relevant part:

"§ 311.2 Sending or bringing into state for sale or distribution; printing, exhibiting, distributing or possessing within state"

"(a) Every person who knowingly: sends or causes to be sent, or brings or causes to be brought, into this state for sale or distribution, or in this state prepares, publishes, prints, exhibits, distributes, or offers to distribute, or has in his possession with intent to distribute or to exhibit or offer to distribute, any obscene matter is guilty of a misdemeanor. . . ."

"§ 311. Definitions"

"As used in this chapter: "

"(a) 'Obscene' means that to the average person, applying contemporary standards, the predominant appeal of the matter, taken as a whole, is to prurient interest, i.e., a shameful or morbid interest in nudity, sex, or excretion, which goes substantially beyond customary limits of candor in description or representation of such matters and is matter which is utterly without redeeming social importance."

"(b) 'Matter' means any book, magazine, newspaper, or other printed or written material or any picture, drawing, photograph, motion picture, or other pictorial representation or any statue or other figure, or any recording, transcription or mechanical, chemical or electrical reproduction or any other articles, equipment, machines or materials."

"(c) 'Person' means any individual, partnership, firm, association, corporation, or other legal entity."

"(d) 'Distribute' means to transfer possession of, whether with or without consideration."

"(e) 'Knowingly' means having knowledge that the matter is obscene."

Section 311(e) of the California Penal Code, *supra,* was amended on June 25, 1969, to read as follows:

"(e) 'Knowingly' means being aware of the character of the matter."

Cal. Amended Stats.1969, c. 249, § 1, p. 598. Despite appellant's contentions to the contrary, the record indicates that the new § 311(e) was not applied *ex post facto* to his case, but only the old § 311(e) as construed by state decisions prior to the commission of the alleged offense. *See People v. Pinkus,* 256 Cal.App.2d 941, 948-950, 63 Cal.Rptr. 680, 685-686 (App. Dept., Superior Ct., Los Angeles, 1967);*People v. Campise,* 242 Cal.App.2d 905, 914, 51 Cal.Rptr. 815, 821 (App.Dept., Superior Ct., San Diego, 1966). *Cf. Bouie v. City of Columbia,*378 U. S. 347 (1964). Nor did § 311.2, *supra,* as applied, create any "direct, immediate burden on the performance of the postal functions," or infringe on congressional commerce powers under Art. I, § 8, cl. 3. *Roth v. United States,*354 U. S. 476, 354 U. S. 494 (1957), quoting *Railway Mail Assn. v. Corsi,*326 U. S. 88, 326 U. S. 96 (1945). *See also Mishkin v. New York,*383 U. S. 502, 383 U. S. 506 (1966); *Smith v. California,*361 U. S. 147, 361 U. S. 150-152 (1959).

[Footnote 2]

This Court has defined "obscene material" as "material which deals with sex in a manner appealing to prurient interest," *Roth v. United States, supra,* at 354 U. S. 487, but the *Roth* definition does not reflect the precise meaning of "obscene" as traditionally used in the English language. Derived from the Latin *obscaenus ob,* to, plus *caenum,* filth, "obscene" is defined in the Webster's Third New International Dictionary (Unabridged 1969) as

"1a: disgusting to the senses . . . b: grossly repugnant to the generally accepted notions of what is appropriate . . . 2: offensive or revolting as countering or violating some ideal or principle."

The Oxford English Dictionary (1933 ed.) gives a similar definition, "[o]ffensive to the senses, or to taste or refinement; disgusting, repulsive, filthy, foul, abominable, loathsome."

The material we are discussing in this case is more accurately defined as "pornography" or "pornographic material." "Pornography" derives from the Greek (porne, harlot, and graphos, writing). The word now means

"1: a description of prostitutes or prostitution 2: a depiction (as in writing or painting) of licentiousness or lewdness: a portrayal of erotic behavior designed to cause sexual excitement."

Webster's Third New International Dictionary, *supra.* Pornographic material which is obscene forms a sub-group of all "obscene" expression, but not the whole, at least as the word "obscene" is now used in our language. We note, therefore, that the words "obscene material," as used in this case, have a specific judicial meaning which derives from the *Roth* case, *i.e.,* obscene material "which deals with sex." *Roth, supra,* at 354 U. S. 487. *See also* ALI Model Penal Code § 251.4(1) "Obscene Defined." (Official Draft 1962.)

[Footnote 3]

In the absence of a majority view, this Court was compelled to embark on the practice of summarily reversing convictions for the dissemination of materials that, at least five members of the Court, applying their separate tests, found to be protected by the First Amendment. *Redrup v. New York,*386 U. S. 767 (1967). Thirty-one cases have been decided in this manner. Beyond the necessity of circumstances, however, no justification has ever been offered in support of the *Redrup* "policy." *See Walker v. Ohio,* 398 U.S. at 398 U. S. 434-435 (1970) (dissenting opinions of BURGER, C.J., and Harlan, J.). The *Redrup* procedure has cast us in the role of an unreviewable board of censorship for the 50 States, subjectively judging each piece of material brought before us.

[Footnote 4]

See the dissenting opinion of MR. JUSTICE BRENNAN in *Paris Adult Theatre I v. Slaton, post,* p. 413 U. S. 73.

[Footnote 5]

As Mr. Chief Justice Warren stated, dissenting, in *Jacobellis v. Ohio,*378 U. S. 184, 378 U. S. 200 (1964):

"For all the sound and fury that the *Roth* test has generated, it has not been proved unsound, and I believe that we should try to live with it -- at least until a more satisfactory definition is evolved. No government -- be it federal, state, or local -- should be forced to choose between repressing all material, including that within the realm of decency, and allowing unrestrained license to publish any material, no matter how vile. There must be a rule of reason in this as in other areas of the law, and we have attempted in the *Roth* case to provide such a rule."

[Footnote 6]

See, e.g., Oregon Laws 1971, c. 743, Art. 29, §§ 255-262, and Hawaii Penal Code, Tit. 37, §§ 1210-1216, 1972 Hawaii Session Laws, Act 9, c. 12, pt.. II, pp. 126-129, as examples of state laws directed at depiction of defined physical conduct, as opposed to expression. Other state formulations could be equally valid in this respect. In giving the Oregon and Hawaii statutes as examples, we do not wish to be understood as approving of them in all other respects nor as establishing their limits as the extent of state power.

We do not hold, as MR. JUSTICE BRENNAN intimates, that all States other than Oregon must now enact new obscenity statutes. Other existing state statutes, as construed heretofore or hereafter, may well be adequate. *See United States v. 12 200-ft. Reel of Film, post,* at413 U. S. 130 n. 7.

[Footnote 7]

"A quotation from Voltaire in the flyleaf of a book will not constitutionally redeem an otherwise obscene publication. . . ." *Kois v. Wisconsin,*408 U. S. 229, 408 U. S. 231 (1972). *See Memoirs v. Massachusetts,*383 U. S. 413, 383 U. S. 461 (1966) (WHITE, J., dissenting). We also reject, as a constitutional standard, the ambiguous concept of "social importance." *See id.* at 383 U. S. 462 (WHITE, J., dissenting).

[Footnote 8]

Although we are not presented here with the problem of regulating lewd public conduct itself, the States have greater power to regulate nonverbal, physical conduct than to suppress depictions or descriptions of the same behavior. In *United States v. O'Brien*,391 U. S. 367,391 U. S. 377 (1968), a case not dealing with obscenity, the Court held a State regulation of conduct which itself embodied both speech and nonspeech elements to be

"sufficiently justified if . . . it furthers an important or substantial governmental interest; if the governmental interest is unrelated to the suppression of free expression; and if the incidental restriction on alleged First Amendment freedoms is no greater than is essential to the furtherance of that interest."

See California v. LaRue,409 U. S. 109, 409 U. S. 117-118 (1972).

[Footnote 9]

The mere fact juries may reach different conclusions as to the same material does not mean that constitutional rights are abridged. As this Court observed in *Roth v. United States*, 354 U.S. at 354 U. S. 492 n. 30,

"it is common experience that different juries may reach different results under any criminal statute. That is one of the consequences we accept under our jury system. *Cf. Dunlop v. United States*,165 U. S. 486, 165 U. S. 499-500."

[Footnote 10]

As MR. JUSTICE BRENNAN stated for the Court in *Roth v. United States, supra* at 354 U. S. 491-492:

"Many decisions have recognized that these terms of obscenity statutes are not precise. [Footnote omitted.] This Court, however, has consistently held that lack of precision is not itself offensive to the requirements of due process. '. . . [T]he Constitution does not require impossible standards;' all that is required is that the language 'conveys sufficiently definite warning as to the proscribed conduct when measured by common understanding and practices. . . .' *United States v. Petrillo*,332 U. S. 1, 332 U. S. 7-8. These words, applied according to the proper standard for judging obscenity, already discussed, give adequate warning of the conduct proscribed and mark"

". . . boundaries sufficiently distinct for judges and juries fairly to administer the law. . . . That there may be marginal cases in which it is difficult to determine the side of the line on which a particular fact situation falls is no sufficient reason to hold the language too ambiguous to define a criminal offense. . . ."

"*Id.* at 332 U. S. 7. *See also United States v. Harriss*,347 U. S. 612, 347 U. S. 624, n. 15; *Boyce Motor Lines, Inc. v. United States*,342 U. S. 337, 342 U. S. 340; *United States v. Ragen*,314 U. S. 513, 314 U. S. 523-524; *United States v. Wurzbach*,280 U. S. 396;*Hygrade Provision Co. v. Sherman*,266 U. S. 497; *Fox v. Washington*,236 U. S. 273; *Nash v. United States*,229 U. S. 373."

[Footnote 11]

We must note, in addition, that any assumption concerning the relative burdens of the past and the probable burden under the standards now adopted is pure speculation.

[Footnote 12]

The record simply does not support appellant's contention, belatedly raised on appeal, that the State's expert was unqualified to give evidence on California "community standards." The expert, a police officer with many years of specialization in obscenity offenses, had conducted an extensive state-wide survey and had given expert evidence on 26 occasions in the year prior to this trial. Allowing such expert testimony was certainly not constitutional error. *Cf. United States v. Augenblick*,393 U. S. 348, 393 U. S. 356 (1969).

[Footnote 13]

In *Jacobellis v. Ohio*,378 U. S. 184 (1964), two Justices argued that application of "local" community standards would run the risk of preventing dissemination of materials in some places because sellers would be unwilling to risk criminal conviction by testing variations in standards from place to place. *Id.* at 378 U. S. 193-195 (opinion of BRENNAN, J., joined by

Goldberg, J.). The use of "national" standards, however, necessarily implies that materials found tolerable in some places, but not under the "national" criteria, will nevertheless be unavailable where they are acceptable. Thus, in terms of danger to free expression, the potential for suppression seems at least as great in the application of a single nationwide standard as in allowing distribution in accordance with local tastes, a point which Mr. Justice Harlan often emphasized. *See Roth v. United States*, 354 U.S. at 354 U. S. 506.

Appellant also argues that adherence to a "national standard" is necessary "in order to avoid unconscionable burdens on the free flow of interstate commerce." As noted *supra* at 413 U. S. 18 n. 1, the application of domestic state police powers in this case did not intrude on any congressional powers under Art. I, § 8, cl. 3, for there is no indication that appellant's materials were ever distributed interstate. Appellant's argument would appear without substance in any event. Obscene material may be validly regulated by a State in the exercise of its traditional local power to protect the general welfare of its population despite some possible incidental effect on the flow of such materials across state lines. *See, e.g., Head v. New Mexico Board,*374 U. S. 424 (1963); *Huron Portland Cement Co. v. Detroit,*362 U. S. 440 (1960); *Breard v. Alexandria,*341 U. S. 622 (1951); *H. P. Hood & Sons v. Du Mond,*336 U. S. 525 (1949); *Southern Pacific Co. v. Arizona,*325 U. S. 761 (1945); *Baldwin v. G.A.F. Seelig, Inc.,*294 U. S. 511 (1935); *Sligh v. Kirkwood,*237 U. S. 52 (1915).

[Footnote 14]

Appellant's jurisdictional statement contends that he was subjected to "double jeopardy" because a Los Angeles County trial judge dismissed, before trial, a prior prosecution based on the same brochures, but apparently alleging exposures at a different time in a different setting. Appellant argues that, once material has been found not to be obscene in one proceeding, the State is "collaterally estopped" from ever alleging it to be obscene in a different proceeding. It is not clear from the record that appellant properly raised this issue, better regarded as a question of procedural due process than a "double jeopardy" claim, in the state courts below. Appellant failed to address any portion of his brief on the merits to this issue, and appellee contends that the question was waived under California law because it was improperly pleaded at trial. Nor is it totally clear from the record before us what collateral effect the pretrial dismissal might have under state law. The dismissal was based, at least in part, on a failure of the prosecution to present affirmative evidence required by state law, evidence which was apparently presented in this case. Appellant's contention, therefore, is best left to the California courts for further consideration on remand. The issue is not, in any event, a proper subject for appeal. *See Mishkin v. New York,*383 U. S. 502, 383 U. S. 512-514 (1966).

[Footnote 15]

In the apt words of Mr. Chief Justice Warren, appellant in this case was

"plainly engaged in the commercial exploitation of the morbid and shameful craving for materials with prurient effect. I believe that the State and Federal Governments can constitutionally punish such conduct. That is all that these cases present to us, and that is all we need to decide."

Roth v. United States, supra, at 354 U. S. 496 (concurring opinion).

[Footnote 16]

See 2 V. Parrington, Main Currents in American Thought *ix et seq.* (1930). As to the latter part of the 19th century, Parrington observed

"A new age had come and other dreams -- the age and the dreams of a middle-class sovereignty. . . . From the crude and vast romanticisms of that vigorous sovereignty emerged eventually a spirit of realistic criticism, seeking to evaluate the worth of this new America, and discover if possible other philosophies to take the place of those which had gone down in the fierce battles of the Civil War."

Id. at 474. *Cf.* 2 S. Morison, H. Commager & W. Leuchtenburg, The Growth of the American Republic 197-233 (6th ed.1969); Paths of American Thought 123-166, 203-290 (A. Schlesinger & M. White ed.1963) (articles of Fleming, Lerner, Morton & Lucia White, E. Rostow, Samuelson, Kazin, Hofstadter); and H. Wish, Society and Thought in Modern America 337-386 (1952).

[Footnote 17]

"[W]e have indicated . . . that, because of its strong and abiding interest in youth, a State may regulate the dissemination to juveniles of, and their access to, material objectionable as to them, but which a State clearly could not regulate as to adults. *Ginsberg v. New York*, . . . [390 U.S. 629 (1968)]."

*Interstate Circuit, Inc. v. Dallas,*390 U. S. 676, 390 U. S. 690 (1968) (footnote omitted).

MR. JUSTICE DOUGLAS, dissenting.

I

Today we leave open the way for California [Footnote 2/1] to send a man to prison for distributing brochures that advertise books and a movie under freshly written standards defining obscenity which until today is decision were never the part of any law.

The Court has worked hard to define obscenity and concededly has failed. In *Roth v. United States,*354 U. S. 476, it ruled that "[o]bscene material is material which deals with sex in a manner appealing to prurient interest." *Id.* at 354 U. S. 487. Obscenity, it was said, was rejected by the First Amendment because it is "utterly without redeeming social importance." *Id.* at 354 U. S. 484. The presence of a "prurient interest" was to be determined by "contemporary community standards." *Id.* at 354 U. S. 489. That test, it has been said, could not be determined by one standard here and another standard there,*Jacobellis v. Ohio,*378 U. S. 184, 378 U. S. 194, but "on the basis of a national standard." *Id.* at 378 U. S. 195. My Brother STEWART, in*Jacobellis,* commented that the difficulty of the Court in giving content to obscenity was that it was "faced with the task of trying to define what may be indefinable." *Id.* at 378 U. S. 197.

In *Memoirs v. Massachusetts,*383 U. S. 413, 383 U. S. 418, the *Roth* test was elaborated to read as follows:

"[T]hree elements must coalesce: it must be established that (a) the dominant theme of the material taken as a whole appeals to a prurient interest in sex; (b) the material is patently offensive because it affronts contemporary community standards relating to the description or representation of sexual matters; and (c) the material is utterly without redeeming social value."

In *Ginzburg v. United States,*383 U. S. 463, a publisher was sent to prison, not for the kind of books and periodicals he sold, but for the manner in which the publications were advertised. The "leer of the sensualist" was said to permeate the advertisements. *Id.* at 383 U. S. 468. The Court said,

"Where the purveyor's sole emphasis is on the sexually provocative aspects of his publications, that fact may be decisive in the determination of obscenity."

Id. at 383 U. S. 470. As Mr. Justice Black said in dissent,

". . . Ginzburg . . . is now finally and authoritatively condemned to serve five years in prison for distributing printed matter about sex which neither Ginzburg nor anyone else could possibly have known to be criminal."

Id. at 383 U. S. 476. That observation by Mr. Justice Black is underlined by the fact that the *Ginzburg* decision was five to four.

A further refinement was added by *Ginsberg v. New York,*390 U. S. 629, 390 U. S. 641, where the Court held that "it was not irrational for the legislature to find that exposure to material condemned by the statute is harmful to minors."

But even those members of this Court who had created the new and changing standards of "obscenity" could not agree on their application. And so we adopted a per curiam treatment of so-called obscene publications that seemed to pass constitutional muster under the several constitutional tests which had been formulated. *See Redrup v. New York,*386 U. S. 767. Some condemn it if its "dominant tendency might be to *deprave or corrupt'* a reader." *[Footnote 2/2] Others look not to the content of the book, but to whether it is advertised "'to appeal to the erotic interests of customers."' [Footnote 2/3] Some condemn only "hard-core pornography," but even then a true definition is lacking. It has indeed been said of that definition, "I could never succeed in [defining it] intelligibly," but "I know it when I see it." [Footnote 2/4]*

Today we would add a new three-pronged test:

"(a) whether 'the average person, applying contemporary community standards,' would find that the work, taken as a whole, appeals to the prurient interest, . . . (b) whether the work depicts or describes, in a patently offensive way, sexual conduct specifically defined by the applicable state law, and (c) whether the work, taken as a whole, lacks serious literary, artistic, political, or scientific value."

Those are the standards we ourselves have written into the Constitution. [Footnote 2/5] Yet how under these vague tests can we sustain convictions for the sale of an article prior to the time when some court has declared it to be obscene?

Today the Court retreats from the earlier formulations of the constitutional test and undertakes to make new definitions. This effort, like the earlier ones, is earnest and well intentioned. The difficulty is that we do not deal with constitutional terms, since "obscenity" is not mentioned in the Constitution or Bill of Rights. And the First Amendment makes no such exception from "the press" which it undertakes to protect nor, as I have said on other occasions, is an exception necessarily implied, for there was no recognized exception to the free press at the time the Bill of Rights was adopted which treated "obscene" publications differently from other types of papers, magazines, and books. So there are no constitutional guidelines for deciding what is and what is not "obscene." The Court is at large because we deal with tastes and standards of literature. What shocks me may be sustenance for my neighbor. What causes one person to boil up in rage over one pamphlet or movie may reflect only his neurosis, not shared by others. We deal here with a regime of censorship which, if adopted, should be done by constitutional amendment after full debate by the people.

Obscenity cases usually generate tremendous emotional outbursts. They have no business being in the courts. If a constitutional amendment authorized censorship, the censor would probably be an administrative agency. Then criminal prosecutions could follow as, if, and when publishers defied the censor and sold their literature. Under that regime, a publisher would know when he was on dangerous ground. Under the present regime -- whether the old standards or the new ones are used -- the criminal law becomes a trap. A brand new test would put a publisher behind bars under a new law improvised by the courts after the publication. That was done in *Ginzburg,* and has all the evils of an *ex post facto* law.

My contention is that, until a civil proceeding has placed a tract beyond the pale, no criminal prosecution should be sustained. For no more vivid illustration of vague and uncertain laws could be designed than those we have fashioned. As Mr. Justice Harlan has said:

"The upshot of all this divergence in viewpoint is that anyone who undertakes to examine the Court's decisions since *Roth* which have held particular material obscene or not obscene would find himself in utter bewilderment."

*Interstate Circuit, Inc. v. Dallas,*390 U. S. 676, 390 U. S. 707.

In *Bouie v. City of Columbia,*378 U. S. 347, we upset a conviction for remaining on property after being asked to leave, while the only unlawful act charged by the statute was entering. We held that the defendants had received no "fair warning, at the time of their conduct" while on the property "that the act for which they now stand convicted was rendered criminal" by the state statute. *Id.* at 378 U. S. 355. The same requirement of "fair warning" is due here, as much as in *Bouie.* The latter involved racial discrimination; the present case involves rights earnestly urged as being protected by the First Amendment. In any case -- certainly when constitutional rights are concerned -- we should not allow men to go to prison or be fined when they had no "fair warning" that what they did was criminal conduct.

II

If a specific book, play, paper, or motion picture has in a civil proceeding been condemned as obscene and review of that finding has been completed, and thereafter a person publishes, shows, or displays that particular book or film, then a vague law has been made specific. There would remain the underlying question whether the First Amendment allows an implied exception in the case of obscenity. I do not think it does, [Footnote 2/6] and my views on the issue have been stated over and over again. [Footnote 2/7] But at least a criminal prosecution brought at that juncture would not violate the time-honored "void for vagueness" test. [Footnote 2/8]

No such protective procedure has been designed by California in this case. Obscenity -- which even we cannot define with precision -- is a hodge-podge. To send men to jail for violating standards they cannot understand, construe, and apply is a monstrous thing to do in a Nation dedicated to fair trials and due process.

III

While the right to know is the corollary of the right to speak or publish, no one can be forced by government to listen to disclosure that he finds offensive. That was the basis of my dissent in *Public Utilities Comm'n v. Pollak,*343 U. S. 451, 343 U. S. 467, where I protested against making streetcar passengers a "captive" audience. There is no "captive audience" problem in these obscenity cases. No one is being compelled to look or to listen. Those who enter newsstands or bookstalls may be offended by what they see. But they are not compelled by the State to frequent those places; and it is only state or governmental action against which the First Amendment, applicable to the States by virtue of the Fourteenth, raises a ban.

The idea that the First Amendment permits government to ban publications that are "offensive" to some people puts an ominous gloss on freedom of the press. That test would make it possible to ban any paper or any journal or magazine in some benighted place. The First Amendment was designed "to invite dispute," to induce "a condition of unrest," to "create dissatisfaction with conditions as they are," and even to stir "people to anger." *Terminiello v. Chicago,*337 U. S. 1, 337 U. S. 4. The idea that the First Amendment permits punishment for ideas that are "offensive" to the particular judge or jury sitting in judgment is astounding. No greater leveler of speech or literature has ever been designed. To give the power to the censor, as we do today, is to make a sharp and radical break with the traditions of a free society. The First Amendment was not fashioned as a vehicle for dispensing tranquilizers to the people. Its prime function was to keep debate open to "offensive" as well as to "staid" people. The tendency throughout history has been to subdue the individual and to exalt the power of government. The use of the standard "offensive" gives authority to government that cuts the very vitals out of the First Amendment. [Footnote 2/9] As is intimated by the Court's opinion, the materials before us may be garbage. But so is much of what is said in political campaigns, in the daily press, on TV, or over the radio. By reason of the First Amendment -- and solely because of it -- speakers and publishers have not been threatened or subdued because their thoughts and ideas may be "offensive" to some.

The standard "offensive" is unconstitutional in yet another way. In *Coates v. City of Cincinnati,*402 U. S. 611, we had before us a municipal ordinance that made it a crime for three or more persons to assemble on a street and conduct themselves "in a manner annoying to persons passing by." We struck it down, saying:

"If three or more people meet together on a sidewalk or street corner, they must conduct themselves so as not to annoy any police officer or other person who should happen to pass by. In our opinion, this ordinance is unconstitutionally vague because it subjects the exercise of the right of assembly to an unascertainable standard, and unconstitutionally broad because it authorizes the punishment of constitutionally protected conduct."

"Conduct that annoys some people does not annoy others. Thus, the ordinance is vague not in the sense that it requires a person to conform his conduct to an imprecise but comprehensive normative standard, but rather in the sense that no standard of conduct is specified at all."

How we can deny Ohio the convenience of punishing people who "annoy" others and allow California power to punish people who publish materials "offensive" to some people is difficult to square with constitutional requirements.

If there are to be restraints on what is obscene, then a constitutional amendment should be the way of achieving the end. There are societies where religion and mathematics are the only free segments. It would be a dark day for America if that were our destiny. But the people can make it such if they choose to write obscenity into the Constitution and define it.

We deal with highly emotional, not rational, questions. To many, the Song of Solomon is obscene. I do not think we, the judges, were ever given the constitutional power to make definitions of obscenity. If it is to be defined, let the people debate and decide by a constitutional amendment what they want to ban as obscene and what standards they want the legislatures and the courts to apply. Perhaps the people will decide that the path towards a mature, integrated society requires that all ideas competing for acceptance must have no censor. Perhaps they will decide otherwise. Whatever the choice, the courts will have some guidelines. Now we have none except our own predilections.

[Footnote 2/1]
California defines "obscene matter" as "matter, taken as a whole, the predominant appeal of which to the average person, applying contemporary standards, is to prurient interest, *i.e.*, a shameful or morbid interest in nudity, sex, or excretion; and is matter which taken as a whole goes substantially beyond customary limits of candor in description or representation of such matters; and is matter which taken as a whole is utterly without redeeming social importance." Calif. Penal Code § 311(a).

[Footnote 2/2]
*Roth v. United States,*354 U. S. 476, 354 U. S. 502 (opinion of Harlan, J.).

[Footnote 2/3]
*Ginzburg v. United States,*383 U. S. 463, 383 U. S. 467.

[Footnote 2/4]
*Jacobellis v. Ohio,*378 U. S. 184, 378 U. S. 197 (STEWART, J., concurring).

[Footnote 2/5]
At the conclusion of a two-year study, the U.S. Commission on Obscenity and Pornography determined that the standards we have written interfere with constitutionally protected materials:

"Society's attempts to legislate for adults in the area of obscenity have not been successful. Present laws prohibiting the consensual sale or distribution of explicit sexual materials to adults are extremely unsatisfactory in their practical application. The Constitution permits material to be deemed 'obscene' for adults only if, as a whole, it appeals to the 'prurient' interest of the average person, is 'patently offensive' in light of 'community standards,' and lacks 'redeeming social value.' These vague and highly subjective aesthetic, psychological and moral tests do not provide meaningful guidance for law enforcement officials, juries or courts. As a result, law is inconsistently and sometimes erroneously applied, and the distinctions made by courts between prohibited and permissible materials often appear indefensible. Errors in the application of the law and uncertainty about its scope also cause interference with the communication of constitutionally protected materials."

Report of the Commission on Obscenity and Pornography 53 (1970).

[Footnote 2/6]
It is said that "obscene" publications can be banned on authority of restraints on communications incident to decrees restraining unlawful business monopolies or unlawful restraints of trade, *Sugar Institute v. United States,*297 U. S. 553, 297 U. S. 597, or communications respecting the sale of spurious or fraudulent securities. *Hall v. Geier-Jones Co.,*242 U. S. 539, 242 U. S. 549; *Caldwell v. Sioux Falls Stock Yards Co.,*242 U. S. 559, 242 U. S.

567; *Merrick v. Halsey & Co.,*242 U. S. 568, 242 U. S. 584. The First Amendment answer is that, whenever speech and conduct are brigaded -- as they are when one shouts "Fire" in a crowded theater -- speech can be outlawed. Mr. Justice Black, writing for a unanimous Court in *Giboney v. Empire Storage Co.,*336 U. S. 490, stated that labor unions could be restrained from picketing a firm in support of a secondary boycott which a State had validly outlawed. Mr. Justice Black said:

"It rarely has been suggested that the constitutional freedom for speech and press extends its immunity to speech or writing used as an integral part of conduct in violation of a valid criminal statute. We reject the contention now."

Id. at 336 U. S. 498.

[Footnote 2/7]

See United States v. 12 200-ft. Reels of Film, post, p. 413 U. S. 123; *United States v. Orito, post,* p. 413 U. S. 139; *Kois v. Wisconsin,*408 U. S. 229; *Byrne v. Karalexis,*396 U. S. 976, 977; *Ginsberg v. New York,*390 U. S. 629, 390 U. S. 650; *Jacobs v. New York,*388 U. S. 431, 388 U. S. 436; *Ginzburg v. United States,*383 U. S. 463, 383 U. S. 482; *Memoirs v. Massachusetts,*383 U. S. 413, 383 U. S. 424; *Bantam Books, Inc. v. Sullivan,*372 U. S. 58, 372 U. S. 72; *Times Film Corp. v. Chicago,*365 U. S. 43, 365 U. S. 78; *Smith v. California,*361 U. S. 147, 361 U. S. 167; *Kingsley Pictures Corp. v. Regents,*360 U. S. 684, 360 U. S. 697; *Roth v. United States,*354 U. S. 476, 354 U. S. 508; *Kingsley Books, Inc. v. Brown,*354 U. S. 436, 354 U. S. 446; *Superior Films, Inc. v. Department of Education,*346 U. S. 587, 346 U. S. 588; *Gelling v. Texas,*343 U. S. 60.

[Footnote 2/8]

The Commission on Obscenity and Pornography has advocated such a procedure:

"The Commission recommends the enactment, in all jurisdictions which enact or retain provisions prohibiting the dissemination of sexual materials to adults or young persons, of legislation authorizing prosecutors to obtain declaratory judgments as to whether particular materials fall within existing legal prohibitions. . . ."

"A declaratory judgment procedure . . . would permit prosecutors to proceed civilly, rather than through the criminal process, against suspected violations of obscenity prohibition. If such civil procedures are utilized, penalties would be imposed for violation of the law only with respect to conduct occurring after a civil declaration is obtained. The Commission believes this course of action to be appropriate whenever there is any existing doubt regarding the legal status of materials; where other alternatives are available, the criminal process should not ordinarily be invoked against persons who might have reasonably believed, in good faith, that the books or films they distributed were entitled to constitutional protection, for the threat of criminal sanctions might otherwise deter the free distribution of constitutionally protected material."

Report of the Commission on Obscenity and Pornography 63 (1970).

[Footnote 2/9]

Obscenity law has had a capricious history:

"The white slave traffic was first exposed by W. T. Stead in a magazine article, 'The Maiden Tribute.' The English law did absolutely nothing to the profiteers in vice, but put Stead in prison for a year for writing about an indecent subject. When the law supplies no definite standard of criminality, a judge, in deciding what is indecent or profane, may consciously disregard the sound test of present injury, and proceeding upon an entirely different theory may condemn the defendant because his words express ideas which are thought liable to cause bad future consequences. Thus, musical comedies enjoy almost unbridled license, while a problem play is often forbidden because opposed to our views of marriage. In the same way, the law of blasphemy has been used against Shelley's Queen Mab and the decorous promulgation of pantheistic ideas on the ground that to attack religion is to loosen the bonds of society and endanger the state. This is simply a round-about modern method to make heterodoxy in sex matters and even in religion a crime."

Z. Chafee, Free Speech in the United States 151 (1942).

MR. JUSTICE BRENNAN, with whom MR. JUSTICE STEWART and MR. JUSTICE MARSHALL join, dissenting.

In my dissent in *Paris Adult Theatre I v. Slaton, post,* p. 413 U. S. 73, decided this date, I noted that I had no occasion to consider the extent of state power to regulate the distribution of sexually oriented material to juveniles or the offensive exposure of such material to unconsenting adults. In the case before us, appellant was convicted of distributing obscene matter in violation of California Penal Code § 311.2, on the basis of evidence that he had caused to be mailed unsolicited brochures advertising various books and a movie. I need not now decide whether a statute might be drawn to impose, within the requirements of the First Amendment, criminal penalties for the precise conduct at issue here. For it is clear that, under my dissent in *Paris Adult Theatre I,* the statute under which the prosecution was brought is unconstitutionally overbroad, and therefore invalid on its face. *

"[T]he transcendent value to all society of constitutionally protected expression is deemed to justify allowing 'attacks on overly broad statutes with no requirement that the person making the attack demonstrate that his own conduct could not be regulated by a statute drawn with the requisite narrow specificity."

*Gooding v. Wilson,*405 U. S. 518, 405 U. S. 521 (1972), quoting from *Dombrowski v. Pfister,*380 U. S. 479, 380 U. S. 486 (1965). *See also Baggett v. Bullitt,*377 U. S. 360, 377 U. S. 366 (1964);*Coates v. City of Cincinnati,*402 U. S. 611, 402 U. S. 616 (1971); *id.* at 402 U. S. 619-620 (WHITE, J., dissenting); *United States v. Raines,*362 U. S. 17, 362 U. S. 21-22 (1960); *NAACP v. Button,*371 U. S. 415, 371 U. S. 433 (1963). Since my view in *Paris Adult Theatre I* represents a substantial departure from the course of our prior decisions, and since the state courts have as yet had no opportunity to consider whether a "readily apparent construction suggests itself as a vehicle for rehabilitating the [statute] in a single prosecution," *Dombrowski v. Pfister, supra,* at 380 U. S. 491, I would reverse the judgment of the Appellate Department of the Superior Court and remand the case for proceedings not inconsistent with this opinion. *See Coates v. City of Cincinnati, supra,* at 402 U. S. 616.

---

* Cal. Penal Code § 311.2(a) provides that

"Every person who knowingly: sends or causes to be sent, or brings or causes to be brought, into this state for sale or distribution, or in this state prepares, publishes, prints, exhibits, distributes, or offers to distribute, or has in his possession with intent to distribute or to exhibit or offer to distribute, any obscene matter is guilty of a misdemeanor."

19 PITTSBURGH PRESS CO. V. HUMAN REL. COMM'N, 413 U.S. 376 (1973)

Pittsburgh Press Co. v. Pittsburgh Commission on Human Relations
No. 72-419
Argued March 20, 1973
Decided June 21, 1973
413 U.S. 376

CERTIORARI TO THE COMMONWEALTH COURT OF PENNSYLVANIA

Syllabus

Following a complaint and hearing, respondent Pittsburgh Commission on Human Relations held that petitioner had violated a city ordinance by using an advertising system in its daily newspaper whereby employment opportunities are published under headings designating job preference by sex. On appeal from affirmance of the Commission's cease and desist order, the court below barred petitioner from referring to sex in employment headings, unless the want ads placed beneath them relate to employment opportunities not subject to the ordinance's prohibition against sex discrimination. Petitioner contends that the ordinance contravenes its constitutional rights to freedom of the press.

Held: The Pittsburgh ordinance, as construed to forbid newspapers to carry sex-designated advertising columns for nonexempt job opportunities, does not violate petitioner's First Amendment rights. Pp. 413 U. S. 381-391.

(a) The advertisements here, which did not implicate the newspaper's freedom of expression or its financial viability, were "purely commercial advertising," which is not protected by the First Amendment. *Valentine v. Chrestensen,*316 U. S. 52, 316 U. S. 54. *New York Times Co. v. Sullivan,*376 U. S. 254, distinguished. Pp. 413 U. S. 384-387.

(b) Petitioner's argument against maintaining the *Chrestensen* distinction between commercial and other speech is unpersuasive in the context of a case like this, where the regulation of the want ads was incidental to and coextensive with the regulation of employment discrimination. Pp. 413 U. S. 387-389.

(c) The Commission's order, which was clear and no broader than necessary, is not a prior restraint endangering arguably protected speech. Pp. 413 U. S. 389-390.

4 Pa.Commw. 448, 287 A.2d 161, affirmed.

POWELL, .J., delivered the opinion of the Court, in which BRENNAN, WHITE, MARSHALL, and REHNQUIST, JJ., joined. BURGER, C.J., *post*, and DOUGLAS, J., *post*, p. 413 U. S. 397, filed dissenting opinions. STEWART, J., filed a dissenting opinion, in which DOUGLAS, J., joined, *post*, p. 413 U. S. 400. BLACKMUN, J., filed a dissenting opinion, *post*, p. 413 U. S. 404.

MR. JUSTICE POWELL delivered the opinion of the Court.

The Human Relations Ordinance of the City of Pittsburgh (the Ordinance) has been construed below by the courts of Pennsylvania as forbidding newspapers to carry "help wanted" advertisements in sex-designated columns except where the employer or advertiser is free to make hiring or employment referral decisions on the basis of sex. We are called upon to decide whether the Ordinance, as so construed, violates the freedoms of speech and of the press guaranteed by the First and Fourteenth Amendments. This issue is a sensitive one, and a full understanding of the context in which it arises is critical to its resolution.

I

The Ordinance proscribes discrimination in employment on the basis of race, color, religion, ancestry, national origin, place of birth, or sex. [Footnote 1] In relevant part, § 8 of the Ordinance declares it to be unlawful employment practice, "except where based upon a *bona fide* occupational exemption certified by the Commission":

"(a) For any employer to refuse to hire any person or otherwise discriminate against any person with respect to hiring . . . because of . . . sex."
"* * * *"

"(e) For any 'employer,' employment agency or labor organization to publish or circulate, or to cause to be published or circulated, any notice or advertisement relating to 'employment' or membership which indicates any discrimination because of . . . sex."
"* * * *"

"(j) For any person, whether or not an employer, employment agency or labor organization, to aid . . . in the doing of any act declared to be an unlawful employment practice by this ordinance. . . . "

The present proceedings were initiated on October 9, 1969, when the National Organization for Women, Inc. (NOW) filed a complaint with the Pittsburgh Commission on Human Relations (the Commission), which is charged with implementing the Ordinance. The complaint alleged that the Pittsburgh Press Co. (Pittsburgh Press) was violating § 8(j) of the Ordinance by "allowing employers to place advertisements in the male or female columns, when the jobs advertised obviously do not have *bona fide*occupational qualifications or exceptions. . . ."

Finding probable cause to believe that Pittsburgh Press was violating the Ordinance, the Commission held a hearing, at which it received evidence and heard argument from the parties and from other interested organizations. Among the exhibits introduced at the hearing were clippings from the help wanted advertisements carried in the January 4, 1970, edition of the Sunday Pittsburgh Press, arranged by column. [Footnote 2] In many cases, the advertisements consisted simply of the job title, the salary, and the employment agency carrying the listing, while others included somewhat more extensive job descriptions. [Footnote 3]

On July 23, 1970, the Commission issued a Decision and Order. [Footnote 4] It found that, during 1969, Pittsburgh Press carried a total of 248,000 help wanted advertisements; that its practice before October, 1969, was to use columns captioned "Male Help Wanted," "Female Help Wanted," and "Male-Female Help Wanted"; that it thereafter used the captions "Jobs -- Male Interest," "Jobs -- Female Interest," and "Male-Female"; and that the advertisements were placed in the respective columns according to the advertiser's wishes, either volunteered by the advertiser or offered in response to inquiry by Pittsburgh Press. [Footnote 5] The Commission first concluded that § 8(e) of the Ordinance forbade employers, employment agencies, and labor organizations to submit advertisements for placement in sex-designated columns. It then held that Pittsburgh Press, in violation of § 8(j), aided the advertisers by maintaining a sex-designated classification system. After specifically considering and rejecting the argument that the Ordinance violated the First Amendment, the Commission ordered Pittsburgh Press to cease and desist such violations and to utilize a classification system with no reference to sex. This order was affirmed in all relevant respects by the Court of Common Pleas. [Footnote 6] On appeal in the Commonwealth Court, the scope of the order was narrowed to allow Pittsburgh Press to carry advertisements in sex-designated columns for jobs exempt from the antidiscrimination provisions of the Ordinance. As pointed out in that court's opinion, the Ordinance does not apply to employers of fewer than five persons, to employers outside the city of Pittsburgh, or to religious, fraternal, charitable, or sectarian organizations, nor does it apply to employment in domestic service or in jobs for which the Commission has certified a *bona fide* occupational exception. The modified order bars "all reference to sex in employment advertising column headings, except as may be exempt under said Ordinance, or as may be certified as exempt by said Commission." 4 Pa.Commw. 448, 470, 287 A.2d 161, 172 (1972). The Pennsylvania Supreme Court denied review, and we granted certiorari to decide whether, as Pittsburgh Press contends, the modified order violates the First Amendment by restricting its editorial judgment. 409 U.S. 1036 (1972). [Footnote 7] We affirm.

II

There is little need to reiterate that the freedoms of speech and of the press rank among our most cherished liberties. As Mr. Justice Black put it:

"In the First Amendment, the Founding Fathers gave the free press the protection it must have to fulfill its essential role in our democracy."

New York Times Co. v. United States, 403 U. S. 713, 403 U. S. 717 (1971) (concurring opinion). The durability of our system of self-government hinges upon the preservation of these freedoms.

"[S]ince informed public opinion is the most potent of all restraints upon misgovernment, the suppression or abridgement of the publicity afforded by a free press cannot be regarded otherwise than with grave concern. . . . A free press stands as one of the great interpreters between the government and the people. To allow it to be fettered is to fetter ourselves."

*Grosjean v. American Press Co.,*297 U. S. 233, 297 U. S. 250 (1936). The repeated emphasis accorded this theme in the decisions of this Court serves to underline the narrowness of the recognized exceptions to the principle that the press may not be regulated by the Government. Our inquiry must therefore be whether the challenged order falls within any of these exceptions.

At the outset, however, it is important to identify with some care the nature of the alleged abridgment. This is not a case in which the challenged law arguably disables the press by undermining its institutional viability. As the press has evolved from an assortment of small printers into a diverse aggregation including large publishing empires as well, the parallel growth and complexity of the economy have led to extensive regulatory legislation from which "[t]he publisher of a newspaper has no special immunity." *Associated Press v. NLRB,*301 U. S. 103, 301 U. S. 132 (1937). Accordingly, this Court has upheld application to the press of the National Labor Relations Act, *ibid.;* the Fair Labor Standards Act, *Mabee v. White Plains Publishing Co.,*327 U. S. 178 (1946); *Oklahoma Press Publishing Co. v. Walling,*327 U. S. 186 (1946); and the Sherman Antitrust Act, *Associated Press v. United States,*326 U. S. 1 (1945); *Citizen Publishing Co. v. United States,*394 U. S. 131 (1969). *See also Branzburg v. Hayes,*408 U. S. 665(1972). Yet the Court has recognized on several occasions the special institutional needs of a vigorous press by striking down laws taxing the advertising revenue of newspapers with circulations in excess of 20,000, *Grosjean v. American Press Co., supra;* requiring a license for the distribution of printed matter, *Lovell v. Griffin,*303 U. S. 444 (1938); and prohibiting the door-to-door distribution of leaflets, *Martin v. Struthers,*319 U. S. 141 (1043). [Footnote 8]

But no suggestion is made in this case that the Ordinance was passed with any purpose of muzzling or curbing the press. Nor does Pittsburgh Press argue that the Ordinance threatens its financial viability [Footnote 9] or impairs in any significant way its ability to publish and distribute its newspaper. In any event, such a contention would not be supported by the record.

III

In a limited way, however, the Ordinance, as construed, does affect the makeup of the help wanted section of the newspaper. Under the modified order, Pittsburgh Press will be required to abandon its present policy of providing sex-designated columns and allowing advertisers to select the columns in which their help wanted advertisements will be placed. In addition, the order does not allow Pittsburgh Press to substitute a policy under which it would make an independent decision regarding placement in sex-designated columns.

Respondents rely principally on the argument that this regulation is permissible because the speech is commercial speech unprotected by the First Amendment. The commercial speech doctrine is traceable to the brief opinion in *Valentine v. Chrestensen,*316 U. S. 52(1942), sustaining a city ordinance which had been interpreted to ban the distribution by handbill of an advertisement soliciting customers to pay admission to tour a submarine. Mr. Justice Roberts, speaking for a unanimous Court, said:

"We are . . . clear that the Constitution imposes no such restraint on government as respects purely commercial advertising."

Id. at 316 U. S. 54.

Subsequent cases have demonstrated, however, that speech is not rendered commercial by the mere fact that it relates to an advertisement. In *New York Times Co. v. Sullivan,*376 U. S. 254 (1964), a city official of Montgomery, Alabama, brought a libel action against four clergymen and the New York Times. The names of the clergymen had appeared in an advertisement, carried in the Times, criticizing police action directed against members of the civil rights movement. In holding that this political advertisement was entitled to the same degree of protection as ordinary speech, the Court stated:

"That the Times was paid for publishing the advertisement is as immaterial in this connection as is the fact that newspapers and books are sold."

Id. at 376 U. S. 266. *See also Smith v. California,*361 U. S. 147 (1959); *Ginzburg v. United States,*383 U. S. 463, 383 U. S. 474(1966). If a newspaper's profit motive were determinative, all aspects of its operations -- from the selection of news stories to the choice of editorial position -- would be subject to regulation if it could be established that they were conducted with a view toward increased sales. Such a basis for regulation clearly would be incompatible with the First Amendment.

The critical feature of the advertisement in *Valentine v. Chrestensen* was that, in the Court's view, it did no more than propose a commercial transaction, the sale of admission to a submarine. In *New York Times Co. v. Sullivan,* MR. JUSTICE BRENNAN, for the Court, found the *Chrestensen* advertisement easily distinguishable:

"The publication here was not a 'commercial' advertisement in the sense in which the word was used in *Chrestensen.* It communicated information, expressed opinion, recited grievances, protested claimed abuses, and sought financial support on behalf of a movement whose existence and objectives are matters of the highest public interest and concern."

376 U.S. at 376 U. S. 266. In the crucial respects, the advertisements in the present record resemble the *Chrestensen* rather than the *Sullivan* advertisement. None expresses a position on whether, as a matter of social policy, certain positions ought to be filled by members of one or the other sex, nor does any of them criticize the Ordinance or the Commission's enforcement practices. Each is no more than a proposal of possible employment. The advertisements are thus classic examples of commercial speech.

But Pittsburgh Press contends that *Chrestensen* is not applicable, as the focus in this case must be upon the exercise of editorial judgment by the newspaper as to where to place the advertisement, rather than upon its commercial content. The Commission made a finding of fact that Pittsburgh Press defers in every case to the advertiser's wishes regarding the column in which a want and should be placed. It is nonetheless true, however, that the newspaper does make a judgment whether or not to allow the advertiser to select the column. We must therefore consider whether this degree of judgmental discretion by the newspaper with respect to a purely commercial advertisement is distinguishable, for the purposes of First Amendment analysis, from the content of the advertisement itself. Or, to put the question differently, is the conduct of the newspaper with respect to the employment want and entitled to a protection under the First Amendment which the Court held in *Chrestensen* was not available to a commercial advertiser?

Under some circumstances, at least, a newspaper's editorial judgments in connection with an advertisement take on the character of the advertisement and, in those cases, the scope of the newspaper's First Amendment protection may be affected by the content of the advertisement. In the context of a libelous advertisement, for example, this Court has held that the First Amendment does not shield a newspaper from punishment for libel when with actual malice it publishes a falsely defamatory advertisement. *New York Times Co. v. Sullivan, supra,* at 376 U. S. 279-280. Assuming the requisite state of mind, then, nothing in a newspaper's editorial decision to accept an advertisement changes the character of the falsely defamatory statements. The newspaper may not defend a libel suit on the ground that the falsely defamatory statements are not its own.

Similarly, a commercial advertisement remains commercial in the hands of the media, at least under some circumstances. [Footnote 10] In *Capital Broadcasting Co. v. Acting Attorney General,* 405 U.S. 1000 (1972), *aff'g* 333 F.Supp. 582 (DC 1971), this Court summarily affirmed a district court decision sustaining the constitutionality of 15 U.S.C. § 1335, which prohibits the electronic media from carrying cigarette advertisements. The District Court there found that the advertising should be treated as commercial speech, even though the First Amendment challenge was mounted by radio broadcasters, rather than by advertisers. Because of the peculiar characteristics of the electronic media, *National Broadcasting Co. v. United States,* 319 U. S. 190, 319 U. S. 226-227 (1943), *Capital Broadcasting* is not dispositive here on the ultimate question of the constitutionality of the Ordinance. Its significance lies, rather, in its recognition that the exercise of this kind of editorial judgment does not necessarily strip commercial advertising of its commercial character. [Footnote 11]

As for the present case, we are not persuaded that either the decision to accept a commercial advertisement which the advertiser directs to be placed in a sex-designated column or the actual placement there lifts the newspaper's actions from the category of commercial speech. By implication at least, an advertiser whose want and appears in the "Jobs -- Male Interest" column is likely to discriminate against women in his hiring decisions. Nothing in a sex-designated column heading sufficiently dissociates the designation from the want ads placed beneath it to make the placement severable for First Amendment purposes from the want ads themselves. The combination, which conveys essentially the same message as an overtly discriminatory want ad, is, in practical effect, an integrated commercial statement.

Pittsburgh Press goes on to argue that, if this package of advertisement and placement is commercial speech, then commercial speech should be accorded a higher level of protection than *Chrestensen* and its progeny would suggest. Insisting that the exchange of information is as important in the commercial realm as in any other, the newspaper here would have us abrogate the distinction between commercial and other speech.

Whatever the merits of this contention may be in other contexts, it is unpersuasive in this case. Discrimination in employment is not only commercial activity, it is *illegal* commercial activity under the Ordinance. [Footnote 12] We have no doubt that a newspaper constitutionally could be forbidden to publish a want and proposing a sale of narcotics or soliciting prostitutes. Nor would the result be different if the nature of the transaction were indicated by placement under columns captioned "Narcotics for Sale" and "Prostitutes Wanted," rather than stated within the four corners of the advertisement.

The illegality in this case may be less overt, but we see no difference in principle here. Sex discrimination in nonexempt employment has been declared illegal under

§ 8(a) of the Ordinance, a provision not challenged here. And § 8(e) of the Ordinance forbids any employer, employment agency, or labor union to publish or cause to be published any advertisement "indicating" sex discrimination. This, too, is unchallenged. Moreover, the Commission specifically concluded that it is an unlawful employment practice for an advertiser to cause an employment advertisement to be published in a sex-designated column.

Section 8(j) of the Ordinance, the only provision which Pittsburgh Press was found to have violated and the only provision under attack here, makes it unlawful for "any person . . . to aid . . . in the doing of any act declared to be an unlawful employment practice by this ordinance." The Commission and the courts below concluded that the practice of placing want ads for nonexempt employment in sex-designated columns did indeed "aid" employers to indicate illegal sex preferences. The advertisements, as embroidered by their placement, signaled that the advertisers were likely to show an illegal sex preference in their hiring decisions. Any First Amendment interest which might be served by advertising an ordinary commercial proposal and which might arguably outweigh the governmental interest supporting the regulation is altogether absent when the commercial activity itself is illegal, and the restriction on advertising is incidental to a valid limitation on economic activity.

IV

It is suggested, in the brief of an *amicus curiae,* that, apart from other considerations, the Commission's order should be condemned as a prior restraint on expression. [Footnote 13] As described by Blackstone, the protection against prior restraint at common law barred only a system of administrative censorship:

"To subject the press to the restrictive power of a licenser, as was formerly done, both before and since the revolution, . . . is to subject all freedom of sentiment to the prejudices of one man, and make him the arbitrary and infallible judge of all controverted points in learning, religion, and government."

4 W. Blackstone, Commentaries *152. While the Court boldly stepped beyond this narrow doctrine in *Near v. Minnesota,* 283 U. S. 697(1931), in striking down an injunction against further publication of a newspaper found to be a public nuisance, it has never held that all injunctions are impermissible. *See Lorain Journal Co. v. United States,* 342 U. S. 143 (1951). The special vice of a prior restraint is that communication will be suppressed, either directly or by inducing excessive caution in the speaker, before an adequate determination that it is unprotected by the First Amendment.

The present order does not endanger arguably protected speech. Because the order is based on a continuing course of repetitive conduct, this is not a case in which the Court is asked to speculate as to the effect of publication. *Cf. New York Times Co. v. United States,* 403 U. S. 713 (1971). Moreover, the order is clear, and sweeps no more broadly than necessary. And because no interim relief was granted, the order will not have gone into effect before our final determination that the actions of *Pittsburgh Press* were unprotected. [Footnote 14]

V

We emphasize that nothing in our holding allows government at any level to forbid Pittsburgh Press to publish and distribute advertisements commenting on the Ordinance, the enforcement practices of the Commission, or the propriety of sex preferences in employment. Nor, *a fortiori*, does our decision authorize any restriction whatever, whether of content or layout, on stories or commentary originated by Pittsburgh Press, its columnists, or its contributors. On the contrary, we reaffirm unequivocally the protection afforded to editorial judgment and to the free expression of views on these and other issues, however controversial. We hold only that the Commission's modified order, narrowly drawn to prohibit placement in sex-designated columns of advertisements for nonexempt job opportunities, does not infringe the First Amendment rights of Pittsburgh Press.

Affirmed.

APPENDIX TO OPINION OF THE COURT

Among the advertisements carried in the Sunday Pittsburgh Press on January 4, 1970, was the following one, submitted by an employment agency and placed in the "JOBS -- MALE INTEREST" column:

```
------------------------------------
ACAD. INSTRUCTORS. . . . . .$13,000
ACCOUNTANTS. . . . . . . . . . . 10,000
ADM. ASS'T, CPA . . . . . . . .. ... 15,000
ADVERTISING MGR. . . . . . . 10,000
BOOKKEEPER F-C. . . . . . .. . 9,000
FINANCIAL CONSULTANT . 12,000
MARKETING MANAGER. . . . 15,000
MGMT. TRAINEE. . . . . . . . .. . 8,400
OFFICE MGR. TRAINEE. . . ... 7,200
LAND DEVELOPMENT . . . . .30,000
PRODUCT. MANAGER . . . . . . 18,000
PERSONNEL MANAGER . . .... . OPEN
SALES-ADVERTISING. . . . . . . . 8,400
SALES-CONSUMER . . . . . . . . . 9,600
SALES-INDUSTRIAL . . . . . . ... 12,000
SALES-MACHINERY. . . . . . . . . 8,400
RETAIL MGR . . . . . . . . . . . .. .... 15,000
Most Positions Fee Paid
EMPLOYMENT SPECIALISTS
2248 Oliver Bldg. 261-2250
Employment Agency
------------------------------------
```

App. 311a.

On the same day, the same agency's advertisement in the "JOBS -- FEMALE INTEREST" column was as follows:

```
------------------------------------
ACAD. INSTRUCTORS. . . . . . .$13,000
```

ACCOUNTANTS. 6,000
AUTO-INS. UNDERWRITER. .. OPEN
BOOKKEEPER-INS 5,000
CLERK-TYPIST 4,200
DRAFTSMAN. 6,000
KEYPUNCH D. T. 6,720
KEYPUNCH BEGINNER. 4,500
PROOFREADER. 4,900
RECEPTIONIST -- Mature D. T. OPEN
EXEC. SEC. 6,300
SECRETARY. 4,800
SECRETARY, Equal Oppor. 6,000
SECRETARY D. T. 5,400
TEACHERS-Pt. Time. . . . . day 33.
TYPIST-Statistical 5,000
Most Positions Fee Paid
EMPLOYMENT SPECIALISTS
2248 Oliver Bldg. 261-2250
Employment Agency

Ibid.

Characteristic of those offering fuller job descriptions was the following advertisement, carried in the "JOBS -- MALE INTEREST" column:

STAFF MANAGEMENT TRAINEE
TO $12,000
If you have had background in the management of small business then this could be
the stepping stone you have been waiting
for. You will be your own boss with no
cash outlay. Call or write today.

App. 313a.
[Footnote 1]
For the full text of the Ordinance and the 1969 amendment adding sex to the list of proscribed classifications, *see* App. 410a-436a.
[Footnote 2]
These exhibits are reproduced in App. 299a-333a.
[Footnote 3]
For examples of these want ads, *see* the Appendix to this opinion, *infra* at 413 U. S. 392-393.
[Footnote 4]
The full text of the Commission's Decision and Order is set forth in the Appendix to the Petition for Certiorari at 1a-18a.
[Footnote 5]
The Commission specifically found that:
"5. The Pittsburgh Press permits the advertiser to select the column within which its advertisement is to be inserted."

"6. When an advertiser does not indicate a column, the Press asks the advertiser whether it wants a male or female for the job and then inserts the advertisement in the jobs -- male interest or jobs -- female interest column accordingly."

Id. at 16a.

[Footnote 6]

See id. at 19a.

[Footnote 7]

Pittsburgh Press also argues that the Ordinance violates due process in that there is no rational connection between sex-designated column headings and sex discrimination in employment. It draws attention to a disclaimer which it runs at the beginning of each of the "Jobs -- Male Interest" and "Jobs -- Female Interest" columns:

"Notice to Job Seekers"

"Jobs are arranged under Male and Female classifications for the convenience of our readers. This is done because most jobs generally appeal more to persons of one sex than the other. Various laws and ordinances -- local, state, and federal, prohibit discrimination in employment because of sex unless sex is a *bona fide* occupational requirement. Unless the advertisement itself specifies one sex or the other, job seekers should assume that the advertiser will consider applicants of either sex in compliance with the laws against discrimination."

It suffices to dispose of this contention by noting that the Commission's common sense recognition that the two are connected is supported by evidence in the present record. *See* App. 236a-239a. *See also Hailes v. United Air Lines,* 464 F.2d 1006, 1009 (CA5 1972). The Guidelines on Discrimination Because of Sex of the Federal Equal Employment Opportunity Commission reflect a similar conclusion. *See* 9 CFR § 1604.4.

[Footnote 8]

See also Jones v. Opelika, 319 U. S. 103 (1943); *Murdock v. Pennsylvania,* 319 U. S. 105 (1943).

[Footnote 9]

In response to questioning at oral argument, counsel for Pittsburgh Press stated only:

"Now, I'm not prepared to answer whether the company makes money on [want ads] or not. I suspect it does. They charge for want ads, and they do make a lot of their revenue in the newspaper through advertising, of course, and I suspect it is profitable."

Tr. of Oral Arg. 10.

[Footnote 10]

In *Head v. New Mexico Board,* 374 U. S. 424 (1963), this Court upheld an injunction prohibiting a newspaper and a radio station from carrying optometrists' advertisements which violated New Mexico law. But because the issue had not been raised in the lower courts, this Court did not consider the appellant's First Amendment challenge. *Id.* at 374 U. S. 432 n. 12.

[Footnote 11]

See also New York State Broadcasters Assn. v. United States, 414 F.2d 990 (CA2 1969), *cert. denied,* 396 U.S. 1061 (1970) (refusing to strike down a ban on broadcasts promoting a lottery).

[Footnote 12]

See Note, Freedom of Expression in a Commercial Context, 78 Harv.L.Rev. 1191, 1195-1196 (1965). *Cf. Capital Broadcasting Co. v. Mitchell,* 333 F.Supp. 582, 593 n. 42 (D.C.1971) (Wright, J., dissenting); *Camp-of-the-Pines, Inc. v. New York Times Co.,* 184 Misc. 389, 53 N.Y.S.2d 475 (1945).

[Footnote 13]

Brief for *Amicus Curiae* American Newspaper Publishers Association 22 n. 32.

[Footnote 14]

The dissent of THE CHIEF JUSTICE argues that *Pittsburgh Press* is in danger of being "subject to summary punishment for contempt for having made an *unlucky' legal guess." Post at 413 U. S. 396-397. The Commission is without power to punish summarily for contempt. When it concludes that its order has been violated,*

"the Commission shall certify the case and the entire record of its proceedings to the City Solicitor, who shall invoke the aid of an appropriate court to secure enforcement or compliance with the order or to impose [a fine of not more than $300] or both."

§ 14 of the Ordinance; Appendix to Pet. for Cert. 103a. But, more fundamentally, it was the newspaper's policy of allowing employers to place advertisements in sex-designated columns without regard to the exceptions or exemptions contained in the Ordinance, not its treatment of particular want ads, which was challenged in the complaint and was found by the Commission and the courts below to be violative of the Ordinance. Nothing in the modified order or the opinions below prohibits the newspaper from relying in good faith on the representation of an advertiser that a particular job falls within an exception to the Ordinance.

20 GERTZ V. ROBERT WELCH, INC.
UNITED STATES SUPREME COURT
418 U.S. 323
Argued November 14, 1973
Decided June 25, 1974

Syllabus

A Chicago policeman named Nuccio was convicted of murder. The victim's family retained petitioner, a reputable attorney, to represent them in civil litigation against Nuccio. An article appearing in respondent's magazine alleged that Nuccio's murder trial was part of a Communist conspiracy to discredit the local police, and it falsely stated that petitioner had arranged Nuccio's "frame-up," implied that petitioner had a criminal record, and labeled him a "Communist-fronter." Petitioner brought this diversity libel action against respondent. After the jury returned a verdict for petitioner, the District Court decided that the standard enunciated in *New York Times Co. v. Sullivan*, 376 U.S. 254, which bars media liability for defamation of a public official absent proof that the defamatory statements were published with knowledge of their falsity or in reckless disregard of the truth, should apply to this suit. The court concluded that that standard protects media discussion of a public issue without regard to whether the person defamed is a public official as in *New York Times Co. v. Sullivan, supra,* or a public figure, as in *Curtis Publishing Co. v. Butts,* 388 U.S. 130. The court found that petitioner had failed to prove knowledge of falsity or reckless disregard for the truth and therefore entered judgment n. o. v. for respondent. The Court of Appeals affirmed. Held:

1. A publisher or broadcaster of defamatory falsehoods about an individual who is neither a public official nor a public figure may not claim the New York Times protection against liability for defamation on the ground that the defamatory statements concern an issue of public or general interest. Pp. 339-348.

(a) Because private individuals characteristically have less effective opportunities for rebuttal than do public officials and public figures, they are more vulnerable to injury from defamation. Because they have not voluntarily exposed themselves to increased risk of injury from defamatory falsehoods, they are also more deserving of recovery. The state interest in compensating [324] injury to the reputation of private individuals is therefore greater than for public officials and public figures. Pp. 343-345.

(b) To extend the New York Times standard to media defamation of private persons whenever an issue of general or public interest is involved would abridge to an unacceptable degree the legitimate state interest in compensating private individuals for injury to reputation and would occasion the additional difficulty of forcing courts to decide on an ad hoc basis which publications and broadcasts address issues of general or public interest and which do not. Pp. 345-346.

(c) So long as they do not impose liability without fault, the States may define for themselves the appropriate standard of liability for a publisher or broadcaster of defamatory falsehood which injures a private individual and whose substance makes substantial danger to reputation apparent. Pp. 347-348.

2. The States, however, may not permit recovery of presumed or punitive damages when liability is not based on knowledge of falsity or reckless disregard for the truth, and the private defamation plaintiff who establishes liability under a less demanding standard than the New York Times test may recover compensation only for actual injury. Pp. 348-350.

3. Petitioner was neither a public official nor a public figure. Pp. 351-352.

(a) Neither petitioner's past service on certain city committees nor his appearance as an attorney at the coroner's inquest into the death of the murder victim made him a public official. P. 351.

(b) Petitioner was also not a public figure. Absent clear evidence of general fame or notoriety in the community and pervasive involvement in ordering the affairs of society, an individual should not be deemed a public figure for all aspects of his life. Rather, the public-figure question should be determined by reference to the individual's participation in the particular controversy giving rise to the defamation. Petitioner's role in the Nuccio affair did not make him a public figure. Pp. 351-352.

471 F.2d 801, reversed and remanded.

POWELL, J., delivered the opinion of the Court, in which STEWART, MARSHALL, BLACKMUN, and REHNQUIST, JJ., joined. BLACKMUN, J., filed a concurring opinion, post, p. 353. BURGER, C. J., post, p. 354, DOUGLAS, J., post, p. 355, BRENNAN, J., post, p. 361, and WHITE, J., post, p. 369, filed dissenting opinions. [325]

MR. JUSTICE POWELL delivered the opinion of the Court.

This Court has struggled for nearly a decade to define the proper accommodation between the law of defamation and the freedoms of speech and press protected by the First Amendment. With this decision we return to that effort. We granted certiorari to reconsider the extent of a publisher's constitutional privilege against liability for defamation of a private citizen. 410 U.S. 925 (1973).

I

In 1968 a Chicago policeman named Nuccio shot and killed a youth named Nelson. The state authorities prosecuted Nuccio for the homicide and ultimately obtained a conviction for murder in the second degree. The Nelson family retained petitioner Elmer Gertz, a reputable attorney, to represent them in civil litigation against Nuccio.

Respondent publishes American Opinion, a monthly outlet for the views of the John Birch Society. Early in the 1960's the magazine began to warn of a nationwide conspiracy to discredit local law enforcement agencies and create in their stead a national police force capable of supporting a Communist dictatorship. As part of the continuing effort to alert the public to this assumed danger, the managing editor of American Opinion commissioned an article on the murder trial of Officer Nuccio. For this purpose he engaged a regular contributor to the magazine. In March 1969 respondent published the resulting article under the title "FRAME-UP: Richard [326] Nuccio And The War On Police." The article purports to demonstrate that the testimony against Nuccio at his criminal trial was false and that his prosecution was part of the Communist campaign against the police.

In his capacity as counsel for the Nelson family in the civil litigation, petitioner attended the coroner's inquest into the boy's death and initiated actions for damages, but he neither discussed Officer Nuccio with the press nor played any part in the criminal proceeding. Notwithstanding petitioner's remote connection with the prosecution of Nuccio, respondent's magazine portrayed him as an architect of the "frame-up." According to the article, the police file on petitioner took "a big, Irish cop to lift." The article stated that petitioner had been an official of the "Marxist League for Industrial Democracy, originally known as the Intercollegiate Socialist Society, which has advocated the violent seizure of our government." It labeled Gertz a "Leninist" and a "Communist-fronter." It also stated that Gertz had been an officer of the National Lawyers Guild, described as a Communist organization that "probably did more than any other outfit to plan the Communist attack on the Chicago police during the 1968 Democratic Convention."

These statements contained serious inaccuracies. The implication that petitioner had a criminal record was false. Petitioner had been a member and officer of the National Lawyers Guild some 15 years earlier, but there was no evidence that he or that organization had taken any part in planning the 1968 demonstrations in Chicago. There was also no basis for the charge that petitioner was a "Leninist" or a "Communist-fronter." And he had never been a member of the "Marxist League for Industrial Democracy" or the "Intercollegiate Socialist Society." [327]

The managing editor of American Opinion made no effort to verify or substantiate the charges against petitioner. Instead, he appended an editorial introduction stating that the author had "conducted extensive research into the Richard Nuccio Case." And he included in the article a photograph of petitioner and wrote the caption that appeared under it: "Elmer Gertz of Red Guild harrasses Nuccio." Respondent placed the issue of American Opinion containing the article on sale at newsstands throughout the country and distributed reprints of the article on the streets of Chicago.

Petitioner filed a diversity action for libel in the United States District Court for the Northern District of Illinois. He claimed that the falsehoods published by respondent injured his reputation as a lawyer and a citizen. Before filing an answer, respondent moved to dismiss the complaint for failure to state a claim upon which relief could be granted, apparently on the ground that petitioner failed to allege special damages. But the court ruled that statements contained in the article constituted libel per se under Illinois law and that consequently petitioner need not plead special damages. 306 F. Supp. 310 (1969).

After answering the complaint, respondent filed a pretrial motion for summary judgment, claiming a constitutional privilege against liability for defamation.[note 1] It asserted that petitioner was a public official or a public figure and that the article concerned an issue of public interest and concern. For these reasons, respondent argued, it was entitled to invoke the privilege enunciated in *New York Times Co. v. Sullivan*, 376 U.S. 254 (1964). Under this rule respondent would escape liability unless [328] petitioner could prove publication of defamatory falsehood "with 'actual malice'--that is, with knowledge that it was false or with reckless disregard of whether it was false or not." *Id.*, at 280. Respondent claimed that petitioner could not make such a showing and submitted a supporting affidavit by the magazine's managing editor. The editor denied any knowledge of the falsity of the statements concerning petitioner and stated that he had relied on the author's reputation and on his prior experience with the accuracy and authenticity of the author's contributions to American Opinion.

The District Court denied respondent's motion for summary judgment in a memorandum opinion of September 16, 1970. The court did not dispute respondent's claim to the protection of the New York Times standard. Rather, it concluded that petitioner might overcome the constitutional privilege by making a factual showing sufficient to prove publication of defamatory falsehood in reckless disregard of the truth. During the course of the trial, however, it became clear that the trial court had not accepted all of respondent's asserted grounds for applying the New York Times rule to this case. It thought that respondent's claim to the protection of the constitutional privilege depended on the contention that petitioner was either a public official under the New York Times decision or a public figure under *Curtis Publishing Co. v. Butts*, 388 U.S. 130 (1967), apparently discounting the argument that a privilege would arise from the presence of a public issue. After all the evidence had been presented but before submission of the case to the jury, the court ruled in effect that petitioner was neither a public official nor a public figure. It added that, if he were, the resulting application of the New York Times standard would require a directed verdict for respondent. Because some statements in the article constituted libel per se [329] under Illinois law, the court submitted the case to the jury under instructions that withdrew from its consideration all issues save the measure of damages. The jury awarded $50,000 to petitioner.

Following the jury verdict and on further reflection, the District Court concluded that the New York Times standard should govern this case even though petitioner was not a public official or public figure. It accepted respondent's contention that that privilege protected discussion of any public issue without regard to the status of a person defamed therein. Accordingly, the court entered judgment for respondent notwithstanding the jury's verdict.[note 2] This conclusion anticipated the reasoning [330] of a plurality of this Court in *Rosenbloom v. Metromedia, Inc.*, 403 U.S. 29 (1971).

Petitioner appealed to contest the applicability of the New York Times standard to this case. Although the Court of Appeals for the Seventh Circuit doubted the correctness of the District Court's determination that petitioner was not a public figure, it did not overturn that finding.[note 3] It agreed with the District Court that respondent could assert the constitutional privilege because the article concerned a matter of public interest, citing this Court's intervening decision in *Rosenbloom v. Metromedia, Inc.*, *supra*. The Court of Appeals read

Rosenbloom to require application of the New York Times standard to any publication or broadcast about an issue of significant public interest, without regard to the position, fame, or anonymity of the person defamed, and it concluded that respondent's statements [331] concerned such an issue.[note 4] After reviewing the record, the Court of Appeals endorsed the District Court's conclusion that petitioner had failed to show by clear and [332] convincing evidence that respondent had acted with "actual malice" as defined by New York Times. There was no evidence that the managing editor of American Opinion knew of the falsity of the accusations made in the article. In fact, he knew nothing about petitioner except what he learned from the article. The court correctly noted that mere proof of failure to investigate, without more, cannot establish reckless disregard for the truth. Rather, the publisher must act with a "'high degree of awareness of . . . probable falsity.'" *St. Amant v. Thompson*, 390 U.S. 727, 731 (1968); accord, *Beckley Newspapers Corp. v. Hanks*, 389 U.S. 81, 84-85 (1967); *Garrison v. Louisiana*, 379 U.S. 64, 75-76 (1964). The evidence in this case did not reveal that respondent had cause for such an awareness. The Court of Appeals therefore affirmed, 471 F.2d 801 (1972). For the reasons stated below, we reverse.

II

The principal issue in this case is whether a newspaper or broadcaster that publishes defamatory falsehoods about an individual who is neither a public official nor a public figure may claim a constitutional privilege against liability for the injury inflicted by those statements. The Court considered this question on the rather different set of facts presented in *Rosenbloom v. Metromedia, Inc.*, 403 U.S. 29 (1971). Rosenbloom, a distributor of nudist magazines, was arrested for selling allegedly obscene material while making [333] a delivery to a retail dealer. The police obtained a warrant and seized his entire inventory of 3,000 books and magazines. He sought and obtained an injunction prohibiting further police interference with his business. He then sued a local radio station for failing to note in two of its newscasts that the 3,000 items seized were only "reportedly" or "allegedly" obscene and for broadcasting references to "the smut literature racket" and to "girliebook peddlers" in its coverage of the court proceeding for injunctive relief. He obtained a judgment against the radio station, but the Court of Appeals for the Third Circuit held the New York Times privilege applicable to the broadcast and reversed. 415 F.2d 892 (1969).

This Court affirmed the decision below, but no majority could agree on a controlling rationale. The eight Justices [note 5] who participated in Rosenbloom announced their views in five separate opinions, none of which commanded more than three votes. The several statements not only reveal disagreement about the appropriate result in that case, they also reflect divergent traditions of thought about the general problem of reconciling the law of defamation with the First Amendment. One approach has been to extend the New York Times test to an expanding variety of situations. Another has been to vary the level of constitutional privilege for defamatory falsehood with the status of the person defamed. And a third view would grant to the press and broadcast media absolute immunity from liability for defamation. To place our holding in the proper context, we preface our discussion of this case with a review of the several Rosenbloom opinions and their antecedents.

In affirming the trial court's judgment in the instant case, the Court of Appeals relied on MR. JUSTICE BRENNAN'S [334] conclusion for the Rosenbloom plurality that "all discussion and communication involving matters of public or general concern," 403 U.S., at 44, warrant the protection from liability for defamation accorded by the rule originally enunciated in *New York Times Co. v. Sullivan*, 376 U.S. 254 (1964). There this Court defined a constitutional privilege intended to free criticism of public officials from the restraints imposed by the common law of defamation. The Times ran a political advertisement endorsing civil rights demonstrations by black students in Alabama and impliedly condemning the performance of local law-enforcement officials. A police commissioner established in state court that certain misstatements in the advertisement referred to him and that they constituted libel per se under Alabama law. This showing left the Times with the single defense of truth, for under Alabama law neither good faith nor reasonable care would protect the newspaper from liability. This Court concluded that a "rule compelling the critic of official conduct to guarantee the truth of all his factual assertions" would deter protected speech, *id.*, at 279, and announced the constitutional privilege designed to counter that effect:

"The constitutional guarantees require, we think, a federal rule that prohibits a public official from recovering damages for a defamatory falsehood relating to his official conduct unless he proves that the statement was made with 'actual malice'--that is, with knowledge that it was false or with reckless disregard of whether it was false or not." *Id.*, at 279-280.6 [335]

Three years after New York Times, a majority of the Court agreed to extend the constitutional privilege to defamatory criticism of "public figures." This extension [336] was announced in *Curtis Publishing Co. v. Butts* and its companion, *Associated Press v. Walker*, 388 U.S. 130, 162 (1967). The first case involved the Saturday Evening Post's charge that Coach Wally Butts of the University of Georgia had conspired with Coach "Bear" Bryant of the University of Alabama to fix a football game between their respective schools. Walker involved an erroneous Associated Press account of former Major General Edwin Walker's participation in a University of Mississippi campus riot. Because Butts was paid by a private alumni association and Walker had resigned from the Army, neither could be classified as a "public official" under New York Times. Although Mr. Justice Harlan announced the result in both cases, a majority of the Court agreed with Mr. Chief Justice Warren's conclusion that the New York Times test should apply to criticism of "public figures" as well as "public officials."7 The Court extended the constitutional [337] privilege announced in that case to protect defamatory criticism of nonpublic persons who "are nevertheless intimately involved in the resolution of important public questions or, by reason of their fame, shape events in areas of concern to society at large." *Id.*, at 164 (Warren, C. J., concurring in result).

In his opinion for the plurality in *Rosenbloom v. Metromedia, Inc.*, 403 U.S. 29 (1971), MR. JUSTICE BRENNAN took the New York Times privilege one step further. He concluded that its protection should extend to defamatory falsehoods relating to private persons if the statements concerned matters of general or public interest. He abjured the suggested distinction between public officials and public figures on the one hand and private individuals on the other. He focused instead on society's interest in learning about certain issues: "If a matter is a subject of public or general interest, it cannot suddenly become less so merely because a private individual is involved, or because in some sense the individual did not 'voluntarily' choose to become involved." *Id.*, at 43. Thus, under the plurality opinion, a private citizen involuntarily associated with a matter of general interest has no recourse for injury to his reputation unless he can satisfy the demanding requirements of the New York Times test.

Two Members of the Court concurred in the result in Rosenbloom but departed from the reasoning of the plurality. Mr. Justice Black restated his view, long shared by MR. JUSTICE DOUGLAS, that the First Amendment cloaks the news media with an absolute and indefeasible immunity from liability for defamation. *Id.,* at 57. MR JUSTICE WHITE concurred on a narrower ground. *Ibid.* He concluded that "the First Amendment gives the press and the broadcast media a privilege to report and comment upon the official actions of public [338] servants in full detail, with no requirement that the reputation or the privacy of an individual involved in or affected by the official action be spared from public view." *Id.,* at 62. He therefore declined to reach the broader questions addressed by the other Justices.

Mr. Justice Harlan dissented. Although he had joined the opinion of the Court in New York Times, in Curtis Publishing Co. he had contested the extension of the privilege to public figures. There he had argued that a public figure who held no governmental office should be allowed to recover damages for defamation "on a showing of highly unreasonable conduct constituting an extreme departure from the standards of investigation and reporting ordinarily adhered to by responsible publishers." 388 U.S., at 155. In his *Curtis Publishing Co.* opinion Mr. Justice Harlan had distinguished New York Times primarily on the ground that defamation actions by public officials "lay close to seditious libel . . . ." *Id.,* at 153. Recovery of damages by one who held no public office, however, could not "be viewed as a vindication of governmental policy." *Id.,* at 154. Additionally, he had intimated that, because most public officials enjoyed absolute immunity from liability for their own defamatory utterances under *Barr v. Matteo,* 360 U.S. 564 (1959), they lacked a strong claim to the protection of the courts.

In *Rosenbloom* Mr. Justice Harlan modified these views. He acquiesced in the application of the privilege to defamation of public figures but argued that a different rule should obtain where defamatory falsehood harmed a private individual. He noted that a private person has less likelihood "of securing access to channels of communication sufficient to rebut falsehoods concerning him" than do public officials and public figures, 403 U.S., at 70, and has not voluntarily placed himself in the [339] public spotlight. Mr. Justice Harlan concluded that the States could constitutionally allow private individuals to recover damages for defamation on the basis of any standard of care except liability without fault.

MR. JUSTICE MARSHALL dissented in Rosenbloom in an opinion joined by MR. JUSTICE STEWART. *Id.,* at 78. He thought that the plurality's "public or general interest" test for determining the applicability of the New York Times privilege would involve the courts in the dangerous business of deciding "what information is relevant to self-government." *Id.,* at 79. He also contended that the plurality's position inadequately served "society's interest in protecting private individuals from being thrust into the public eye by the distorting light of defamation." *Ibid.* MR. JUSTICE MARSHALL therefore reached the conclusion, also reached by Mr. Justice Harlan, that the States should be "essentially free to continue the evolution of the common law of defamation and to articulate whatever fault standard best suits the State's need," so long as the States did not impose liability without fault. *Id.,* at 86. The principal point of disagreement among the three dissenters concerned punitive damages. Whereas Mr. Justice Harlan thought that the States could allow punitive damages in amounts bearing "a reasonable and purposeful relationship to the actual harm done . . . ," *id.,* at 75, MR. JUSTICE MARSHALL concluded that the size and unpredictability of jury awards of exemplary damages unnecessarily exacerbated the problems of media self-censorship and that such damages should therefore be forbidden.

III

We begin with the common ground. Under the First Amendment there is no such thing as a false idea. However pernicious an opinion may seem, we depend for its correction not on the conscience of judges and juries but [340] on the competition of other ideas.[note 8] But there is no constitutional value in false statements of fact. Neither the intentional lie nor the careless error materially advances society's interest in "uninhibited, robust, and wide-open" debate on public issues. *New York Times Co. v. Sullivan*, 376 U.S., at 270. They belong to that category of utterances which "are no essential part of any exposition of ideas, and are of such slight social value as a step to truth that any benefit that may be derived from them is clearly outweighed by the social interest in order and morality." *Chaplinsky v. New Hampshire*, 315 U.S. 568, 572 (1942).

Although the erroneous statement of fact is not worthy of constitutional protection, it is nevertheless inevitable in free debate. As James Madison pointed out in the Report on the Virginia Resolutions of 1798: "Some degree of abuse is inseparable from the proper use of every thing; and in no instance is this more true than in that of the press." 4 J. Elliot, Debates on the Federal Constitution of 1787, p. 571 (1876). And punishment of error runs the risk of inducing a cautious and restrictive exercise of the constitutionally guaranteed freedoms of speech and press. Our decisions recognize that a rule of strict liability that compels a publisher or broadcaster to guarantee the accuracy of his factual assertions may lead to intolerable self-censorship. Allowing the media to avoid liability only by proving the truth of all injurious statements does not accord adequate protection to First Amendment liberties. As the Court stated in *New York Times Co. v. Sullivan, supra*, at 279: "Allowance of the defense of truth, [341] with the burden of proving it on the defendant, does not mean that only false speech will be deterred." The First Amendment requires that we protect some falsehood in order to protect speech that matters.

The need to avoid self-censorship by the news media is, however, not the only societal value at issue. If it were, this Court would have embraced long ago the view that publishers and broadcasters enjoy an unconditional and indefeasible immunity from liability for defamation. See *New York Times Co. v. Sullivan, supra*, at 293 (Black, J., concurring); *Garrison v. Louisiana*, 379 U.S., at 80 (DOUGLAS, J., concurring); *Curtis Publishing Co. v. Butts*, 388 U.S., at 170 (opinion of Black, J.). Such a rule would, indeed, obviate the fear that the prospect of civil liability for injurious falsehood might dissuade a timorous press from the effective exercise of First Amendment freedoms. Yet absolute protection for the communications media requires a total sacrifice of the competing value served by the law of defamation.

The legitimate state interest underlying the law of libel is the compensation of individuals for the harm inflicted on them by defamatory falsehood. We would not lightly require the State to abandon this purpose, for, as MR. JUSTICE STEWART has reminded us, the individual's right to the protection of his own good name "reflects no more than our basic concept of the essential dignity and worth of every human being--a concept at the root of any decent system of ordered liberty. The protection of private personality, like the protection of life itself, is left primarily to the individual States under the Ninth and Tenth Amendments. But this does not mean that the right is entitled to any less recognition by this Court as a basic of our constitutional system." *Rosenblatt v. Baer*, 383 U.S. 75, 92 (1966) (concurring opinion). [342]

Some tension necessarily exists between the need for a vigorous and uninhibited press and the legitimate interest in redressing wrongful injury. As Mr. Justice Harlan stated, "some antithesis between freedom of speech and press and libel actions persists, for libel remains premised on the content of speech and limits the freedom of the publisher to express certain sentiments, at least without guaranteeing legal proof of their substantial accuracy." *Curtis Publishing Co. v. Butts, supra,* at 152. In our continuing effort to define the proper accommodation between these competing concerns, we have been especially anxious to assure to the freedoms of speech and press that "breathing space" essential to their fruitful exercise. *NAACP v. Button,* 371 U.S. 415, 433 (1963). To that end this Court has extended a measure of strategic protection to defamatory falsehood.

The New York Times standard defines the level of constitutional protection appropriate to the context of defamation of a public person. Those who, by reason of the notoriety of their achievements or the vigor and success with which they seek the public's attention, are properly classed as public figures and those who hold governmental office may recover for injury to reputation only on clear and convincing proof that the defamatory falsehood was made with knowledge of its falsity or with reckless disregard for the truth. This standard administers an extremely powerful antidote to the inducement to media self-censorship of the common-law rule of strict liability for libel and slander. And it exacts a correspondingly high price from the victims of defamatory falsehood. Plainly many deserving plaintiffs, including some intentionally subjected to injury, will be unable to surmount the barrier of the New York Times test. Despite this [343] substantial abridgment of the state law right to compensation for wrongful hurt to one's reputation, the Court has concluded that the protection of the New York Times privilege should be available to publishers and broadcasters of defamatory falsehood concerning public officials and public figures. *New York Times Co. v. Sullivan, supra; Curtis Publishing Co. v. Butts, supra.* We think that these decisions are correct, but we do not find their holdings justified solely by reference to the interest of the press and broadcast media in immunity from liability. Rather, we believe that the New York Times rule states an accommodation between this concern and the limited state interest present in the context of libel actions brought by public persons. For the reasons stated below, we conclude that the state interest in compensating injury to the reputation of private individuals requires that a different rule should obtain with respect to them.

Theoretically, of course, the balance between the needs of the press and the individual's claim to compensation for wrongful injury might be struck on a case-by-case basis. As Mr. Justice Harlan hypothesized, "it might seem, purely as an abstract matter, that the most utilitarian approach would be to scrutinize carefully every jury verdict in every libel case, in order to ascertain whether the final judgment leaves fully protected whatever First Amendment values transcend the legitimate state interest in protecting the particular plaintiff who prevailed." *Rosenbloom v. Metromedia, Inc.,* 403 U.S., at 63 (footnote omitted). But this approach would lead to unpredictable results and uncertain expectations, and it could render our duty to supervise the lower courts unmanageable. Because an ad hoc resolution of the competing interests at stake in each particular case is not feasible, we must lay down broad rules of general [344] application. Such rules necessarily treat alike various cases involving differences as well as similarities. Thus it is often true that not all of the considerations which justify adoption of a given rule will obtain in each particular case decided under its authority.

With that caveat we have no difficulty in distinguishing among defamation plaintiffs. The first remedy of any victim of defamation is self-help--using available opportunities to contradict the lie or correct the error and thereby to minimize its adverse impact on reputation. Public officials and public figures usually enjoy significantly greater access to the channels of effective communication and hence have a more realistic opportunity to counteract false statements than private individuals normally enjoy.[note 9] Private individuals are therefore more vulnerable to injury, and the state interest in protecting them is correspondingly greater.

More important than the likelihood that private individuals will lack effective opportunities for rebuttal, there is a compelling normative consideration underlying the distinction between public and private defamation plaintiffs. An individual who decides to seek governmental office must accept certain necessary consequences of that involvement in public affairs. He runs the risk of closer public scrutiny than might otherwise be the case. And society's interest in the officers of government is not strictly limited to the formal discharge of official duties. As the Court pointed out in *Garrison v. Louisiana*, 379 U.S., at 77, the public's interest extends to "anything [345] which might touch on an official's fitness for office . . . . Few personal attributes are more germane to fitness for office than dishonesty, malfeasance, or improper motivation, even though these characteristics may also affect the official's private character."

Those classed as public figures stand in a similar position. Hypothetically, it may be possible for someone to become a public figure through no purposeful action of his own, but the instances of truly involuntary public figures must be exceedingly rare. For the most part those who attain this status have assumed roles of especial prominence in the affairs of society. Some occupy positions of such persuasive power and influence that they are deemed public figures for all purposes. More commonly, those classed as public figures have thrust themselves to the forefront of particular public controversies in order to influence the resolution of the issues involved. In either event, they invite attention and comment.

Even if the foregoing generalities do not obtain in every instance, the communications media are entitled to act on the assumption that public officials and public figures have voluntarily exposed themselves to increased risk of injury from defamatory falsehood concerning them. No such assumption is justified with respect to a private individual. He has not accepted public office or assumed an "influential role in ordering society." *Curtis Publishing Co. v. Butts*, 388 U.S., at 164 (Warren, C. J., concurring in result). He has relinquished no part of his interest in the protection of his own good name, and consequently he has a more compelling call on the courts for redress of injury inflicted by defamatory falsehood. Thus, private individuals are not only more vulnerable to injury than public officials and public figures; they are also more deserving of recovery.

For these reasons we conclude that the States should retain substantial latitude in their efforts to enforce a [346] legal remedy for defamatory falsehood injurious to the reputation of a private individual. The extension of the New York Times test proposed by the Rosenbloom plurality would abridge this legitimate state interest to a degree that we find unacceptable. And it would occasion the additional difficulty of forcing state and federal judges to decide on an ad hoc basis which publications address issues of "general or public interest" and which do not--to determine, in the words of MR. JUSTICE MARSHALL, "what information is relevant to self-government." *Rosenbloom v. Metromedia, Inc.*, 403 U.S., at 79. We doubt the wisdom of committing this task to the conscience of judges. Nor does the Constitution require us to draw so thin a line between the drastic alternatives of the New

York Times privilege and the common law of strict liability for defamatory error. The "public or general interest" test for determining the applicability of the New York Times standard to private defamation actions inadequately serves both of the competing values at stake. On the one hand, a private individual whose reputation is injured by defamatory falsehood that does concern an issue of public or general interest has no recourse unless he can meet the rigorous requirements of New York Times. This is true despite the factors that distinguish the state interest in compensating private individuals from the analogous interest involved in the context of public persons. On the other hand, a publisher or broadcaster of a defamatory error which a court deems unrelated to an issue of public or general interest may be held liable in damages even if it took every reasonable precaution to ensure the accuracy of its assertions. And liability may far exceed compensation for any actual injury to the plaintiff, for the jury may be permitted to presume damages without proof of loss and even to award punitive damages. [347]

We hold that, so long as they do not impose liability without fault, the States may define for themselves the appropriate standard of liability for a publisher or broadcaster of defamatory falsehood injurious to a private individual. [note10] This approach provides a more equitable [348] boundary between the competing concerns involved here. It recognizes the strength of the legitimate state interest in compensating private individuals for wrongful injury to reputation, yet shields the press and broadcast media from the rigors of strict liability for defamation. At least this conclusion obtains where, as here, the substance of the defamatory statement "makes substantial danger to reputation apparent."11 This phrase places in perspective the conclusion we announce today. Our inquiry would involve considerations somewhat different from those discussed above if a State purported to condition civil liability on a factual misstatement whose content did not warn a reasonably prudent editor or broadcaster of its defamatory potential. Cf. *Time, Inc. v. Hill*, 385 U.S. 374 (1967). Such a case is not now before us, and we intimate no view as to its proper resolution.

IV

Our accommodation of the competing values at stake in defamation suits by private individuals allows the States to impose liability on the publisher or broadcaster of defamatory falsehood on a less demanding showing than that required by New York Times. This conclusion is not based on a belief that the considerations which prompted the adoption of the New York Times privilege for defamation of public officials and its extension to public figures are wholly inapplicable to the context of private individuals. Rather, we endorse this approach in recognition of the strong and legitimate state interest in compensating private individuals for injury to reputation. [349] But this countervailing state interest extends no further than compensation for actual injury. For the reasons stated below, we hold that the States may not permit recovery of presumed or punitive damages, at least when liability is not based on a showing of knowledge of falsity or reckless disregard for the truth.

The common law of defamation is an oddity of tort law, for it allows recovery of purportedly compensatory damages without evidence of actual loss. Under the traditional rules pertaining to actions for libel, the existence of injury is presumed from the fact of publication. Juries may award substantial sums as compensation for supposed damage to reputation without any proof that such harm actually occurred. The largely uncontrolled discretion of juries to award damages where there is no loss unnecessarily compounds the potential of any system of liability for defamatory falsehood to inhibit the vigorous exercise of First Amendment freedoms. Additionally, the doctrine of presumed damages invites juries to punish unpopular opinion rather than to compensate individuals for injury sustained by the publication of a false fact. More to the point, the States have no substantial interest in securing for plaintiffs such as this petitioner gratuitous awards of money damages far in excess of any actual injury.

We would not, of course, invalidate state law simply because we doubt its wisdom, but here we are attempting to reconcile state law with a competing interest grounded in the constitutional command of the First Amendment. It is therefore appropriate to require that state remedies for defamatory falsehood reach no farther than is necessary to protect the legitimate interest involved. It is necessary to restrict defamation plaintiffs who do not prove knowledge of falsity or reckless disregard for the truth to compensation for actual injury. We [350] need not define "actual injury," as trial courts have wide experience in framing appropriate jury instructions in tort actions. Suffice it to say that actual injury is not limited to out-of-pocket loss. Indeed, the more customary types of actual harm inflicted by defamatory falsehood include impairment of reputation and standing in the community, personal humiliation, and mental anguish and suffering. Of course, juries must be limited by appropriate instructions, and all awards must be supported by competent evidence concerning the injury, although there need be no evidence which assigns an actual dollar value to the injury.

We also find no justification for allowing awards of punitive damages against publishers and broadcasters held liable under state-defined standards of liability for defamation. In most jurisdictions jury discretion over the amounts awarded is limited only by the gentle rule that they not be excessive. Consequently, juries assess punitive damages in wholly unpredictable amounts bearing no necessary relation to the actual harm caused. And they remain free to use their discretion selectively to punish expressions of unpopular views. Like the doctrine of presumed damages, jury discretion to award punitive damages unnecessarily exacerbates the danger of media self-censorship, but, unlike the former rule, punitive damages are wholly irrelevant to the state interest that justifies a negligence standard for private defamation actions. They are not compensation for injury. Instead, they are private fines levied by civil juries to punish reprehensible conduct and to deter its future occurrence. In short, the private defamation plaintiff who established liability under a less demanding standard than that stated by New York Times may recover only such damages as are sufficient to compensate him for actual injury. [351]

V

Notwithstanding our refusal to extend the New York Times privilege to defamation of private individuals, respondent contends that we should affirm the judgment below on the ground that petitioner is either a public official or a public figure. There is little basis for the former assertion. Several years prior to the present incident, petitioner had served briefly on housing committees appointed by the mayor of Chicago, but at the time of publication he had never held any remunerative governmental position. Respondent admits this but argues that petitioner's appearance at the coroner's inquest rendered him a "de facto public official." Our cases recognize no such concept. Respondent's suggestion would sweep all lawyers under the New York Times rule as officers of the court and distort the plain meaning of the "public official" category beyond all recognition. We decline to follow it.

Respondent's characterization of petitioner as a public figure raises a different question.

That designation may rest on either of two alternative bases. In some instances an individual may achieve such pervasive fame or notoriety that he becomes a public figure for all purposes and in all contexts. More commonly, an individual voluntarily injects himself or is drawn into a particular public controversy and thereby becomes a public figure for a limited range of issues. In either case such persons assume special prominence in the resolution of public questions.

Petitioner has long been active in community and professional affairs. He has served as an officer of local civic groups and of various professional organizations, and he has published several books and articles on legal subjects. Although petitioner was consequently well known in some circles, he had achieved no general fame [352] or notoriety in the community. None of the prospective jurors called at the trial had ever heard of petitioner prior to this litigation, and respondent offered no proof that this response was atypical of the local population. We would not lightly assume that a citizen's participation in community and professional affairs rendered him a public figure for all purposes. Absent clear evidence of general fame or notoriety in the community, and pervasive involvement in the affairs of society, an individual should not be deemed a public personality for all aspects of his life. It is preferable to reduce the public-figure question to a more meaningful context by looking to the nature and extent of an individual's participation in the particular controversy giving rise to the defamation.

In this context it is plain that petitioner was not a public figure. He played a minimal role at the coroner's inquest, and his participation related solely to his representation of a private client. He took no part in the criminal prosecution of Officer Nuccio. Moreover, he never discussed either the criminal or civil litigation with the press and was never quoted as having done so. He plainly did not thrust himself into the vortex of this public issue, nor did he engage the public's attention in an attempt to influence its outcome. We are persuaded that the trial court did not err in refusing to characterize petitioner as a public figure for the purpose of this litigation.

We therefore conclude that the New York Times standard is inapplicable to this case and that the trial court erred in entering judgment for respondent. Because the jury was allowed to impose liability without fault and was permitted to presume damages without proof of injury, a new trial is necessary. We reverse and remand for further proceedings in accord with this opinion.

It is so ordered.

21 COX BROADCASTING CORP. ET AL V. COHN
SUPREME COURT OF THE UNITED STATES
420 U.S. 469
Argued November 11, 1974
Decided March 3, 1975

Syllabus

Appellant reporter, employed by a television station owned by appellant broadcasting company, during a news report of a rape case, broadcast the deceased rape victim's name, which he had obtained from the indictments, which were public records available for inspection. The victim's father, appellee, brought a damages action against appellants in reliance on a Georgia statute making it a misdemeanor to broadcast a rape victim's name, claiming that his right to privacy had been invaded by the broadcast of his daughter's name. The trial court, rejecting appellants' claims that the broadcast was privileged under the First and Fourteenth Amendments, held that the Georgia statute gave a civil remedy to those injured by its violation and granted summary judgment for appellee. On appeal, the Georgia Supreme Court initially held that, while the trial court erred in construing the Georgia statute to extend a cause of action for invasion of privacy, the complaint stated a cause of action for common-law invasion of privacy, and that the First and Fourteenth Amendments did not, as a matter of law, require judgment for appellants. On a motion for rehearing appellants contended that a rape victim's name was a matter of public interest and hence could be published with impunity, but the Supreme Court denied the motion on the ground that the statute declared a state policy that a rape victim's name was not a matter of public concern, and sustained the statute as a legitimate limitation on the First Amendment's freedom of expression.

Held:

1. This Court has jurisdiction over the appeal under 28 U. S. C. § 1257 (2). Pp. 476–487.

(a) The constitutionality of the Georgia statute was "drawn in question" within the meaning of § 1257 (2), since, when the Georgia Supreme Court relied upon it as a declaration of state public policy, the statute was drawn in question in a manner directly bearing upon the merits of the action, and the decision upholding its constitutional validity invokes this Court's appellate jurisdiction. P. 476.

(b) The Georgia Supreme Court's decision is a "final judgment or decree" within the meaning of § 1257. It was plainly final on the federal issue of whether the broadcasts were privileged [471] under the First and Fourteenth Amendments and is not subject to further review in the state courts; and appellants would be liable for damages if the elements of the state cause of action were proved. Moreover, since the litigation could be terminated by this Court's decision on the merits and a failure to decide the free speech question now will leave the Georgia press operating in the shadow of civil and criminal sanctions of a rule of law and statute whose constitutionality is in serious doubt, this Court's reaching the merits comports with its past pragmatic approach in determining finality. Pp. 476-487.

2. The State may not, consistently with the First and Fourteenth Amendments, impose sanctions on the accurate publication of a rape victim's name obtained from judicial records that are maintained in connection with a public prosecution and that themselves are open to public inspection. Here, under circumstances where appellant reporter based his televised report upon notes taken during court proceedings and obtained the rape victim's name from official court documents open to public inspection, the protection of freedom of the press provided by the First and Fourteenth Amendments bars Georgia from making appellants' broadcast the basis of civil liability in a cause of action for invasion of privacy that penalizes pure expression--the content of a publication. Pp. 487-497.

(a) The commission of a crime, prosecutions resulting therefrom, and judicial proceedings arising from the prosecutions are events of legitimate concern to the public and consequently fall within the press' responsibility to report the operations of government. Pp. 492-493.

(b) The interests of privacy fade when the information involved already appears on public record, especially when viewed in terms of the First and Fourteenth Amendments and in light of the public interest in a vigorous press. Pp. 493-495.

231 Ga. 60, 200 S. E. 2d 127, reversed.

MR. JUSTICE WHITE delivered the opinion of the Court.

The issue before us in this case is whether, consistently with the First and Fourteenth Amendments, a State may extend a cause of action for damages for invasion of privacy caused by the publication of the name of a deceased rape victim which was publicly revealed in connection with the prosecution of the crime.

I

In August 1971, appellee's 17-year-old daughter was the victim of a rape and did not survive the incident. Six youths were soon indicted for murder and rape. Although there was substantial press coverage of the crime and of subsequent developments, the identity of the victim was not disclosed pending trial, perhaps because of Ga. Code Ann. § 26-9901 (1972),[note 1] which makes [472] it a misdemeanor to publish or broadcast the name or identity of a rape victim. In April 1972, some eight months later, the six defendants appeared in court. Five pleaded guilty to rape or attempted rape, the charge of murder having been dropped. The guilty pleas were accepted by the court, and the trial of the defendant pleading not guilty was set for a later date.

In the course of the proceedings that day, appellant Wassell,[note 2] a reporter covering the incident for his employer, learned the name of the victim from an examination of the indictments which were made available for his inspection in the courtroom.[note 3] That the name of the [473] victim appears in the indictments and that the indictments were public records available for inspection are not disputed.[note 4] Later that day, Wassell broadcast over the facilities of station WSB-TV, a television station owned by appellant Cox Broadcasting Corp., a news report concerning [474] the court proceedings. The report named the victim of the crime and was repeated the following day.[note 5]

In May 1972, appellee brought an action for money damages against appellants, relying on § 26-9901 and claiming that his right to privacy had been invaded by the television broadcasts giving the name of his deceased daughter. Appellants admitted the broadcasts but claimed that they were privileged under both state law and the First and Fourteenth Amendments. The trial court, rejecting appellants' constitutional claims and holding that the Georgia statute gave a civil remedy to those injured by its violation, granted summary judgment to appellee as to liability, with the determination of damages to await trial by jury.

On appeal, the Georgia Supreme Court, in its initial opinion, held that the trial court had erred in construing § 26-9901 to extend a civil cause of action for invasion of privacy and thus found it unnecessary to consider the constitutionality of the statute. 231 Ga. 60, 200 S. E. 2d 127 (1973). The court went on to rule, however, that the complaint stated a cause of action "for the invasion of the appellee's right of privacy, or for the tort of public disclosure"--a "common law tort [existing] in this jurisdiction without the help of the statute that the trial judge in this case relied on." Id., at 62, 200 S. E. 2d, at 130. Although the privacy invaded was not that of the deceased victim, the father was held to have stated a claim for invasion of his own privacy by reason of the publication of his daughter's name. The court explained, however, that liability did not follow as a matter of law and that summary judgment was improper; whether the public disclosure of the name actually invaded appellee's "zone of privacy," and if so, to what extent, were issues to be determined by the trier of fact. Also, "in formulating such an issue for determination by the fact-finder, it is reasonable to require the appellee to prove that the appellants invaded his privacy with wilful or negligent disregard for the fact that reasonable men would find the invasion highly offensive." Id., at 64, 200 S. E. 2d, at 131. The Georgia Supreme Court did agree with the trial court, however, that the First and Fourteenth Amendments did not, as a matter of law, require judgment for appellants. The court concurred with the statement in *Briscoe v. Reader's Digest Assn.*, Inc., 4 Cal. 3d 529, 541, 483 P. 2d 34, 42 (1971), that "the rights guaranteed by the First Amendment do not require total abrogation of the right to privacy. The goals sought by each may be achieved with a minimum of intrusion upon the other."

Upon motion for rehearing the Georgia court countered the argument that the victim's name was a matter of public interest and could be published with impunity by relying on § 26-9901 as an authoritative declaration of state policy that the name of a rape victim was not a matter of public concern. This time the court felt compelled to determine the constitutionality of the statute and sustained it as a "legitimate limitation on the right of freedom of expression contained in the First Amendment." The court could discern "no public interest or general concern about the identity of the victim of such a crime as will make the right to disclose the identity of the victim rise to the level of First Amendment protection." 231 Ga., at 68, 200 S. E. 2d, at 134.

[476] We postponed decision as to our jurisdiction over this appeal to the hearing on the merits. 415 U.S. 912 (1974). We conclude that the Court has jurisdiction, and reverse the judgment of the Georgia Supreme Court.

II

Appellants invoke the appellate jurisdiction of this Court under 28 U. S. C. § 1257 (2) and, if that jurisdictional basis is found to be absent, through a petition for certiorari under 28 U. S. C. § 2103. Two questions concerning our jurisdiction must be resolved: (1) whether the constitutional validity of § 26-9901 was "drawn in question," with the Georgia Supreme Court upholding its validity, and (2) whether the decision from which this appeal has been taken is a "[final] judgment or decree."

A

Appellants clearly raised the issue of the constitutionality of § 26-9901 in their motion for rehearing in the Georgia Supreme Court. In denying that motion that court held: "A majority of this court does not consider this statute to be in conflict with the First Amendment." 231 Ga., at 68, 200 S. E. 2d, at 134. Since the court relied upon the statute as a declaration of the public policy of Georgia that the disclosure of a rape victim's name was not to be protected expression, the statute was drawn in question in a manner directly bearing upon the merits of the action, and the decision in favor of its constitutional validity invokes this Court's appellate jurisdiction. Cf. *Garrity v. New Jersey*, 385 U.S. 493, 495-496 (1967).

B

Since 1789, Congress has granted this Court appellate jurisdiction with respect to state litigation only after the highest state court in which judgment could be had has [477] rendered a "[final] judgment or decree." Title 28 U. S. C. § 1257 retains this limitation on our power to review cases coming from state courts. The Court has noted that "[considerations] of English usage as well as those of judicial policy" would justify an interpretation of the final-judgment rule to preclude review "where anything further remains to be determined by a State court, no matter how dissociated from the only federal issue that has finally been adjudicated by the highest court of the State." *Radio Station WOW, Inc. v. Johnson*, 326 U.S. 120, 124 (1945). But the Court there observed that the rule had not been administered in such a mechanical fashion and that there were circumstances in which there has been "a departure from this requirement of finality for federal appellate jurisdiction." Ibid.

These circumstances were said to be "very few," ibid.; but as the cases have unfolded, the Court has recurringly encountered situations in which the highest court of a State has finally determined the federal issue present in a particular case, but in which there are further proceedings in the lower state courts to come. There are now at least four categories of such cases in which the Court has treated the decision on the federal issue as a final judgment for the purposes of 28 U. S. C. § 1257 and has taken jurisdiction without awaiting the completion of the additional proceedings anticipated in the lower state courts. In most, if not all, of the cases in these categories, these additional proceedings would not require the decision of other federal questions that might also require review by the Court at a later date,[note 6] and immediate [478] rather than delayed review would be the best way to avoid "the mischief of economic waste and of delayed justice," *Radio Station WOW, Inc. v. Johnson*, *supra*, at 124, as well as precipitate interference with state litigation.[note 7] In the cases in the first two categories considered below, the federal issue would not be mooted or otherwise affected by the proceedings yet to be had because those proceedings have little substance, their outcome is certain, or they are wholly unrelated to the federal question. In the other two categories, however, the federal issue would be mooted if the petitioner or appellant seeking to bring the action here prevailed on the merits in the later state-court proceedings, but there is nevertheless [479] sufficient justification for immediate review of the federal question finally determined in the state courts.

In the first category are those cases in which there are further proceedings--even entire trials--yet to occur in the state courts but where for one reason or another the federal issue is conclusive or the outcome of further proceedings preordained. In these circumstances, because the case is for all practical purposes concluded, the judgment of the state court on the federal issue is deemed final. In *Mills v. Alabama*, 384 U.S. 214 (1966), for example, a demurrer to a criminal complaint was sustained on federal constitutional grounds by a state trial court. The State Supreme Court reversed, remanding for jury trial. This Court took jurisdiction on the reasoning that the appellant had no defense other than his federal claim and could not prevail at trial on the facts or any nonfederal ground. To dismiss the appeal "would not only be an inexcusable delay of the benefits Congress intended to grant by providing for appeal to this Court, but it would also result in a completely unnecessary waste of time and energy in judicial systems already troubled by delays due to congested dockets." *Id.,* at 217-218 (footnote omitted).[note 8] [480]

Second, there are cases such as Radio Station WOW, *supra*, and *Brady v. Maryland*, 373 U.S. 83 (1963), in which the federal issue, finally decided by the highest court in the State, will survive and require decision regardless of the outcome of future state-court proceedings. In Radio Station WOW, the Nebraska Supreme Court directed the transfer of the properties of a federally licensed radio station and ordered an accounting, rejecting the claim that the transfer order would interfere with the federal license. The federal issue was held reviewable here despite the pending accounting on the "presupposition . . . that the federal questions that could come here have been adjudicated by the State court, and that the accounting which remains to be taken could not remotely give rise to a federal question . . . that may later come here . . . ." 326 U.S., at 127. The judgment rejecting the federal claim and directing the transfer was deemed "dissociated from a provision for an accounting even though that is decreed in the same order." *Id.,* at 126. Nothing that could happen in the course of the accounting, short of settlement of the case, would foreclose or make unnecessary decision on the federal question. Older cases in the Court had reached the same result on similar facts. *Carondelet Canal & Nav. Co. v. Louisiana*, 233 U.S. 362 (1914); *Forgay v. Conrad*, 6 How. 201 (1848). In the latter case, the Court, in an opinion by Mr. Chief Justice Taney, stated that the Court had not understood the final-judgment rule "in this strict and technical sense, but has given [it] a more liberal, and, as we think, a more reasonable construction, [481] and one more consonant to the intention of the legislature." *Id.,* at 203.[note 9]

In the third category are those situations where the federal claim has been finally decided, with further proceedings on the merits in the state courts to come, but in which later review of the federal issue cannot be had, whatever the ultimate outcome of the case. Thus, in these cases, if the party seeking interim review ultimately prevails on the merits, the federal issue will be mooted; if he were to lose on the merits, however, the governing state law would not permit him again to present his federal claims for review. The Court has taken jurisdiction in these circumstances prior to completion of the case in the state courts. *California v. Stewart*, 384 U.S. 436 (1966) (decided with *Miranda v. Arizona*), epitomizes this category. There the state court reversed a conviction on federal constitutional grounds and remanded for a new trial. Although the State might have prevailed at trial, we granted its petition for certiorari and affirmed, explaining that the state judgment was "final" since an acquittal of the defendant at trial would preclude, under state law, an appeal by the State. *Id.*, at 498 n. 71.

A recent decision in this category is *North Dakota State Board of Pharmacy v. Snyder's Drug Stores, Inc.*, 414 U.S. 156 (1973), in which the Pharmacy Board rejected an application for a pharmacy operating permit relying on a state statute specifying ownership requirements which the applicant did not meet. The State Supreme [482] Court held the statute unconstitutional and remanded the matter to the Board for further consideration of the application, freed from the constraints of the ownership statute. The Board brought the case here, claiming that the statute was constitutionally acceptable under modern cases. After reviewing the various circumstances under which the finality requirement has been deemed satisfied despite the fact that litigation had not terminated in the state courts, we entertained the case over claims that we had no jurisdiction. The federal issue would not survive the remand, whatever the result of the state administrative proceedings. The Board might deny the license on state-law grounds, thus foreclosing the federal issue, and the Court also ascertained that under state law the Board could not bring the federal issue here in the event the applicant satisfied the requirements of state law except for the invalidated ownership statute. Under these circumstances, the issue was ripe for review. [note 10]

Lastly, there are those situations where the federal issue has been finally decided in the state courts with further proceedings pending in which the party seeking review here might prevail on the merits on nonfederal grounds, thus rendering unnecessary review of the federal issue by this Court, and where reversal of the state court on the federal issue would be preclusive of any further [483] litigation on the relevant cause of action rather than merely controlling the nature and character of, or determining the admissibility of evidence in, the state proceedings still to come. In these circumstances, if a refusal immediately to review the state-court decision might seriously erode federal policy, the Court has entertained and decided the federal issue, which itself has been finally determined by the state courts for purposes of the state litigation.

In *Construction Laborers v. Curry*, 371 U.S. 542 (1963), the state courts temporarily enjoined labor union picketing over claims that the National Labor Relations Board had exclusive jurisdiction of the controversy. The Court took jurisdiction for two independent reasons. First, the power of the state court to proceed in the face of the preemption claim was deemed an issue separable from the merits and ripe for review in this Court, particularly "when postponing review would seriously erode the national labor policy requiring the subject matter of respondents' cause to be heard by the . . . Board, not by the state courts." *Id.*, at 550. Second, the Court was convinced that in any event the union had no defense to the entry of a permanent injunction other than the preemption claim that had already been ruled on in the state courts. Hence the case was for all practical purposes concluded in the state tribunals.

In *Mercantile National Bank v. Langdeau*, 371 U.S. 555 (1963), two national banks were sued, along with others, in the courts of Travis County, Tex. The claim asserted was conspiracy to defraud an insurance company. The banks as a preliminary matter asserted that a special federal venue statute immunized them from suit in Travis County and that they could properly be sued only in another county. Although trial was still to be had and the banks might well prevail on the merits, the Court, relying on *Curry,* entertained the issue as a "separate [484] and independent matter, anterior to the merits and not enmeshed in the factual and legal issues comprising the plaintiff's cause of action." *Id.,* at 558. Moreover, it would serve the policy of the federal statute "to determine now in which state court appellants may be tried rather than to subject them . . . to long and complex litigation which may all be for naught if consideration of the preliminary question of venue is postponed until the conclusion of the proceedings." Ibid.

Miami Herald Publishing Co. v. Tornillo, 418 U.S. 241 (1974), is the latest case in this category.[note 11] There a candidate for public office sued a newspaper for refusing, allegedly contrary to a state statute, to carry his reply to the paper's editorial critical of his qualifications. The trial court held the act unconstitutional, denying both injunctive relief and damages. The State Supreme Court reversed, sustaining the statute against the challenge based upon the First and Fourteenth Amendments and remanding the case for a trial and appropriate relief, including damages. The newspaper brought the case here. We sustained our jurisdiction, relying on the principles elaborated in the North Dakota case and observing:

"Whichever way we were to decide on the merits, it [485] would be intolerable to leave unanswered, under these circumstances, an important question of freedom of the press under the First Amendment; an uneasy and unsettled constitutional posture of § 104.38 could only further harm the operation of a free press. *Mills v. Alabama,* 384 U.S. 214, 221-222 (1966) (DOUGLAS, J., concurring). See also *Organization for a Better Austin v. Keefe,* 402 U.S. 415, 418 n. (1971)." 418 U.S., at 247 n. 6.[note 12]

In light of the prior cases, we conclude that we have jurisdiction to review the judgment of the Georgia Supreme Court rejecting the challenge under the First and Fourteenth Amendments to the state law authorizing damage suits against the press for publishing the name of a rape victim whose identity is revealed in the course of a public prosecution. The Georgia Supreme Court's judgment is plainly final on the federal issue and is not subject to further review in the state courts. Appellants will be liable for damages if the elements of the state cause of action are proved. They may prevail at trial on nonfederal grounds, it is true, but if the Georgia court erroneously upheld the statute, there should be no trial at all. Moreover, even if appellants prevailed at trial and made unnecessary further consideration of the constitutional question, there would remain in effect the unreviewed decision of the State Supreme Court that a civil action for publishing the name of a rape victim disclosed in a public judicial proceeding may go forward despite the First and Fourteenth Amendments. Delaying final [486] decision of the First Amendment claim until after trial will "leave unanswered . . . an important question of freedom of the press under the First Amendment," "an uneasy and unsettled constitutional posture [that] could only further harm the operation of a free press." *Tornillo, supra,* at 247 n. 6. On the other hand, if we now hold that the First and Fourteenth Amendments bar civil liability for broadcasting the victim's name, this litigation ends. Given these factors--that the litigation could be terminated by our decision on the merits [note 13] and that a failure to decide the question now will leave the press in Georgia operating in the shadow of the civil and criminal sanctions of a rule of law and a statute the constitutionality of which is in serious doubt--we find that reaching the merits is consistent with the pragmatic approach that we have followed in the past in determining finality. [487] See *Gillespie v. United States Steel Corp.*, 379 U.S. 148 (1964); *Radio Station WOW, Inc. v. Johnson*, 326 U.S., at 124; *Mills v. Alabama*, 384 U.S., at 221-222 (DOUGLAS, J., concurring).[note 14]

III

Georgia stoutly defends both § 26-9901 and the State's common-law privacy action challenged here. Its claims are not without force, for powerful arguments can be made, and have been made, that however it may be ultimately defined, there is a zone of privacy surrounding every individual, a zone within which the State may protect him from intrusion by the press, with all its attendant publicity.[note 15] Indeed, the central thesis of the root article by Warren and Brandeis, The Right to Privacy, 4 Harv. L. Rev. 193, 196 (1890), was that the press was overstepping its prerogatives by publishing essentially private information and that there should be a remedy for the alleged abuses.[note 16] [488]

More compellingly, the century has experienced a strong tide running in favor of the so-called right of privacy. In 1967, we noted that "[it] has been said that a 'right of privacy' has been recognized at common law in 30 States plus the District of Columbia and by statute in four States." *Time, Inc. v. Hill*, 385 U.S. 374, 383 n. 7. We there cited the 1964 edition of Prosser's Law of Torts. The 1971 edition of that same source states that "[in] one form or another, the right of privacy is by this time recognized and accepted in all but a very few jurisdictions." W. Prosser, Law of Torts 804 (4th ed.) (footnote omitted). Nor is it irrelevant [489] here that the right of privacy is no recent arrival in the jurisprudence of Georgia, which has embraced the right in some form since 1905 when the Georgia Supreme Court decided the leading case of *Pavesich v. New England Life Ins. Co.*, 122 Ga. 190, 50 S. E. 68.

These are impressive credentials for a right of privacy, [note 17] but we should recognize that we do not have at issue here an action for the invasion of privacy involving the appropriation of one's name or photograph, a physical or other tangible intrusion into a private area, or a publication of otherwise private information that is also false although perhaps not defamatory. The version of the privacy tort now before us--termed in Georgia "the tort of public disclosure," 231 Ga., at 60, 200 S. E. 2d, at 130--is that in which the plaintiff claims the right to be free from unwanted publicity about his private affairs, which, although wholly true, would be offensive to a person of ordinary sensibilities. Because the gravamen of the claimed injury is the publication of information, whether true or not, the dissemination of which is embarrassing or otherwise painful to an individual, it is here that claims of privacy most directly confront the constitutional freedoms of speech and press. The face-off is apparent, and the appellants urge upon us the broad holding that the press may not be made criminally or civilly liable for publishing information that is neither false nor misleading but absolutely accurate, however damaging it may be to reputation or individual sensibilities.

It is true that in defamation actions, where the protected interest is personal reputation, the prevailing view is that truth is a defense; [note 18] and the message of *New York* [490] *Times Co. v. Sullivan*, 376 U.S. 254 (1964); *Garrison v. Louisiana*, 379 U.S. 64 (1964); *Curtis Publishing Co. v. Butts*, 388 U.S. 130 (1967), and like cases is that the defense of truth is constitutionally required where the subject of the publication is a public official or public figure. What is more, the defamed public official or public figure must prove not only that the publication is false but that it was knowingly so or was circulated with reckless disregard for its truth or falsity. Similarly, where the interest at issue is privacy rather than reputation and the right claimed is to be free from the publication of false or misleading information about one's affairs, the target of the publication must prove knowing or reckless falsehood where the materials published, although assertedly private, are "matters of public interest." *Time, Inc. v. Hill, supra,* at 387-388.[note 19]

The Court has nevertheless carefully left open the question whether the First and Fourteenth Amendments require that truth be recognized as a defense in a defamation action brought by a private person as distinguished from a public official or public figure. Garrison held that where criticism is of a public official and his conduct of public business, "the interest in private reputation is overborne [491] by the larger public interest, secured by the Constitution, in the dissemination of truth," 379 U.S., at 73 (footnote omitted), but recognized that "different interests may be involved where purely private libels, totally unrelated to public affairs, are concerned; therefore, nothing we say today is to be taken as intimating any views as to the impact of the constitutional guarantees in the discrete area of purely private libels." *Id.,* at 72 n. 8. In similar fashion, *Time, Inc. v. Hill, supra,* expressly saved the question whether truthful publication of very private matters unrelated to public affairs could be constitutionally proscribed. 385 U.S., at 383 n. 7.

Those precedents, as well as other considerations, counsel similar caution here. In this sphere of collision between claims of privacy and those of the free press, the interests on both sides are plainly rooted in the traditions and significant concerns of our society. Rather than address the broader question whether truthful publications may ever be subjected to civil or criminal liability consistently with the First and Fourteenth Amendments, or to put it another way, whether the State may ever define and protect an area of privacy free from unwanted publicity in the press, it is appropriate to focus on the narrower interface between press and privacy that this case presents, namely, whether the State may impose sanctions on the accurate publication of the name of a rape victim obtained from public records--more specifically, from judicial records which are maintained in connection with a public prosecution and which themselves are open to public inspection. We are convinced that the State may not do so.

In the first place, in a society in which each individual has but limited time and resources with which to observe at first hand the operations of his government, he relies necessarily upon the press to bring to him in convenient form the facts of those operations. Great responsibility [492] is accordingly placed upon the news media to report fully and accurately the proceedings of government, and official records and documents open to the public are the basic data of governmental operations. Without the information provided by the press most of us and many of our representatives would be unable to vote intelligently or to register opinions on the administration of government generally. With respect to judicial proceedings in particular, the function of the press serves to guarantee the fairness of trials and to bring to bear the beneficial effects of public scrutiny upon the administration of justice. See *Sheppard v. Maxwell,* 384 U.S. 333, 350 (1966).

Appellee has claimed in this litigation that the efforts of the press have infringed his right to privacy by broadcasting to the world the fact that his daughter was a rape victim. The commission of crime, prosecutions resulting from it, and judicial proceedings arising from the prosecutions, however, are without question events of legitimate concern to the public and consequently fall within the responsibility of the press to report the operations of government.

The special protected nature of accurate reports of judicial proceedings has repeatedly been recognized. This Court, in an opinion written by MR. JUSTICE DOUGLAS, has said:

"A trial is a public event. What transpires in the court room is public property. If a transcript of the court proceedings had been published, we suppose none would claim that the judge could punish the publisher for contempt. And we can see no difference though the conduct of the attorneys, of the jury, or even of the judge himself, may have reflected on the court. Those who see and hear what transpired can report it with impunity. There is no special perquisite of the judiciary which enables [493] it, as distinguished from other institutions of democratic government, to suppress, edit, or censor events which transpire in proceedings before it." *Craig v. Harney*, 331 U.S. 367, 374 (1947) (emphasis added).

See also *Sheppard v. Maxwell, supra,* at 362-363; *Estes v. Texas*, 381 U.S. 532, 541-542 (1965); *Pennekamp v. Florida*, 328 U.S. 331 (194 6); *Bridges v. California*, 314 U.S. 252 (1941).

The developing law surrounding the tort of invasion of privacy recognizes a privilege in the press to report the events of judicial proceedings. The Warren and Brandeis article, *supra,* noted that the proposed new right would be limited in the same manner as actions for libel and slander where such a publication was a privileged communication: "the right to privacy is not invaded by any publication made in a court of justice . . . and (at least in many jurisdictions) reports of any such proceedings would in some measure be accorded a like privilege."[note 20]

The Restatement of Torts, § 867, embraced an action for privacy.[note 21] Tentative Draft No. 13 of the Second Restatement of Torts, §§ 652A-652E, divides the privacy tort into four branches;[note 22] and with respect to the wrong of giving unwanted publicity about private life, the commentary [494] to § 652D states: "There is no liability when the defendant merely gives further publicity to information about the plaintiff which is already public. Thus there is no liability for giving publicity to facts about the plaintiff's life which are matters of public record . . . ."[note 23] The same is true of the separate tort of physically or otherwise intruding upon the seclusion or private affairs of another. Section 652B, Comment c, provides that "there is no liability for the examination of a public record concerning the plaintiff, or of documents which the plaintiff is required to keep and make available for public inspection."[note 24] According to this draft, ascertaining and publishing the contents of public records are simply not within the reach of these kinds of privacy actions.[note 25]

Thus even the prevailing law of invasion of privacy generally recognizes that the interests in privacy fade [495] when the information involved already appears on the public record. The conclusion is compelling when viewed in terms of the First and Fourteenth Amendments and in light of the public interest in a vigorous press. The Georgia cause of action for invasion of privacy through public disclosure of the name of a rape victim imposes sanctions on pure expression--the content of a publication--and not conduct or a combination of speech and nonspeech elements that might otherwise be open to regulation or prohibition. See *United States v. O'Brien*, 391 U.S. 367, 376-377 (1968). The publication of truthful information available on the public record contains none of the indicia of those limited categories of expression, such as "fighting" words, which "are no essential part of any exposition of ideas, and are of such slight social value as a step to truth that any benefit that may be derived from them is clearly outweighed by the social interest in order and morality." *Chaplinsky v. New Hampshire*, 315 U.S. 568, 572 (1942) (footnote omitted).

By placing the information in the public domain on official court records, the State must be presumed to have concluded that the public interest was thereby being served. Public records by their very nature are of interest to those concerned with the administration of government, and a public benefit is performed by the reporting of the true contents of the records by the media. The freedom of the press to publish that information appears to us to be of critical importance to our type of government in which the citizenry is the final judge of the proper conduct of public business. In preserving that form of government the First and Fourteenth Amendments command nothing less than that the States may not impose sanctions on the publication of truthful information contained in official court records open to public inspection.

We are reluctant to embark on a course that would make public records generally available to the media but forbid their publication if offensive to the sensibilities of the supposed reasonable man. Such a rule would make it very difficult for the media to inform citizens about the public business and yet stay within the law. The rule would invite timidity and self-censorship and very likely lead to the suppression of many items that would otherwise be published and that should be made available to the public. At the very least, the First and Fourteenth Amendments will not allow exposing the press to liability for truthfully publishing information released to the public in official court records. If there are privacy interests to be protected in judicial proceedings, the States must respond by means which avoid public documentation or other exposure of private information. Their political institutions must weigh the interests in privacy with the interests of the public to know and of the press to publish.[note 26] Once true information is disclosed in public court documents open to public inspection, the press cannot be sanctioned for publishing it. In this instance as in others reliance must rest upon the judgment of those who decide what to publish or broadcast. See *Miami Herald Publishing Co. v. Tornillo*, 418 U.S., at 258.

Appellant Wassell based his televised report upon notes taken during the court proceedings and obtained the name of the victim from the indictments handed to him at his request during a recess in the hearing. Appellee has not contended that the name was obtained in an improper fashion or that it was not on an official court document open to public inspection. Under these circumstances, [497] the protection of freedom of the press provided by the First and Fourteenth Amendments bars the State of Georgia from making appellants' broadcast the basis of civil liability.[note 27]

Reversed.

22 ZACCHINI V. SCRIPPS-HOWARD BROADCASTING CO.
SUPREME COURT OF THE UNITED STATES
433 U.S. 562
Argued April 25, 1977
Decided June 28, 1977

Syllabus

Petitioner's 15-second "human cannonball" act, in which he is shot from a cannon into a net some 200 feet away, was, without his consent, videotaped in its entirety at a county fair in Ohio by a reporter for respondent broadcasting company and shown on a television news program later the same day. Petitioner then brought a damages action in state court against respondent, alleging an "unlawful appropriation" of his "professional property." The trial court's summary judgment for respondent was reversed by the Ohio Court of Appeals on the ground that the complaint stated a cause of action. The Ohio Supreme Court, while recognizing that petitioner had a cause of action under state law on his "right to the publicity value of his performance," nevertheless, relying on *Time, Inc. v. Hill*, 385 U.S. 374, rendered judgment for respondent on the ground that it is constitutionally privileged to include in its newscasts matters of public interest that would otherwise be protected by the right of publicity, absent an intent to injure or to appropriate for some nonprivileged purpose. Held:

1. It appears from the Ohio Supreme Court's opinion syllabus (which is to be looked to for the rule of law in the case), as clarified by the opinion itself, that the judgment below did not rest on an adequate and independent state ground but rested solely on federal grounds in that the court considered the source of respondent's privilege to be the First and Fourteenth Amendments, and therefore this Court has jurisdiction to decide the federal issue. Pp. 566-568.

2. The First and Fourteenth Amendments do not immunize the news media when they broadcast a performer's entire act without his consent, and the Constitution no more prevents a State from requiring respondent to compensate petitioner for broadcasting his act on television than it would privilege respondent to film and broadcast a copyrighted dramatic work without liability to the copyright owner, or to film or broadcast a prize fight or a baseball game, where the promoters or participants had other plans for publicizing the event. *Time, Inc. v. Hill, supra,* distinguished. Pp. 569-579.

(a) The broadcast of a film of petitioner's entire act poses a substantial threat to the economic value of that performance, since (1) if the public can see the act free on television it will be less willing [563] to pay to see it at the fair, and (2) the broadcast goes to the heart of petitioner's ability to earn a living as an entertainer. Pp. 575-576.

(b) The protection of petitioner's right of publicity provides an economic incentive for him to make the investment required to produce a performance of interest to the public. Pp. 576-577.

(c) While entertainment, as well as news, enjoys First Amendment protection, and entertainment itself can be important news, neither the public nor respondent will be deprived of the benefit of petitioner's performance as long as his commercial stake in his act is appropriately recognized. P. 578.

(d) Although the State may as a matter of its own law privilege the press in the circumstances of this case, the First and Fourteenth Amendments do not require it to do so. Pp. 578-579.

47 Ohio St. 2d 224, 351 N.E. 2d 454, reversed.

WHITE, J., delivered the opinion of the Court, in which BURGER, C.J., and STEWART, BLACKMUN, and REHNQUIST, JJ., joined. POWELL, J., filed a dissenting opinion, in which BRENNAN and MARSHALL, JJ., joined, post, p. 579. STEVENS, J., filed a dissenting opinion, post, p. 582.

MR. JUSTICE WHITE delivered the opinion of the Court.

Petitioner, Hugo Zacchini, is an entertainer. He performs a "human cannonball" act in which he is shot from a cannon into a net some 200 feet away. Each performance occupies some 15 seconds. In August and September 1972, petitioner was engaged to perform his act on a regular basis at the Geauga County Fair in Burton, Ohio. He performed in a fenced area, surrounded by grandstands, at the fair grounds. Members of the public attending the fair were not charged a separate admission fee to observe his act.

On August 30, a free-lance reporter for Scripps-Howard Broadcasting Co., the operator of a television broadcasting station and respondent in this case, attended the fair. He [564] carried a small movie camera. Petitioner noticed the reporter and asked him not to film the performance. The reporter did not do so on that day; but on the instructions of the producer of respondent's daily newscast, he returned the following day and videotaped the entire act. This film clip, approximately 15 seconds in length, was shown on the 11 o'clock news program that night, together with favorable commentary.[note 1]

Petitioner then brought this action for damages, alleging that he is "engaged in the entertainment business," that the act he performs is one "invented by his father and. . . performed only by his family for the last fifty years," that respondent "showed and commercialized the film of his act without his consent," and that such conduct was an "unlawful appropriation of plaintiff's professional property." App. 4-5. Respondent answered and moved for summary judgment, which was granted by the trial court.

The Court of Appeals of Ohio reversed. The majority held that petitioner's complaint stated a cause of action for conversion and for infringement of a common-law copyright, and one judge concurred in the judgment on the ground that the complaint stated a cause of action for appropriation of petitioner's "right of publicity" in the film of his act. All three judges agreed that the First Amendment did not privilege the press to show the entire performance on a news program without compensating petitioner for any financial injury he could prove at trial. [565]

Like the concurring judge in the Court of Appeals, the Supreme Court of Ohio rested petitioner's cause of action under state law on his "right to publicity value of his performance." 47 Ohio St. 2d 224, 351 N.E. 2d 454, 455 (1976). The opinion syllabus, to which we are to look for the rule of law used to decide the case,[note 2] declared first that one may not use for his own benefit the name or likeness of another, whether or not the use or benefit is a commercial one, and second that respondent would be liable for the appropriation, over petitioner's objection and in the absence of license or privilege, of petitioner's right to the publicity value of his performance. Ibid. The court nevertheless gave judgment for respondent because, in the words of the syllabus:

"A TV station has a privilege to report in its newscasts matters of legitimate public interest which would otherwise be protected by an individual's right of publicity, unless the actual intent of the TV station was to appropriate the benefit of the publicity for some non-privileged private use, or unless the actual intent was to injure the individual." *Ibid.*

We granted certiorari, 429 U.S. 1037 (1977), to consider an issue unresolved by this Court: whether the First and Fourteenth Amendments immunized respondent from damages for its alleged infringement of petitioner's state-law "right of publicity." Pet. for Cert. 2. Insofar as the Ohio Supreme Court held that the First and Fourteenth Amendments of the [566] United States Constitution required judgment for respondent, we reverse the judgment of that court.

I

If the judgment below rested on an independent and adequate state ground, the writ of certiorari should be dismissed as improvidently granted, *Wilson v. Loew's Inc.,* 355 U.S. 597 (1958), for "[o]ur only power over state judgments is to correct them to the extent that they incorrectly adjudge federal rights. And our power is to correct wrong judgments, not to revise opinions. We are not permitted to render an advisory opinion, and if the same judgment would be rendered by the state court after we corrected its views of federal laws, our review could amount to nothing more than an advisory opinion." *Herb v. Pitcairn,* 324 U.S. 117, 125-126 (1945). We are confident, however, that the judgment below did not rest on an adequate and independent state ground and that we have jurisdiction to decide the federal issue presented in this case.

There is no doubt that petitioner's complaint was grounded in state law and that the right of publicity which petitioner was held to possess was a right arising under Ohio law. It is also clear that respondent's claim of constitutional privilege was sustained. The source of this privilege was not identified in the syllabus. It is clear enough from the opinion of the Ohio Supreme Court, which we are permitted to consult for understanding of the syllabus, *Perkins v. Benguet Consolidated Mining Co.,* 342 U.S. 437, 441-443 (1952),[note 3] that in adjudicating

[567] the crucial question of whether respondent had a privilege to film and televise petitioner's performance, the court placed principal reliance on *Time, Inc. v. Hill*, 385 U.S. 374 (1967), a case involving First Amendment limitations on state tort actions. It construed the principle of that case, along with that of *New York Times Co. v. Sullivan*, 376 U.S. 254 (1964), to be that "the press has a privilege to report matters of legitimate public interest even though such reports might intrude on matters otherwise private," and concluded, therefore, that the press is also "privileged when an individual seeks to publicly exploit his talents while keeping the benefits private." 47 Ohio St. 2d, at 234, 351 N.E. 2d, at 461. The privilege thus exists in cases "where appropriation of a right of publicity is claimed." The court's opinion also referred to Draft 21 of the relevant portion of Restatement (Second) of Torts (1975), which was understood to make room for reasonable press appropriations by limiting the reach of the right of privacy rather than by creating a privileged invasion. The court preferred the notion of privilege over the Restatement's formulation, however, reasoning that "since the gravamen of the issue in this case is not whether the degree of intrusion is reasonable, but whether First Amendment principles require that the [568] right of privacy give way to the public right to be informed of matters of public interest and concern, the concept of privilege seems the more useful and appropriate one." 47 Ohio St. 2d, at 234 n. 5, 351 N.E. 2d, at 461 n. 5. (Emphasis added.)

Had the Ohio court rested its decision on both state and federal grounds, either of which would have been dispositive, we would have had no jurisdiction. *Fox Film Corp. v. Muller*, 296 U.S. 207 (1935); *Enterprise Irrigation Dist. v. Farmers Mutual Canal Co.*, 243 U.S. 157, 164 (1917). But the opinion, like the syllabus, did not mention the Ohio Constitution, citing instead this Court's First Amendment cases as controlling. It appears to us that the decision rested solely on federal grounds. That the Ohio court might have, but did not, invoke state law does not foreclose jurisdiction here. *Steele v. Louisville & Nashville R. Co.*, 323 U.S. 192, 197 n. 1 (1944); *Indiana ex rel. Anderson v. Brand*, 303 U.S. 95, 98 (1938).

Even if the judgment in favor of respondent must nevertheless be understood as ultimately resting on Ohio law, it appears that at the very least the Ohio court felt compelled by what it understood to be federal constitutional considerations to construe and apply its own law in the manner it did. In this event, we have jurisdiction and should decide the federal issue; for if the state court erred in its understanding of our cases and of the First and Fourteenth Amendments, we should so declare, leaving the state court free to decide the privilege issue solely as a matter of Ohio law. *Perkins v. Benguet Consolidated Mining Co., supra.* If the Supreme Court of Ohio "held as it did because it felt under compulsion of federal law as enunciated by this Court so to hold, it should be relieved of that compulsion. It should be freed to decide. . . these suits according to its own local law." *Missouri ex rel. Southern R. Co. v. Mayfield*, 340 U.S. 1, 5 (1950). [569]

II

The Ohio Supreme Court held that respondent is constitutionally privileged to include in its newscasts matters of public interest that would otherwise be protected by the right of publicity, absent an intent to injure or to appropriate for some nonprivileged purpose. If under this standard respondent had merely reported that petitioner was performing at the fair and described or commented on his act, with or without showing his picture on television, we would have a very different case. But petitioner is not contending that his appearance at the fair and his performance could not be reported by the press as newsworthy items. His complaint is that respondent filmed his entire act and displayed that film on television for the public to see and enjoy. This, he claimed, was an appropriation of his professional property. The Ohio Supreme Court agreed that petitioner had "a right of publicity" that gave him "personal control over commercial display and exploitation of his personality and the exercise of his talents."[note 4] This right of "exclusive control over the publicity given to his performances" was said to be such a "valuable part of the benefit which may be attained by his talents and efforts" that it was entitled to legal protection. It was [570] also observed, or at least expressly assumed, that petitioner had not abandoned his rights by performing under the circumstances present at the Geauga County Fair Grounds.

The Ohio Supreme Court nevertheless held that the challenged invasion was privileged, saying that the press "must be accorded broad latitude in its choice of how much it presents of each story or incident, and of the emphasis to be given to such presentation. No fixed standard which would bar the press from reporting or depicting either an entire occurrence or an entire discrete part of a public performance can be formulated which would not unduly restrict the 'breathing room' in reporting which freedom of the press requires." 47 Ohio St. 2d, at 235, 351 N.E. 2d, at 461. Under this view, respondent was thus constitutionally free to film and display petitioner's entire act.[note 5]

The Ohio Supreme Court relied heavily on *Time, Inc. v. Hill*, 385 U.S. 374 (1967), but that case does not mandate a media privilege to televise a performer's entire act without his consent. Involved in *Time, Inc. v. Hill* was a claim under the New York "Right of Privacy" statute [note 6] that Life Magazine, in [571] the course of reviewing a new play, had connected the play with a long-past incident involving petitioner and his family and had falsely described their experience and conduct at that time. The complaint sought damages for humiliation and suffering flowing from these nondefamatory falsehoods that allegedly invaded Hill's privacy. The Court held, however, that the opening of a new play linked to an actual incident was a matter of public interest and that Hill could not recover without showing that the Life report was knowingly false or was published with reckless disregard for the truth--the same rigorous standard that had been applied in *New York Times Co. v. Sullivan*, 376 U.S. 254 (1964).

Time, Inc. v. Hill, which was hotly contested and decided by a divided Court, involved an entirely different tort from the "right of publicity" recognized by the Ohio Supreme Court. As the opinion reveals in *Time, Inc. v. Hill*, the Court was steeped in the literature of privacy law and was aware of the developing distinctions and nuances in this branch of the law. The Court, for example, cited W. Prosser, Law of Torts 831-832 (3d ed. 1964), and the same author's well-known article, Privacy, 48 Calif. L. Rev. 383 (1960), both of which divided privacy into four distinct branches. [note 7] The Court was aware that it was adjudicating a "false light" privacy case involving a matter of public interest, not a case involving "intrusion," 385 U.S., at 384-385, n. 9, "appropriation" of a [572] name or likeness for the purposes of trade, *id.*, at 381, or "private details" about a non-newsworthy person or event, *id.*, at 383 n. 7. It is also abundantly clear that *Time, Inc. v. Hill* did not involve a performer, a person with a name having commercial value, or any claim to a "right of publicity." This discrete kind of "appropriation" case was plainly identified in the literature cited by the Court [note 8] and had been adjudicated in the reported cases. [note 9] [573]

The differences between these two torts are important. First, the State's interests in providing a cause of action in each instance are different. "The interest protected" in permitting recovery for placing the plaintiff in a false light "is clearly that of reputation, with the same overtones of mental distress as in defamation." Prosser, *supra*, 48 Calif. L. Rev., at 400. By contrast, the State's interest in permitting a "right of publicity" is in protecting the proprietary interest of the individual in his act in part to encourage such entertainment.[note 10] As we later note, the State's interest is closely analogous to the goals of patent and copyright law, focusing on the right of the individual to reap the reward of his endeavors and having little to do with protecting feelings or reputation. Second, the two torts differ in the degree to which they intrude on dissemination of information to the public. In "false light" cases the only way to protect the interests involved is to attempt to minimize publication of the damaging matter, while in "right of publicity" cases the only question is who gets to do the publishing. An entertainer such as petitioner usually has no objection to the widespread publication of his act as long as he gets the commercial benefit of such publication. Indeed, in the present case petitioner did not seek to enjoin the broadcast of his act; he simply [574] sought compensation for the broadcast in the form of damages.

Nor does it appear that our later cases, such as *Rosenbloom v. Metromedia, Inc.*, 403 U.S. 29 (1971); *Gertz v. Robert Welch, Inc.*, 418 U.S. 323 (1974); and *Time, Inc. v. Firestone*, 424 U.S. 448 (1976), require or furnish substantial support for the Ohio court's privilege ruling. These cases, like New York Times, emphasize the protection extended to the press by the First Amendment in defamation cases, particularly when suit is brought by a public official or a public figure. None of them involve an alleged appropriation by the press of a right of publicity existing under state law.

Moreover, *Time, Inc. v. Hill*, *New York Times*, *Metromedia*, *Gertz*, and *Firestone* all involved the reporting of events; in none of them was there an attempt to broadcast or publish an entire act for which the performer ordinarily gets paid. It is evident, and there is no claim here to the contrary, that petitioner's state-law right of publicity would not serve to prevent respondent from reporting the newsworthy facts about petitioner's act.[note 11] Wherever the line in particular situations is to be drawn between media reports that are protected and [575] those that are not, we are quite sure that the First and Fourteenth Amendments do not immunize the media when they broadcast a performer's entire act without his consent. The Constitution no more prevents a State from requiring respondent to compensate petitioner for broadcasting his act on television than it would privilege respondent to film and broadcast a copyrighted dramatic work without liability to the copyright owner, Copyrights Act, 17 U.S.C. App. § 101 et seq. (1976 ed.); cf. *Kalem Co. v. Harper Bros.*, 222 U.S. 55 (1911); *Manners v. Morosco*, 252 U.S. 317 (1920), or to film and broadcast a prize fight, *Ettore v. Philco Television Broadcasting Corp.*, 229 F.2d 481 (CA3), cert. denied, 351 U.S. 926 (1956); or a baseball game, *Pittsburgh Athletic Co. v. KQV Broadcasting Co.*, 24 F.Supp. 490 (WD Pa. 1938), where the promoters or the participants had other plans for publicizing the event. There are ample reasons for reaching this conclusion.

The broadcast of a film of petitioner's entire act poses a substantial threat to the economic value of that performance. As the Ohio court recognized, this act is the product of petitioner's own talents and energy, the end result of much time, effort, and expense. Much of its economic value lies in the "right of exclusive control over the publicity given to his performance"; if the public can see the act free on television, it will be less willing to pay to see it at the fair.[note 12] The [576] effect of a public broadcast of the performance is similar to preventing petitioner from charging an admission fee. "The rationale for [protecting the right of publicity] is the straight-forward one of preventing unjust enrichment by the theft of good will. No social purpose is served by having the defendant get free some aspect of the plaintiff that would have market value and for which he would normally pay." Kalven, Privacy in Tort Law--Were Warren and Brandeis Wrong?, 31 Law & Contemp. Prob. 326, 331 (1966). Moreover, the broadcast of petitioner's entire performance, unlike the unauthorized use of another's name for purposes of trade or the incidental use of a name or picture by the press, goes to the heart of the petitioner's ability to earn a living as an entertainer. Thus, in the case, Ohio has recognized what may be the strongest case for a "right of publicity"--involving, not the appropriation of an entertainer's reputation, but the appropriation of the very activity by which the entertainer acquired his reputation in the first place.

Of course, Ohio's decision to protect petitioner's right of publicity here rests on more than a desire to compensate the performer for the time and effort invested in his act; the protection provides an economic incentive for him to make the investment required to produce a performance of interest to the public. This same consideration underlies the patent and copyright laws long enforced by this Court. As the Court stated in *Mazer v. Stein*, 347 U.S. 201, 219 (1954):

"The economic philosophy behind the clause empowering Congress to grant patents and copyrights is the conviction that encouragement of individual effort by personal gain is the best way to advance public welfare through the talents of authors and inventors in 'Science and useful Arts.' Sacrificial days devoted to such creative activities deserve rewards commensurate with the services rendered." [577]

These laws perhaps regard the "reward to the owner [as] a secondary consideration," *United States v. Paramount Pictures*, 334 U.S. 131, 158 (1948), but they were "intended definitely to grant valuable, enforceable rights" in order to afford greater encouragement to the production of works of benefit to the public. *Washingtonian Publishing Co. v. Pearson*, 306 U.S. 30, 36 (1939). The Constitution does not prevent Ohio from making a similar choice here in deciding to protect the entertainer's incentive in order to encourage the production of this type of work. Cf. *Goldstein v. California*, 412 U.S. 546 (1973); *Kewanee Oil Co. v. Bicron Corp.*, 416 U.S. 470 (1974).[note 13] [578]

There is no doubt that entertainment, as well as news, enjoys First Amendment protection. It is also true that entertainment itself can be important news. *Time, Inc. v. Hill.* But it is important to note that neither the public nor respondent will be deprived of the benefit of petitioner's performance as long as his commercial stake in his act is appropriately recognized. Petitioner does not seek to enjoin the broadcast of his performance; he simply wants to be paid for it. Nor do we think that a state-law damages remedy against respondent would represent a species of liability without fault contrary to the letter or spirit of *Gertz v. Robert Welch, Inc.*, 418 U.S. 323 (1974). Respondent knew that petitioner objected to televising his act but nevertheless displayed the entire film.

We conclude that although the State of Ohio may as a [579] matter of its own law privilege the press in the circumstances of this case, the First and Fourteenth Amendments do not require it to do so.

Reversed.

23 CBS, INC. V. FCC
SUPREME COURT OF THE UNITED STATES
453 U.S. 367
Argued March 3, 1981
Decided July 1, 1981

Together with No. 80-213, *American Broadcasting Cos., Inc. v. Federal Communications Commission et al.*, and No. 80-214, *National Broadcasting Co., Inc. v. Federal Communications Commission et al.*, also on certiorari to the same court.

Syllabus

Section 312 (a) (7) of the Communications Act of 1934, as added by Title I of the Federal Election Campaign Act of 1971, authorizes the Federal Communications Commission (FCC) to revoke any broadcasting station license "for willful or repeated failure to allow reasonable access to or to permit purchase of reasonable amounts of time for the use of a broadcasting station by a legally qualified candidate for Federal elective office on behalf of his candidacy." On October 11, 1979, the Carter-Mondale Presidential Committee (Committee) requested each of the three major television networks (petitioners) to provide time for a 30-minute program between 8 p. m. and 10:30 p. m. on any day from the 4th through the 7th of December 1979. The Committee intended to present, in conjunction with President Carter's formal announcement of his candidacy, a documentary outlining the record of his administration. The petitioners refused to make the requested time available. CBS emphasized the large number of candidates for the Presidential nominations and the potential disruption of regular programming to accommodate requests for equal treatment, but offered to sell a 5-minute segment at 10:55 p. m. on December 8 and a 5-minute segment in the daytime; American Broadcasting Cos. replied that it had not yet decided when it would begin selling political time for the 1980 Presidential campaign, but later indicated that it would allow such sales in January 1980; and National Broadcasting Co., noting the number of potential requests for time from Presidential candidates, stated that it was not prepared to sell time for political programs as early as December 1979. The Committee then filed a complaint with the FCC, charging that the networks had violated their obligation to provide "reasonable access" under 312 (a) (7). The FCC ruled that the networks had violated the statute, concluding that their reasons for refusing to sell the time requested were "deficient" under the FCC's standards [368] of reasonableness, and directing the networks to indicate by a specified date how they intended to fulfill their statutory obligations. On the networks' petition for review, the Court of Appeals affirmed the FCC's orders, holding that the statute created a new, affirmative right of access to the broadcast media for individual candidates for federal elective office and that the FCC has the authority to independently evaluate whether a campaign has begun for purposes of the statute. The court approved the FCC's insistence that in responding to a candidate's request for time broadcasters must weigh certain factors, including the individual needs of the candidate (as expressed by the candidate); the amount of time previously provided to the candidate; potential disruption of regular programming; the number of other candidates likely to invoke equal opportunity rights if the broadcaster granted the request before it; and the timing of the request. The court determined that the record supported the FCC's conclusion that the networks failed to apply the proper standards and had thus violated the statute's "reasonable access" requirement. The court also rejected petitioners' First Amendment challenge to 312 (a) (7) as applied.

Held:

1. Section 312 (a) (7) created an affirmative, promptly enforceable right of reasonable access to the use of broadcast stations for individual candidates seeking federal elective office. It went beyond merely codifying prior FCC policies developed under the public interest standard. Pp. 376-386.

(a) It is clear on the face of the statute that Congress did not prescribe simply a general duty to afford some measure of political programming, which the public interest obligation of broadcasters already provided for. Rather, 312 (a) (7) focuses on the individual "legally qualified candidate" seeking air time to advocate "his candidacy," and guarantees him "reasonable access" enforceable by specific governmental sanction. Further, the sanction may be imposed for either "willful or repeated" failure to afford reasonable access. Pp. 377-379.

(b) The legislative history confirms that 312 (a) (7) created a right of access that enlarged the political broadcasting responsibilities of licensees. Pp. 379-382.

(c) Since the enactment of 312 (a) (7), the FCC has consistently construed the statute as extending beyond the prior public interest policy and as imposing the additional requirement that reasonable access and purchase of reasonable amounts of time be afforded candidates for federal office. This repeated construction of the statute comports with its language and legislative history and has received congressional review, so that departure from that construction is unwarranted. Pp. 382-385. [369]

(d) The qualified observation in *Columbia Broadcasting System, Inc. v. Democratic National Committee*, 412 U.S. 94, 113-114, n. 12, relied on by petitioners, that 312 (a) (7) "essentially codified" existing FCC practice was not a conclusion that the statute was in all respects coextensive with that practice and imposed no additional duties on broadcasters. That case did not purport to rule on the precise contours of the responsibilities created by 312 (a) (7) since that issue was not before the Court. Pp. 385-386.

2. Contrary to petitioners' contentions, certain of the FCC's standards to effectuate the guarantees of 312 (a) (7)--which standards evolved principally on a case-by-case basis and are not embodied in formalized rules--do not contravene the statutory objectives or unduly

intrude on petitioners' editorial discretion, and the statute was properly applied to petitioners in determining that they had failed to grant the "reasonable access" required by the statute. Pp. 386-394.

(a) The FCC's practice of independently determining--by examining objective evidence and considering the position of both the candidate and the networks as well as other factors--whether a campaign has begun and the obligations imposed by the statute have attached does not improperly involve the FCC in the electoral process or significantly impair broadcasters' editorial discretion. Nor is the FCC's standard requiring broadcasters to evaluate access requests on an individualized basis improper on the alleged ground that it attaches inordinate significance to candidates' needs, thereby precluding fair assessment of broadcasters' concerns. The FCC mandates careful consideration of, not blind assent to, candidates' desires for air time. Although the standard does proscribe blanket rules concerning access, such as broadcaster's rule of granting only time spots of a fixed duration to all candidates, the standard is consistent with 312 (a) (7)'s guarantee of reasonable access to individual candidates for federal elective office. The FCC's standards are not arbitrary and capricious, but represent a reasoned attempt to effectuate the statute's access requirement, giving broadcasters room to exercise their discretion but demanding that they act in good faith. Pp. 388-390.

(b) On the basis of prior FCC decisions and interpretations, petitioners had adequate notice that their conduct in responding to the Committee's request for access would contravene the statute. The FCC's conclusion about the status of the campaign accorded with its announced position on the vesting of 312 (a) (7) rights and was adequately supported by the objective factors on which it relied. And under the circumstances here, it cannot be concluded that the FCC abused its discretion in finding that petitioners failed to grant the "reasonable access" required by 312 (a) (7). Pp. 390-394. [370]

3. The right of access to the media under 312 (a) (7), as defined by the FCC and applied here, does not violate the First Amendment rights of broadcasters by unduly circumscribing their editorial discretion, but instead properly balances the First Amendment rights of federal candidates, the public, and broadcasters. Although the broadcasting industry is entitled under the First Amendment to exercise "the widest journalistic freedom consistent with its public [duties]," *Columbia Broadcasting System, Inc. v. Democratic National Committee, supra,* at 110, "[i]t is the right of the viewers and listeners, not the right of the broadcasters, which is paramount." *Red Lion Broadcasting Co. v. FCC,* 395 U.S. 367, 390. Section 312 (a) (7), which creates only a limited right of access to the media, makes a significant contribution to freedom of expression by enhancing the ability of candidates to present, and the public to receive, information necessary for the effective operation of the democratic process. Pp. 394-397.

202 U.S. App. D.C. 369, 629 F.2d 1, affirmed.

BURGER, C. J., delivered the opinion of the Court, in which BRENNAN, STEWART, MARSHALL, BLACKMUN, and POWELL, JJ., joined. WHITE, J., filed a dissenting opinion, in which REHNQUIST and STEVENS, JJ., joined, post, p. 397. STEVENS, J., filed a dissenting opinion, post, p. 418.

CHIEF JUSTICE BURGER delivered the opinion of the Court.

We granted certiorari to consider whether the Federal Communications Commission properly construed 47 U.S.C. 312 (a) (7) and determined that petitioners failed to provide "reasonable access to . . . the use of a broadcasting station" as required by the statute. 449 U.S. 950 (1980).

I

A

On October 11, 1979, Gerald M. Rafshoon, President of the Carter-Mondale Presidential Committee, requested each of the three major television networks to provide time for a 30-minute program between 8 p. m. and 10:30 p. m. on either the 4th, 5th, 6th, or 7th of December 1979.[note 1] The Committee [372] intended to present, in conjunction with President Carter's formal announcement of his candidacy, a documentary outlining the record of his administration.

The networks declined to make the requested time available. Petitioner CBS emphasized the large number of candidates for the Republican and Democratic Presidential nominations and the potential disruption of regular programming to accommodate requests for equal treatment, but it offered to sell two 5-minute segments to the Committee, one at 10:55 p. m. on December 8 and one in the daytime.[note 2] Petitioner [373] American Broadcasting Cos. replied that it had not yet decided when it would begin selling political time for the 1980 Presidential campaign,[note 3] but subsequently indicated that it would allow such sales in January 1980. App. 58. Petitioner National Broadcasting Co., noting the number of potential requests for time from Presidential candidates, stated that it was not prepared to sell time for political programs as early as December 1979.[note 4]

On October 29, 1979, the Carter-Mondale Presidential Committee filed a complaint with the Federal Communications Commission, charging that the networks had violated [374] their obligation to provide "reasonable access" under 312 (a) (7) of the Communications Act of 1934, as amended. Title 47 U.S.C. 312 (a) (7), as added to the Act, 86 Stat. 4, states:

"The Commission may revoke any station license or construction permit -

. . . . .

"(7) for willful or repeated failure to allow reasonable access to or to permit purchase of reasonable amounts of time for the use of a broadcasting station by a legally qualified candidate for Federal elective office on behalf of his candidacy."

At an open meeting on November 20, 1979, the Commission, by a 4-to-3 vote, ruled that the networks had violated 312 (a) (7). In its memorandum opinion and order, the Commission concluded that the networks' reasons for refusing to sell the time requested were "deficient" under its standards of reasonableness, and directed the networks to indicate by November 26, 1979, how they intended to fulfill their statutory obligations. 74 F. C. C. 2d 631.

Petitioners sought reconsideration of the FCC's decision. The reconsideration petitions were denied by the same 4-to-3 vote, and, on November 28, 1979, the Commission issued a second memorandum opinion and order clarifying its previous decision. It rejected petitioners' arguments that 312 (a) (7) was not intended to create a new right of access to the broadcast media and that the Commission had improperly substituted its judgment for that of the networks in evaluating the Carter-Mondale Presidential Committee's request for time. November 29, 1979, was set as the date for the networks to file their plans for compliance with the statute. 74 F. C. C. 2d 657.

The networks, pursuant to 47 U.S.C. 402, then petitioned for review of the Commission's orders in the United States Court of Appeals for the District of Columbia Circuit. The [375] court allowed the Committee and the National Association of Broadcasters to intervene, and granted a stay of the Commission's orders pending review.

Following the seizure of American Embassy personnel in Iran, the Carter-Mondale Presidential Committee decided to postpone to early January 1980 the 30-minute program it had planned to broadcast during the period of December 4-7, 1979. However, believing that some time was needed in conjunction with the President's announcement of his candidacy, the Committee sought and subsequently obtained from CBS the purchase of five minutes of time on December 4. In addition, the Committee sought and obtained from ABC and NBC offers of time for a 30-minute program in January, and the ABC offer eventually was accepted. Throughout these negotiations, the Committee and the networks reserved all rights relating to the appeal.

B

The Court of Appeals affirmed the Commission's orders, 202 U.S. App. D.C. 369, 629 F.2d 1 (1980), holding that the statute created a new, affirmative right of access to the broadcast media for individual candidates for federal elective office. As to the implementation of 312 (a) (7), the court concluded that the Commission has the authority to independently evaluate whether a campaign has begun for purposes of the statute, and approved the Commission's insistence that "broadcasters consider and address all non-frivolous matters in responding to a candidate's request for time." Id., at 386, 629 F.2d, at 18. For example, a broadcaster must weigh such factors as: "(a) the individual needs of the candidate (as expressed by the candidate); (b) the amount of time previously provided to the candidate; (c) potential disruption of regular programming; (d) the number of other candidates likely to invoke equal opportunity rights if the broadcaster grants the request before him; and. (e) the timing of the request." Id., at 387, 629 F.2d. at 19. And in reviewing a broadcaster's decision, the Commission will confine [376] itself to two questions: "(1) has the broadcaster adverted to the proper standards in deciding whether to grant a request for access, and (2) is the broadcaster's explanation for his decision reasonable in terms of those standards?" Id., at 386, 629 F.2d, at 18.

Applying these principles, the Court of Appeals sustained the Commission's determination that the Presidential campaign had begun by November 1979, and, accordingly, the obligations imposed by 312 (a) (7) had attached. Further, the court decided that "the record . . . adequately supports the Commission's conclusion that the networks failed to apply the proper standards." Id., at 389, 629 F.2d, at 21. In particular, the "across-the-board" policies of all three networks failed to address the specific needs asserted by the Carter-Mondale Presidential Committee. Id., at 390, 629 F.2d, at 22. From this the court concluded that the Commission was correct in holding that the networks had violated the statute's "reasonable access" requirement.

Finally, the Court of Appeals rejected petitioners' First Amendment challenge to 312 (a)

(7) as applied, reasoning that the statute as construed by the Commission "is a constitutionally acceptable accommodation between, on the one hand, the public's right to be informed about elections and the right of candidates to speak and, on the other hand, the editorial rights of broadcasters." Id., at 389, 629 F.2d, at 25. In a concurring opinion adopted by the majority, id., at 389, n. 117, 629 F.2d, at 25, n. 117, Judge Tamm expressed the view that 312 (a) (7) is saved from constitutional infirmity "as long as the [Commission] . . . maintains a very limited 'overseer' role consistent with its obligation of careful neutrality . . . ." Id., at 402, 629 F.2d, at 34.

II

We consider first the scope of 312 (a) (7). Petitioners CBS and NBC contend that the statute did not impose any [377] additional obligations on broadcasters, but merely codified prior policies developed by the Federal Communications Commission under the public interest standard. The Commission, however, argues that 312 (a) (7) created an affirmative, promptly enforceable right of reasonable access to the use of broadcast stations for individual candidates seeking federal elective office.

A

The Federal Election Campaign Act of 1971, which Congress enacted in 1972, included as one of its four Titles the Campaign Communications Reform Act (Title I). Title I contained the provision that was codified as 47 U.S.C. 312 (a) (7).[note 5]

We have often observed that the starting point in every case involving statutory construction is "the language employed by Congress." *Reiter v. Sonotone Corp.*, 442 U.S. 330, 337 (1979). In unambiguous language, 312 (a) (7) authorizes the Commission to revoke a broadcaster's license

"for willful or repeated failure to allow reasonable access to or to permit purchase of reasonable amounts of time for the use of a broadcasting station by a legally qualified candidate for Federal elective office on behalf of his candidacy."

It is clear on the face of the statute that Congress did not prescribe merely a general duty to afford some measure of political programming, which the public interest obligation [378] of broadcasters already provided for. Rather, 312 (a) (7) focuses on the individual "legally qualified candidate" seeking air time to advocate "his candidacy," and guarantees him "reasonable access" enforceable by specific governmental sanction. Further, the sanction may be imposed for "willful or repeated" failure to afford reasonable access. This suggests that, if a legally qualified candidate for federal office is denied a reasonable amount of broadcast time, license revocation may follow even a single instance of such denial so long as it is willful; where the denial is recurring, the penalty may be imposed in the absence of a showing of willfulness.

The command of 312 (a) (7) differs from the limited duty of broadcasters under the public interest standard. The practice preceding the adoption of 312 (a) (7) has been described by the Commission as follows:

"Prior to the enactment of the [statute], we recognized political broadcasting as one of the fourteen basic elements necessary to meet the public interest, needs and desires of the community. No legally qualified candidate had, at that time, a specific right of access to a broadcasting station. However, stations were required to make reasonable, good faith judgments about the importance and interest of particular races. Based upon those judgments, licensees were to 'determine how much time should be made available for candidates in each race on either a paid or unpaid basis.' There was no requirement that such time be made available for specific 'uses' of a broadcasting station to which Section 315 'equal opportunities' would be applicable." (Footnotes omitted.) *Report and Order: Commission Policy in Enforcing Section 312 (a) (7) of the Communications Act*, 68 F. C. C. 2d 1079, 1087-1088 (1978) (1978 Report and Order).

Under the pre-1971 public interest requirement, compliance with which was necessary to assure license renewal, some time [379] had to be given to political issues, but an individual candidate could claim no personal right of access unless his opponent used the station and no distinction was drawn between federal, state, and local elections.[note 6] See *Farmers Educational & Cooperative Union v. WDAY, Inc.*, 360 U.S. 525, 534 (1959). By its terms however, 312 (a) (7) singles out legally qualified candidates for federal elective office and grants them a special right of access on an individual basis, violation of which carries the serious consequence of license revocation. The conclusion is inescapable that the statute did more than simply codify the pre-existing public interest standard.

B

The legislative history confirms that 312 (a) (7) created a right of access that enlarged the political broadcasting responsibilities of licensees. When the subject of campaign reform was taken up by Congress in 1971, three bills were introduced in the Senate--S. 1, S. 382, and S. 956. All three measures, while differing in approach, were "intended to increase a candidate's accessibility to the media and to reduce the level of spending for its use." Federal Election Campaign Act of 1971: Hearings on S. 1. S. 382, and S. 956 before the Subcommittee on Communications of the Senate Committee on Commerce, 92d Cong., 1st Sess., 2 (1971) (remarks of Sen. Pastore). The subsequent Report of the Senate Commerce Committee stated that one of the primary purposes of the Federal Election Campaign Act of 1971 was to "give candidates for public office greater access to the media so that they may better explain their stand on the issues, and thereby more fully and completely inform the voters." S. Rep. No. 92-96, p. 20 (1971) (emphasis added). The Report contained [380] neither an explicit interpretation of the provision that became 312 (a) (7) nor a discussion of its intended impact, but simply noted:

"[The amendment] provide[s] that willful or repeated failure by a broadcast licensee to allow reasonable access to or to permit purchase of reasonable amounts of time for the use of his station's facilities by a lagally [sic] qualified candidate for Federal elective office on behalf of his candidacy shall be grounds for adverse action by the FCC.

"The duty of broadcast licensees generally to permit the use of their facilities by legally qualified candidates for these public offices is inherent in the requirement that licensees serve the needs and interests of the [communities] of license. The Federal Communications Commission has recognized this obligation . . . ." Id., at 34.

While acknowledging the "general" public interest requirement, the Report treated it separately from the specific obligation prescribed by the proposed legislation. See also id., at 28.

As initially reported in the Senate, 312 (a) (7) applied broadly to "the use of a broadcasting station by any person who is a legally qualified candidate on behalf of his candidacy." Id., at 3. The Conference Committee confined the provision to candidates seeking federal elective office. S. Conf. Rep. No. 92-580, p. 22 (1971); H. Conf. Rep. No. 92-752, p. 22 (1971). During floor debate on the Conference Report in the House, attention was called to the substantial impact 312 (a) (7) would have on the broadcasting industry:

"[B]roadcasters [are required] to permit any legally qualified candidate [for federal office] to purchase a 'reasonable amount of time' for his campaign advertising. Any broadcaster found in willful or repeated violation of this requirement could lose his license and be [381] thrown out of business, his total record of public service notwithstanding.

. . . . .

"[U]nder this provision, a broadcaster, whose license is obtained and retained on basis of performance in the public interest, may be charged with being unreasonable and, therefore, fall subject to revocation of his license." 118 Cong. Rec. 326 (1972) (remarks of Rep. Keith).

Such emphasis on the thrust of the statute would seem unnecessary if it did nothing more than reiterate the public interest standard.

Perhaps the most telling evidence of congressional intent, however, is the contemporaneous amendment of 315 (a) of the Communications Act.[note 7] That amendment was described by the Conference Committee as a "conforming amendment" necessitated by the enactment of 312 (a) (7). S. Conf. Rep. No. 92-580, *supra*, at 22; H. Conf. Rep. No. 92-752, *supra*, at 22. Prior to the "conforming amendment," the second sentence of 47 U.S.C. 315 (a) (1970 ed.) read: "No obligation is imposed upon any licensee to allow the use of its station by any such candidate." This language made clear that broadcasters were not common carriers as to affirmative, rather than responsive, requests for access. As a result of the amendment, the second sentence now contains an important qualification: "No obligation is imposed under this subsection upon any licensee to allow the use of its station by any such candidate." 47 U.S.C. 315 (a) (emphasis added). Congress retreated from its statement that "no obligation" exists to afford individual access presumably because 312 (a) (7) compels such access in the context of federal elections. If 312 (a) (7) simply reaffirmed the pre-existing public interest [382] requirement with the added sanction of license revocation, no conforming amendment to 315 (a) would have been needed.

Thus, the legislative history supports the plain meaning of the statute that individual candidates for federal elective office have a right of reasonable access to the use of stations for paid political broadcasts on behalf of their candidacies,[note 8] without reference to whether an opponent has secured time.

C

We have held that "the construction of a statute by those charged with its execution should be followed unless there are compelling indications that it is wrong, especially when Congress has refused to alter the administrative construction." *Red Lion Broadcasting Co. v. FCC*, 395 U.S. 367, 381 (1969) (footnotes omitted). Accord *Columbia Broadcasting System, Inc. v. Democratic National Committee*, 412 U.S. 94, 121 (1973). Such deference "is particularly appropriate where, as here, an agency's interpretation involves issues of considerable public controversy, and Congress has not acted to correct any misperception of its statutory objectives." *United States v. Rutherford*, 442 U.S. 544, 554 (1979).

Since the enactment of 312 (a) (7), the Commission has consistently construed the statute as extending beyond the prior public interest policy. In 1972, the Commission made clear that 312 (a) (7) "now imposes on the overall obligation to operate in the public interest the additional specific requirement that reasonable access and purchase of reasonable amounts of time be afforded candidates for Federal office." Use of Broadcast and Cablecast Facilities by Candidates for Public Office, 34 F. C. C. 2d 510, 537-538 (1972) [383] (1972 Policy Statement) (emphasis added). Accord, *Public Notice Concerning Licensee Responsibility Under Amendments to the Communications Act Made by the Federal Election Campaign Act of 1971*, 47 F. C. C. 2d 516 (1974). In its 1978 Report and Order, the Commission stated:

"When Congress enacted Section 312 (a) (7), it imposed an additional obligation on the general mandate to operate in the public interest. Licensees were specifically required to afford reasonable access to or to permit the purchase of reasonable amounts of broadcast time for the 'use' of Federal candidates.

"We see no merit to the contention that Section 312 (a) (7) was meant merely as a codification of the Commission's already existing policy concerning political broadcasts. There was no reason to commit that policy to statute since it was already being enforced by the Commission. . . ." 68 F. C. C. 2d, at 1088.

See also 1978 Primer, 69 F. C. C. 2d, at 2286-2289. The Commission has adhered to this view of the statute in its rulings on individual inquiries and complaints. See, e. g., The Labor Party, 67 F. C. C. 2d 589, 590 (1978); Ken Bauder, 62 F. C. C. 2d 849 (Broadcast Bureau 1976); Don C. Smith, 49 F. C. C. 2d 678, 679 (Broadcast Bureau 1974); Summa Corp., 43 F. C. C. 2d 602, 603-605 (1973); Robert H. Hauslein, 39 F. C. C. 2d 1064, 1065 (Broadcast Bureau 1973).

Congress has been made aware of the Commission's interpretation of 312 (a) (7). In 1973, hearings were conducted to review the operation of the Federal Election Campaign Act of 1971. Federal Election Campaign Act of 1973: Hearings on S. 372 before the Subcommittee on Communications of the Senate Committee on Commerce, 93d Cong., 1st Sess. (1973). Commission Chairman Dean Burch testified regarding the agency's experience with 312 (a) (7). Id., at 136-137. He noted that the Commission's 1972 Policy Statement was "widely distributed and represented our best judgment as to [384] the requirements of the law and the intent of Congress." Id., at 135. Chairman Burch discussed some of the difficult questions implicit in determining whether a station has afforded "reasonable access" to a candidate for federal office, and in conclusion stated: "We have brought our approach to these problems in the form of the 1972 Public Notice to the attention of Congress. If we have erred in some important construction, we would, of course, welcome congressional guidance." Id., at 137. Senator Pastore, Chairman of the Communications Subcommittee, replied:

"We didn't draw the provision any differently than we did because when you begin to legislate on guidelines, and on standards, and on criteria, you know what you run up against. I think what we did was reasonable enough, and I think what you did was reasonable enough as well.

. . . . .

"I would suppose that in cases of that kind, you would get some complaints. But, frankly, I think it has worked out pretty well." Id., at 137-138.

The issue was joined when CBS Vice Chairman Frank Stanton also testified at the hearings and objected to the fact that 312 (a) (7) "grants rights to all legally qualified candidates for Federal office . . . ." Id., at 190. He strongly urged "repeal" of the statute, but his plea was unsuccessful. Ibid.[note 9]

The Commission's repeated construction of 312 (a) (7) as affording an affirmative right of reasonable access to individual [385] candidates for federal elective office comports with the statute's language and legislative history and has received congressional review. Therefore, departure from that construction is unwarranted. "Congress' failure to repeal or revise [the statute] in the face of such administrative interpretation [is] persuasive evidence that that interpretation is the one intended by Congress." *Zemel v. Rusk*, 381 U.S. 1, 11 (1965).

D

In support of their narrow reading of 312 (a) (7) as simply a restatement of the public interest obligation, petitioners cite our decision in *Columbia Broadcasting System, Inc. v. Democratic National Committee*, 412 U.S. 94 (1973), which held that neither the First Amendment nor the Communications Act requires broadcasters to accept paid editorial advertisements from citizens at large. The Court in Democratic National Committee observed that "the Commission on several occasions has ruled that no private individual or group has a right to command the use of broadcast facilities," and that Congress has not altered that policy even though it has amended the Communications Act several times. Id., at 113. In a footnote, on which petitioners here rely, we referred to the then recently enacted 312 (a) (7) as one such amendment, stating that it had "essentially codified the Commission's prior interpretation of 315 (a) as requiring broadcasters to make time available to political candidates." Id., at 113-114, n. 12.

However, "the language of an opinion is not always to be parsed as though we were dealing with language of a statute." *Reiter v. Sonotone Corp.*, 442 U.S., at 341. The qualified observation that 312 (a) (7) "essentially codified" existing Commission practice was not a conclusion that the statute was in all respects coextensive with that practice and imposed no additional duties on broadcasters. In Democratic National Committee, we did not purport to rule on the precise contours [386] of the responsibilities created by 312 (a) (7) since that issue was not before us. Like the general public interest standard and the equal opportunities provision of 315 (a), 312 (a) (7) reflects the importance attached to the use of the public airwaves by political candidates. Yet we now hold that 312 (a) (7) expanded on those predecessor requirements and granted a new right of access to persons seeking election to federal office.[note 10]

III
A

Although Congress provided in 312 (a) (7) for greater use of broadcasting stations by federal candidates, it did not give guidance on how the Commission should implement the statute's access requirement. Essentially, Congress adopted a "rule of reason" and charged the Commission with its enforcement. Pursuant to 47 U.S.C. 303 (r), which empowers the Commission to "[m]ake such rules and regulations and prescribe such restrictions and conditions, not inconsistent with law, as may be necessary to carry out the provisions of [the Communications Act]," the agency has developed standards to effectuate the guarantees of 312 (a) (7). See also 47 U.S.C. 154 (i). The Commission has issued some general interpretative statements, but its standards implementing 312 (a) (7) have evolved principally on a case-by-case basis and are not embodied in formalized rules. The relevant criteria broadcasters must employ in evaluating access requests under the statute can be summarized from the Commission's 1978 Report and Order and the memorandum opinions and orders in these cases.

Broadcasters are free to deny the sale of air time prior to [387] the commencement of a campaign, but once a campaign has begun they must give reasonable and good-faith attention to access requests from "legally qualified" candidates [note 11] for federal elective office. Such requests must be considered on an individualized basis, and broadcasters are required to tailor their responses to accommodate, as much as reasonably possible, a candidate's stated purposes in seeking air time. In responding to access requests, however, broadcasters may also give weight to such factors as the amount of time previously sold to the candidate, the disruptive impact on regular programming, and the likelihood of requests for time by rival candidates under the equal opportunities provision of 315 (a). These considerations may not be invoked as pretexts for denying access; to justify a negative response, broadcasters must cite a realistic danger of substantial program disruption-- perhaps caused by insufficient notice to allow adjustments in the schedule--or of an excessive number of equal time requests. Further, in order to facilitate review by the Commission, broadcasters must explain their reasons for refusing time or making a more limited counteroffer. If broadcasters take the appropriate factors into account and act reasonably and in good faith, their decisions will be entitled to deference even if the Commission's analysis would have differed in the first instance. But if broadcasters adopt "across-the-board policies" and do not attempt to respond to [388] the individualized situation of a particular candidate, the Commission is not compelled to sustain their denial of access. See 74 F. C. C. 2d, at 665-674; 74 F. C. C. 2d, at 642-651; 1978 Report and Order, 68 F. C. C. 2d, at 1089-1092, 1094. Petitioners argue that certain of these standards are contrary to the statutory objectives of 312 (a) (7).

(1)

The Commission has concluded that, as a threshold matter, it will independently determine whether a campaign has begun and the obligations imposed by 312 (a) (7) have attached. 74 F. C. C. 2d, at 665-666. Petitioners assert that, in undertaking such a task, the Commission becomes improperly involved in the electoral process and seriously impairs broadcaster discretion.

However, petitioners fail to recognize that the Commission does not set the starting date for a campaign. Rather, on review of a complaint alleging denial of "reasonable access," it examines objective evidence to find whether the campaign has already commenced, "taking into account the position of the candidate and the networks as well as other factors." Id., at 665 (emphasis added). As the Court of Appeals noted, the "determination of when the statutory obligations attach does not control the electoral process. . . . the determination is controlled by the process." 202 U.S. App. D.C., at 384, 629 F.2d, at 16. Such a decision is not, and cannot be, purely one of editorial judgment.

Moreover, the Commission's approach serves to narrow 312 (a) (7), which might be read as vesting access rights in an individual candidate as soon as he becomes "legally qualified" without regard to the status of the campaign. See n. 11, supra. By confining the applicability of the statute to the period after a campaign commences, the Commission has limited its impact on broadcasters and given substance to its command of reasonable access. [389]

(2)

Petitioners also challenge the Commission's requirement that broadcasters evaluate and respond to access requests on an individualized basis. In petitioners' view, the agency has attached inordinate significance to candidates' needs, thereby precluding fair assessment of broadcasters' concerns and prohibiting the adoption of uniform policies regarding requests for access.

While admonishing broadcasters not to "'second guess' the 'political' wisdom or . . . effectiveness" of the particular format sought by a candidate, the Commission has clearly acknowledged that "the candidate's . . . request is by no means conclusive of the question of how much time, if any, is appropriate. Other . . . factors, such as the disruption or displacement of regular programming (particularly as affected by a reasonable probability of requests by other candidates), must be considered in the balance." 74 F. C. C. 2d, at 667-668. Thus, the Commission mandates careful consideration of, not blind assent to, candidates' desires for air time.

Petitioners are correct that the Commission's standards proscribe blanket rules concerning access; each request must be examined on its own merits. While the adoption of uniform policies might well prove more convenient for broadcasters, such an approach would allow personal campaign strategies and the exigencies of the political process to be ignored. A broadcaster's "evenhanded" response of granting only time spots of a fixed duration to candidates may be "unreasonable" where a particular candidate desires less time for an advertisement or a longer format to discuss substantive issues. In essence, petitioners seek the unilateral right to determine in advance how much time to afford all candidates. Yet 312 (a) (7) assures a right of reasonable access to individual candidates for federal elective office, and the Commission's requirement that their requests be considered on an individualized basis is consistent with that guarantee. [390]

(3)

The Federal Communications Commission is the experienced administrative agency long entrusted by Congress with the regulation of broadcasting, and the Commission is responsible for implementing and enforcing 312 (a) (7) of the Communications Act. Accordingly, its construction of the statute is entitled to judicial deference "unless there are compelling indications that it is wrong." *Red Lion Broadcasting Co. v. FCC*, 395 U.S., at 381. As we held in *Columbia Broadcasting System, Inc. v. Democratic National Committee*, 412 U.S., at 120, the Commission must be allowed to "remain in a posture of flexibility to chart a workable 'middle course' in its quest to preserve a balance between the essential public accountability and the desired private control of the media." Like the Court of Appeals, we cannot say that the Commission's standards are arbitrary and capricious or at odds with the language and purposes of 312 (a) (7). See 5 U.S.C. 706 (2) (A). Indeed, we are satisfied that the Commission's action represents a reasoned attempt to effectuate the statute's access requirement, giving broadcasters room to exercise their discretion but demanding that they act in good faith.[note 12]

B

There can be no doubt that the Commission's standards have achieved greater clarity as a result of the orders in these cases.[note 13] However laudable that may be, it raises the question [391] whether 312 (a) (7) was properly applied to petitioners.[note 14] Based upon the Commission's prior decisions and 1978 Report and Order, however, we must conclude that petitioners had adequate notice that their conduct in responding to the Carter-Mondale Presidential Committee's request for access would contravene the statute.

In the 1978 Report and Order, the Commission stated that it could not establish a precise point at which 312 (a) (7) obligations would attach for all campaigns because each is unique:

"For instance, a presidential campaign may be in full swing almost a year before an election; other campaigns may be limited to a short concentrated period. . . . [W]e believe that, generally, a licensee would be unreasonable if it refused to afford access to Federal candidates at least during those time periods [when the 'lowest unit charge' provision of 315 applied]. Moreover, it may be required to afford reasonable access before these periods; however, the determination of whether 'reasonable access' must be afforded before these periods for particular races must be made in each case under all the facts and circumstances present. . . . [W]e expect licensees to afford access at a reasonable time prior to a convention or caucus. We will review a licensee's decisions in [392] this area on a case-by-case basis." 68 F. C. C. 2d, at 1091-1092 (emphasis added).

In Anthony R. Martin-Trigona, 67 F. C. C. 2d 743 (1978), the Commission observed: "[T]he licensee, and ultimately the Commission, must look to the circumstances of each particular case to determine when it is reasonable for a candidate's access to begin . . . ." Id., at 746, n. 4 (emphasis added). Further, the 1978 Report and Order made clear that "Federal candidates are the intended beneficiary of Section 312 (a) (7) and therefore a candidate's desires as to the method of conducting his or her media campaign should be considered by licensees in granting reasonable access." 68 F. C. C. 2d, at 1089, n. 14. The agency also stated:

"[A]n arbitrary 'blanket' ban on the use by a candidate of a particular class or length of time in a particular period cannot be considered reasonable. A Federal candidate's decisions as to the best method of pursuing his or her media campaign should be honored as much as possible under the 'reasonable' limits imposed by the licensee." Id., at 1090.

Here, the Carter-Mondale Presidential Committee sought broadcast time approximately 11 months before the 1980 Presidential election and 8 months before the Democratic National Convention. In determining that a national campaign was underway at that point, the Commission stressed: (a) that 10 candidates formally had announced their intention to seek the Republican nomination, and 2 candidates had done so for the Democratic nomination; (b) that various states had started the delegate selection process; (c) that candidates were traveling across the country making speeches and attempting to raise funds; (d) that national campaign organizations were established and operating; (e) that the Iowa caucus would be held the following month; (f) that public officials and private groups were making endorsements; and (g) that the national print media had given campaign [393] activities prominent coverage for almost two months. 74 F. C. C. 2d, at 645-647. The Commission's conclusion about the status of the campaign accorded with its announced position on the vesting of 312 (a) (7) rights and was adequately supported by the objective factors on which it relied.

Nevertheless, petitioners ABC and NBC refused to sell the Carter-Mondale Presidential Committee any time in December 1979 on the ground that it was "too early in the political season." App. 41-43, 52-74; nn. 3 and 4, supra. These petitioners made no counteroffers, but adopted "blanket" policies refusing access despite the admonition against such an approach in the 1978 Report and Order. Cf. Donald W. Riegle, 59 F. C. C. 2d 1314 (1976); WALB-TV, Inc., 59 F. C. C. 2d 1246 (1976). Likewise, petitioner CBS, while not barring access completely, had an across-the-board policy of selling only 5-minute spots to all candidates, notwithstanding the Commission's directive in the 1978 Report and Order that broadcasters consider "a candidate's desires as to the method of conducting his or her media campaign." 68 F. C. C. 2d, at 1089, n. 14. See App. 44-45, 75-93; n. 2, supra. Petitioner CBS responded with its standard offer of separate 5-minute segments, even though the Carter-Mondale Presidential Committee sought 30 minutes of air time to present a comprehensive statement launching President Carter's re-election campaign. Moreover, the Committee's request was made almost two months before the intended date of broadcast, was flexible in that it could be satisfied with any prime time slot during a 4-day period, was accompanied by an offer to pay the normal commercial rate, and was not preceded by other requests from President Carter for access. See App. 27-40; n. 1, supra. Although petitioners adverted to the disruption of regular programming and the potential equal time requests from rival candidates in their responses to the Carter-Mondale Presidential Committee's complaint, the Commission rejected these claims as "speculative and unsubstantiated at best." 74 F. C. C. 2d, at 674. [394]

Under these circumstances, we cannot conclude that the Commission abused its discretion in finding that petitioners failed to grant the "reasonable access" required by 312 (a) (7).[note 15] See 5 U.S.C. 706 (2) (A). "[T]he fact that we might not have made the same determination on the same facts does not warrant a substitution of judicial for administrative discretion since Congress has confided the problem to the latter." *FCC v. WOKO, Inc.*, 329 U.S. 223, 229 (1946). "[C]ourts should not overrule an administrative decision merely because they disagree with its wisdom." *Radio Corp. of America v. United States*, 341 U.S. 412, 420 (1951).

IV

Finally, petitioners assert that 312 (a) (7) as implemented by the Commission violates the First Amendment rights of broadcasters by unduly circumscribing their editorial discretion. In *Columbia Broadcasting System, Inc. v. Democratic National Committee*, 412 U.S., at 117, we stated:

"Th[e] role of the Government as an 'overseer' and ultimate arbiter and guardian of the public interest and the role of the license as a journalistic 'free agent' call for a delicate balancing of competing interests. The maintenance of this balance for more than 40 years has called on both the regulators and the licensees to walk a 'tight-rope' to preserve the First Amendment values written [395] into the Radio Act and its successor, the Communications Act."

Petitioners argue that the Commission's interpretation of 312 (a) (7)'s access requirement disrupts the "delicate balanc[e]" that broadcast regulation must achieve. We disagree.

A licensed broadcaster is "granted the free and exclusive use of a limited and valuable part of the public domain; when he accepts that franchise it is burdened by enforceable public obligations." *Office of Communication of the United Church of Christ v. FCC*, 123 U.S. App. D.C. 328, 337, 359 F.2d 994, 1003 (1966). This Court has noted the limits on a broadcast license:

"A license permits broadcasting, but the licensee has no constitutional right to be the one who holds the license or to monopolize a . . . frequency to the exclusion of his fellow citizens. There is nothing in the First Amendment which prevents the Government from requiring a licensee to share his frequency with others . . . ." *Red Lion Broadcasting Co. v. FCC*, 395 U.S., at 389.

See also *FCC v. National Citizens Comm. for Broadcasting*, 436 U.S. 775, 799-800 (1978). Although the broadcasting industry is entitled under the First Amendment to exercise "the widest journalistic freedom consistent with its public [duties]," *Columbia Broadcasting System, Inc. v. Democratic National Committee, supra*, at 110, the Court has made clear that:

"*It is the right of the viewers and listeners, not the right of the broadcasters, which is paramount.* It is the purpose of the First Amendment to preserve an uninhibited marketplace of ideas in which truth will ultimately prevail, rather than to countenance monopolization of that market . . . . It is the right of the public to receive suitable access to social, political, esthetic, moral, and other ideas and experiences which is crucial here." *Red [396] Lion Broadcasting Co. v. FCC, supra*, at 390 (citations omitted) (emphasis added).

The First Amendment interests of candidates and voters, as well as broadcasters, are implicated by 312 (a) (7). We have recognized that "it is of particular importance that candidates have the . . . opportunity to make their views known so that the electorate may intelligently evaluate the candidates' personal qualities and their positions on vital public issues before choosing among them on election day." *Buckley v. Valeo*, 424 U.S. 1, 52-53 (1976). Indeed, "speech concerning public affairs is . . . the essence of self-government." *Garrison v. Louisiana*, 379 U.S. 64, 74-75 (1964). The First Amendment "has its fullest and most urgent application precisely to the conduct of campaigns for political office." *Monitor Patriot Co. v. Roy*, 401 U.S. 265, 272 (1971). Section 312 (a) (7) thus makes a significant contribution to freedom of expression by enhancing the ability of candidates to present, and the public to receive, information necessary for the effective operation of the democratic process.

Petitioners are correct that the Court has never approved a general right of access to the media. See, e. g., *FCC v. Midwest Vedio Corp.*, 440 U.S. 689 (1979); *Miami Herald Publishing Co. v. Tornillo*, 418 U.S. 241 (1974); *Columbia Broadcasting System, Inc. v. Democratic National Committee*, supra. Nor do we do so today. Section 312 (a) (7) creates a limited right to "reasonable" access that pertains only to legally qualified federal candidates and may be invoked by them only for the purpose of advancing their candidacies once a campaign has commenced. The Commission has stated that, in enforcing the statute, it will "provide leeway to broadcasters and not merely attempt de novo to determine the reasonableness of their judgments . . . ." 74 F. C. C. 2d, at 672. If broadcasters have considered the relevant factors in good faith, the Commission will uphold their decisions. See 202 U.S. App. D.C., at 393, 629 F.2d, at 25. Further, 312 [397] (a) (7) does not impair the discretion of broadcasters to present their views on any issue or to carry any particular type of programming.

Section 312 (a) (7) represents an effort by Congress to assure that an important resource-

-the airwaves--will be used in the public interest. We hold that the statutory right of access, as defined by the Commission and applied in these cases, properly balances the First Amendment rights of federal candidates, the public, and broadcasters.

The judgment of the Court of Appeal is

Affirmed.

24 HUSTLER MAGAZINE, INC. ET AL. V. JERRY FALWELL
SUPREME COURT OF THE UNITED STATES
485 U.S. 46
Argued December 2, 1987
Decided February 24, 1988

Syllabus

Respondent, a nationally known minister and commentator on politics and public affairs, filed a diversity action in Federal District Court against petitioners, a nationally circulated magazine and its publisher, to recover damages for, inter alia, libel and intentional infliction of emotional distress arising from the publication of an advertisement "parody" which, among other things, portrayed respondent as having engaged in a drunken incestuous rendezvous with his mother in an outhouse. The jury found against respondent on the libel claim, specifically finding that the parody could not "reasonably be understood as describing actual facts . . . or events," but ruled in his favor on the emotional distress claim, stating that he should be awarded compensatory and punitive damages. The Court of Appeals affirmed, rejecting petitioners' contention that the "actual malice" standard of *New York Times Co. v. Sullivan*, 376 U. S. 254, must be met before respondent can recover for emotional distress. Rejecting as irrelevant the contention that, because the jury found that the parody did not describe actual facts, the ad was an opinion protected by the First Amendment to the Federal Constitution, the court ruled that the issue was whether the ad's publication was sufficiently outrageous to constitute intentional infliction of emotional distress.

Held: In order to protect the free flow of ideas and opinions on matters of public interest and concern, the First and Fourteenth Amendments prohibit public figures and public officials from recovering damages for the tort of intentional infliction of emotional distress by reason of the publication of a caricature such as the ad parody at issue without showing in addition that the publication contains a false statement of fact which was made with "actual malice," i.e., with knowledge that the statement was false or with reckless disregard as to whether or not it was true. The State's interest in protecting public figures from emotional distress is not sufficient to deny First Amendment protection to speech that is patently offensive and is intended to inflict emotional injury when that speech could not reasonably have been interpreted as stating actual facts about the public figure involved. Here, respondent is clearly a "public figure" for First Amendment purposes, and the lower courts' finding that the ad parody was not reasonably believable must be accepted.

"Outrageousness" [47] in the area of political and social discourse has an inherent subjectiveness about it which would allow a jury to impose liability on the basis of the jurors' tastes or views, or perhaps on the basis of their dislike of a particular expression, and cannot, consistently with the First Amendment, form a basis for the award of damages for conduct such as that involved here. Pp. 50-57.

797 F. 2d 1270, reversed.

REHNQUIST, C.J., delivered the opinion of the Court, in which BRENNAN, MARSHALL, BLACKMUN, STEVENS, O'CONNOR, AND SCALIA, JJ., joined. WHITE, J., filed an opinion concurring in the judgment, post, p. 57. KENNEDY, J., took no part in the consideration or decision of the case.

CHIEF JUSTICE REHNQUIST delivered the opinion of the Court.

Petitioner Hustler Magazine, Inc., is a magazine of nationwide circulation. Respondent Jerry Falwell, a nationally known minister who has been active as a commentator on politics and public affairs, sued petitioner and its publisher, petitioner Larry Flynt, to recover damages for invasion of [48] privacy, libel, and intentional infliction of emotional distress. The District Court directed a verdict against respondent on the privacy claim, and submitted the other two claims to a jury. The jury found for petitioners on the defamation claim, but found for respondent on the claim for intentional infliction of emotional distress and awarded damages. We now consider whether this award is consistent with the First and Fourteenth Amendments of the United States Constitution.

The inside front cover of the November 1983 issue of Hustler Magazine featured a "parody" of an advertisement for Campari Liqueur that contained the name and picture of respondent and was entitled "Jerry Falwell talks about his first time." This parody was modeled after actual Campari ads that included interviews with various celebrities about their "first times." Although it was apparent by the end of each interview that this meant the first time they sampled Campari, the ads clearly played on the sexual double entendre of the general subject of "first times." Copying the form and layout of these Campari ads, Hustler's editors chose respondent as the featured celebrity and drafted an alleged "interview" with him in which he states that his "first time" was during a drunken incestuous rendezvous with his mother in an outhouse. The Hustler parody portrays respondent and his mother as drunk and immoral, and suggests that respondent is a hypocrite who preaches only when he is drunk. In small print at the bottom of the page, the ad contains the disclaimer, "ad parody-- not to be taken seriously." The magazine's table of contents also lists the ad as "Fiction; Ad and Personality Parody."

Soon after the November issue of Hustler became available to the public, respondent brought this diversity action in the United States District Court for the Western District of Virginia against Hustler Magazine, Inc., Larry C. Flynt, and Flynt Distributing Co. Respondent stated in his complaint that publication of the ad parody in Hustler entitled [49] him to recover damages for libel, invasion of privacy, and intentional infliction of emotional distress. The case proceeded to trial.[note 1] At the close of the evidence, the District Court granted a directed verdict for petitioners on the invasion of privacy claim. The jury then found against respondent on the libel claim, specifically finding that the ad parody could not "reasonably be understood as describing actual facts about [respondent] or actual events in which [he] participated." App. to Pet. for Cert. C1. The jury ruled for respondent on the intentional infliction of emotional distress claim, however and stated that he should be awarded $100,000 in compensatory damages, as well as $50,000 each in punitive damages from petitioners.[note 2] Petitioners' motion for judgment notwithstanding the verdict was denied.

On appeal, the United States Court of Appeals for the Fourth Circuit affirmed the judgment against petitioners. *Falwell v. Flynt*, 797 F. 2d 1270 (CA4 1986). The court rejected petitioners' argument that the "actual malice" standard of *New York Times Co. v. Sullivan*, 376 U. S. 254 (1964), must be met before respondent can recover for emotional distress. The court agreed that because respondent is concededly a public figure, petitioners are "entitled to the same level of first amendment protection in the claim for intentional infliction of emotional distress that they received in [respondent's] claim for libel." 797 F. 2d, at 1274. But this does not mean that a literal application of the actual malice rule is appropriate in the context of an emotional distress claim. In the court's view, the *New York Times* decision emphasized the constitutional importance not of the falsity of the statement or the defendant's disregard for the truth, but of the heightened level of culpability embodied in the requirement of "knowing . . . or reckless" conduct. Here, the New York [50] Times standard is satisfied by the state-law requirement, and the jury's finding, that the defendants have acted intentionally or recklessly.[note 3] The Court of Appeals then went on to reject the contention that because the jury found that the ad parody did not describe actual facts about respondent, the ad was an opinion that is protected by the First Amendment. As the court put it, this was "irrelevant," as the issue is "whether [the ad's] publication was sufficiently outrageous to constitute intentional infliction of emotional distress." *Id.*, at 1276.[note 4]Petitioners then filed a petition for rehearing en banc, but this was denied by a divided court. Given the importance of the constitutional issues involved, we granted certiorari. 480 U.S. 945 (1987).

This case presents us with a novel question involving First Amendment limitations upon a State's authority to protect its citizens from the intentional infliction of emotional distress. We must decide whether a public figure may recover damages for emotional harm caused by the publication of an ad parody offensive to him, and doubtless gross and repugnant in the eyes of most. Respondent would have us find that a State's interest in protecting public figures from emotional distress is sufficient to deny First Amendment protection to speech that is patently offensive and is intended to inflict emotional injury, even when that speech could not reasonably have been interpreted as stating actual facts about the public figure involved. This we decline to do.

At the heart of the First Amendment is the recognition of the fundamental importance of the free flow of ideas and opinions on matters of public interest and concern. "The [51] freedom to speak one's mind is not only an aspect of individual liberty--and thus a good unto itself--but also is essential to the common quest for truth and the vitality of society as a whole." *Bose Corp. v. Consumers Union of United States, Inc.*, 466 U. S. 485, 503-504 (1984). We have therefore been particularly vigilant to ensure that individual expressions of ideas remain free from governmentally imposed sanctions. The First Amendment recognizes no such thing as a "false" idea. *Gertz v. Robert Welch, Inc.*, 418 U. S. 323, 339 (1974). As Justice Holmes wrote, "When men have realized that time has upset many fighting faiths, they may come to believe even more than they believe the very foundations of their own conduct that the ultimate good desired is better reached by free trade in ideas--that the best test of truth is the power of the thought to get itself accepted in the competition of the market . . . ." *Abrams v.*

United States, 250 U. S. 616, 630 (1919) (dissenting opinion).

The sort of robust political debate encouraged by the First Amendment is bound to produce speech that is critical of those who hold public office or those public figures who are "intimately involved in the resolution of important public questions or, by reason of their fame, shape events in areas of concern to society at large." *Associated Press v. Walker* decided with *Curtis Publishing Co. v. Butts,* 388 U. S. 130, 164 (1967) (Warren, C.J., concurring in result). Justice Frankfurter put it succinctly in *Baumgartner v. United States,* 322 U. S. 665, 673-674 (1944), when he said that "one of the prerogatives of American citizenship is the right to criticize public men and measures." Such criticism, inevitably, will not always be reasoned or moderate; public figures as well as public officials will be subject to "vehement, caustic, and sometimes unpleasantly sharp attacks," *New York Times, supra,* at 270. "The candidate who vaunts his spotless record and sterling integrity cannot convincingly cry 'Foul!' when an opponent or an industrious reporter attempts [52] to demonstrate the contrary." *Monitor Patriot Co. v. Roy,* 401 U. S. 265, 274 (1971).

Of course, this does not mean that any speech about a public figure is immune from sanction in the form of damages. Since *New York Times Co. v. Sullivan, supra,* we have consistently ruled that a public figure may hold a speaker liable for the damage to reputation caused by publication of a defamatory falsehood, but only if the statement was made "with knowledge that it was false or with reckless disregard of whether it was false or not." *Id.,* at 279-280. False statements of fact are particularly valueless; they interfere with the truth-seeking function of the marketplace of ideas, and they cause damage to an individual's reputation that cannot easily be repaired by counterspeech, however persuasive or effective. See *Gertz,* 418 U. S., at 340, 344, n. 9. But even though falsehoods have little value in and of themselves, they are "nevertheless inevitable in free debate," *id.,* at 340, and a rule that would impose strict liability on a publisher for false factual assertions would have an undoubted "chilling" effect on speech relating to public figures that does have constitutional value. "Freedoms of expression require " breathing space.'" *Philadelphia Newspapers, Inc. v. Hepps,* 475 U. S. 767, 772 (1986) (quoting *New York Times,* 376 U. S., at 272). This breathing space is provided by a constitutional rule that allows public figures to recover for libel or defamation only when they can prove both that the statement was false and that the statement was made with the requisite level of culpability.

Respondent argues, however, that a different standard should apply in this case because here the State seeks to prevent not reputational damage, but the severe emotional distress suffered by the person who is the subject of an offensive publication. Cf. *Zacchini v. Scripps-Howard Broadcasting Co.,* 433 U. S. 562 (1977) (ruling that the "actual malice" standard does not apply to the tort of appropriation of a right of publicity). In respondent's view, and in the view of the [53] Court of Appeals, so long as the utterance was intended to inflict emotional distress, was outrageous, and did in fact inflict serious emotional distress, it is of no constitutional import whether the statement was a fact or an opinion, or whether it was true or false. It is the intent to cause injury that is the gravamen of the tort, and the State's interest in preventing emotional harm simply outweighs whatever interest a speaker may have in speech of this type.

Generally speaking the law does not regard the intent to inflict emotional distress as one which should receive much solicitude, and it is quite understandable that most if not all jurisdictions have chosen to make it civilly culpable where the conduct in question is sufficiently "outrageous." But in the world of debate about public affairs, many things done with motives that are less than admirable are protected by the First Amendment. In *Garrison v. Louisiana*, 379 U. S. 64 (1964), we held that even when a speaker or writer is motivated by hatred or ill-will his expression was protected by the First Amendment:

"Debate on public issues will not be uninhibited if the speaker must run the risk that it will be proved in court that he spoke out of hatred; even if he did speak out of hatred, utterances honestly believed contribute to the free interchange of ideas and the ascertainment of truth." *Id.,* at 73.

Thus while such a bad motive may be deemed controlling for purposes of tort liability in other areas of the law, we think the First Amendment prohibits such a result in the area of public debate about public figures.

Were we to hold otherwise, there can be little doubt that political cartoonists and satirists would be subjected to damages awards without any showing that their work falsely defamed its subject. Webster's defines a caricature as "the deliberately distorted picturing or imitating of a person, literary style, etc. by exaggerating features or mannerisms for satirical effect." Webster's New Unabridged Twentieth [54] Century Dictionary of the English Language 275 (2d ed. 1979). The appeal of the political cartoon or caricature is often based on exploration of unfortunate physical traits or politically embarrassing events--an exploration often calculated to injure the feelings of the subject of the portrayal. The art of the cartoonist is often not reasoned or evenhanded, but slashing and one-sided. One cartoonist expressed the nature of the art in these words:

"The political cartoon is a weapon of attack, of scorn and ridicule and satire; it is least effective when it tries to pat some politician on the back. It is usually as welcome as a bee sting and is always controversial in some quarters." Long, The Political Cartoon: Journalism's Strongest Weapon, The Quill, 56, 57 (Nov. 1962).

Several famous examples of this type of intentionally injurious speech were drawn by Thomas Nast, probably the greatest American cartoonist to date, who was associated for many years during the post-Civil War era with Harper's Weekly. In the pages of that publication Nast conducted a graphic vendetta against William M. "Boss" Tweed and his corrupt associates in New York City's "Tweed Ring." It has been described by one historian of the subject as "a sustained attack which in its passion and effectiveness stands alone in the history of American graphic art." M. Keller, The Art and Politics of Thomas Nast 177 (1968). Another writer explains that the success of the Nast cartoon was achieved "because of the emotional impact of its presentation. It continuously goes beyond the bounds of good taste and conventional manners." C. Press, The Political Cartoon 251 (1981).

Despite their sometimes caustic nature, from the early cartoon portraying George Washington as an ass down to the present day, graphic depictions and satirical cartoons have played a prominent role in public and political debate. Nast's castigation of the Tweed Ring, Walt McDougall's characterization of presidential candidate James G. Blaine's banquet with the millionaires at Delmonico's as "The Royal [55] Feast of Belshazzar," and numerous other efforts have undoubtedly had an effect on the course and outcome of contemporaneous debate. Lincoln's tall, gangling posture, Teddy Roosevelt's glasses and teeth, and Franklin D. Roosevelt's jutting jaw and cigarette holder have been memorialized by political cartoons with an effect that could not have been obtained by the photographer or the portrait artist. From the viewpoint of history it is clear that our political discourse would have been considerably poorer without them.

Respondent contends, however, that the caricature in question here was so "outrageous" as to distinguish it from more traditional political cartoons. There is no doubt that the caricature of respondent and his mother published in Hustler is at best a distant cousin of the political cartoons described above, and a rather poor relation at that. If it were possible by laying down a principled standard to separate the one from the other, public discourse would probably suffer little or no harm. But we doubt that there is any such standard, and we are quite sure that the pejorative description " outrageous" does not supply one. "Outrageousness" in the area of political and social discourse has an inherent subjectiveness about it which would allow a jury to impose liability on the basis of the jurors' tastes or views, or perhaps on the basis of their dislike of a particular expression. An "outrageousness" standard thus runs afoul of our longstanding refusal to allow damages to be awarded because the speech in question may have an adverse emotional impact on the audience. See *NAACP v. Claiborne Hardware Co.*, 458 U. S. 886, 910 (1982) ("Speech does not lose its protected character . . . simply because it may embarrass others or coerce them into action"). And, as we stated in *FCC v. Pacifica Foundation*, 438 U. S. 726 (1978):

"[T]he fact that society may find speech offensive is not a sufficient reason for sup pressing it. Indeed, if it is the speaker's opinion that gives offense, that con sequence is a reason for according it constitutional protection. [56] For it is a central tenet of the First Amendment that the government must remain neutral in the marketplace of ideas." *Id.*, at 745-746.

See also *Street v. New York*, 394 U. S. 576, 592 (1969) ("It is firmly settled that . . . the public expression of ideas may not be prohibited merely because the ideas are themselves offensive to some of their hearers").

Admittedly, these oft-repeated First Amendment principles, like other principles, are subject to limitations. We recognized in Pacifica Foundation, that speech that is " vulgar,' offensive,' and shocking'" is "not entitled to absolute constitutional protection under all circumstances." 438 U. S., at 747. In *Chaplinsky v. New Hampshire*, 315 U. S. 568 (1942), we held that a state could lawfully punish an individual for the use of insulting " fighting' words- -those which by their very utterance inflict injury or tend to incite an immediate breach of the peace." *Id.*, at 571-572. These limitations are but recognition of the observation in *Dun & Bradstreet, Inc. v. Greenmoss Builders, Inc.*, 472 U. S. 749, 758 (1985), that this Court has "long recognized that not all speech is of equal First Amendment importance." But the sort of expression involved in this case does not seem to us to be governed by any exception to the general First Amendment principles stated above.

We conclude that public figures and public officials may not recover for the tort of intentional infliction of emotional distress by reason of publications such as the one here at issue without showing in addition that the publication contains a false statement of fact which was made with "actual malice," i.e., with knowledge that the statement was false or with reckless disregard as to whether or not it was true. This is not merely a "blind application" of the *New York Times* standard, see *Time, Inc. v. Hill*, 385 U. S. 374, 390 (1967), it reflects our considered judgment that such a standard is necessary to give adequate "breathing space" to the freedoms protected by the First Amendment. [57]

Here it is clear that respondent Falwell is a "public figure" for purposes of First Amendment law.[note 5] The jury found against respondent on his libel claim when it decided that the Hustler ad parody could not "reasonably be understood as describing actual facts about [respondent] or actual events in which [he] participated." App. to Pet. for Cert. C1. The Court of Appeals interpreted the jury's finding to be that the ad parody "was not reasonably believable," 797 F. 2d, at 1278, and in accordance with our custom we accept this finding. Respondent is thus relegated to his claim for damages awarded by the jury for the intentional infliction of emotional distress by "outrageous" conduct. But for reasons heretofore stated this claim cannot, consistently with the First Amendment, form a basis for the award of damages when the conduct in question is the publication of a caricature such as the ad parody involved here.

The judgment of the Court of Appeals is accordingly Reversed.

25 Texas v. Johnson
SUPREME COURT OF THE UNITED STATES
491 U.S. 397
Argued March 21, 1989
Decided June 21, 1989

Syllabus

During the 1984 Republican National Convention in Dallas, Texas, respondent Johnson participated in a political demonstration to protest the policies of the Reagan administration and some Dallas-based corporations. After a march through the city streets, Johnson burned an American flag while protesters chanted. No one was physically injured or threatened with injury, although several witnesses were seriously offended by the flag burning. Johnson was convicted of desecration of a venerated object in violation of a Texas statute, and a State Court of Appeals affirmed. However, the Texas Court of Criminal Appeals reversed, holding that the State, consistent with the First Amendment, could not punish Johnson for burning the flag in these circumstances. The court first found that Johnson's burning of the flag was expressive conduct protected by the First Amendment. The court concluded that the State could not criminally sanction flag desecration in order to preserve the flag as a symbol of national unity. It also held that the statute did not meet the State's goal of preventing breaches of the peace, since it was not drawn narrowly enough to encompass only those flag burnings that would likely result in a serious disturbance, and since the flag burning in this case did not threaten such a reaction. Further, it stressed that another Texas statute prohibited breaches of the peace and could be used to prevent disturbances without punishing this flag desecration.

Held: Johnson's conviction for flag desecration is inconsistent with the First Amendment. Pp. 402-420.

(a) Under the circumstances, Johnson's burning of the flag constituted expressive conduct, permitting him to invoke the First Amendment. The State conceded that the conduct was expressive. Occurring as it did at the end of a demonstration coinciding with the Republican National Convention, the expressive, overtly political nature of the conduct was both intentional and overwhelmingly apparent. Pp. 402-406.

(b) Texas has not asserted an interest in support of Johnson's conviction that is unrelated to the suppression of expression and would therefore permit application of the test set forth in *United States v. O'Brien*, 391 U.S. 367, whereby an important governmental interest in regulating nonspeech can justify incidental limitations on First Amendment freedoms when speech and nonspeech elements are combined in the same course of conduct. An interest in preventing breaches of the peace is not implicated on this record. Expression may not be prohibited [398] on the basis that an audience that takes serious offense to the expression may disturb the peace, since the government cannot assume that every expression of a provocative idea will incite a riot but must look to the actual circumstances surrounding the expression. Johnson's expression of dissatisfaction with the Federal Government's policies also does not fall within the class of "fighting words" likely to be seen as a direct personal insult or an invitation to exchange fisticuffs. This Court's holding does not forbid a State to prevent "imminent lawless action" and, in fact, Texas has a law specifically prohibiting breaches of the peace. Texas' interest in preserving the flag as a symbol of nationhood and national unity is related to expression in this case and, thus, falls outside the *O'Brien* test. Pp. 406-410.

(c) The latter interest does not justify Johnson's conviction. The restriction on Johnson's political expression is content based, since the Texas statute is not aimed at protecting the physical integrity of the flag in all circumstances, but is designed to protect it from intentional and knowing abuse that causes serious offense to others. It is therefore subject to "the most exacting scrutiny." *Boos v. Barry*, 485 U.S. 312. The government may not prohibit the verbal or nonverbal expression of an idea merely because society finds the idea offensive or disagreeable, even where our flag is involved. Nor may a State foster its own view of the flag by prohibiting expressive conduct relating to it, since the government may not permit designated symbols to be used to communicate a limited set of messages. Moreover, this Court will not create an exception to these principles protected by the First Amendment for the American flag alone. Pp. 410-422.

755 S. W. 2d 92, affirmed.

JUDGES: Brennan, J., delivered the opinion of the Court, in which Marshall, Blackmun, Scalia, and Kennedy, JJ., joined. Kennedy, J., filed a concurring opinion, *post*, p. 420. Rehnquist, C. J., filed a dissenting opinion, in which White and O'Connor, JJ., joined, *post*, p. 421. Stevens, J., filed a dissenting opinion, *post*, p. 436. [399]

JUSTICE BRENNAN delivered the opinion of the Court.

After publicly burning an American flag as a means of political protest, Gregory Lee Johnson was convicted of desecrating a flag in violation of Texas law. This case presents the question whether his conviction is consistent with the First Amendment. We hold that it is not.

I

While the Republican National Convention was taking place in Dallas in 1984, respondent Johnson participated in a political demonstration dubbed the "Republican War Chest Tour." As explained in literature distributed by the demonstrators and in speeches made by them, the purpose of this event was to protest the policies of the Reagan administration and of certain Dallas-based corporations. The demonstrators marched through the Dallas streets, chanting political slogans and stopping at several corporate locations to stage "die-ins" intended to dramatize the consequences of nuclear war. On several occasions they spray-painted the walls of buildings and overturned potted plants, but Johnson himself took no part in such activities. He did, however, accept an American flag handed to him by a fellow protestor who had taken it from a flagpole outside one of the targeted buildings.

The demonstration ended in front of Dallas City Hall, where Johnson unfurled the American flag, doused it with kerosene, and set it on fire. While the flag burned, the protestors chanted: "America, the red, white, and blue, we spit on you." After the demonstrators dispersed, a witness to the flag burning collected the flag's remains and buried them in his backyard. No one was physically injured or threatened with injury, though several witnesses testified that they had been seriously offended by the flag burning. [400]

Of the approximately 100 demonstrators, Johnson alone was charged with a crime. The only criminal offense with which he was charged was the desecration of a venerated object in violation of Tex. Penal Code Ann. § 42.09(a)(3) (1989). [note 1] After a trial, he was convicted, sentenced to one year in prison, and fined $2,000. The Court of Appeals for the Fifth District of Texas at Dallas affirmed Johnson's conviction, 706 S. W. 2d 120 (1986), but the Texas Court of Criminal Appeals reversed, 755 S. W. 2d 92 (1988), holding that the State could not, consistent with the First Amendment, punish Johnson for burning the flag in these circumstances.

The Court of Criminal Appeals began by recognizing that Johnson's conduct was symbolic speech protected by the First Amendment: "Given the context of an organized demonstration, speeches, slogans, and the distribution of literature, anyone who observed appellant's act would have understood the message that appellant intended to convey. The act for which appellant was convicted was clearly 'speech' contemplated by the First Amendment." *Id.,* at 95. To justify Johnson's conviction for engaging in symbolic speech, the State asserted two interests: preserving the flag as a symbol of national unity and preventing breaches of the peace. The Court of Criminal Appeals held that neither interest supported his conviction. [401]

Acknowledging that this Court had not yet decided whether the Government may criminally sanction flag desecration in order to preserve the flag's symbolic value, the Texas court nevertheless concluded that our decision in *West Virginia Board of Education v. Barnette,* 319 U.S. 624 (1943), suggested that furthering this interest by curtailing speech was impermissible. "Recognizing that the right to differ is the centerpiece of our First Amendment freedoms," the court explained, "a government cannot mandate by fiat a feeling of unity in its citizens. Therefore, that very same government cannot carve out a symbol of unity and prescribe a set of approved messages to be associated with that symbol when it cannot mandate the status or feeling the symbol purports to represent." 755 S. W. 2d, at 97. Noting that the State had not shown that the flag was in "grave and immediate danger," *Barnette, supra,* at 639, of being stripped of its symbolic value, the Texas court also decided that the flag's special status was not endangered by Johnson's conduct. 755 S. W. 2d, at 97.

As to the State's goal of preventing breaches of the peace, the court concluded that the flag-desecration statute was not drawn narrowly enough to encompass only those flag burnings that were likely to result in a serious disturbance of the peace. And in fact, the court emphasized, the flag burning in this particular case did not threaten such a reaction. "'Serious offense' occurred," the court admitted, "but there was no breach of peace nor does the record reflect that the situation was potentially explosive. One cannot equate 'serious offense' with incitement to breach the peace." *Id.*, at 96. The court also stressed that another Texas statute, Tex. Penal Code Ann. § 42.01 (1989), prohibited breaches of the peace. Citing *Boos v. Barry*, 485 U.S. 312 (1988), the court decided that § 42.01 demonstrated Texas' ability to prevent disturbances of the peace without punishing this flag desecration. 755 S. W. 2d, at 96. [402]

Because it reversed Johnson's conviction on the ground that § 42.09 was unconstitutional as applied to him, the state court did not address Johnson's argument that the statute was, on its face, unconstitutionally vague and overbroad. We granted certiorari, 488 U.S. 907 (1988), and now affirm.

II

Johnson was convicted of flag desecration for burning the flag rather than for uttering insulting words. [note 2] This fact [403] somewhat complicates our consideration of his conviction under the First Amendment. We must first determine whether Johnson's burning of the flag constituted expressive conduct, permitting him to invoke the First Amendment in challenging his conviction. See, e.g., *Spence v. Washington*, 418 U.S. 405, 409-411 (1974). If his conduct was expressive, we next decide whether the State's regulation is related to the suppression of free expression. See, e.g., *United States v. O'Brien*, 391 U.S. 367, 377 (1968); *Spence, supra*, at 414, n. 8. If the State's regulation is not related to expression, then the less stringent standard we announced in *United States v. O'Brien* for regulations of noncommunicative conduct controls. See *O'Brien, supra*, at 377. If it is, then we are outside of *O'Brien's* test, and we must ask whether this interest justifies Johnson's conviction under a more demanding standard. [note 3] See *Spence, supra*, at 411. A [404] third possibility is that the State's asserted interest is simply not implicated on these facts, and in that event the interest drops out of the picture. See 418 U.S., at 414, n. 8.

The First Amendment literally forbids the abridgment only of "speech," but we have long recognized that its protection does not end at the spoken or written word. While we have rejected "the view that an apparently limitless variety of conduct can be labeled 'speech' whenever the person engaging in the conduct intends thereby to express an idea," *United States v. O'Brien, supra*, at 376, we have acknowledged that conduct may be "sufficiently imbued with elements of communication to fall within the scope of the First and Fourteenth Amendments," *Spence, supra*, at 409.

In deciding whether particular conduct possesses sufficient communicative elements to bring the First Amendment into play, we have asked whether "[a]n intent to convey a particularized message was present, and [whether] the likelihood was great that the message would be understood by those who viewed it." 418 U.S., at 410-411. Hence, we have recognized the expressive nature of students' wearing of black armbands to protest American military involvement in Vietnam, *Tinker v. Des Moines Independent Community School Dist.*, 393 U.S. 503, 505 (1969); of a sit-in by blacks in a "whites only" area to protest segregation, *Brown v. Louisiana*, 383 U.S. 131, 141-142 (1966); of the wearing of American military uniforms in a dramatic presentation criticizing American involvement in Vietnam, *Schacht v. United States*, 398 U.S. 58 (1970); and of picketing about a wide variety of causes, see, e.g., *Food Employees v. Logan Valley Plaza, Inc.*, 391 U.S. 308, 313-314 (1968); *United States v. Grace*, 461 U.S. 171, 176 (1983).

Especially pertinent to this case are our decisions recognizing the communicative nature of conduct relating to flags. Attaching a peace sign to the flag, *Spence, supra,* at 409-410; refusing to salute the flag, *Barnette,* 319 U.S., at 632; and displaying a red flag, *Stromberg v. California,* 283 U.S. 359, 368-369 [405] (1931), we have held, all may find shelter under the First Amendment. See also *Smith v. Goguen,* 415 U.S. 566, 588 (1974) (White, J., concurring in judgment) (treating flag "contemptuously" by wearing pants with small flag sewn into their seat is expressive conduct). That we have had little difficulty identifying an expressive element in conduct relating to flags should not be surprising. The very purpose of a national flag is to serve as a symbol of our country; it is, one might say, "the one visible manifestation of two hundred years of nationhood." *Id.,* at 603 (Rehnquist, J., dissenting). Thus, we have observed:

"[T]he flag salute is a form of utterance. Symbolism is a primitive but effective way of communicating ideas. The use of an emblem or flag to symbolize some system, idea, institution, or personality, is a short cut from mind to mind. Causes and nations, political parties, lodges and ecclesiastical groups seek to knit the loyalty of their followings to a flag or banner, a color or design." *Barnette, supra,* at 632.

Pregnant with expressive content, the flag as readily signifies this Nation as does the combination of letters found in "America."

We have not automatically concluded, however, that any action taken with respect to our flag is expressive. Instead, in characterizing such action for First Amendment purposes, we have considered the context in which it occurred. In *Spence,* for example, we emphasized that Spence's taping of a peace sign to his flag was "roughly simultaneous with and concededly triggered by the Cambodian incursion and the Kent State tragedy." 418 U.S., at 410. The State of Washington had conceded, in fact, that Spence's conduct was a form of communication, and we stated that "the State's concession is inevitable on this record." *Id.,* at 409.

The State of Texas conceded for purposes of its oral argument in this case that Johnson's conduct was expressive conduct, Tr. of Oral Arg. 4, and this concession seems to us as [406] prudent as was Washington's in *Spence.* Johnson burned an American flag as part--indeed, as the culmination--of a political demonstration that coincided with the convening of the Republican Party and its renomination of Ronald Reagan for President. The expressive, overtly political nature of this conduct was both intentional and overwhelmingly apparent. At his trial, Johnson explained his reasons for burning the flag as follows: "The American Flag was burned as Ronald Reagan was being renominated as President. And a more powerful statement of symbolic speech, whether you agree with it or not, couldn't have been made at that time. It's quite a just position [juxtaposition]. We had new patriotism and no patriotism." 5 Record 656. In these circumstances, Johnson's burning of the flag was conduct "sufficiently imbued with elements of communication," *Spence,* 418 U.S., at 409, to implicate the First Amendment.

III

The government generally has a freer hand in restricting expressive conduct than it has in restricting the written or spoken word. See *O'Brien,* 391 U.S. at 376-377; *Clark v. Community for Creative Non-Violence,* 468 U.S. 288, 293 (1984); *Dallas v. Stanglin,* 490 U.S. 19, 25 (1989). It may not, however, proscribe particular conduct because it has expressive elements. "[W]hat might be termed the more generalized guarantee of freedom of expression makes the communicative nature of conduct an inadequate basis for singling out that conduct for proscription. A law directed at the communicative nature of conduct must, like a law directed at speech itself, be justified by the substantial showing of need that the First Amendment requires." *Community for Creative Non-Violence v. Watt*, 227 U. S. App. D. C. 19, 55-56, 703 F. 2d 586, 622-623 (1983) (Scalia, J., dissenting) (emphasis in original), rev'd sub nom. *Clark v. Community for Creative Non-Violence, supra*. It is, in short, not simply the verbal or nonverbal nature of the expression, but the governmental [407] interest at stake, that helps to determine whether a restriction on that expression is valid.

Thus, although we have recognized that where "'speech' and 'nonspeech' elements are combined in the same course of conduct, a sufficiently important governmental interest in regulating the nonspeech element can justify incidental limitations on First Amendment freedoms," *O'Brien, supra*, at 376, we have limited the applicability of *O'Brien's* relatively lenient standard to those cases in which "the governmental interest is unrelated to the suppression of free expression." *Id.*, at 377; see also *Spence, supra*, at 414, n. 8. In stating, moreover, that *O'Brien's* test "in the last analysis is little, if any, different from the standard applied to time, place, or manner restrictions," *Clark, supra*, at 298, we have highlighted the requirement that the governmental interest in question be unconnected to expression in order to come under *O'Brien's* less demanding rule.

In order to decide whether *O'Brien's* test applies here, therefore, we must decide whether Texas has asserted an interest in support of Johnson's conviction that is unrelated to the suppression of expression. If we find that an interest asserted by the State is simply not implicated on the facts before us, we need not ask whether *O'Brien's* test applies. See *Spence, supra*, at 414, n. 8. The State offers two separate interests to justify this conviction: preventing breaches of the peace and preserving the flag as a symbol of nationhood and national unity. We hold that the first interest is not implicated on this record and that the second is related to the suppression of expression.

A

Texas claims that its interest in preventing breaches of the peace justifies Johnson's conviction for flag desecration. [note 4] [408] However, no disturbance of the peace actually occurred or threatened to occur because of Johnson's burning of the flag. Although the State stresses the disruptive behavior of the protestors during their march toward City Hall, Brief for Petitioner 34-36, it admits that "no actual breach of the peace occurred at the time of the flagburning or in response to the flagburning." *Id.*, at 34. The State's emphasis on the protestors' disorderly actions prior to arriving at City Hall is not only somewhat surprising given that no charges were brought on the basis of this conduct, but it also fails to show that a disturbance of the peace was a likely reaction to Johnson's conduct. The only evidence offered by the State at trial to show the reaction to Johnson's actions was the testimony of several persons who had been seriously offended by the flag burning. *Id.*, at 6-7.

The State's position, therefore, amounts to a claim that an audience that takes serious offense at particular expression is necessarily likely to disturb the peace and that the expression may be prohibited on this basis. [note 5] Our precedents do not countenance such a presumption. On the contrary, they recognize that a principal "function of free speech under our system of government is to invite dispute. It may indeed best serve its high purpose when it induces a condition of unrest, creates dissatisfaction with conditions as they are, or [409] even stirs people to anger." *Terminiello v. Chicago*, 337 U.S. 1, 4 (1949). See also

Cox v. Louisiana, 379 U.S. 536, 551 (1965); *Tinker v. Des Moines Independent Community School Dist.*, 393 U.S., at 508-509; *Coates v. Cincinnati*, 402 U.S. 611, 615 (1971); *Hustler Magazine, Inc. v. Falwell*, 485 U.S. 46, 55-56 (1988). It would be odd indeed to conclude both that "if it is the speaker's opinion that gives offense, that consequence is a reason for according it constitutional protection," *FCC v. Pacifica Foundation*, 438 U.S. 726, 745 (1978) (opinion of Stevens, J.), and that the government may ban the expression of certain disagreeable ideas on the unsupported presumption that their very disagreeableness will provoke violence.

Thus, we have not permitted the government to assume that every expression of a provocative idea will incite a riot, but have instead required careful consideration of the actual circumstances surrounding such expression, asking whether the expression "is directed to inciting or producing imminent lawless action and is likely to incite or produce such action." *Brandenburg v. Ohio*, 395 U.S. 444, 447 (1969) (reviewing circumstances surrounding rally and speeches by Ku Klux Klan). To accept Texas' arguments that it need only demonstrate "the potential for a breach of the peace," Brief for Petitioner 37, and that every flag burning necessarily possesses that potential, would be to eviscerate our holding in Brandenburg. This we decline to do.

Nor does Johnson's expressive conduct fall within that small class of "fighting words" that are "likely to provoke the average person to retaliation, and thereby cause a breach of the peace." *Chaplinsky v. New Hampshire*, 315 U.S. 568, 574 (1942). No reasonable onlooker would have regarded Johnson's generalized expression of dissatisfaction with the policies of the Federal Government as a direct personal insult or an invitation to exchange fisticuffs. See *id.*, at 572-573; *Cantwell v. Connecticut*, 310 U.S. 296, 309 (1940); *FCC v. Pacifica Foundation, supra*, at 745 (opinion of Stevens, J.). [410]

We thus conclude that the State's interest in maintaining order is not implicated on these facts. The State need not worry that our holding will disable it from preserving the peace. We do not suggest that the First Amendment forbids a State to prevent "imminent lawless action." Brandenburg, *supra*, at 447. And, in fact, Texas already has a statute specifically prohibiting breaches of the peace, Tex. Penal Code Ann. § 42.01 (1989), which tends to confirm that Texas need not punish this flag desecration in order to keep the peace. See *Boos v. Barry*, 485 U.S., at 327-329.

B

The State also asserts an interest in preserving the flag as a symbol of nationhood and national unity. In *Spence*, we acknowledged that the government's interest in preserving the flag's special symbolic value "is directly related to expression in the context of activity" such as affixing a peace symbol to a flag. 418 U.S., at 414, n. 8. We are equally persuaded that this interest is related to expression in the case of Johnson's burning of the flag. The State, apparently, is concerned that such conduct will lead people to believe either that the flag does not stand for nationhood and national unity, but instead reflects other, less positive concepts, or that the concepts reflected in the flag do not in fact exist, that is, that we do not enjoy unity as a Nation. These concerns blossom only when a person's treatment of the flag communicates some message, and thus are related "to the suppression of free expression" within the meaning of *O'Brien*. We are thus outside of *O'Brien's* test altogether.

IV

It remains to consider whether the State's interest in preserving the flag as a symbol of nationhood and national unity justifies Johnson's conviction.

As in *Spence*, "[w]e are confronted with a case of prosecution for the expression of an idea through activity," and "[a]ccordingly, we must examine with particular care the interests [411] advanced by [petitioner] to support its prosecution." 418 U.S., at 411. Johnson was not, we add, prosecuted for the expression of just any idea; he was prosecuted for his expression of dissatisfaction with the policies of this country, expression situated at the core of our First Amendment values. See, e.g., *Boos v. Barry, supra*, at 318; *Frisby v. Schultz*, 487 U.S. 474, 479 (1988).

Moreover, Johnson was prosecuted because he knew that his politically charged expression would cause "serious offense." If he had burned the flag as a means of disposing of it because it was dirty or torn, he would not have been convicted of flag desecration under this Texas law: federal law designates burning as the preferred means of disposing of a flag "when it is in such condition that it is no longer a fitting emblem for display," 36 U. S. C. § 176(k), and Texas has no quarrel with this means of disposal. Brief for Petitioner 45. The Texas law is thus not aimed at protecting the physical integrity of the flag in all circumstances, but is designed instead to protect it only against impairments that would cause serious offense to others. [note 6] Texas concedes as much: "Section 42.09(b) reaches only those severe acts of physical abuse of the flag carried out in a way likely to be offensive. The statute mandates intentional or knowing abuse, that is, the kind of mistreatment that is not innocent, but rather is intentionally designed to seriously offend other individuals." *Id.*, at 44.

Whether Johnson's treatment of the flag violated Texas law thus depended on the likely communicative impact of his expressive conduct. [note 7] Our decision in *Boos v. Barry, supra*, [412] tells us that this restriction on Johnson's expression is content based. In Boos, we considered the constitutionality of a law prohibiting "the display of any sign within 500 feet of a foreign embassy if that sign tends to bring that foreign government into 'public odium' or 'public disrepute.'" *Id.*, at 315. Rejecting the argument that the law was content neutral because it was justified by "our international law obligation to shield diplomats from speech that offends their dignity," *id.*, at 320, we held that "[t]he emotive impact of speech on its audience is not a 'secondary effect'" unrelated to the content of the expression itself. *Id.*, at 321 (plurality opinion); see also *id.*, at 334 (Brennan, J., concurring in part and concurring in judgment).

According to the principles announced in Boos, Johnson's political expression was restricted because of the content of the message he conveyed. We must therefore subject the State's asserted interest in preserving the special symbolic character of the flag to "the most exacting scrutiny." *Boos v. Barry, supra*, at 321. [note 8] [413]

Texas argues that its interest in preserving the flag as a symbol of nationhood and national unity survives this close analysis. Quoting extensively from the writings of this Court chronicling the flag's historic and symbolic role in our society, the State emphasizes the "'special place'" reserved for the flag in our Nation. Brief for Petitioner 22, quoting *Smith v. Goguen*, 415 U.S., at 601 (Rehnquist, J., dissenting). The State's argument is not that it has an interest simply in maintaining the flag as a symbol of something, no matter what it symbolizes; indeed, if that were the State's position, it would be difficult to see how that interest is endangered by highly symbolic conduct such as Johnson's. Rather, the State's claim is that it has an interest in preserving the flag as a symbol of *nationhood* and *national unity*, a symbol with a determinate range of meanings. Brief for Petitioner 20-24. According to Texas, if one physically treats the flag in a way that would tend to cast doubt on either the idea that nationhood and national unity are the flag's referents or that national unity actually exists, the message conveyed thereby is a harmful one and therefore may be prohibited. [note 9] [414]

If there is a bedrock principle underlying the First Amendment, it is that the government may not prohibit the expression of an idea simply because society finds the idea itself offensive or disagreeable. See, e.g., *Hustler Magazine, Inc. v. Falwell*, 485 U.S., at 55-56; *City Council of Los Angeles v. Taxpayers for Vincent*, 466 U.S. 789, 804 (1984); *Bolger v. Youngs Drug Products Corp.*, 463 U.S. 60, 65, 72 (1983); *Carey v. Brown*, 447 U.S. 455, 462-463 (1980); *FCC v. Pacifica Foundation*, 438 U.S., at 745-746; *Young v. American Mini Theatres, Inc.*, 427 U.S. 50, 63-65, 67-68 (1976) (plurality opinion); *Buckley v. Valeo*, 424 U.S. 1, 16-17 (1976); *Grayned v. Rockford*, 408 U.S. 104, 115 (1972); *Police Dept. of Chicago v. Mosley*, 408 U.S. 92, 95 (1972); *Bachellar v. Maryland*, 397 U.S. 564, 567 (1970); *O'Brien*, 391 U.S., at 382; *Brown v. Louisiana*, 383 U.S., at 142-143; *Stromberg v. California*, 283 U.S., at 368-369.

We have not recognized an exception to this principle even where our flag has been involved. In *Street v. New York*, 394 U.S. 576 (1969), we held that a State may not criminally punish a person for uttering words critical of the flag. Rejecting the argument that the conviction could be sustained on the ground that Street had "failed to show the respect for our national symbol which may properly be demanded of every citizen," we concluded that "the constitutionally guaranteed 'freedom to be intellectually . . . diverse or even contrary,' and the 'right to differ as to things that touch the heart of the existing order,' encompass the freedom to express publicly one's opinions about our flag, including those opinions which are defiant or contemptuous." *Id.*, at 593, quoting *Barnette*, 319 U.S., at 642. Nor may the government, we have held, compel conduct that would evince respect for the flag. "To sustain the compulsory flag salute we are required to say that a Bill of Rights which guards the individual's right to speak his own mind, left it open to public authorities to compel him to utter what is not in his mind." *Id.*, at 634. [415]

In holding in *Barnette* that the Constitution did not leave this course open to the government, Justice Jackson described one of our society's defining principles in words deserving of their frequent repetition: "If there is any fixed star in our constitutional constellation, it is that no official, high or petty, can prescribe what shall be orthodox in politics, nationalism, religion, or other matters of opinion or force citizens to confess by word or act their faith therein." *Id.*, at 642. In *Spence*, we held that the same interest asserted by Texas here was insufficient to support a criminal conviction under a flag-misuse statute for the taping of a peace sign to an American flag. "Given the protected character of [Spence's] expression and in light of the fact that no interest the State may have in preserving the physical integrity of a privately owned flag was significantly impaired on these facts," we held, "the conviction must be invalidated." 418 U.S., at 415. See also *Goguen*, *supra*, at 588 (White, J., concurring in judgment) (to convict person who had sewn a flag onto the seat of his pants for "contemptuous" treatment of the flag would be "[t]o convict not to protect the physical integrity or to protect against acts interfering with the proper use of the flag, but to punish for communicating ideas unacceptable to the controlling majority in the legislature").

In short, nothing in our precedents suggests that a State may foster its own view of the flag by prohibiting expressive conduct relating to it. [note 10] To bring its argument outside our [416] precedents, Texas attempts to convince us that even if its interest in preserving the flag's symbolic role does not allow it to prohibit words or some expressive conduct critical of the flag, it does permit it to forbid the outright destruction of the flag. The State's argument cannot depend here on the distinction between written or spoken words and nonverbal conduct. That distinction, we have shown, is of no moment where the nonverbal conduct is expressive, as it is here, and where the regulation of that conduct is related to expression, as it is here. See *supra*, at 402-403. In addition, both *Barnette* and *Spence* involved expressive conduct, not only verbal communication, and both found that conduct protected.

Texas' focus on the precise nature of Johnson's expression, moreover, misses the point of our prior decisions: their enduring lesson, that the government may not prohibit expression simply because it disagrees with its message, is not dependent on the particular mode in which one chooses to express an idea. [note 11] If we were to hold that a State may forbid flag burning wherever it is likely to endanger the flag's symbolic role, but allow it wherever burning a flag promotes that role--as where, for example, a person ceremoniously burns a dirty flag--we would be saying that when it comes to impairing the flag's physical integrity, the flag itself may be used as [417] a symbol--as a substitute for the written or spoken word or a "short cut from mind to mind"--only in one direction. We would be permitting a State to "prescribe what shall be orthodox" by saying that one may burn the flag to convey one's attitude toward it and its referents only if one does not endanger the flag's representation of nationhood and national unity.

We never before have held that the Government may ensure that a symbol be used to express only one view of that symbol or its referents. Indeed, in *Schacht v. United States*, we invalidated a federal statute permitting an actor portraying a member of one of our Armed Forces to "'wear the uniform of that armed force if the portrayal does not tend to discredit that armed force.'" 398 U.S., at 60, quoting 10 U. S. C. § 772(f). This proviso, we held, "which leaves Americans free to praise the war in Vietnam but can send persons like Schacht to prison for opposing it, cannot survive in a country which has the First Amendment." *Id.*, at 63.

We perceive no basis on which to hold that the principle underlying our decision in *Schacht* does not apply to this case. To conclude that the government may permit designated symbols to be used to communicate only a limited set of messages would be to enter territory having no discernible or defensible boundaries. Could the government, on this theory, prohibit the burning of state flags? Of copies of the Presidential seal? Of the Constitution? In evaluating these choices under the First Amendment, how would we decide which symbols were sufficiently special to warrant this unique status? To do so, we would be forced to consult our own political preferences, and impose them on the citizenry, in the very way that the First Amendment forbids us to do. See *Carey v. Brown*, 447 U.S., at 466-467.

There is, moreover, no indication--either in the text of the Constitution or in our cases interpreting it--that a separate juridical category exists for the American flag alone. Indeed, we would not be surprised to learn that the persons [418] who framed our Constitution and wrote the Amendment that we now construe were not known for their reverence for the Union Jack. The First Amendment does not guarantee that other concepts virtually sacred to our Nation as a whole--such as the principle that discrimination on the basis of race is odious and destructive--will go unquestioned in the market-place of ideas. See *Brandenburg v. Ohio*, 395 U.S. 444 (1969). We decline, therefore, to create for the flag an exception to the joust of principles protected by the First Amendment.

It is not the State's ends, but its means, to which we object. It cannot be gainsaid that there is a special place reserved for the flag in this Nation, and thus we do not doubt that the government has a legitimate interest in making efforts to "preserv[e] the national flag as an unalloyed symbol of our country." *Spence*, 418 U.S., at 412. We reject the suggestion, urged at oral argument by counsel for Johnson, that the government lacks "any state interest whatsoever" in regulating the manner in which the flag may be displayed. Tr. of Oral Arg. 38. Congress has, for example, enacted precatory regulations describing the proper treatment of the flag, see 36 U. S. C. §§ 173-177, and we cast no doubt on the legitimacy of its interest in making such recommendations. To say that the government has an interest in encouraging proper treatment of the flag, however, is not to say that it may criminally punish a person for burning a flag as a means of political protest. "National unity as an end which officials may foster by persuasion and example is not in question. The problem is whether under our Constitution compulsion as here employed is a permissible means for its achievement." *Barnette*, 319 U.S., at 640.

We are fortified in today's conclusion by our conviction that forbidding criminal punishment for conduct such as Johnson's will not endanger the special role played by our flag or the feelings it inspires. To paraphrase Justice Holmes, we submit that nobody can suppose that this one gesture of an unknown [419] man will change our Nation's attitude towards its flag. See *Abrams v. United States*, 250 U.S. 616, 628 (1919) (Holmes, J., dissenting). Indeed, Texas' argument that the burning of an American flag "'is an act having a high likelihood to cause a breach of the peace,'" Brief for Petitioner 31, quoting *Sutherland v. DeWulf*, 323 F. Supp. 740, 745 (SD Ill. 1971) (citation omitted), and its statute's implicit assumption that physical mistreatment of the flag will lead to "serious offense," tend to confirm that the flag's special role is not in danger; if it were, no one would riot or take offense because a flag had been burned.

We are tempted to say, in fact, that the flag's deservedly cherished place in our community will be strengthened, not weakened, by our holding today. Our decision is a reaffirmation of the principles of freedom and inclusiveness that the flag best reflects, and of the conviction that our toleration of criticism such as Johnson's is a sign and source of our strength. Indeed, one of the proudest images of our flag, the one immortalized in our own national anthem, is of the bombardment it survived at Fort McHenry. It is the Nation's resilience, not its rigidity, that Texas sees reflected in the flag--and it is that resilience that we reassert today.

The way to preserve the flag's special role is not to punish those who feel differently about these matters. It is to persuade them that they are wrong. "To courageous, self-reliant men, with confidence in the power of free and fearless reasoning applied through the processes of popular government, no danger flowing from speech can be deemed clear and present, unless the incidence of the evil apprehended is so imminent that it may befall before there is opportunity for full discussion. If there be time to expose through discussion the falsehood and fallacies, to avert the evil by the processes of education, the remedy to be applied is more speech, not enforced silence." *Whitney v. California*, 274 U.S. 357, 377 (1927) (Brandeis, J., concurring). And, precisely because it is our flag that is involved, one's response to the flag [420] burner may exploit the uniquely persuasive power of the flag itself. We can imagine no more appropriate response to burning a flag than waving one's own, no better way to counter a flag burner's message than by saluting the flag that burns, no surer means of preserving the dignity even of the flag that burned than by--as one witness here did--according its remains a respectful burial. We do not consecrate the flag by punishing its desecration, for in doing so we dilute the freedom that this cherished emblem represents.

V

Johnson was convicted for engaging in expressive conduct. The State's interest in preventing breaches of the peace does not support his conviction because Johnson's conduct did not threaten to disturb the peace. Nor does the State's interest in preserving the flag as a symbol of nationhood and national unity justify his criminal conviction for engaging in political expression. The judgment of the Texas Court of Criminal Appeals is therefore

Affirmed.

26 CITY OF ERIE V. PAP'S A. M.
SUPREME COURT OF THE UNITED STATES
529 U.S. 277
Argued November 10, 1999
Decided March 29, 2000

Syllabus

Erie, Pennsylvania, enacted an ordinance making it a summary offense to knowingly or intentionally appear in public in a "state of nudity." Respondent Pap's A. M. (hereinafter Pap's), a Pennsylvania corporation, operated "Kandyland," an Erie establishment featuring totally nude erotic dancing by women. To comply with the ordinance, these dancers had to wear, at a minimum, "pasties" and a "G-string." Pap's filed suit against Erie and city officials, seeking declaratory relief and a permanent injunction against the ordinance's enforcement. The Court of Common Pleas struck down the ordinance as unconstitutional, but the Commonwealth Court reversed. The Pennsylvania Supreme Court in turn reversed, finding that the ordinance's public nudity sections violated Pap's right to freedom of expression as protected by the First and Fourteenth Amendments. The Pennsylvania court held that nude dancing is expressive conduct entitled to some quantum of protection under the First Amendment, a view that the court noted was endorsed by eight Members of this Court in *Barnes* v. *Glen Theatre, Inc.,* 501 U. S. 560 . The Pennsylvania court explained that, although one stated purpose of the ordinance was to combat negative secondary effects, there was also an unmentioned purpose to "impact negatively on the erotic message of the dance." Accordingly, the Pennsylvania court concluded that the ordinance was related to the suppression of expression. Because the ordinance was not content neutral, it was subject to strict scrutiny. The court held that the ordinance failed the narrow tailoring requirement of strict scrutiny. After this Court granted certiorari, Pap's filed a motion to dismiss the case as moot, noting that Kandyland no longer operated as a nude dancing club, and that Pap's did not operate such a club at any other location. This Court denied the motion.

Held: The judgment is reversed, and the case is remanded.

553 Pa. 348, 719 A. 2d 273, reversed and remanded.

Justice O'Connor, delivered the opinion of the Court with respect to Parts I and II, concluding that the case is not moot. A case is moot when the issues presented are no longer "live" or the parties lack a legally cognizable interest in the outcome. *County of Los Angeles* v. *Davis* , 440 U. S. 625, 631 . Simply closing Kandyland is not sufficient to moot the case because Pap's is still incorporated under Pennsylvania law, and could again decide to operate a nude dancing establishment in Erie. Moreover, Pap's failed, despite its obligation to the Court, to mention the potential mootness issue in its brief in opposition, which was filed after Kandyland was closed and the property sold. See *Board of License Comm'rs of Tiverton* v. *Pastore*, 469 U. S. 238 , 240 . In any event, this is not a run of the mill voluntary cessation case. Here it is the plaintiff who, having prevailed below, seeks to have the case declared moot. And it is the defendant city that seeks to invoke the federal judicial power to obtain this Court's review of the decision. Cf. *ASARCO Inc.* v. *Kadish* , 490 U. S. 605 , 617-618. The city has an ongoing injury because it is barred from enforcing the ordinance's public nudity provisions. If the ordinance is found constitutional, then Erie can enforce it, and the availability of such relief is sufficient to prevent the case from being moot. See *Church of Scientology of Cal.* v. *United States* , 506 U. S. 9, 13 . And Pap's still has a concrete stake in the case's outcome because, to the extent it has an interest in resuming operations, it has an interest in preserving the judgment below. This Court's interest in preventing litigants from attempting to manipulate its jurisdiction to insulate a favorable decision from review further counsels against a finding of mootness. See, *e.g.*, *United States* v. *W. T. Grant Co.* , 345 U. S. 629, 632 . Pp. 5-7.

Justice O'Connor, joined by *The Chief Justice, Justice Kennedy*, and *Justice Breyer*, concluded in Parts III and IV that:

1. Government restrictions on public nudity such as Erie's ordinance should be evaluated under the framework set forth in *United States* v. *O'Brien*, 391 U. S. 367 , for content-neutral restrictions on symbolic speech. Although being "in a state of nudity" is not an inherently expressive condition, nude dancing of the type at issue here is expressive conduct that falls within the outer ambit of the First Amendment's protection. See, *e.g.*, *Barnes, supra*, at 565-566 (plurality opinion). What level of scrutiny applies is determined by whether the ordinance is related to the suppression of expression. *E.g.*, *Texas* v. *Johnson*, 491 U. S. 397, 403 . If the governmental purpose in enacting the ordinance is unrelated to such suppression, the ordinance need only satisfy the "less stringent," intermediate *O'Brien* standard. *E.g.*, *Johnson, supra*, at 403 . If the governmental interest is related to the expression's content, however, the ordinance falls outside *O'Brien* and must be justified under the more demanding, strict scrutiny standard. *Johnson, supra*, at 403. An almost identical public nudity ban was held not to violate the First Amendment in *Barnes* , although no five Members of the Court agreed on a single rationale for that conclusion. The ordinance here, like the statute in *Barnes* , is on its face a general prohibition on public nudity. By its terms, it regulates conduct alone. It does not target nudity that contains an erotic message; rather, it bans all public nudity, regardless of whether that nudity is accompanied by expressive activity. Although Pap's contends that the ordinance is related to the suppression of expression because its preamble suggests that its actual purpose is to prohibit erotic dancing of the type performed at Kandyland, that is not how the Pennsylvania Supreme Court interpreted that language. Rather, the Pennsylvania Supreme Court construed the preamble to mean that one purpose of the ordinance was to combat negative secondary effects. That is, the ordinance is aimed at combating crime and other negative secondary effects caused by the presence of adult entertainment establishments like Kandyland and not at suppressing the erotic message conveyed by this type of nude dancing. See 391 U. S., at 382 ; see also *Boos* v. *Barry*, 485 U. S. 312, 321 . The Pennsylvania Supreme Court's ultimate conclusion that the ordinance was nevertheless content based relied on Justice White's position in dissent in *Barnes* that a ban of this type *necessarily* has the purpose of suppressing the erotic message of the dance. That view was rejected by a majority of the Court in *Barnes* , and is here rejected again. Pap's argument that the ordinance is "aimed" at suppressing expression through a ban on nude dancing is really an argument that Erie also had an illicit motive in enacting the ordinance. However, this Court will not strike down an otherwise constitutional statute on the basis of an alleged illicit motive. *O'Brien* , *supra,* 391 U. S., at 382 -383. Even if Erie's public nudity ban has some minimal effect on the erotic message by muting that portion of the expression that occurs when the last stitch is dropped, the dancers at Kandyland and other such establishments are free to perform wearing pasties and G-strings. Any effect on the overall expression is therefore *de minimis* . If States are to be able to regulate secondary effects, then such *de minimis* intrusions on expression cannot be sufficient to render the ordinance content based. See, *e.g., Clark* v. *Community for Creative Non-Violence,* 468 U. S. 288, 299 . Thus, Erie's ordinance is valid if it satisfies the *O'Brien* test. Pp. 7-15.

2. Erie's ordinance satisfies *O'Brien* 's four-factor test. First, the ordinance is within Erie's constitutional power to enact because the city's efforts to protect public health and safety are clearly within its police powers. Second, the ordinance furthers the important government interests of regulating conduct through a public nudity ban and of combating the harmful secondary effects associated with nude dancing. In terms of demonstrating that such secondary effects pose a threat, the city need not conduct new studies or produce evidence independent of that already generated by other cities, so long as the evidence relied on is reasonably believed to be relevant to the problem addressed. *Renton* v. *Playtime Theatres, Inc.,* 475 U. S. 41 , 51-52. Erie could reasonably rely on the evidentiary foundation set forth in *Renton* and *Young* v. *American Mini Theatres, Inc.,* 427 U. S. 50 , to the effect that secondary effects are caused by the presence of even one adult entertainment establishment in a given neighborhood. See *Renton, supra* , at 51-52. In fact, Erie expressly relied on *Barnes* and its discussion of secondary effects, including its reference to *Renton* and *American Mini Theatres* . The evidentiary standard described in *Renton* controls here, and Erie meets that standard. In any event, the ordinance's preamble also relies on the city council's express findings that "certain lewd, immoral activities carried on in public places for profit are highly detrimental to the public health, safety and welfare ... ." The council members, familiar with commercial downtown Erie, are the individuals who would likely have had first-hand knowledge of what took place at and around nude dancing establishments there, and can make particularized, expert judgments about the resulting harmful secondary effects. Cf., *e.g.,* FCC v. *National Citizens Comm. for Broadcasting,* 436 U. S. 775 . The fact that this sort of leeway is appropriate in this case, which involves a content-neutral restriction that regulates conduct, says nothing whatsoever about its appropriateness in a case involving actual regulation of First Amendment expression. Also, although requiring dancers to wear pasties and G-strings may not greatly reduce these secondary effects, *O'Brien* requires only that the regulation further the interest in combating such effects. The ordinance also satisfies *O'Brien* 's third factor, that the government interest is unrelated to the suppression of free expression, as discussed *supra.* The fourth *O'Brien* factor--that the restriction is no greater than is essential to the furtherance of the government interest--is satisfied as well. The ordinance regulates conduct, and any incidental impact on the expressive element of nude dancing is *de minimis* . The pasties and G-string requirement is a minimal restriction in furtherance of the asserted government interests, and the restriction leaves ample capacity to convey the dancer's erotic message. See, *e.g., Barnes, supra,* at 572. Pp. 15-21.

Justice Scalia, joined by *Justice Thomas*, agreed that the Pennsylvania Supreme Court's decision must be reversed, but disagreed with the mode of analysis that should be applied. Erie self-consciously modeled its ordinance on the public nudity statute upheld in *Barnes* v. *Glen Theatre, Inc.*, 501 U. S. 560 , calculating (one would have supposed reasonably) that the Pennsylvania courts would consider themselves bound by this Court's judgment on a question of federal constitutional law. That statute was constitutional not because it survived some lower level of First Amendment scrutiny, but because, as a general law regulating conduct and not specifically directed at expression, it was not subject to First Amendment scrutiny at all. *Id.*, at 572 (*Scalia, J.* , concurring in judgment). Erie's ordinance, too, by its terms prohibits not merely nude dancing, but the act--irrespective of whether it is engaged in for expressive purposes--of going nude in public. The facts that the preamble explains the ordinance's purpose, in part, as limiting a recent increase in nude live entertainment, that city councilmembers in supporting the ordinance commented to that effect, and that the ordinance includes in the definition of nudity the exposure of devices simulating that condition, neither make the law any less general in its reach nor demonstrate that what the municipal authorities *really* find objectionable is expression rather than public nakedness. That the city made no effort to enforce the ordinance against a production of Equus involving nudity that was being staged in Erie at the time the ordinance became effective does not render the ordinance discriminatory on its face. The assertion of the city's counsel in the trial court that the ordinance would not cover theatrical productions to the extent their expressive activity rose to a higher level of protected expression simply meant that the ordinance would not be enforceable against such productions if the Constitution forbade it. That limitation does not cause the ordinance to be not generally applicable, in the relevant sense of being *targeted* against expressive conduct. Moreover, even if it could be concluded that Erie specifically singled out the activity of nude dancing, the ordinance still would not violate the First Amendment unless it could be proved (as on this record it could not) that it was the communicative character of nude dancing that prompted the ban. See *id.*, at 577. There is no need to identify "secondary effects" associated with nude dancing that Erie could properly seek to eliminate. The traditional power of government to foster good morals, and the acceptability of the traditional judgment that nude public dancing *itself* is immoral, have not been repealed by the First Amendment. Pp. 6-10.

O'Connor, J., announced the judgment of the Court and delivered the opinion of the Court with respect to Parts I and II, in which *Rehnquist, C. J.*, and *Kennedy, Souter*, and *Breyer*, JJ., joined, and an opinion with respect to Parts III and IV, in which *Rehnquist, C. J.*, and *Kennedy*, and *Breyer*, JJ., joined. *Scalia, J.*, filed an opinion concurring in the judgment, in which *Thomas, J.*, joined. *Souter, J.*, filed an opinion concurring in part and dissenting in part. *Stevens, J.*, filed a dissenting opinion, in which *Ginsburg, J.*, joined.

Justice O'Connor announced the judgment of the Court and delivered the opinion of the Court with respect to Parts I and II, and an opinion with respect to Parts III and IV, in which *The Chief Justice, Justice Kennedy*, and *Justice Breyer* join.

The city of Erie, Pennsylvania, enacted an ordinance banning public nudity. Respondent Pap's A. M. (hereinafter Pap's), which operated a nude dancing establishment in Erie, challenged the constitutionality of the ordinance and sought a permanent injunction against its enforcement. The Pennsylvania Supreme Court, although noting that this Court in *Barnes* v. *Glen Theatre, Inc.*, 501 U. S. 560 (1991), had upheld an Indiana ordinance that was "strikingly similar" to Erie's, found that the public nudity sections of the ordinance violated respondent's right to freedom of expression under the United States Constitution. 553 Pa. 348, 356, 719 A. 2d 273, 277 (1998). This case raises the question whether the Pennsylvania Supreme Court properly evaluated the ordinance's constitutionality under the First Amendment. We hold that Erie's ordinance is a content-neutral regulation that satisfies the four-part test of *United States* v. *O'Brien*, 391 U. S. 367 (1968). Accordingly, we reverse the decision of the Pennsylvania Supreme Court and remand for the consideration of any remaining issues.

I

On September 28, 1994, the city council for the city of Erie, Pennsylvania, enacted Ordinance 75-1994, a public indecency ordinance that makes it a summary offense to knowingly or intentionally appear in public in a "state of nudity."* [1] Respondent Pap's, a Pennsylvania corporation, operated an establishment in Erie known as "Kandyland" that featured totally nude erotic dancing performed by women. To comply with the ordinance, these dancers must wear, at a minimum, "pasties" and a "G-string." On October 14, 1994, two days after the ordinance went into effect, Pap's filed a complaint against the city of Erie, the mayor of the city, and members of the city council, seeking declaratory relief and a permanent injunction against the enforcement of the ordinance.

The Court of Common Pleas of Erie County granted the permanent injunction and struck down the ordinance as unconstitutional. Civ. No. 60059-1994 (Jan. 18, 1995), Pet. for Cert. 40a. On cross appeals, the Commonwealth Court reversed the trial court's order. 674 A. 2d 338 (1996).

The Pennsylvania Supreme Court granted review and reversed, concluding that the public nudity provisions of the ordinance violated respondent's rights to freedom of expression as protected by the First and Fourteenth Amendments. 553 Pa. 348, 719 A. 2d 273 (1998). The Pennsylvania court first inquired whether nude dancing constitutes expressive conduct that is within the protection of the First Amendment. The court noted that the act of being nude, in and of itself, is not entitled to First Amendment protection because it conveys no message. *Id.*, at 354 , 719 A. 2d, at 276. Nude dancing, however, is expressive conduct that is entitled to some quantum of protection under the First Amendment, a view that the Pennsylvania Supreme Court noted was endorsed by eight Members of this Court in *Barnes* . 553 Pa., at 354, 719 A. 2d, at 276.

The Pennsylvania court next inquired whether the government interest in enacting the ordinance was content neutral, explaining that regulations that are unrelated to the suppression of expression are not subject to strict scrutiny but to the less stringent standard of *United States* v. *O'Brien, supra*, at 377. To answer the question whether the ordinance is content based, the court turned to our decision in *Barnes* . 553 Pa., at 355-356, 719 A. 2d, at 277. Although the Pennsylvania court noted that the Indiana statute at issue in *Barnes* "is strikingly similar to the Ordinance we are examining," it concluded that "[u]nfortunately for our purposes, the *Barnes* Court splintered and produced four separate, non-harmonious opinions." 553 Pa., at 356, 719 A. 2d, at 277. After canvassing these separate opinions, the Pennsylvania court concluded that, although it is permissible to find precedential effect in a fragmented decision, to do so a majority of the Court must have been in agreement on the concept that is deemed to be the holding. See *Marks* v. *United States*, 430 U. S. 188 (1977). The Pennsylvania court noted that "aside from the agreement by a majority of the *Barnes* Court that nude dancing is entitled to some First Amendment protection, we can find no point on which a majority of the *Barnes* Court agreed." 553 Pa., at 358, 719 A. 2d, at 278. Accordingly, the court concluded that "no clear precedent arises out of *Barnes* on the issue of whether the [Erie] ordinance ... passes muster under the First Amendment." *Ibid*.

Having determined that there was no United States Supreme Court precedent on point, the Pennsylvania court conducted an independent examination of the ordinance to ascertain whether it was related to the suppression of expression. The court concluded that although one of the purposes of the ordinance was to combat negative secondary effects, "[i]nextricably bound up with this stated purpose is an unmentioned purpose ... to impact negatively on the erotic message of the dance." *Id.*, at 359, 719 A. 2d, at 279. As such, the court determined the ordinance was content based and subject to strict scrutiny. The ordinance failed the narrow tailoring requirement of strict scrutiny because the court found that imposing criminal and civil sanctions on those who commit sex crimes would be a far narrower means of combating secondary effects than the requirement that dancers wear pasties and G-strings. *Id.*, at 361-362, 719 A. 2d, at 280.

Concluding that the ordinance unconstitutionally burdened respondent's expressive conduct, the Pennsylvania court then determined that, under Pennsylvania law, the public nudity provisions of the ordinance could be severed rather than striking the ordinance in its entirety. Accordingly, the court severed §§1(c) and 2 from the ordinance and reversed the order of the Commonwealth Court. *Id.*, at 363-364, 719 A. 2d, at 281. Because the court determined that the public nudity provisions of the ordinance violated Pap's right to freedom of expression under the United States Constitution, it did not address the constitutionality of the ordinance under the Pennsylvania Constitution or the claim that the ordinance is unconstitutionally overbroad. *Ibid.*

In a separate concurrence, two justices of the Pennsylvania court noted that, because this Court upheld a virtually identical statute in *Barnes*, the ordinance should have been upheld under the United States Constitution. 553 Pa., at 364, 719 A. 2d, at 281. They reached the same result as the majority, however, because they would have held that the public nudity sections of the ordinance violate the Pennsylvania Constitution. *Id.*, at 370, 719 A. 2d, at 284.

The city of Erie petitioned for a writ of certiorari, which we granted. 526 U. S. 1111 (1999). Shortly thereafter, Pap's filed a motion to dismiss the case as moot, noting that Kandyland was no longer operating as a nude dancing club, and Pap's was not operating a nude dancing club at any other location. Respondent's Motion to Dismiss as Moot 1. We denied the motion. 527 U. S. 1034 (1999).

II

As a preliminary matter, we must address the justiciability question. " `[A] case is moot when the issues presented are no longer `live' or the parties lack a legally cognizable interest in the outcome.' " *County of Los Angeles* v. *Davis* , 440 U. S. 625, 631 (1979) (quoting *Powell* v. *McCormack* , 395 U. S. 486, 496 (1969)). The underlying concern is that, when the challenged conduct ceases such that " `there is no reasonable expectation that the wrong will be repeated,' " *United States* v. *W. T. Grant Co.* , 345 U. S. 629, 633 (1953), then it becomes impossible for the court to grant " `any effectual relief whatever' to [the] prevailing party," *Church of Scientology of Cal.* v. *United States* , 506 U. S. 9, 12 (1992) (quoting *Mills* v. *Green* , 159 U. S. 651, 653 (1895)). In that case, any opinion as to the legality of the challenged action would be advisory.

Here, Pap's submitted an affidavit stating that it had "ceased to operate a nude dancing establishment in Erie." Status Report Re Potential Issue of Mootness 1 (Sept. 8, 1999). Pap's asserts that the case is therefore moot because "[t]he outcome of this case will have no effect upon Respondent." Respondent's Motion to Dismiss as Moot 1. Simply closing Kandyland is not sufficient to render this case moot, however. Pap's is still incorporated under Pennsylvania law, and it could again decide to operate a nude dancing establishment in Erie. See Petitioner's Brief in Opposition to Motion to Dismiss 3. J *ustice S calia* differs with our assessment as to the likelihood that Pap's may resume its nude dancing operation. Several Members of this Court can attest, however, that the "advanced age" of Pap's owner (72) does not make it "absolutely clear" that a life of quiet retirement is his only reasonable expectation. Cf. *Friends of Earth, Inc.* v. *Laidlaw Environmental Services (TOC), Inc.* , 528 U. S. ___ (2000). Moreover, our appraisal of Pap's affidavit is influenced by Pap's failure, despite its obligation to the Court, to mention a word about the potential mootness issue in its brief in opposition to the petition for writ of certiorari, which was filed in April 1999, even though, as *Justice Scalia* points out, Kandyland was closed and that property sold in 1998. See *Board of License Comm'rs of Tiverton* v. *Pastore*, 469 U. S. 238, 240 (1985) *(per curiam)* . Pap's only raised the issue after this Court granted certiorari.

In any event, this is not a run of the mill voluntary cessation case. Here it is the plaintiff who, having prevailed below, now seeks to have the case declared moot. And it is the city of Erie that seeks to invoke the federal judicial power to obtain this Court's review of the Pennsylvania Supreme Court decision. Cf. *ASARCO Inc.* v. *Kadish* , 490 U. S. 605, 617-618 (1989). The city has an ongoing injury because it is barred from enforcing the public nudity provisions of its ordinance. If the challenged ordinance is found constitutional, then Erie can enforce it, and the availability of such relief is sufficient to prevent the case from being moot. See *Church of Scientology of Cal.* v. *United States* , *supra* , at 13. And Pap's still has a concrete stake in the outcome of this case because, to the extent Pap's has an interest in resuming operations, it has an interest in preserving the judgment of the Pennsylvania Supreme Court. Our interest in preventing litigants from attempting to manipulate the Court's jurisdiction to insulate a favorable decision from review further counsels against a finding of mootness here. See *United States* v. *W. T. Grant Co.* , *supra* , at 632; cf. *Arizonans for Official English* v. *Arizona*, 520 U. S. 43, 74 (1997). Although the issue is close, we conclude that the case is not moot, and we turn to the merits.

III

Being "in a state of nudity" is not an inherently expressive condition. As we explained in *Barnes* , however, nude dancing of the type at issue here is expressive conduct, although we think that it falls only within the outer ambit of the First Amendment's protection. See *Barnes* v. *Glen Theatre, Inc.*, 501 U. S., at 565 -566 (plurality opinion); *Schad* v. *Mount Ephraim*, 452 U. S. 61, 66 (1981).

To determine what level of scrutiny applies to the ordinance at issue here, we must decide "whether the State's regulation is related to the suppression of expression." *Texas* v. *Johnson*, 491 U. S. 397, 403 (1989); see also *United States* v. *O'Brien*, 391 U. S., at 377 . If the governmental purpose in enacting the regulation is unrelated to the suppression of expression, then the regulation need only satisfy the "less stringent" standard from *O'Brien* for evaluating restrictions on symbolic speech. *Texas* v. *Johnson* , *supra* , at 403; *United States* v. *O'Brien, supra* , at 377. If the government interest is related to the content of the expression, however, then the regulation falls outside the scope of the *O'Brien* test and must be justified under a more demanding standard. *Texas* v. *Johnson*, *supra*, at 403.

In *Barnes*, we analyzed an almost identical statute, holding that Indiana's public nudity ban did not violate the First Amendment, although no five Members of the Court agreed on a single rationale for that conclusion. We now clarify that government restrictions on public nudity such as the ordinance at issue here should be evaluated under the framework set forth in *O'Brien* for content-neutral restrictions on symbolic speech.

The city of Erie argues that the ordinance is a content-neutral restriction that is reviewable under *O'Brien* because the ordinance bans conduct, not speech; specifically, public nudity. Respondent counters that the ordinance targets nude dancing and, as such, is aimed specifically at suppressing expression, making the ordinance a content-based restriction that must be subjected to strict scrutiny.

The ordinance here, like the statute in *Barnes*, is on its face a general prohibition on public nudity. 553 Pa., at 354, 719 A. 2d, at 277. By its terms, the ordinance regulates conduct alone. It does not target nudity that contains an erotic message; rather, it bans all public nudity, regardless of whether that nudity is accompanied by expressive activity. And like the statute in *Barnes*, the Erie ordinance replaces and updates provisions of an "Indecency and Immorality" ordinance that has been on the books since 1866, predating the prevalence of nude dancing establishments such as Kandyland. Pet. for Cert. 7a; see *Barnes* v. *Glen Theatre, Inc.*, *supra*, at 568.

Respondent and *Justice Stevens* contend nonetheless that the ordinance is related to the suppression of expression because language in the ordinance's preamble suggests that its actual purpose is to prohibit erotic dancing of the type performed at Kandyland. *Post*, at 1 (dissenting opinion). That is not how the Pennsylvania Supreme Court interpreted that language, however. In the preamble to the ordinance, the city council stated that it was adopting the regulation " 'for the purpose of limiting a recent increase in nude live entertainment within the City, which activity adversely impacts and threatens to impact on the public health, safety and welfare by providing an atmosphere conducive to violence, sexual harassment, public intoxication, prostitution, the spread of sexually transmitted diseases and other deleterious effects.' " 553 Pa., at 359, 719 A. 2d, at 279.

The Pennsylvania Supreme Court construed this language to mean that one purpose of the ordinance was "to combat negative secondary effects." *Ibid.*

As *Justice Souter* noted in *Barnes*, "on its face, the governmental interest in combating prostitution and other criminal activity is not at all inherently related to expression." 501 U. S., at 585 (opinion concurring in judgment). In that sense, this case is similar to *O'Brien*. *O'Brien* burned his draft registration card as a public statement of his antiwar views, and he was convicted under a statute making it a crime to knowingly mutilate or destroy such a card. This Court rejected his claim that the statute violated his First Amendment rights, reasoning that the law punished him for the "noncommunicative impact of his conduct, and for nothing else." 391 U. S., at 382. In other words, the Government regulation prohibiting the destruction of draft cards was aimed at maintaining the integrity of the Selective Service System and not at suppressing the message of draft resistance that O'Brien sought to convey by burning his draft card. So too here, the ordinance prohibiting public nudity is aimed at combating crime and other negative secondary effects caused by the presence of adult entertainment establishments like Kandyland and not at suppressing the erotic message conveyed by this type of nude dancing. Put another way, the ordinance does not attempt to regulate the primary effects of the expression, *i.e.*, the effect on the audience of watching nude erotic dancing, but rather the secondary effects, such as the impacts on public health, safety, and welfare, which we have previously recognized are "caused by the presence of even one such" establishment. *Renton* v. *Playtime Theatres, Inc.*, 475 U. S. 41, 47-48, 50 (1986); see also *Boos* v. *Barry*, 485 U. S. 312, 321 (1988).

Although the Pennsylvania Supreme Court acknowledged that one goal of the ordinance was to combat the negative secondary effects associated with nude dancing establishments, the court concluded that the ordinance was nevertheless content based, relying on Justice White's position in dissent in *Barnes* for the proposition that a ban of this type *necessarily* has the purpose of suppressing the erotic message of the dance. Because the Pennsylvania court agreed with Justice White's approach, it concluded that the ordinance must have another, "unmentioned" purpose related to the suppression of expression. 553 Pa., at 359, 719 A. 2d, at 279. That is, the Pennsylvania court adopted the dissent's view in *Barnes* that " `[s]ince the State permits the dancers to perform if they wear pasties and G-strings but forbids nude dancing, it is precisely because of the distinctive, expressive content of the nude dancing performances at issue in this case that the State seeks to apply the statutory prohibition." 553 Pa., at 359, 719 A. 2d, at 279 (quoting *Barnes*, *supra*, at 592 (White, J., dissenting)). A majority of the Court rejected that view in *Barnes*, and we do so again here.

Respondent's argument that the ordinance is "aimed" at suppressing expression through a ban on nude dancing--an argument that respondent supports by pointing to statements by the city attorney that the public nudity ban was not intended to apply to "legitimate" theater productions--is really an argument that the city council also had an illicit motive in enacting the ordinance. As we have said before, however, this Court will not strike down an otherwise constitutional statute on the basis of an alleged illicit motive. *O'Brien*, 391 U. S., at 382-383; *Renton* v. *Playtime Theatres, Inc.*, *supra*, at 47-48 (that the "predominate" purpose of the statute was to control secondary effects was "more than adequate to establish" that the city's interest was unrelated to the suppression of expression). In light of the Pennsylvania court's determination that one purpose of the ordinance is to combat harmful secondary effects, the ban on public nudity here is no different from the ban on burning draft registration cards in *O'Brien*, where the Government sought to prevent the means of the expression and not the expression of antiwar sentiment itself.

Justice Stevens argues that the ordinance enacts a complete ban on expression. We respectfully disagree with that characterization. The public nudity ban certainly has the effect of limiting one particular means of expressing the kind of erotic message being disseminated at Kandyland. But simply to define what is being banned as the "message" is to assume the conclusion. We did not analyze the regulation in *O'Brien* as having enacted a total ban on expression. Instead, the Court recognized that the regulation against destroying one's draft card was justified by the Government's interest in preventing the harmful "secondary effects" of that conduct (disruption to the Selective Service System), even though that regulation may have some incidental effect on the expressive element of the conduct. Because this justification was unrelated to the suppression of O'Brien's antiwar message, the regulation was content neutral. Although there may be cases in which banning the means of expression so interferes with the message that it essentially bans the message, that is not the case here.

Even if we had not already rejected the view that a ban on public nudity is necessarily related to the suppression of the erotic message of nude dancing, we would do so now because the premise of such a view is flawed. The State's interest in preventing harmful secondary effects is not related to the suppression of expression. In trying to control the secondary effects of nude dancing, the ordinance seeks to deter crime and the other deleterious effects caused by the presence of such an establishment in the neighborhood. See *Renton, supra,* at 50-51. In *Clark* v. *Community for Creative Non-Violence,* 468 U. S. 288 (1984), we held that a National Park Service regulation prohibiting camping in certain parks did not violate the First Amendment when applied to prohibit demonstrators from sleeping in Lafayette Park and the Mall in Washington, D. C., in connection with a demonstration intended to call attention to the plight of the homeless. Assuming, *arguendo,* that sleeping can be expressive conduct, the Court concluded that the Government interest in conserving park property was unrelated to the demonstrators' message about homelessness. *Id.,* at 299. So, while the demonstrators were allowed to erect "symbolic tent cities," they were not allowed to sleep overnight in those tents. Even though the regulation may have directly limited the expressive element involved in actually sleeping in the park, the regulation was nonetheless content neutral.

Similarly, even if Erie's public nudity ban has some minimal effect on the erotic message by muting that portion of the expression that occurs when the last stitch is dropped, the dancers at Kandyland and other such establishments are free to perform wearing pasties and G-strings. Any effect on the overall expression is *de minimis* . And as *Justice Stevens* eloquently stated for the plurality in *Young* v. *American Mini Theatres, Inc.,* 427 U. S. 50, 70 (1976), "even though we recognize that the First Amendment will not tolerate the total suppression of erotic materials that have some arguably artistic value, it is manifest that society's interest in protecting this type of expression is of a wholly different, and lesser, magnitude than the interest in untrammeled political debate," and "few of us would march our sons or daughters off to war to preserve the citizen's right to see" specified anatomical areas exhibited at establishments like Kandyland. If States are to be able to regulate secondary effects, then *de minimis* intrusions on expression such as those at issue here cannot be sufficient to render the ordinance content based. See *Clark* v. *Community for Creative Non-Violence, supra* , at 299; *Ward* v. *Rock Against Racism,* 491 U. S. 781, 791 (1989) (even if regulation has an incidental effect on some speakers or messages but not others, the regulation is content neutral if it can be justified without reference to the content of the expression).

This case is, in fact, similar to *O'Brien* , *Community for Creative Non-Violence* , and *Ward* . The justification for the government regulation in each case prevents harmful "secondary" effects that are unrelated to the suppression of expression. See, *e.g., Ward* v. *Rock Against Racism, supra* , at 791-792 (noting that "[t]he principal justification for the sound-amplification guideline is the city's desire to control noise levels at bandshell events, in order to retain the character of [the adjacent] Sheep Meadow and its more sedate activities," and citing *Renton* for the proposition that "[a] regulation that serves purposes unrelated to the content of expression is deemed neutral, even if it has an incidental effect on some speakers or messages but not others"). While the doctrinal theories behind "incidental burdens" and "secondary effects" are, of course, not identical, there is nothing objectionable about a city passing a general ordinance to ban public nudity (even though such a ban may place incidental burdens on some protected speech) and at the same time recognizing that one specific occurrence of public nudity--nude erotic dancing--is particularly problematic because it produces harmful secondary effects.

Justice Stevens claims that today we "[f]or the first time" extend *Renton* 's secondary effects doctrine to justify restrictions other than the location of a commercial enterprise. *Post* , at 1. Our reliance on *Renton* to justify other restrictions is not new, however. In *Ward* , the Court relied on *Renton* to evaluate restrictions on sound amplification at an outdoor bandshell, rejecting the dissent's contention that *Renton* was inapplicable. See *Ward* v. *Rock Against Racism, supra*, at 804, n. 1 (Marshall , *J.*, dissenting) ("Today, for the first time, a majority of the Court applies *Renton* analysis to a category of speech far afield from that decision's original limited focus"). Moreover, Erie's ordinance does not effect a "total ban" on protected expression. *Post* , at 3.

In *Renton,* the regulation explicitly treated "adult" movie theaters differently from other theaters, and defined "adult" theaters solely by reference to the content of their movies. 475 U. S., at 44 . We nonetheless treated the zoning regulation as content neutral because the ordinance was aimed at the secondary effects of adult theaters, a justification unrelated to the content of the adult movies themselves. *Id.* , at 48. Here, Erie's ordinance is on its face a content-neutral restriction on conduct. Even if the city thought that nude dancing at clubs like Kandyland constituted a particularly problematic instance of public nudity, the regulation is still properly evaluated as a content-neutral restriction because the interest in combating the secondary effects associated with those clubs is unrelated to the suppression of the erotic message conveyed by nude dancing.

We conclude that Erie's asserted interest in combating the negative secondary effects associated with adult entertainment establishments like Kandyland is unrelated to the suppression of the erotic message conveyed by nude dancing. The ordinance prohibiting public nudity is therefore valid if it satisfies the four-factor test from *O'Brien* for evaluating restrictions on symbolic speech.

IV

Applying that standard here, we conclude that Erie's ordinance is justified under *O'Brien* . The first factor of the *O'Brien* test is whether the government regulation is within the constitutional power of the government to enact. Here, Erie's efforts to protect public health and safety are clearly within the city's police powers. The second factor is whether the regulation furthers an important or substantial government interest. The asserted interests of regulating conduct through a public nudity ban and of combating the harmful secondary effects associated with nude dancing are undeniably important. And in terms of demonstrating that such secondary effects pose a threat, the city need not "conduct new studies or produce evidence independent of that already generated by other cities" to demonstrate the problem of secondary effects, "so long as whatever evidence the city relies upon is reasonably believed to be relevant to the problem that the city addresses." *Renton* v. *Playtime Theatres, Inc., supra*, at 51-52. Because the nude dancing at Kandyland is of the same character as the adult entertainment at issue in *Renton* , *Young* v. *American Mini Theatres, Inc.,* 427 U. S. 50 (1976), and *California* v. *LaRue*, 409 U. S. 109 (1972), it was reasonable for Erie to conclude that such nude dancing was likely to produce the same secondary effects. And Erie could reasonably rely on the evidentiary foundation set forth in *Renton* and *American Mini Theatres* to the effect that secondary effects are caused by the presence of even one adult entertainment establishment in a given neighborhood. See *Renton* v. *Playtime Theatres, Inc.* , *supra* , at 51-52 (indicating that reliance on a judicial opinion that describes the evidentiary basis is sufficient). In fact, Erie expressly relied on *Barnes* and its discussion of secondary effects, including its reference to *Renton* and *American Mini Theatres* . Even in cases addressing regulations that strike closer to the core of First Amendment values, we have accepted a state or local government's reasonable belief that the experience of other jurisdictions is relevant to the problem it is addressing. See *Nixon* v. *Shrink Missouri Government PAC* , 528 U. S. ___ (2000) (slip op., at 13, n. 6). Regardless of whether J *ustice Souter* now wishes to disavow his opinion in *Barnes* on this point, see *post*, at 8 (opinion concurring in part and dissenting in part), the evidentiary standard described in *Renton* controls here, and Erie meets that standard.

In any event, Erie also relied on its own findings. The preamble to the ordinance states that "the Council of the City of Erie *has, at various times over more than a century, expressed its findings* that certain lewd, immoral activities carried on in public places for profit are highly detrimental to the public health, safety and welfare, and lead to the debasement of both women and men, promote violence, public intoxication, prostitution and other serious criminal activity." Pet. for Cert. 6a (emphasis added). The city council members, familiar with commercial downtown Erie, are the individuals who would likely have had first-hand knowledge of what took place at and around nude dancing establishments in Erie, and can make particularized, expert judgments about the resulting harmful secondary effects. Analogizing to the administrative agency context, it is well established that, as long as a party has an opportunity to respond, an administrative agency may take official notice of such "legislative facts" within its special knowledge, and is not confined to the evidence in the record in reaching its expert judgment. See *FCC* v. *National Citizens Comm. for Broadcasting,* 436 U. S. 775 (1978); *Republic Aviation Corp.* v. *NLRB,* 324 U. S. 793 (1945); 2 K. Davis & R. Pierce, Administrative Law Treatise §10.6 (3d ed. 1994). Here, Kandyland has had ample opportunity to contest the council's findings about secondary effects--before the council itself, throughout the state proceedings, and before this Court. Yet to this day, Kandyland has never challenged the city council's findings or cast any specific doubt on the validity of those findings. Instead, it has simply asserted that the council's evidentiary proof was lacking. In the absence of any reason to doubt it, the city's expert judgment should be credited. And the study relied on by *amicus curiae* does not cast any legitimate doubt on the Erie city council's judgment about Erie. See Brief for First Amendment Lawyers Association as *Amicus Curiae* 16-23.

Finally, it is worth repeating that Erie's ordinance is on its face a content neutral restriction that regulates conduct, not First Amendment expression. And the government should have sufficient leeway to justify such a law based on secondary effects. On this point, *O'Brien* is especially instructive. The Court there did not require evidence that the integrity of the Selective Service System would be jeopardized by the knowing destruction or mutilation of draft cards. It simply reviewed the Government's various administrative interests in issuing the cards, and then concluded that "Congress has a legitimate and substantial interest in preventing their wanton and unrestrained destruction and assuring their continuing availability by punishing people who knowingly and willfully destroy or mutilate them." 391 U. S., at 378 -380. There was no study documenting instances of draft card mutilation or the actual effect of such mutilation on the Government's asserted efficiency interests. But the Court permitted Congress to take official notice, as it were, that draft card destruction would jeopardize the system. The fact that this sort of leeway is appropriate in a case involving conduct says nothing whatsoever about its appropriateness in a case involving actual regulation of First Amendment expression. As we have said, so long as the regulation is unrelated to the suppression of expression, "[t]he government generally has a freer hand in restricting expressive conduct than it has in restricting the written or spoken word." *Texas* v. *Johnson*, 491 U. S., at 406 . See, *e.g* ., *United States* v. *O'Brien, supra* , at 377; *United States* v. *Albertini* , 472 U. S. 675, 689 (1985) (finding sufficient the Government's assertion that those who had previously been barred from entering the military installation pose a threat to the security of that installation); *Clark* v. *Community for Creative Non-Violence*, 468 U. S., at 299 (finding sufficient the Government's assertion that camping overnight in the park poses a threat to park property).

Justice Souter , however, would require Erie to develop a specific evidentiary record supporting its ordinance. *Post,* at 7-8. *Justice Souter* agrees that Erie's interest in combating the negative secondary effects associated with nude dancing establishments is a legitimate government interest unrelated to the suppression of expression, and he agrees that the ordinance should therefore be evaluated under *O'Brien* . *O'Brien* , of course, required no evidentiary showing at all that the threatened harm was real. But that case is different, *Justice Souter* contends, because in *O'Brien* "there could be no doubt" that a regulation prohibiting the destruction of draft cards would alleviate the harmful secondary effects flowing from the destruction of those cards. *Post,* at 2, n. 1.

But whether the harm is evident to our "intuition," *ibid* , is not the proper inquiry. If it were, we would simply say there is no doubt that a regulation prohibiting public nudity would alleviate the harmful secondary effects associated with nude dancing. In any event, J *ustice Souter* conflates two distinct concepts under *O'Brien* : whether there is a substantial government interest and whether the regulation furthers that interest. As to the government interest, *i.e.* , whether the threatened harm is real, the city council relied on this Court's opinions detailing the harmful secondary effects caused by establishments like Kandyland, as well as on its own experiences in Erie. *Justice Souter* attempts to denigrate the city council's conclusion that the threatened harm was real, arguing that we cannot accept Erie's findings because the subject of nude dancing is "fraught with some emotionalism," *post,* at 5. Yet surely the subject of drafting our citizens into the military is "fraught" with more emotionalism than the subject of regulating nude dancing. J *ustice Souter* next hypothesizes that the reason we cannot accept Erie's conclusion is that, since the question whether these secondary effects occur is "amenable to empirical treatment," we should ignore Erie's actual experience and instead require such an empirical analysis. *Post,* at 6, n. 4 (referring to a "scientifically sound" study offered by an *amicus curiae* to show that nude dancing establishments do not cause secondary effects). In *Nixon* , however, we flatly rejected that idea. 528 U. S., at ___ (slip op., at 14-15) (noting that the "invocation of academic studies said

to indicate" that the threatened harms are not real is insufficient to cast doubt on the experience of the local government).

As to the second point--whether the regulation furthers the government interest--it is evident that, since crime and other public health and safety problems are caused by the presence of nude dancing establishments like Kandyland, a ban on such nude dancing would further Erie's interest in preventing such secondary effects. To be sure, requiring dancers to wear pasties and G-strings may not greatly reduce these secondary effects, but *O'Brien* requires only that the regulation further the interest in combating such effects. Even though the dissent questions the wisdom of Erie's chosen remedy, *post* , at 7 (opinion of *Stevens, J.*), the " `city must be allowed a reasonable opportunity to experiment with solutions to admittedly serious problems,' " *Renton* v. *Playtime Theatres, Inc.*, 475 U. S., at 52 (quoting *American Mini Theatres* , 427 U. S., at 71 (plurality opinion)). It also may be true that a pasties and G-string requirement would not be as effective as, for example, a requirement that the dancers be fully clothed, but the city must balance its efforts to address the problem with the requirement that the restriction be no greater than necessary to further the city's interest.

The ordinance also satisfies *O'Brien* 's third factor, that the government interest is unrelated to the suppression of free expression, as discussed *supra*, at 7-15. The fourth and final *O'Brien* factor--that the restriction is no greater than is essential to the furtherance of the government interest--is satisfied as well. The ordinance regulates conduct, and any incidental impact on the expressive element of nude dancing is *de minimis* . The requirement that dancers wear pasties and G-strings is a minimal restriction in furtherance of the asserted government interests, and the restriction leaves ample capacity to convey the dancer's erotic message. See *Barnes* v. *Glen Theatre, Inc.*, 501 U. S., at 572 (plurality opinion of *Rehnquist, C. J.* , joined by *O'Connor* and *Kennedy* , *JJ* .); *id.*, at 587 (*Souter, J.*, concurring in judgment). *Justice Souter* points out that zoning is an alternative means of addressing this problem. It is far from clear, however, that zoning imposes less of a burden on expression than the minimal requirement implemented here. In any event, since this is a content-neutral restriction, least restrictive means analysis is not required. See *Ward*, 491 U. S., at 798 -799, n. 6.

We hold, therefore, that Erie's ordinance is a content-neutral regulation that is valid under *O'Brien* . Accordingly, the judgment of the Pennsylvania Supreme Court is reversed, and the case is remanded for further proceedings not inconsistent with this opinion.

It is so ordered.

27 VIRGINIA *V.* BLACK *ET AL.*

Certiorari to the Supreme Court of Virginia
Argued December 11, 2002
Decided April 7, 2003

Respondents were convicted separately of violating a Virginia statute that makes it a felony "for any person ... , with the intent of intimidating any person or group ... , to burn ... a cross on the property of another, a highway or other public place," and specifies that "[a]ny such burning ... shall be prima facie evidence of an intent to intimidate a person or group." When respondent Black objected on First Amendment grounds to his trial court's jury instruction that cross burning by itself is sufficient evidence from which the required "intent to intimidate" could be inferred, the prosecutor responded that the instruction was taken straight out of the Virginia Model Instructions. Respondent O'Mara pleaded guilty to charges of violating the statute, but reserved the right to challenge its constitutionality. At respondent Elliott's trial, the judge instructed the jury as to what the Commonwealth had to prove, but did not give an instruction on the meaning of the word "intimidate," nor on the statute's prima facie evidence provision. Consolidating all three cases, the Virginia Supreme Court held that the cross-burning statute is unconstitutional on its face; that it is analytically indistinguishable from the ordinance found unconstitutional in *R. A. V. v. St. Paul,* 505 U. S. 377; that it discriminates on the basis of content and viewpoint since it selectively chooses only cross burning because of its distinctive message; and that the prima facie evidence provision renders the statute overbroad because the enhanced probability of prosecution under the statute chills the expression of protected speech.

Held: The judgment is affirmed in part, vacated in part, and remanded.
262 Va. 764, 553 S. E. 2d 738, affirmed in part, vacated in part, and remanded.

Justice O'Connor delivered the opinion of the Court with respect to Parts I, II, and III, concluding that a State, consistent with the First Amendment, may ban cross burning carried out with the intent to intimidate. Pp. 6–17.

(a) Burning a cross in the United States is inextricably intertwined with the history of the Ku Klux Klan, which, following its formation in 1866, imposed a reign of terror throughout the South, whipping, threatening, and murdering blacks, southern whites who disagreed with the Klan, and "carpetbagger" northern whites. The Klan has often used cross burnings as a tool of intimidation and a threat of impending violence, although such burnings have also remained potent symbols of shared group identity and ideology, serving as a central feature of Klan gatherings. To this day, however, regardless of whether the message is a political one or is also meant to intimidate, the burning of a cross is a "symbol of hate." *Capitol Square Review and Advisory Bd.* v. *Pinette*, 515 U. S. 753, 771. While cross burning does not inevitably convey a message of intimidation, often the cross burner intends that the recipients of the message fear for their lives. And when a cross burning is used to intimidate, few if any messages are more powerful. Pp. 6-11.

(b) The protections the First Amendment affords speech and expressive conduct are not absolute. This Court has long recognized that the government may regulate certain categories of expression consistent with the Constitution. See, *e.g., Chaplinsky* v. *New Hampshire*, 315 U. S. 568, 571-572. For example, the First Amendment permits a State to ban "true threats," *e.g., Watts* v. *United States*, 394 U. S. 705, 708 *(per curiam)*, which encompass those statements where the speaker means to communicate a serious expression of an intent to commit an act of unlawful violence to a particular individual or group of individuals, see, *e.g., id.*, at 708. The speaker need not actually intend to carry out the threat. Rather, a prohibition on true threats protects individuals from the fear of violence and the disruption that fear engenders, as well as from the possibility that the threatened violence will occur. *R. A. V., supra*, at 388. Intimidation in the constitutionally proscribable sense of the word is a type of true threat, where a speaker directs a threat to a person or group of persons with the intent of placing the victim in fear of bodily harm or death. Respondents do not contest that some cross burnings fit within this meaning of intimidating speech, and rightly so. As the history of cross burning in this country shows, that act is often intimidating, intended to create a pervasive fear in victims that they are a target of violence. Pp. 11-14.

(c) The First Amendment permits Virginia to outlaw cross burnings done with the intent to intimidate because burning a cross is a particularly virulent form of intimidation. Instead of prohibiting all intimidating messages, Virginia may choose to regulate this subset of intimidating messages in light of cross burning's long and pernicious history as a signal of impending violence. A ban on cross burning carried out with the intent to intimidate is fully consistent with this Court's holding in *R. A. V.* Contrary to the Virginia Supreme Court's ruling, *R. A. V.* did not hold that the First Amendment prohibits *all* forms of content-based discrimination within a proscribable area of speech. Rather, the Court specifically stated that a particular type of content discrimination does not violate the First Amendment when the basis for it consists entirely of the very reason its entire class of speech is proscribable. 505 U. S., at 388. For example, it is permissible to prohibit only that obscenity that is most patently offensive in its prurience--*i.e.*, that which involves the most lascivious displays of sexual activity. *Ibid.* Similarly, Virginia's statute does not run afoul of the First Amendment insofar as it bans cross burning with intent to intimidate. Unlike the statute at issue in *R. A. V.*, the Virginia statute does not single out for opprobrium only that speech directed toward "one of the specified disfavored topics." *Id.*, at 391. It does not matter whether an individual burns a cross with intent to intimidate because of the victim's race, gender, or religion, or because of the victim's "political affiliation, union membership, or homosexuality." *Ibid.* Thus, just as a State may regulate only that obscenity which is the most obscene due to its prurient content, so too may a State choose to prohibit only those forms of intimidation that are most likely to inspire fear of bodily harm. Pp. 14-17.

Justice O'Connor, joined by *The Chief Justice, Justice Stevens,* and *Justice Breyer,* concluded in Parts IV and V that the Virginia statute's prima facie evidence provision, as interpreted through the jury instruction given in respondent Black's case and as applied therein, is unconstitutional on its face. Because the instruction is the same as the Commonwealth's Model Jury Instruction, and because the Virginia Supreme Court had the opportunity to expressly disavow it, the instruction's construction of the prima facie provision is as binding on this Court as if its precise words had been written into the statute. E.g., Terminiello v. Chicago, 337 U. S. 1, 4. As construed by the instruction, the prima facie provision strips away the very reason why a State may ban cross burning with the intent to intimidate. The provision permits a jury to convict in every cross burning case in which defendants exercise their constitutional right not to put on a defense. And even where a defendant like Black presents a defense, the provision makes it more likely that the jury will find an intent to intimidate regardless of the particular facts of the case. It permits the Commonwealth to arrest, prosecute, and convict a person based solely on the fact of cross burning itself. As so interpreted, it would create an unacceptable risk of the suppression of ideas. E.g., Secretary of State of Md. v. Joseph H. Munson Co., 467 U. S. 947, 965, n. 13. The act of burning a cross may mean that a person is engaging in constitutionally proscribable intimidation, or it may mean only that the person is engaged in core political speech. The prima facie evidence provision blurs the line between these meanings, ignoring all of the contextual factors that are necessary to decide whether a particular cross burning is intended to intimidate. The First Amendment does not permit such a shortcut. Thus, Black's conviction cannot stand, and the judgment as to him is affirmed. Conversely, Elliott's jury did not receive any instruction on the prima facie provision, and the provision was not an issue in O'Mara's case because he pleaded guilty. The possibility that the provision is severable, and if so, whether Elliott and O'Mara could be retried under the statute, is left open. Also left open is the theoretical possibility that, on remand, the Virginia Supreme Court could interpret the prima facie provision in a manner that would avoid the constitutional objections described above. Pp. 17-22.

Justice Scalia agreed that this Court should vacate and remand the judgment of the Virginia Supreme Court with respect to respondents Elliott and O'Mara so that that court can have an opportunity authoritatively to construe the cross-burning statute's prima-facie-evidence provision. Pp. 1, 12.

Justice Souter, joined by *Justice Kennedy* and *Justice Ginsburg*, concluded that the Virginia statute is unconstitutional and cannot be saved by any exception under R. A. V. v. St. Paul, 505 U. S. 377, and therefore concurred in the Court's judgment insofar as it affirms the invalidation of respondent Black's conviction. Pp. 1, 8.

O'Connor, J., announced the judgment of the Court and delivered the opinion of the Court with respect to Parts I, II, and III, in which *Rehnquist, C. J.*, and *Stevens, Scalia*, and *Breyer, JJ.*, joined, and an opinion with respect to Parts IV and V, in which *Rehnquist, C. J*, and *Stevens* and *Breyer, JJ.*, joined. *Stevens, J.*, filed a concurring opinion. *Scalia, J.*, filed an opinion concurring in part, concurring in the judgment in part, and dissenting in part, in which *Thomas, J.*, joined as to Parts I and II. *Souter, J.*, filed an opinion concurring in the judgment in part and dissenting in part, in which *Kennedy* and *Ginsburg, JJ.*, joined. *Thomas, J.*, filed a dissenting opinion.

---

*VIRGINIA, PETITIONER v. BARRY ELTON BLACK, RICHARD J. ELLIOTT, and
JONATHAN O'MARA*
on writ of certiorari to the supreme court of Virginia
[April 7, 2003]

Justice O'Connor announced the judgment of the Court and delivered the opinion of the Court with respect to Parts I, II, and III, and an opinion with respect to Parts IV and V, in which *The Chief Justice, Justice Stevens,* and *Justice Breyer* join.

In this case we consider whether the Commonwealth of Virginia's statute banning cross burning with "an intent to intimidate a person or group of persons" violates the First Amendment. Va. Code Ann. §18.2-423 (1996). We conclude that while a State, consistent with the First Amendment, may ban cross burning carried out with the intent to intimidate, the provision in the Virginia statute treating any cross burning as prima facie evidence of intent to intimidate renders the statute unconstitutional in its current form.

I

Respondents Barry Black, Richard Elliott, and Jonathan O'Mara were convicted separately of violating Virginia's cross-burning statute, §18.2-423. That statute provides:

"It shall be unlawful for any person or persons, with the intent of intimidating any person or group of persons, to burn, or cause to be burned, a cross on the property of another, a highway or other public place. Any person who shall violate any provision of this section shall be guilty of a Class 6 felony.

"Any such burning of a cross shall be prima facie evidence of an intent to intimidate a person or group of persons."

On August 22, 1998, Barry Black led a Ku Klux Klan rally in Carroll County, Virginia. Twenty-five to thirty people attended this gathering, which occurred on private property with the permission of the owner, who was in attendance. The property was located on an open field just off Brushy Fork Road (State Highway 690) in Cana, Virginia.

When the sheriff of Carroll County learned that a Klan rally was occurring in his county, he went to observe it from the side of the road. During the approximately one hour that the sheriff was present, about 40 to 50 cars passed the site, a "few" of which stopped to ask the sheriff what was happening on the property. App. 71. Eight to ten houses were located in the vicinity of the rally. Rebecca Sechrist, who was related to the owner of the property where the rally took place, "sat and watched to see wha[t] [was] going on" from the lawn of her in-laws' house. She looked on as the Klan prepared for the gathering and subsequently conducted the rally itself. *Id.*, at 103.

During the rally, Sechrist heard Klan members speak about "what they were" and "what they believed in." *Id.*, at 106. The speakers "talked real bad about the blacks and the Mexicans." *Id.*, at 109. One speaker told the assembled gathering that "he would love to take a .30/.30 and just random[ly] shoot the blacks." *Ibid.* The speakers also talked about "President Clinton and Hillary Clinton," and about how their tax money "goes to ... the black people." *Ibid.* Sechrist testified that this language made her "very ... scared." *Id.*, at 110.

At the conclusion of the rally, the crowd circled around a 25- to 30-foot cross. The cross was between 300 and 350 yards away from the road. According to the sheriff, the cross "then all of a sudden ... went up in a flame." *Id.*, at 71. As the cross burned, the Klan played Amazing Grace over the loudspeakers. Sechrist stated that the cross burning made her feel "awful" and "terrible." *Id.*, at 110.

When the sheriff observed the cross burning, he informed his deputy that they needed to "find out who's responsible and explain to them that they cannot do this in the State of Virginia." *Id.*, at 72. The sheriff then went down the driveway, entered the rally, and asked "who was responsible for burning the cross." *Id.*, at 74. Black responded, "I guess I am because I'm the head of the rally." *Ibid.* The sheriff then told Black, "[T]here's a law in the State of Virginia that you cannot burn a cross and I'll have to place you under arrest for this." *Ibid.*

Black was charged with burning a cross with the intent of intimidating a person or group of persons, in violation of §18.2-423. At his trial, the jury was instructed that "intent to intimidate means the motivation to intentionally put a person or a group of persons in fear of bodily harm. Such fear must arise from the willful conduct of the accused rather than from some mere temperamental timidity of the victim." *Id.*, at 146. The trial court also instructed the jury that "the burning of a cross by itself is sufficient evidence from which you may infer the required intent." *Ibid.* When Black objected to this last instruction on First Amendment grounds, the prosecutor responded that the instruction was "taken straight out of the [Virginia] Model Instructions." *Id.*, at 134. The jury found Black guilty, and fined him $2,500. The Court of Appeals of Virginia affirmed Black's conviction. Rec. No. 1581-99-3 (Va. App., Dec. 19, 2000), App. 201.

On May 2, 1998, respondents Richard Elliott and Jonathan O'Mara, as well as a third individual, attempted to burn a cross on the yard of James Jubilee. Jubilee, an African-American, was Elliott's next-door neighbor in Virginia Beach, Virginia. Four months prior to the incident, Jubilee and his family had moved from California to Virginia Beach. Before the cross burning, Jubilee spoke to Elliott's mother to inquire about shots being fired from behind the Elliott home. Elliott's mother explained to Jubilee that her son shot firearms as a hobby, and that he used the backyard as a firing range.

On the night of May 2, respondents drove a truck onto Jubilee's property, planted a cross, and set it on fire. Their apparent motive was to "get back" at Jubilee for complaining about the shooting in the backyard. *Id.*, at 241. Respondents were not affiliated with the Klan. The next morning, as Jubilee was pulling his car out of the driveway, he noticed the partially burned cross approximately 20 feet from his house. After seeing the cross, Jubilee was "very nervous" because he "didn't know what would be the next phase," and because "a cross burned in your yard ... tells you that it's just the first round." *Id.*, at 231.

Elliott and O'Mara were charged with attempted cross burning and conspiracy to commit cross burning. O'Mara pleaded guilty to both counts, reserving the right to challenge the constitutionality of the cross-burning statute. The judge sentenced O'Mara to 90 days in jail and fined him $2,500. The judge also suspended 45 days of the sentence and $1,000 of the fine.

At Elliott's trial, the judge originally ruled that the jury would be instructed "that the burning of a cross by itself is sufficient evidence from which you may infer the required intent." *Id.*, at 221-222. At trial, however, the court instructed the jury that the Commonwealth must prove that "the defendant intended to commit cross burning," that "the defendant did a direct act toward the commission of the cross burning," and that "the defendant had the intent of intimidating any person or group of persons."*Id.*, at 250. The court did not instruct the jury on the meaning of the word "intimidate," nor on the prima facie evidence provision of §18.2-423. The jury found Elliott guilty of attempted cross burning and acquitted him of conspiracy to commit cross burning. It sentenced Elliott to 90 days in jail and a $2,500 fine. The Court of Appeals of Virginia affirmed the convictions of both Elliott and O'Mara.*O'Mara* v. *Commonwealth*, 33 Va. App. 525, 535 S. E. 2d 175 (2000).

Each respondent appealed to the Supreme Court of Virginia, arguing that §18.2-423 is facially unconstitutional. The Supreme Court of Virginia consolidated all three cases, and held that the statute is unconstitutional on its face. 262 Va. 764, 553 S. E. 2d 738 (2001). It held that the Virginia cross-burning statute "is analytically indistinguishable from the ordinance found unconstitutional in *R. A. V.*[v. *St. Paul*, 505 U. S. 377 (1992)]." *Id.*, at 772, 553 S. E. 2d, at 742. The Virginia statute, the court held, discriminates on the basis of content since it "selectively chooses only cross burning because of its distinctive message." *Id.*, at 774, 553 S. E. 2d, at 744. The court also held that the prima facie evidence provision renders the statute overbroad because "[t]he enhanced probability of prosecution under the statute chills the expression of protected speech." *Id.*, at 777, 553 S. E. 2d, at 746.

Three justices dissented, concluding that the Virginia cross-burning statute passes constitutional muster because it proscribes only conduct that constitutes a true threat. The justices noted that unlike the ordinance found unconstitutional in *R. A. V.* v. *St. Paul*, 505 U. S. 377 (1992), the Virginia statute does not just target cross burning "on the basis of race, color, creed, religion or gender." 262 Va., at 791, 553 S. E. 2d, at 791. Rather, "the Virginia statute applies to any individual who burns a cross for any reason provided the cross is burned with the intent to intimidate." *Ibid.* The dissenters also disagreed with the majority's analysis of the prima facie provision because the inference alone "is clearly insufficient to establish beyond a reasonable doubt that a defendant burned a cross with the intent to intimidate." *Id.*, at 795, 553 S. E. 2d, at 756. The dissent noted that the burden of proof still remains on the Commonwealth to prove intent to intimidate. We granted certiorari. 535 U. S. 1094(2002).[1]

II

Cross burning originated in the 14th century as a means for Scottish tribes to signal each other. See M. Newton & J. Newton, The Ku Klux Klan: An Encyclopedia 145 (1991). Sir Walter Scott used cross burnings for dramatic effect in The Lady of the Lake, where the burning cross signified both a summons and a call to arms. See W. Scott, The Lady of The Lake, canto third. Cross burning in this country, however, long ago became unmoored from its Scottish ancestry. Burning a cross in the United States is inextricably intertwined with the history of the Ku Klux Klan.

The first Ku Klux Klan began in Pulaski, Tennessee, in the spring of 1866. Although the Ku Klux Klan started as a social club, it soon changed into something far different. The Klan fought Reconstruction and the corresponding drive to allow freed blacks to participate in the political process. Soon the Klan imposed "a veritable reign of terror" throughout the South. S. Kennedy, Southern Exposure 31 (1991) (hereinafter Kennedy). The Klan employed tactics such as whipping, threatening to burn people at the stake, and murder. W. Wade, The Fiery Cross: The Ku Klux Klan in America 48-49 (1987) (hereinafter Wade). The Klan's victims included blacks, southern whites who disagreed with the Klan, and "carpetbagger" northern whites.

The activities of the Ku Klux Klan prompted legislative action at the national level. In 1871, "President Grant sent a message to Congress indicating that the Klan's reign of terror in the Southern States had rendered life and property insecure." *Jett* v. *Dallas Independent School Dist.*, 491 U. S. 701, 722 (1989) (internal quotation marks and alterations omitted). In response, Congress passed what is now known as the Ku Klux Klan Act. See "An Act to enforce the Provisions of the Fourteenth Amendment to the Constitution of the United States, and for other Purposes," 17 Stat. 13 (now codified at 42 U. S. C. §§1983, 1985, and 1986). President Grant used these new powers to suppress the Klan in South Carolina, the effect of which severely curtailed the Klan in other States as well. By the end of Reconstruction in 1877, the first Klan no longer existed.

The genesis of the second Klan began in 1905, with the publication of Thomas Dixon's The Clansmen: An Historical Romance of the Ku Klux Klan. Dixon's book was a sympathetic portrait of the first Klan, depicting the Klan as a group of heroes "saving" the South from blacks and the "horrors" of Reconstruction. Although the first Klan never actually practiced cross burning, Dixon's book depicted the Klan burning crosses to celebrate the execution of former slaves. *Id.*, at 324–326; see also *Capitol Square Review and Advisory Bd.* v. *Pinette*, 515 U. S. 753, 770-771 (1995) (*Thomas, J.*, concurring). Cross burning thereby became associated with the first Ku Klux Klan. When D. W. Griffith turned Dixon's book into the movie The Birth of a Nation in 1915, the association between cross burning and the Klan became indelible. In addition to the cross burnings in the movie, a poster advertising the film displayed a hooded Klansman riding a hooded horse, with his left hand holding the reins of the horse and his right hand holding a burning cross above his head. Wade 127. Soon thereafter, in November 1915, the second Klan began.

From the inception of the second Klan, cross burnings have been used to communicate both threats of violence and messages of shared ideology. The first initiation ceremony occurred on Stone Mountain near Atlanta, Georgia. While a 40-foot cross burned on the mountain, the Klan members took their oaths of loyalty. See Kennedy 163. This cross burning was the second recorded instance in the United States. The first known cross burning in the country had occurred a little over one month before the Klan initiation, when a Georgia mob celebrated the lynching of Leo Frank by burning a "gigantic cross" on Stone Mountain that was "visible throughout" Atlanta. Wade 144 (internal quotation marks omitted).

The new Klan's ideology did not differ much from that of the first Klan. As one Klan publication emphasized, "We avow the distinction between [the] races, ... and we shall ever be true to the faithful maintenance of White Supremacy and will strenuously oppose any compromise thereof in any and all things." *Id.*, at 147-148 (internal quotation marks omitted). Violence was also an elemental part of this new Klan. By September 1921, the New York World newspaper documented 152 acts of Klan violence, including 4 murders, 41 floggings, and 27 tar-and-featherings. Wade 160.

Often, the Klan used cross burnings as a tool of intimidation and a threat of impending violence. For example, in 1939 and 1940, the Klan burned crosses in front of synagogues and churches. See Kennedy 175. After one cross burning at a synagogue, a Klan member noted that if the cross burning did not "shut the Jews up, we'll cut a few throats and see what happens." *Ibid.* (internal quotation marks omitted). In Miami in 1941, the Klan burned four crosses in front of a proposed housing project, declaring, "We are here to keep niggers out of your town ... . When the law fails you, call on us." *Id.*, at 176 (internal quotation marks omitted). And in Alabama in 1942, in "a whirlwind climax to weeks of flogging and terror," the Klan burned crosses in front of a union hall and in front of a union leader's home on the eve of a labor election. *Id.*, at 180. These cross burnings embodied threats to people whom the Klan deemed antithetical to its goals. And these threats had special force given the long history of Klan violence.

The Klan continued to use cross burnings to intimidate after World War II. In one incident, an African-American "school teacher who recently moved his family into a block formerly occupied only by whites asked the protection of city police ... after the burning of a cross in his front yard." Richmond News Leader, Jan. 21, 1949, p. 19, App. 312. And after a cross burning in Suffolk, Virginia during the late 1940's, the Virginia Governor stated that he would "not allow any of our people of any race to be subjected to terrorism or intimidation in any form by the Klan or any other organization." D. Chalmers, Hooded Americanism: The History of the Ku Klux Klan 333 (1980) (hereinafter Chalmers). These incidents of cross burning, among others, helped prompt Virginia to enact its first version of the cross-burning statute in 1950.

The decision of this Court in *Brown* v. *Board of Education*, 347 U. S. 483 (1954), along with the civil rights movement of the 1950's and 1960's, sparked another outbreak of Klan violence. These acts of violence included bombings, beatings, shootings, stabbings, and mutilations. See, *e.g.*, Chalmers 349-350; Wade 302-303. Members of the Klan burned crosses on the lawns of those associated with the civil rights movement, assaulted the Freedom Riders, bombed churches, and murdered blacks as well as whites whom the Klan viewed as sympathetic toward the civil rights movement.

Throughout the history of the Klan, cross burnings have also remained potent symbols of shared group identity and ideology. The burning cross became a symbol of the Klan itself and a central feature of Klan gatherings. According to the Klan constitution (called the kloran), the "fiery cross" was the "emblem of that sincere, unselfish devotedness of all klansmen to the sacred purpose and principles we have espoused." The Ku Klux Klan Hearings before the House Committee on Rules, 67th Cong., 1st Sess., 114, Exh. G (1921); see also Wade 419. And the Klan has often published its newsletters and magazines under the name The Fiery Cross. See Wade 226, 489.

At Klan gatherings across the country, cross burning became the climax of the rally or the initiation. Posters advertising an upcoming Klan rally often featured a Klan member holding a cross. See N. MacLean, Behind the Mask of Chivalry: The Making of the Second Ku Klux Klan 142-143 (1994). Typically, a cross burning would start with a prayer by the "Klavern" minister, followed by the singing of Onward Christian Soldiers. The Klan would then light the cross on fire, as the members raised their left arm toward the burning cross and sang The Old Rugged Cross. Wade 185. Throughout the Klan's history, the Klan continued to use the burning cross in their ritual ceremonies.

For its own members, the cross was a sign of celebration and ceremony. During a joint Nazi-Klan rally in 1940, the proceeding concluded with the wedding of two Klan members who "were married in full Klan regalia beneath a blazing cross." *Id.*, at 271. In response to antimasking bills introduced in state legislatures after World War II, the Klan burned crosses in protest. See Chalmers 340. On March 26, 1960, the Klan engaged in rallies and cross burnings throughout the South in an attempt to recruit 10 million members. See Wade 305. Later in

1960, the Klan became an issue in the third debate between Richard Nixon and John Kennedy, with both candidates renouncing the Klan. After this debate, the Klan reiterated its support for Nixon by burning crosses. See *id.*, at 309. And cross burnings featured prominently in Klan rallies when the Klan attempted to move toward more nonviolent tactics to stop integration. See *id.*, at 323; cf. Chalmers 368-369, 371-372, 380, 384. In short, a burning cross has remained a symbol of Klan ideology and of Klan unity.

To this day, regardless of whether the message is a political one or whether the message is also meant to intimidate, the burning of a cross is a "symbol of hate." *Capitol Square Review and Advisory Bd.* v.*Pinette*, 515 U. S., at 771 *(Thomas, J.,* concurring). And while cross burning sometimes carries no intimidating message, at other times the intimidating message is the *only* message conveyed. For example, when a cross burning is directed at a particular person not affiliated with the Klan, the burning cross often serves as a message of intimidation, designed to inspire in the victim a fear of bodily harm. Moreover, the history of violence associated with the Klan shows that the possibility of injury or death is not just hypothetical. The person who burns a cross directed at a particular person often is making a serious threat, meant to coerce the victim to comply with the Klan's wishes unless the victim is willing to risk the wrath of the Klan. Indeed, as the cases of respondents Elliott and O'Mara indicate, individuals without Klan affiliation who wish to threaten or menace another person sometimes use cross burning because of this association between a burning cross and violence.

In sum, while a burning cross does not inevitably convey a message of intimidation, often the cross burner intends that the recipients of the message fear for their lives. And when a cross burning is used to intimidate, few if any messages are more powerful.

III

A

The First Amendment, applicable to the States through the Fourteenth Amendment, provides that "Congress shall make no law ... abridging the freedom of speech." The hallmark of the protection of free speech is to allow "free trade in ideas"--even ideas that the overwhelming majority of people might find distasteful or discomforting. *Abrams* v. *United States,* 250 U. S. 616, 630 (1919) (Holmes, J., dissenting); see also *Texas* v. *Johnson,* 491 U. S. 397, 414 (1989) ("If there is a bedrock principle underlying the First Amendment, it is that the government may not prohibit the expression of an idea simply because society finds the idea itself offensive or disagreeable"). Thus, the First Amendment "ordinarily" denies a State "the power to prohibit dissemination of social, economic and political doctrine which a vast majority of its citizens believes to be false and fraught with evil consequence."*Whitney* v. *California,* 274 U. S. 357, 374 (1927) (Brandeis, J., dissenting). The First Amendment affords protection to symbolic or expressive conduct as well as to actual speech. See, *e.g.,* R. *A. V.* v.*City of St. Paul,* 505 U. S., at 382; *Texas* v. *Johnson, supra,* at 405-406; *United States* v. *O'Brien,* 391 U. S. 367, 376-377 (1968); *Tinker* v. *Des Moines Independent Community School Dist.,* 393 U. S. 503, 505 (1969).

The protections afforded by the First Amendment, however, are not absolute, and we have long recognized that the government may regulate certain categories of expression consistent with the Constitution. See, *e.g., Chaplinsky* v. *New Hampshire,* 315 U. S. 568, 571-572 (1942) ("There are certain well-defined and narrowly limited classes of speech, the prevention and punishment of which has never been thought to raise any Constitutional problem"). The First Amendment permits "restrictions upon the content of speech in a few limited areas, which are 'of such slight social value as a step to truth that any benefit that may be derived from them is clearly outweighed by the social interest in order and morality.' " *R. A. V.* v. *City of St. Paul, supra,* at 382-383 (quoting *Chaplinsky* v. *New Hampshire, supra,* at 572).

Thus, for example, a State may punish those words "which by their very utterance inflict injury or tend to incite an immediate breach of the peace." *Chaplinsky* v. *New Hampshire, supra,* at 572; see also *R. A. V.* v. *City of St. Paul, supra,* at 383 (listing limited areas where the First Amendment permits restrictions on the content of speech). We have consequently held that fighting words--"those personally abusive epithets which, when addressed to the ordinary citizen, are, as a matter of common knowledge, inherently likely to provoke violent reaction"--are generally proscribable under the First Amendment. *Cohen* v. *California,* 403 U. S. 15, 20 (1971); see also *Chaplinsky* v. *New Hampshire, supra,* at 572. Furthermore, "the constitutional guarantees of free speech and free press do not permit a State to forbid or proscribe advocacy of the use of force or of law violation except where such advocacy is directed to inciting or producing imminent lawless action and is likely to incite or produce such action." *Brandenburg* v. *Ohio,* 395 U. S. 444, 447 (1969) *(per curiam).* And the First Amendment also permits a State to ban a "true threat." *Watts* v. *United States,* 394 U. S. 705, 708 (1969) *(per curiam)* (internal quotation marks omitted); accord, *R. A. V.* v. *City of St. Paul, supra,* at 388 ("[T]hreats of violence are outside the First Amendment"); *Madsen* v. *Women's Health Center, Inc.,* 512 U. S. 753, 774 (1994); *Schenck* v. *Pro-Choice Network of Western N. Y.,* 519 U. S. 357, 373 (1997).

"True threats" encompass those statements where the speaker means to communicate a serious expression of an intent to commit an act of unlawful violence to a particular individual or group of individuals. See *Watts* v. *United States, supra,* at 708 ("political hyberbole" is not a true threat); *R. A. V.* v. *City of St. Paul,* 505 U. S., at 388. The speaker need not actually intend to carry out the threat. Rather, a prohibition on true threats "protect[s] individuals from the fear of violence" and "from the disruption that fear engenders," in addition to protecting people "from the possibility that the threatened violence will occur." *Ibid.* Intimidation in the constitutionally proscribable sense of the word is a type of true threat, where a speaker directs a threat to a person or group of persons with the intent of placing the victim in fear of bodily harm or death. Respondents do not contest that some cross burnings fit within this meaning of intimidating speech, and rightly so. As noted in Part II, *supra,* the history of cross burning in this country shows that cross burning is often intimidating, intended to create a pervasive fear in victims that they are a target of violence.

B

The Supreme Court of Virginia ruled that in light of *R. A. V.* v. *City of St. Paul, supra,* even if it is constitutional to ban cross burning in a content-neutral manner, the Virginia cross-burning statute is unconstitutional because it discriminates on the basis of content and viewpoint. 262 Va., at 771-776, 553 S. E. 2d, at 742-745. It is true, as the Supreme Court of Virginia held, that the burning of a cross is symbolic expression. The reason why the Klan burns a cross at its rallies, or individuals place a burning cross on someone else's lawn, is that the burning cross represents the message that the speaker wishes to communicate. Individuals burn crosses as opposed to other means of communication because cross burning carries a message in an effective and dramatic manner.[2]

The fact that cross burning is symbolic expression, however, does not resolve the constitutional question. The Supreme Court of Virginia relied upon *R. A. V.* v. *City of St. Paul, supra,* to conclude that once a statute discriminates on the basis of this type of content, the law is unconstitutional. We disagree.

In *R. A. V.*, we held that a local ordinance that banned certain symbolic conduct, including cross burning, when done with the knowledge that such conduct would " 'arouse anger, alarm or resentment in others on the basis of race, color, creed, religion or gender' " was unconstitutional. *Id.*, at 380 (quoting the St. Paul Bias-Motivated Crime Ordinance, St. Paul, Minn., Legis. Code §292.02 (1990)). We held that the ordinance did not pass constitutional muster because it discriminated on the basis of content by targeting only those individuals who "provoke violence" on a basis specified in the law. 505 U. S., at 391. The ordinance did not cover "[t]hose who wish to use 'fighting words' in connection with other ideas--to express hostility, for example, on the basis of political affiliation, union membership, or homosexuality." *Ibid.* This content-based discrimination was unconstitutional because it allowed the city "to impose special prohibitions on those speakers who express views on disfavored subjects." *Ibid.*

We did not hold in *R. A. V.* that the First Amendment prohibits *all* forms of content-based discrimination within a proscribable area of speech. Rather, we specifically stated that some types of content discrimination did not violate the First Amendment:

"When the basis for the content discrimination consists entirely of the very reason the entire class of speech at issue is proscribable, no significant danger of idea or viewpoint discrimination exists. Such a reason, having been adjudged neutral enough to support exclusion of the entire class of speech from First Amendment protection, is also neutral enough to form the basis of distinction within the class." *Id.*, at 388.

Indeed, we noted that it would be constitutional to ban only a particular type of threat: "[T]he Federal Government can criminalize only those threats of violence that are directed against the President ... since the reasons why threats of violence are outside the First Amendment ... have special force when applied to the person of the President." *Ibid.* And a State may "choose to prohibit only that obscenity which is the most patently offensive *in its prurience--i.e.*, that which involves the most lascivious displays of sexual activity." *Ibid.* (emphasis in original). Consequently, while the holding of *R. A. V.* does not permit a State to ban only obscenity based on "offensive *political* messages," *ibid.*, or "only those threats against the President that mention his policy on aid to inner cities," *ibid.*, the First Amendment permits content discrimination "based on the very reasons why the particular class of speech at issue ... is proscribable," *id.*, at 393.

Similarly, Virginia's statute does not run afoul of the First Amendment insofar as it bans cross burning with intent to intimidate. Unlike the statute at issue in *R. A. V.*, the Virginia statute does not single out for opprobrium only that speech directed toward "one of the specified disfavored topics." *Id.*, at 391. It does not matter whether an individual burns a cross with intent to intimidate because of the victim's race, gender, or religion, or because of the victim's "political affiliation, union membership, or homosexuality." *Ibid.* Moreover, as a factual matter it is not true that cross burners direct their intimidating conduct solely to racial or religious minorities. See, *e.g.*, *supra*, at 8 (noting the instances of cross burnings directed at union members); *State* v. *Miller*, 6 Kan. App. 2d 432, 629 P. 2d 748 (1981) (describing the case of a defendant who burned a cross in the yard of the lawyer who had previously represented him and who was currently prosecuting him). Indeed, in the case of Elliott and O'Mara, it is at least unclear whether the respondents burned a cross due to racial animus. See 262 Va., at 791, 553 S. E. 2d, at 753 (Hassell, J., dissenting) (noting that "these defendants burned a cross because they were angry that their neighbor had complained about the presence of a firearm shooting range in the Elliott's yard, not because of any racial animus").

The First Amendment permits Virginia to outlaw cross burnings done with the intent to intimidate because burning a cross is a particularly virulent form of intimidation. Instead of prohibiting all intimidating messages, Virginia may choose to regulate this subset of intimidating messages in light of cross burning's long and pernicious history as a signal of impending violence. Thus, just as a State may regulate only that obscenity which is the most obscene due to its prurient content, so too may a State choose to prohibit only those forms of intimidation that are most likely to inspire fear of bodily harm. A ban on cross burning carried out with the intent to intimidate is fully consistent with our holding in R. A. V. and is proscribable under the First Amendment.

IV

The Supreme Court of Virginia ruled in the alternative that Virginia's cross-burning statute was unconstitutionally overbroad due to its provision stating that "[a]ny such burning of a cross shall be prima facie evidence of an intent to intimidate a person or group of persons." Va. Code Ann. §18.2-423 (1996). The Commonwealth added the prima facie provision to the statute in 1968. The court below did not reach whether this provision is severable from the rest of the cross-burning statute under Virginia law. See §1-17.1 ("The provisions of all statutes are severable unless ... it is apparent that two or more statutes or provisions must operate in accord with one another"). In this Court, as in the Supreme Court of Virginia, respondents do not argue that the prima facie evidence provision is unconstitutional as applied to any one of them. Rather, they contend that the provision is unconstitutional on its face.

The Supreme Court of Virginia has not ruled on the meaning of the prima facie evidence provision. It has, however, stated that "the act of burning a cross alone, with no evidence of intent to intimidate, will nonetheless suffice for arrest and prosecution and will insulate the Commonwealth from a motion to strike the evidence at the end of its case-in-chief." 262 Va., at 778, 553 S. E. 2d, at 746. The jury in the case of Richard Elliott did not receive any instruction on the prima facie evidence provision, and the provision was not an issue in the case of Jonathan O'Mara because he pleaded guilty. The court in Barry Black's case, however, instructed the jury that the provision means: "The burning of a cross, by itself, is sufficient evidence from which you may infer the required intent." App. 196. This jury instruction is the same as the Model Jury Instruction in the Commonwealth of Virginia. See Virginia Model Jury Instructions, Criminal, Instruction No. 10.250 (1998 and Supp. 2001).

The prima facie evidence provision, as interpreted by the jury instruction, renders the statute unconstitutional. Because this jury instruction is the Model Jury Instruction, and because the Supreme Court of Virginia had the opportunity to expressly disavow the jury instruction, the jury instruction's construction of the prima facie provision "is a ruling on a question of state law that is as binding on us as though the precise words had been written into" the statute. E.g., *Terminiello* v. *Chicago*, 337 U. S. 1, 4 (1949) (striking down an ambiguous statute on facial grounds based upon the instruction given to the jury); see also *New York* v. *Ferber*, 458 U. S. 747, 768 n. 21 (1982) (noting that *Terminiello* involved a facial challenge to the statute); *Secretary of State of Md.* v. *Joseph H. Munson Co.*, 467 U. S. 947, 965, n. 13 (1984); Note, The First Amendment Overbreadth Doctrine, 83 Harv. L. Rev. 844, 845-846, n. 8 (1970); Monaghan, Overbreadth, 1981 S. Ct. Rev. 1, 10-12; Blakey & Murray, Threats, Free Speech, and the Jurisprudence of the Federal Criminal Law, 2002 B. Y. U. L. Rev. 829, 883, n. 133. As construed by the jury instruction, the prima facie provision strips away the very reason why a

State may ban cross burning with the intent to intimidate. The prima facie evidence provision permits a jury to convict in every cross-burning case in which defendants exercise their constitutional right not to put on a defense. And even where a defendant like Black presents a defense, the prima facie evidence provision makes it more likely that the jury will find an intent to intimidate regardless of the particular facts of the case. The provision permits the Commonwealth to arrest, prosecute, and convict a person based solely on the fact of cross burning itself.

It is apparent that the provision as so interpreted " 'would create an unacceptable risk of the suppression of ideas.' " *Secretary of State of Md.* v. *Joseph H. Munson Co., supra*, at 965, n. 13 (quoting *Members of City Council of Los Angeles* v. *Taxpayers for Vincent*, 466 U. S. 789, 797 (1984)). The act of burning a cross may mean that a person is engaging in constitutionally proscribable intimidation. But that same act may mean only that the person is engaged in core political speech. The prima facie evidence provision in this statute blurs the line between these two meanings of a burning cross. As interpreted by the jury instruction, the provision chills constitutionally protected political speech because of the possibility that a State will prosecute-- and potentially convict--somebody engaging only in lawful political speech at the core of what the First Amendment is designed to protect.

As the history of cross burning indicates, a burning cross is not always intended to intimidate. Rather, sometimes the cross burning is a statement of ideology, a symbol of group solidarity. It is a ritual used at Klan gatherings, and it is used to represent the Klan itself. Thus, "[b]urning a cross at a political rally would almost certainly be protected expression." *R. A. V.* v. *St. Paul*, 505 U. S., at 402, n. 4 (White, J., concurring in judgment) (citing *Brandenburg* v. *Ohio*, 395 U. S., at 445). Cf. *National Socialist Party of America* v. *Skokie*, 432 U. S. 43 (1977) *(per curiam)*. Indeed, occasionally a person who burns a cross does not intend to express either a statement of ideology or intimidation. Cross burnings have appeared in movies such as Mississippi Burning, and in plays such as the stage adaptation of Sir Walter Scott's The Lady of the Lake.

The prima facie provision makes no effort to distinguish among these different types of cross burnings. It does not distinguish between a cross burning done with the purpose of creating anger or resentment and a cross burning done with the purpose of threatening or intimidating a victim. It does not distinguish between a cross burning at a public rally or a cross burning on a neighbor's lawn. It does not treat the cross burning directed at an individual differently from the cross burning directed at a group of like-minded believers. It allows a jury to treat a cross burning on the property of another with the owner's acquiescence in the same manner as a cross burning on the property of another without the owner's permission. To this extent I agree with *Justice Souter* that the prima facie evidence provision can "skew jury deliberations toward conviction in cases where the evidence of intent to intimidate is relatively weak and arguably consistent with a solely ideological reason for burning." *Post*, at 6 (opinion concurring in judgment and dissenting in part).

It may be true that a cross burning, even at a political rally, arouses a sense of anger or hatred among the vast majority of citizens who see a burning cross. But this sense of anger or hatred is not sufficient to ban all cross burnings. As Gerald Gunther has stated, "The lesson I have drawn from my childhood in Nazi Germany and my happier adult life in this country is the need to walk the sometimes difficult path of denouncing the bigot's hateful ideas with all my power, yet at the same time challenging any community's attempt to suppress hateful ideas by force of law." Casper, Gerry, 55 Stan. L. Rev. 647, 649 (2002) (internal quotation marks omitted). The prima facie evidence provision in this case ignores all of the contextual factors that are necessary to decide whether a particular cross burning is intended to intimidate. The First Amendment does not permit such a shortcut.

For these reasons, the prima facie evidence provision, as interpreted through the jury instruction and as applied in Barry Black's case, is unconstitutional on its face. We recognize that the Supreme Court of Virginia has not authoritatively interpreted the meaning of the prima facie evidence provision. Unlike *Justice Scalia*, we refuse to speculate on whether *any* interpretation of the prima facie evidence provision would satisfy the First Amendment. Rather, all we hold is that because of the interpretation of the prima facie evidence provision given by the jury instruction, the provision makes the statute facially invalid at this point. We also recognize the theoretical possibility that the court, on remand, could interpret the provision in a manner different from that so far set forth in order to avoid the constitutional objections we have described. We leave open that possibility. We also leave open the possibility that the provision is severable, and if so, whether Elliott and O'Mara could be retried under §18.2-423.

V

With respect to Barry Black, we agree with the Supreme Court of Virginia that his conviction cannot stand, and we affirm the judgment of the Supreme Court of Virginia. With respect to Elliott and O'Mara, we vacate the judgment of the Supreme Court of Virginia, and remand the case for further proceedings.

It is so ordered.

III. Appendices

A. THEORIES FOR INTERPRETING THE CONSTITUTION
BY DANIEL S. BROWN, JR.

The First Amendment to the Constitution of the United States includes a declaration protecting public and private speech. It announces that "Congress shall make no law respecting an establishment of religion, or prohibiting the free exercise thereof; or abridging the freedom of speech, or of the press; or the right of the people peaceably to assemble, and to petition the government for a redress of grievances."

While the Amendment appears to be clear cut and absolute when it pledges that "no law . . . abridging the freedom of speech, or of the press" will be made by Congress, the hard course of life has proven otherwise. In fact, the federal, state, and local systems of government in the United States do make laws that keep speech from being unabridged. There are many categories of unprotected speech some of which are obvious to thinking citizens in our representative form of government. We do not, for example, have the freedom to load our automobiles with loudspeakers and blare out messages in support of our political agenda, party, or candidate. At least, we cannot do this in a residential neighborhood at 2 a.m. Such laws are called "time, place, and manner" restrictions on our speech.

Other forms of unprotected speech include obscenity. Vulgarity is protected, but not obscenity. The legal difference between these concepts is murkier than one might think. Of course, being vulgar rarely endears others to our point of view. It is nonetheless protected speech as can be demonstrated by the careers of numerous radio "shock jocks" who find listeners ready to engage with them.

The United States does not permit the manufacture or distribution of pornography involving children without severe penalties. Inciting a gathering to engage in violent behavior is not permitted. Certain logos and graphics retain trademark or copyright protections and it is illegal for someone to communicate using them without the permission of the owner.

The Constitution does not permit false advertising. While this protects consumers, is there any doubt that the charlatan's liberty of express is abridged by federal legislation? Congress regulates this type of communication, also called "commercial speech." Americans have the freedom to advertise products that are legal and goods that are safe. But, through the Federal Trade Commission, false and misleading commercial speech is abridged. Through the Federal Communications Commission, false and misleading broadcast commercial speech is abridged. Our economic system does encourage "Buyer beware," or as the Romans used to cry "Caveat

Emptor." Nonetheless, it is in the interest of public safety that advertisements for food, vitamins, automobiles, and nearly every other product or service has its advertisements regulated by the government.

What the Founding Fathers had in mind when they agreed to the free speech clause of the Constitution may be lost forever. We know that the writers did have a favorable opinion toward inquiry and science, both of which were central to the Enlightenment Era of which they were products. It is left to us to discern how the First Amendment should be applied and what it means to contemporary communicators. What we do know is that determining appropriate or inappropriate speech – requiring an act of Congress, or any other branch of the government – was not on the agenda of those who drafted the Constitution. *changes w/ nature & time of today*

Perhaps we understand tacitly and fully that Congress does make laws regualteing or abridging our speech. It is for the public good, the common cause. Why might such policies or laws exist? How far might they reach? Is there any issue that the Government may not restrict? To answer these questions about where the line is drawn regarding government interference with the speech of the people, consider five traditions that have emerged from the legal professions over the last centuries.

The Absolutist Tradition

The absolutists include the libertarians who argue for no government interference with speech. When the Constitution says "no law," it actually means "no law." No smoke and mirrors here. The Founding Fathers meant what they wrote and wrote what they meant. The impracticality of this approach is obvious especially when considering the broadcast media. If not the FCC, then what group will step in to regulate the technology of the broadcasting industry? Who will establish broadcast spectrum and censure those who violate another broadcaster's air space? Will anyone be able to eavesdrop on your telephone calls without fear of reprisal? The early history of radio and television broadcasting in America is replete with examples of business empires that were unable to cooperate with others who targeted the same audiences. In theory, the Absolutist is on solid ground; in practice, the people require protections that can be supervised by the Government.

Ad Hoc Balancing Theories

Often used by the government – especially the judicial system –as a way to negotiate through the nuanced requirements of competing or clashing rights, balancing theories appear in several forms. Two approaches are considered here. Balancing Theory refers to the courts balancing any number of competing rights against each other. The image of the scales of justice applies. The two sides of a case are considered carefully. The risks and benefits are measured or weighed. A decision is rendered. In this approach to interpreting the First Amendment's free speech clause, speech enjoys no special privilege. Let me illustrate. In a case that involves the publication and distribution of state secrets – national security issues, let's say – a newspaper publisher is halted and restricted from doing his job. Charges are filed. Friends of the court briefs are invited. Arguments are made and examined. Here the competing values are both solidly American values. We value the freedom to speak, but we also value the inalienable rights granted by the Creator, as the Constitution's Preamble records, to life. If speaking out on these national security issues undercuts the public's right to life, or liberty, or its pursuit of happiness, the courts typically will be asked to decide which value takes precedence. Sometime speech or the press wins; sometimes the other set of values wins. It is an Ad Hoc, case-by-case decision-making process.

Preferred Balancing Theory

A second Balancing Theory is referred to by different names, but is commonly known as Preferred Balancing. Similar in application to the Ad Hoc Balance Approach, this approach simply prefers or privileges freedom of expression over other social values with which it may conflict. This is not to say that speech is automatically the controlling value. The values in conflict with speech may ultimately triumph and speech be censored. All other things being equal, the scales of justice tip in favor of freedom of speech. This is not an insignificant difference. It is, however, still a balancing approach.

Meiklejohnian Theory

Alexander Meiklejohn, a professor of philosophy, college dean, and free-speech advocate, proposed that free speech is not an end in itself. It is, rather, a means to an end. The ultimate purpose of free speech is to foster and promote self-governance. Meiklejohn's theory distinguishes between private speech, about which the Constitution is silent, and public speech, about which the Founding Fathers were concerned enough to include it in the Bill of Rights. The Meiklejohnian Theory is a type of Absolutist Theory that applies specifically to political speech. Even speech that is critical of the government and its policies – perhaps especially such speech – must be protected if the electorate is to remain informed and democracy to remain healthy.

Marketplace of Ideas Approach

The great jurist Oliver Wendell Holmes, while serving as a Justice of the United States, wrote in a dissenting opinion that "the best test of truth is the power of the thought to get itself accepted in the competition of the market." Holmes is credited with articulating and advancing this theory of free speech. While he never argued that Truth would triumph over all pretenders, he did argue that the best test of Truth was to let it engage a country's collective intellect, thoughts, and minds freely and openly. This approach to free speech values Truth and its pursuit; it is used more frequently in federal court decisions than the other approaches discussed here.

These theories of how the free speech and free press clauses operate and what they mean did not emerge in a vacuum. That is why this book includes several historic essays. To understand how speech and press freedoms evolved, one must study their roots.

The articulated freedoms enjoyed by Americans are enshrined in the Constitution of the United States. Caution is called for at this point. Note well that the interpretations and applications of the freedoms of expression in the first decade of the twenty-first century differ significantly and mightily from the interpretations and applications of those same rights in the late eighteenth century, at the dawn of Constitutional rule. Let me illustrate with four simple examples. First, in the eighteenth century, learned men were familiar with church law, also called canon law. Church law and church courts influenced the content and intent of the Constitution's authors. Today, canon law is irrelevant to most speech and press debates. Second, the framers of the Constitution were also salving the wounds inflicted by a malnificent monarch. The King had ruled his colonies harshly from a distance. He has insisted on publishers receiving his official sanction and approval before publishing a word. Those who processed without royal charter were fined, imprisoned or worse. Third, legislators worked under the tacit assumption that publishers and public speakers shared with them desire to create a better life in the New World. Criticism could be expected from some, but it would surely be mild. Anarchy and terrorist threats, on the other hand, were not addressed because there was no perceived need to do so. Finally, the U.S. Constitution was crafted by representatives of the various states. As such they were apparently committed to the federal Congress making "no law respecting an establishment of religion, or prohibiting the free exercise thereof; or abridging the freedom of speech, or of the press; or the right of the people peaceably to assemble, and to petition the government for a redress of grievances," their individual state governments did restrict religious practice, liberty of expression, freedoms to assemble and to petition the state government.

The application of the First Amendment to the local and state governments was a long time in coming. Not incidentally, the freedoms expressed in the Bill of Rights, including the First Amendment, now applies to state agencies and agents. Public school educators and state-supported universities may not abridge "the freedom of speech, or of the press" today. "Congress," so the Supreme Court has concluded, is simply a short-hand for "all government systems and entities," in the case of the First Amendment.

B. SECTION 215 OF THE USA PATRIOT ACT
SEC. 215. ACCESS TO RECORDS AND OTHER ITEMS UNDER THE FOREIGN INTELLIGENCE SURVEILLANCE ACT.

Title V of the Foreign Intelligence Surveillance Act of 1978 (50 U.S.C. 1861 et seq.) is amended by striking sections 501 through 503 and inserting the following:

SEC. 501. ACCESS TO CERTAIN BUSINESS RECORDS FOR FOREIGN INTELLIGENCE AND INTERNATIONAL TERRORISM INVESTIGATIONS.

(a)

(1) The Director of the Federal Bureau of Investigation or a designee of the Director (whose rank shall be no lower than Assistant Special Agent in Charge) may make an application for an order requiring the production of any tangible things (including books, records, papers, documents, and other items) for an investigation to protect against international terrorism or clandestine intelligence activities, provided that such investigation of a United States person is not conducted solely upon the basis of activities protected by the first amendment to the Constitution.

(2) An investigation conducted under this section shall—
    (A) be conducted under guidelines approved by the Attorney General under Executive Order 12333 (or a successor order); and
    (B) not be conducted of a United States person solely upon the basis of activities protected by the first amendment to the Constitution of the United States.

(b)
Each application under this section—
(1) shall be made to—
    (A) a judge of the court established by section 103(a); or
    (B) a United States Magistrate Judge under chapter 43 of title 28, United States Code, who is publicly designated by the Chief Justice of the United States to have the power to hear applications and grant orders for the production of tangible things under this section on behalf of a judge of that court; and
(2) shall specify that the records concerned are sought for an authorized investigation conducted in accordance with subsection (a)(2) to protect against international terrorism or clandestine intelligence activities.

(c)

(1) Upon an application made pursuant to this section, the judge shall enter an ex parte order as requested, or as modified, approving the release of records if the judge finds that the application meets the requirements of this section.

(2) An order under this subsection shall not disclose that it is issued for purposes of an investigation described in subsection (a).

(d)

No person shall disclose to any other person (other than those persons necessary to produce the tangible things under this section) that the Federal Bureau of Investigation has sought or obtained tangible things under this section.

(e)

A person who, in good faith, produces tangible things under an order pursuant to this section shall not be liable to any other person for such production. Such production shall not be deemed to constitute a waiver of any privilege in any other proceeding or context.

SEC. 502. CONGRESSIONAL OVERSIGHT.

(a)

On a semiannual basis, the Attorney General shall fully inform the Permanent Select Committee on Intelligence of the House of Representatives and the Select Committee on Intelligence of the Senate concerning all requests for the production of tangible things under section 402.

(b)

On a semiannual basis, the Attorney General shall provide to the Committees on the Judiciary of the House of Representatives and the Senate a report setting forth with respect to the preceding 6-month period.

C. USA PATRIOT ISSUES FOR CAMPUSES
American Library Association

Policies in the USA PATRIOT Act, Executive Orders, and other federal guidelines that directly pertain to student, faculty and staff life on campus fall into at least
five main areas:

1. privacy of student, staff, faculty and administration records,
2. campus police cooperation with the FBI,
3. surveillance,
4. academic freedom, and
5. immigrants' rights.

Below, the issues are explained in detail. It is important to recognize that this is a list of what could possibly be occurring on your campus; and even if it is not occurring, students, staff, faculty and members of the administration may still institute protection measures to uphold their civil liberties. It is important to get the facts, to find out what is happening on your campus and to then take action.

Privacy of Campus Records
- According to the American Association of Collegiate Registrars and Admissions Officers (AACRAO), about 200 colleges and universities have turned over student information to the FBI, INS, and other law enforcement officials.
- Educational institutions are permitted to disclose "directory information" to anyone who asks. Directory information includes name, phone number, address, date and place of birth, major field of study, participation in activities and sports, dates of attendance, the most recent previous educational institution attended, and other information which would not generally be considered harmful or an invasion of privacy (FERPA).
- Your school also collects a wealth of more personal information ranging from your medical records to your family's finances to disciplinary records; they may also release this information to federal authorities.
- Your school library and bookstore must turn over borrowing and sales records on individuals to the FBI or other law enforcement agency, and they can't tell you they have done so.

Campus Police Cooperation with the FBI
- The FBI is employing campus police on a part-time basis to monitor political and religious activities on campus and investigate student, faculty, and staff backgrounds

and activities.

- Under the guise of "terrorism investigation", campus police may then search your room/office and belongings without notifying you or the college administration.
- Campus police cooperating in FBI investigations on terrorism are prohibited from reporting to the head of campus police or any other member of the university on their activities.

Surveillance

- Universities may be permitted to monitor e-mail and Internet communications, particularly in cases where a student, faculty member or staff person is using university or college-owned equipment.
- Law enforcement agents may obtain 'pen register' and 'trap and trace' orders access to "dialing, routing and signaling information." Because Internet information moves together in packets, law enforcement thereby has the authority to monitor Internet communications of students, faculty or staff who are not a target of a criminal investigation.
- Law enforcement agents may employ video surveillance to track and record an individual's activities on campus.

Academic Freedom

- Universities may institute policies that restrict when and where students, faculty and staff may rally, protest, or speak about a certain issue.
- Universities may sanction students or faculty for written or spoken commentary.
- The government or universities may institute policies that prohibit the research and writing around certain topic areas in the interests of "national security."

Immigrant Rights

- Colleges and universities are required to compile records for all international students and enter them into an INS database, the SEVIS (Student/Exchange Visitor Information System).
- All non-citizen men over the age of sixteen from a specific list of mainly Arab and Muslim nations are required to participate in special registration with the INS. Of those who have registered, some have been arrested without a specific warrant, held without access to a lawyer, and/or deported without the right to an open hearing.
- Students (and perhaps faculty) from some mainly Arab and Muslim countries have been denied visas to return to school after visits home.

Online Source:
http://www.ala.org/advocacy/sites/ala.org.advocacy/files/content/advleg/federallegislation/theusapatriotact/campusissues.pdf

D. Supreme Court to Determine How Free Speech Applies to Social Media
By Natasha Paulmeno

The Supreme Court is finally ruling on free speech relating to social media platforms. Now, before we jump the gun and say putting limitations on free speech is a violation of the First Amendment, let me explain. This conversation was sparked by a recent case — *United States of America v. Anthony Douglas Elonis.* I originally thought the outcome of this case was absurd — the defendant is serving more than three years in prison for a few eccentric Facebook posts. Really? Then I dug deeper and what I found was quite disturbing.

After losing his wife, his kids, and his job, Anthony Elonis was depressed and angry. He turned to Facebook to rant. And the "raps" he posted threatened his former place of work, his wife, innocent children, and an FBI agent. Below are some excerpts from his "rap lyrics":

> *I also found out that it's incredibly illegal,*
> *extremely illegal, to go on Facebook and say*
> *something like the best place to fire a mortar*
> *launcher at her house would be from the*
> *cornfield behind it because of easy access to a*
> *getaway road and you'd have a clear line of*
> *sight through the sun room.*
> *Insanely illegal.*
> *Ridiculously, wrecklessly, insanely illegal.*
> *Yet even more illegal to show an illustrated*
> *diagram.*
> *===[__] =====house*
> *: : : : : : ^ : : : : : : : : : : : :cornfield*
> *: : : : : : : : : : : : : : : : : : : :*
> *: : : : : : : : : : : : : : : : : : : :*
> *: : : : : : : : : : : : : : : : : : : :*
> *###########################getaway road*
> *Insanely illegal.*
> *Ridiculously, horribly felonious.*
> *Cause they will come to my house in the middle*
> *of the night and they will lock me up.*
> *Extremely against the law.*

In another post he "rapped" about shooting up a kindergarten classroom:

> *That's it, I've had about enough*
> *I'm checking out and making a name for myself*
> *Enough elementary schools in a ten mile radius*
> *to initiate the most heinous school shooting ever*
> *imagined*
> *And hell hath no fury like a crazy man in a*
> *kindergarten class*
> *The only question is . . . which one?*

Do you feel uncomfortable yet? You can also check out the hearing transcript for more of Elonis' disconcerting posts. By now, you're probably pretty creeped out by this weird Eminem wannabe. Well, he served his time: a 44-month sentence. What makes me see red is why he was convicted.

Elonis landed in the slammer for "transmit[ting] in interstate or foreign commerce any communication containing any threat to kidnap any person or any threat to injure the person of another…" Anyone else think it's problematic that despite his threats, which blatantly targeted his wife, he was sentenced on a technicality?

Cyber threats are common; Elonis' wife is not alone. Now the media is examining when rap crosses the line from being "gangsta" to being threatening? This issue is at the crux of the case the Supreme Court will hear in the upcoming term.

True Threats

While true threats are not protected by the First Amendment, the Supreme Court is struggling with ambiguities like cyber threats. The last time the court had a case involving threats was the 2003 case *Virginia v. Black et al.* The court defined true threats as "statements where the speaker means to communicate a serious expression of an intent to commit an act of unlawful violence to a particular individual or group of individuals."

Elonis defended his posts as art, saying he therefore lacked intent to actually carry out those threats. But his threats were specific, well thought-out, and frightening. So were his posts true threats or merely artistic expression? That's exactly the question SCOTUS will have to answer.

When Does Rap go too Far?

Elonis is one of many who have been put on trial for violent content in rap lyrics. Now who doesn't love some good ol' fashioned hate-the-world, go burn in hell, Eminem-style rap? I actually love Eminem – my iTunes holds precisely 54 of his songs. Yes, his raps are graphic, violent, angry, and sometimes downright grotesque. But, aside from his mother, whom he actually bought a mansion, he does not outline specific plans for a single person's demise. He's just angry at the world, that's all.

So, this is where Eminem's content differs from Elonis', among others. The debate is tangled — scholars and legal professionals need to consider artistic expression, intent, and how that plays out in the cyber world.

A group of legal scholars are defending Elonis and his "artistic expression" posts on Facebook. Clay Calvert, Erik Nielson, and Charis E. Kubrin argue that the context in which artistic expression is interpreted depends on its vessel of dissemination, in this case, social media. So, higher courts have difficulty determining the context and the intent, which both affect the verdict of threat cases involving social media posts.

The subject is highly complex, but my opinion on this is simple. If you post poorly written yet fear-inducing threats to Facebook, you deserve to be put away. Elonis is clearly not stable, as you can see from the nostalgic posts about his ex-wife, whom he threatened to behead.

Rap is considered an art form, so it's protected by the First Amendment. But throw social media into the mix and our Constitution becomes difficult to apply. So, yes, I'm relieved the Supreme Court will rule on this convoluted case because it will have long-reaching ramifications. I would certainly feel more secure if social media threats were considered more seriously, especially considering the shooting in Santa Barbara last month.

When it comes to threats, there is a fine line between protecting our First Amendment rights and protecting our citizens. My hope is that the Supreme Court will find a solution by defining when threats should be taken literally and when they are artistic ploys.

Used by permission of the author and Law Street Media. This essay originally appeared at this link: http://lawstreetmedia.com/blogs/off-hours/supreme-court-rule-free-speech-social-media/. *In-text hyperlinks appeared in the online version of this essay.*

ABOUT THE AUTHOR

Daniel S. Brown, Jr., is a teacher, administrator, and researcher in higher education. Brown specializes in communication theory and rhetorical criticism, especially as they intersect with religious organizations and people of faith. Other areas he teaches include journalism, editing, and, of course, media law.

Brown began his career teaching business and professional communication in the Florida panhandle. He taught at Bryan College and Indiana Wesleyan University prior to his move to Pennsylvania's Grove City College in 2001. Brown held a visiting professorship in communication at Miami University. He has chaired communication departments at Bryan and Grove City colleges. He is a doctoral thesis examiner for Australia's Macquarie University.

An Ohio native, he was educated at Miami and Edinboro universities before earning his doctor of philosophy degree from Louisiana State University. Brown took post-doctoral work at The Ohio State University and was named a Fellow at Northwestern University's Institute on the Holocaust and Jewish Civilization.